Fodor's

PUERTO VALLARTA

5th Edition

Fodor's Travel Publications   New York, Toronto, London, Sydney, Auckland
www.fodors.com

Be a Fodor's Correspondent

Your opinion matters. It matters to us. It matters to your fellow Fodor's travelers, too. And we'd like to hear it. In fact, we *need* to hear it.

When you share your experiences and opinions, you become an active member of the Fodor's community. That means we'll not only use your feedback to make our books better, but we'll publish your names and comments whenever possible. Throughout our guides, look for "Word of Mouth," excerpts of your unvarnished feedback.

Here's how you can help improve Fodor's for all of us.

Tell us when we're right. We rely on local writers to give you an insider's perspective. But our writers and staff editors—who are the best in the business—depend on you. Your positive feedback is a vote to renew our recommendations for the next edition.

Tell us when we're wrong. We're proud that we update most of our guides every year. But we're not perfect. Things change. Hotels cut services. Museums change hours. Charming cafés lose charm. If our writer didn't quite capture the essence of a place, tell us how you'd do it differently. If any of our descriptions are inaccurate or inadequate, we'll incorporate your changes in the next edition and will correct factual errors at fodors.com *immediately.*

Tell us what to include. You probably have had fantastic travel experiences that aren't yet in Fodor's. Why not share them with a community of like-minded travelers? Maybe you chanced upon a beach or bistro or B&B that you don't want to keep to yourself. Tell us why we should include it. And share your discoveries and experiences with everyone directly at fodors.com. Your input may lead us to add a new listing or highlight a place we cover with a "Highly Recommended" star or with our highest rating, "Fodor's Choice."

Give us your opinion instantly at our feedback center at www.fodors.com/feedback. You may also e-mail editors@fodors.com with the subject line "Puerto Vallarta Editor." Or send your nominations, comments, and complaints by mail to Puerto Vallarta Editor, Fodor's, 1745 Broadway, New York, NY 10019.

You and travelers like you are the heart of the Fodor's community. Make our community richer by sharing your experiences. Be a Fodor's correspondent.

¡Buen viaje!

Tim Jarrell, Publisher

FODOR'S PUERTO VALLARTA

Editors: Kelly Kealy (lead editor), Erica Duecy

By: Jane Onstott

Production Editor: Carolyn Roth
Maps & Illustrations: David Lindroth and Mark Stroud, *cartographers;* Bob Blake, Rebecca Baer, *map editors;* William Wu, *information graphics*
Design: Fabrizio La Rocca, *creative director;* Guido Caroti, Siobhan O'Hare, *art directors;* Tina Malaney, Nora Rosansky, Chie Ushio, Jessica Walsh, Ann McBride, *designers;* Melanie Marin, *senior picture editor*
Cover Photo: (Huichol Art, Malecón) Ken Ross/viestiphoto.com
Production Manager: Amanda Bullock

COPYRIGHT

Copyright © 2011 by Fodor's Travel, a division of Random House, Inc.

Fodor's is a registered trademark of Random House, Inc.

All rights reserved. Published in the United States by Fodor's Travel, a division of Random House, Inc., and simultaneously in Canada by Random House of Canada, Limited, Toronto. Distributed by Random House, Inc., New York.

No maps, illustrations, or other portions of this book may be reproduced in any form without written permission from the publisher.

Portions of Chapter 8, Overnight Excursions, appear in *Fodor's Mexico* in slightly different form.

5th Edition

ISBN 978-1-4000-0482-9

ISSN 1558-8718

SPECIAL SALES

This book is available at special discounts for bulk purchases for sales promotions or premiums. Special editions, including personalized covers, excerpts of existing books, and corporate imprints, can be created in large quantities for special needs. For more information, write to Special Markets/Premium Sales, 1745 Broadway, MD 6-2, New York, New York 10019, or e-mail specialmarkets@randomhouse.com.

AN IMPORTANT TIP & AN INVITATION

Although all prices, opening times, and other details in this book are based on information supplied to us at press time, changes occur all the time in the travel world, and Fodor's cannot accept responsibility for facts that become outdated or for inadvertent errors or omissions. So **always confirm information when it matters**, especially if you're making a detour to visit a specific place. Your experiences—positive and negative—matter to us. If we have missed or misstated something, **please write to us.** We follow up on all suggestions. Contact the Puerto Vallarta editor at editors@fodors.com or c/o Fodor's at 1745 Broadway, New York, NY 10019.

PRINTED IN CHINA

10 9 8 7 6 5 4 3 2

CONTENTS

ABOUT THIS BOOK

Our Ratings

Sometimes you find terrific travel experiences and sometimes they just find you. But usually the burden is on you to select the right combination of experiences. That's where our ratings come in.

As travelers we've all discovered a place so wonderful that its worthiness is obvious. And sometimes that place is so experiential that superlatives don't do it justice: you just have to be there to know. These sights, properties, and experiences get our highest rating, **Fodor's Choice**, indicated by orange stars throughout this book.

Black stars highlight sights and properties we deem **Highly Recommended**, places that our writers, editors, and readers praise again and again for consistency and excellence.

By default, there's another category: any place we include in this book is by definition worth your time, unless we say otherwise. And we will.

Disagree with any of our choices? Care to nominate a place or suggest that we rate one more highly? Visit our feedback center at fodors.com.

Budget Well

Hotel and restaurant price categories from ¢ to $$$$ are defined in the opening pages of chapters 4 and 5. For attractions, we always give standard adult admission fees; reductions are usually available for children, students, and senior citizens. Want to pay with plastic? **AE, D, DC, MC, V** following restaurant and hotel listings indicate if American Express, Discover, Diners Club, MasterCard, and Visa are accepted.

Restaurants

Unless we state otherwise, restaurants are open for lunch and dinner daily. We mention dress only when there's a specific requirement and reservations only when they're essential or not accepted—it's always best to book ahead.

Hotels

Hotels have private bath, phone, TV, and air-conditioning and operate on the European Plan (aka EP, meaning without meals), unless we specify that they use the Continental Plan (CP, with a Continental breakfast), Breakfast Plan (BP, with a full breakfast), or Modified American Plan (MAP, with breakfast and dinner) or are all-inclusive (including all meals and most activities). We always list facilities but not whether you'll be charged an extra fee to use them, so when pricing accomodations, find out what's included.

Listings	
★	Fodor's Choice
★	Highly recommended
⊠	Physical address
✛	Directions or Map coordinates
⑤	Mailing address
☎	Telephone
🖷	Fax
⊕	On the Web
✍	E-mail
☎	Admission fee
☉	Open/closed times
Ⓜ	Metro stations
▭	Credit cards
Hotels & Restaurants	
🏨	Hotel
🛏	Number of rooms
☖	Facilities
❤️⃝	Meal plans
✕	Restaurant
✍	Reservations
🎩	Dress code
☖	Smoking
🍸	BYOB
Outdoors	
🏌	Golf
⚠	Camping
Other	
☺	Family-friendly
⇨	See also
⊠	Branch address
☞	Take note

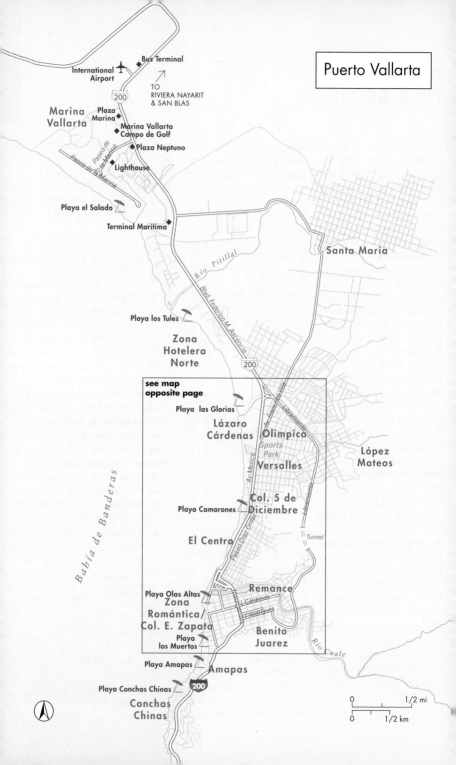

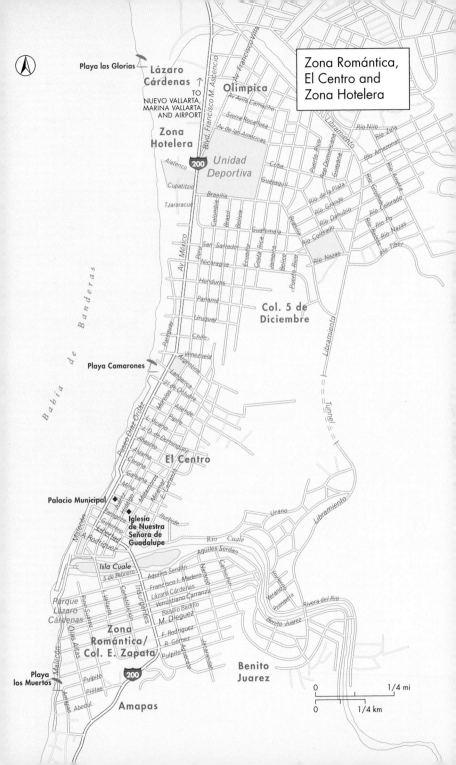

Zona Romántica,
El Centro and
Zona Hotelera

Playa las Glorias

Lázaro
Cárdenas ↑
TO
NUEVO VALLARTA,
MARINA VALLARTA
AND AIRPORT

Olimpica

Av Avila Camacho
Sierra Rocallosa
Av de las Américas

Zona
Hotelera

Río Nilo
Río Zula
Río Amazonas

Puerto Rico
Rep Dominicana
Guayana

Cuba
Guaraguí

Libramiento

Alatenco
200
Unidad
Deportiva

Cupatitzio

Brasilia

Río de la Plata
Río Grande
Río Danubio

Río Colorado

Tzararacue

Colombia
Brasil
Bolivia

Guatemala

Costa Rica

Atlántica
Belice
Puerto Rico

Río Colorado

Río Griyalva
Río Ebro
Río Balsas
Río Po
Río Nazas
Río Tíber

Av. México

San Salvador
Perú

Ecuador

Río Nazas

Nicaragua

Honduras

Panamá

Col. 5 de
Diciembre

Uruguay

Bahía de Banderas

Chile

Paraguay

Venezuela

Playa Camarones

Argentina

Lamarca
31 de Octubre

Morelos

Pipila

Paseo Díaz Ordaz

Allende

L. Lucerio
J. D. de Domínguez

El Centro

Abasolo

Juárez
Corona

Galeana

Mina

Libramiento

Matamoros

Miramar

V. E. Lazaga

Iturbide

Palacio Municipal ◆
◆ Iglesia
de Nuestra
Señora de
Guadalupe

Zaragoza
Hidalgo
Guerrero
Libertad
A. Rodríguez

Urano

Malecón

Río Cuale

Isla Cuale

Aquiles Serdán

5 de Febrero

Aquiles Serdán

Naranjo

Camichín

Jacarandas

Verania

Libramiento

Francisco I. Madero

Primavera

Parque
Lázaro
Cárdenas

Lázaro Cárdenas

Venustiano Carranza

Rivera del Río

Pino Suárez

Vallarta

Constitución

Insurgentes

Basilio Badillo

M. Diéguez

Benito Juárez

F. Rodríguez

Zona
Romántica/
Col. E. Zapata

Olas Altas

R. Gómez

Pulpito

Jacarandas

Aguacate

Benito
Juarez

Malecón

200

Amapas

Pulpito
Pilitas

Playa
los Muertos

Amapas
Abedul

| 0 | | 1/4 mi |
| 0 | | 1/4 km |

The Central Pacific Coast

TO MAZATLÁN

Toll

San Blas

Bahía de San Blas

66

TEPIC ★

15

200

Compostela

Toll

Las Varas

Chacala

Bahía de Jaltemba

SIERRA ZAPOTÁN

Rincón de Guayabitos○ ○La Peñita
Lo de Marcos

San Francisco   200

Sayulita

SIERRA VALLEJO

Dirt

Las Palmas

Dirt

Punta Mita

Bucerías

Las Islas Marietas

La Cruz de
Huanacaxtle

La Estancia

San
Sebastián

Nuevo Vallarta

Ixtapa

Puerto Vallarta

Bahía de Banderas

Mismaloya

Boca de Tomatlán

Mascota

El Chimo

Dirt

200

Talpa

Aquiles Serdan

Dirt

Dirt

El Tuito

Bahía Tehualmixtle

Dirt

Presa
Cajón de Peña

La Cruz de Loreto

El Tequesquite

Dirt

La Cumbre

José María Morelos

Dirt

Perula

Bahía Chamela

Reserva de
la Biosfera
Chamela-
Cuixmala

Chamela

200

Tenacatita

Bahía Tenacatita

San Patricio–Melaque

Barra de Navidad

0   20 mi

0   20 km

Experience
Puerto Vallarta

WELCOME TO PUERTO VALLARTA

TOP REASONS TO GO

★ **Legendary restaurants:** Eat barbecued snapper with your feet in the sand or chateaubriand with a killer ocean view.

★ **Adventure and indulgence:** Ride a horse, mountain-bike or go four-wheeling into the mountains, dive into the sea, and relax at an elegant spa—all in one day.

★ **Natural beauty:** Enjoy the physical beauty of Pacific Mexico's prettiest resort town, where cobblestone streets disappear into emerald green hills with the big, sparkling bay below.

★ **Authentic art:** PV's artists and artisans—from Huichol Indians to expats—produce a huge diversity of exceptional folk treasures and fine art.

★ **Diverse nightlife:** Whether you're old, young, gay, straight, mild, or wild, PV's casual and unpretentious party scene has something to entice you after dark.

1 **Old Vallarta.** Rising abruptly from the sea are the hilly, cobblestone streets of El Centro (Downtown), lined with white-washed homes and shops. South of the Cuale River, the Zona Romántica (Romantic Zone, in Col. E. Zapata) has PV's highest density of restaurants and tourist-oriented shops.

2 **North of Downtown.** Facing a busy avenue, the Zona Hotelera Norte (Northern Hotel Zone) has malls, businesses, and high-rise hotels. The shopping centers and deluxe hotels of Marina Vallarta are sandwiched between a golf course and the city's main yacht marina.

3 Nuevo Vallarta. The southernmost spot in Nayarit State, this planned resort is ideal if you want all-inclusive hotels. It has few restaurants and shops outside the Paradise Plaza mall.

4 The Southern Nayarit Coast. Exclusive Punta Mita (sometimes called Punta *de* Mita) is dominated by the Four Seasons and St. Regis hotels. Sayulita, San Francisco, La Cruz de Huanacaxtle, and Bucerías attract visitors with their pretty beaches and unpretentious charm.

5 South of Puerto Vallarta. To Mismaloya, the hotels of the Zona Hotelera Sur hug the beach or overlook it from cliff-side aeries. South of El Tuito, Cabo Corrientes hides tiny towns and gorgeous, untrammeled beaches, while the Costalegre is a mixture of luxury resorts and earthy seaside hamlets.

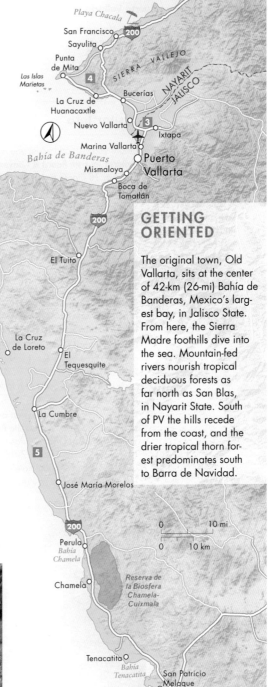

Playa Chacala
San Francisco — 200
Sayulita
Punta de Mita
Las Islas Marietas — 4
SIERRA VALLEJO
NAYARIT — JALISCO
Bucerías
La Cruz de Huanacaxtle
Nuevo Vallarta — 3
Ixtapa
Marina Vallarta
Bahía de Banderas
Mismaloya
Puerto Vallarta
Boca de Tomatlán
El Tuito
La Cruz de Loreto
El Tequesquite
La Cumbre
5
José María Morelos
200
Perula
Bahía Chamela
Chamela
Reserva de la Biosfera Chamela-Cuixmala
0 — 10 mi
0 — 10 km
Tenacatita
Bahía Tenacatita
San Patricio Melaque

GETTING ORIENTED

The original town, Old Vallarta, sits at the center of 42-km (26-mi) Bahía de Banderas, Mexico's largest bay, in Jalisco State. From here, the Sierra Madre foothills dive into the sea. Mountain-fed rivers nourish tropical deciduous forests as far north as San Blas, in Nayarit State. South of PV the hills recede from the coast, and the drier tropical thorn forest predominates south to Barra de Navidad.

PUERTO VALLARTA PLANNER

The Scene

Mexico's second-most-visited destination after the Cancún/ Playa del Carmen area, Puerto Vallarta is touristy. That said, this isn't a spring-break destination. Yes, twentysomethings party all night. But a sense of decorum and civic pride keeps things reasonably restrained. Most tour companies, restaurants, and hotels are run by locals who are happy to have you because tourism is PV's only real industry.

Fast Facts

Nickname: Foreigners call it PV or Vallarta. A *vallartense* (person from Puerto Vallarta), however, is known as a *pata salada* (literally, salty foot).

State: PV is in the state of Jalisco, whose capital is Guadalajara.

Population: 220,368

Latitude: 20°N (same as Cancún, Mexico; Port-au-Prince, Haiti; Hanoi, Vietnam)

Longitude: 105°W (same as Regina, Saskatchewan; Denver, Colorado; El Paso, Texas)

Trivia: Two of the four quadrants in PV's official seal symbolize the tourism industry: a sailfish represents sportfishing, and hands welcome visitors.

Visitor Info

Before you visit and when you arrive, contact the **Puerto Vallarta Tourism Board & Convention and Visitors Bureau** (⊠ *Local 18 Planta Baja, Zona Comercial Hotel Canto del Sol, Zona Hotelera, Las Glorias* ☎ *322/224–1175; 888/384–6822 in U.S.; 01800/719–3276 in Mexico* ⊕ *www.visitpuertovallarta.com*).

The **Municipal Tourist Office** (⊠ *Av. Independencia 123, Centro* ☎ *322/223–2500 Ext. 232*) is open Monday through Saturday 8–8 and Sunday 10–6, although it doesn't always adhere to its stated hours.

The friendly folks at the **Jalisco State Tourism Office** (⊠ *Plaza Marina shopping center, Local 144, Planta Alta, Marina Vallarta* ☎ *322/221–2676*), open weekdays 9–5, have information about PV and other destinations.

Riviera Nayarit Convention & Visitors Bureau (⊠ *Paseo de los Cocoteros 85 Sur, Local Int. 6–A, Paradise Plaza, Nuevo Vallarta* ☎ *322/297–2516* ⊕ *www.rivieranayarit. com*) is a friendly source of info for the area between San Blas and Nuevo Vallarta.

For information about the area between Nuevo Vallarta and Punta de Mita, contact the **Bay of Banderas/Nuevo Vallarta Tourism Office** (⊠ *Paseo de los Cocoteros at Blvd. Nuevo Vallarta* ☎ *322/297–1006*), wedged between the Gran Velas and Maribal hotels. To avoid the small parking fee, tell the attendant you're visiting the tourism office.

Classes and Tours

With so many expats living here, PV and environs have lots of classes conducted in English. Low-cost courses at the Centro Cultural Cuale and other outlets put you in touch with locals as well as other English speakers.

In winter there are house and garden tours and even more cultural activities up and down the coast. A good source of information for current classes is the bimonthly, free *Bay Vallarta*, which always lists a Web page or phone number for further information.

CLASSES

You can matriculate midsession at the informal **Centro Cultural Cuale** (⊠ *East end of Isla Río Cuale, Centro* ☎ *322/223–0095*) for classes like painting, drawing, and acting for children and for adults. Most instructors speak some English; others are fluent. The center also sells the work of local artists and hosts cultural events. Cost of classes is nominal, and cultural events are free.

Biblioteca Los Mangos (⊠ *Av. Francisco Villa 1001, Col. Los Mangos* ☎ *322/224–9966*) has lots of reasonably priced art and Spanish classes and free or inexpensive monthly events, such as dance performances and art films.

Philo's (⊠ *Calle Delfin 15, La Cruz de Huanacaxtle* ☎ *329/295–5068*) is the unofficial cultural center of La Cruz, north of Bucerías. Spanish classes are Tuesday and Thursday at 10 AM. Classes are technically free, but donations are expected. **AmeriSpan Unlimited** (☎ *800/879–6640 in U.S. and Canada* ⊕ *amerispan.com*), based in the United States, specializes in medical and business Spanish; see the Web site for student blogs.

TOURS

Puerto Vallarta Tours (☎ *322/222–4935; 866/217–9704 in U.S. and Canada* ⊕ *www.puertovallartatours. net*) runs many different adventure tours, ecotours, city and ranch tours, tequila tours, and private tours. **Vallarta Adventures** (⊠ *Paseo de las Palmas 39–A, Nuevo Vallarta* ☎ *322/297–1212; 888/303–2653 in U.S. and Canada* ⊠ *Edificio Marina Golf, Local 13–C, Calle Mástil, Marina Vallarta* ☎ *322/221–0657* ⊕ *www.vallarta-adventures. com*) is one of PV's most respected tour operators and offers sea and land adventures; a particularly wonderful tour combines round-trip air transportation to the highlands with a visit to the former mining town of San Sebastián.

When to Go

High season (aka dry season) is December through April; the resorts are most crowded and expensive during this time. If you don't mind afternoon showers, temperatures in the 80s and 90s F (high 20s and 30s C), and high humidity, rainy season (late June through October) is a great time to visit. Hotel rates drop by as much as 40%, and there aren't any crowds.

Summer sees the best diving, snorkeling, and surfing conditions. By August the coast and inland forests are green and bursting with blooms. Afternoon rains clean the streets; waterfalls and rivers outside of town spring into action. On the downside, heat and humidity are high, some businesses close shop in the hottest months (August and September), and nightlife slacks off.

Climate

The proximity of mountains to the coast increases humidity. From Puerto Vallarta north to San Blas there's jungly terrain (officially, tropical deciduous forest). South of PV the mountains recede from the coast, making that area's thorn-forest ecosystem drier but still hot and humid.

TOP EXPERIENCES

Canopy Tours

Canopy tours are action-packed rides, where, fastened to a zip line high off the ground, you fly from tree to tree—blue sky above, ribbons of river below and, in between, a forest of treetops and a healthy shot of adrenaline.

Water Sports

Spend a day on the bay. Dive the varied landscape of Las Marietas Islands, angle for billfish, or take a boat ride for the fun of it. Look for humpbacks in winter and dolphins year-round. Swim, snorkel, or learn to surf or sail. Perhaps just build a sand castle with your kids.

Dining Out

First-time travelers come for the sun and sea, but it's PV's wonderful restaurants that create long-term fans. Dozens of top toques have restaurants here, and each November sees the International Gourmet Festival, with guest chefs, recipes, and ideas from around the globe. Seaside family-owned eateries grill fish right off the boat, and tiny city cafés have great eats at bargain prices. And a number of street-side stalls are as hygienic as five-star-hotel restaurants.

Late Nights, Latino Style

Much of Vallarta is geared to the gringo palate; however, there's plenty of authentic spice for those who crave it. Enjoy a mojito at La Bodeguita del Medio, on the malecón. Dine on roast pork, black beans, and fried plantains before heading for the dance floor at around 9:30, when the house band comes to life. Thursday and Friday, take a taxi to J&B Dance Club, in the Hotel Zone, for $4 dance lessons from 8 to 9 PM. Otherwise hang at La Bodeguita until around 11, when the Latino crowds start to arrive at J&B for a late night of cumbia, salsa, and merengue.

Sensational Sunsets

After a day of activity, you deserve R, R, and R: rest, relaxation, and rewarding views. Sip a fancy cocktail to live music at busy Los Muertos Beach or indulge in dessert from the crow's nest at Bucerías's The Bar Above. For dramatic views from high above the sea head to Barcelona Tapas or Vista Guayabitos (⇨ Chapter 5). All serve dinner and drinks.

Hilltop Retreats

Get away from the gringo trail 4,000 feet above sea level in the mountain towns east of PV. Admire the elegant simplicity of tiny San Sebastián; in Talpa, visit the diminutive Virgin of Talpa statue, revered throughout Mexico for petitions granted. Buy keepsakes and mountain-grown coffee in shops on the square. Road access is relatively easy, but you can still charter a plane to these towns or to Mascota, where you can sample homemade *raicilla*—second cousin of tequila. Hike into tapestry hills and deep green valleys where, on a good day, you can spy PV and a ribbon of the Pacific. For an unforgettable experience (at least until your thigh muscles recover), take a horseback expedition (⇨ Chapter 3) into forests. Rancho Charro and Rancho Ojo de Agua have full-day excursions. For those who prefer motorized horsepower, Wild Vallarta runs full-day ATV tours to San Sebastián.

THE MALECÓN

Puerto Vallarta's **malecón** is its Champs Élysées—only shorter, warmer, and less expensive. On the mile-long cement walkway bordering the sea, small groups of young studs check out their feminine counterparts; cruise-ship passengers stretch their legs; and landlocked visitors stroll before dinner. Even those who have lived here all their lives come out to watch the red sun sink into the gray-blue water beyond the bay.

Every night and weekend is a parade. Vendors sell *agua de tuba,* a refreshing coconut-palm-heart drink. Empanada, corn-on-the-cob, and fried-banana stands congregate on the boardwalk near the mouth of the Cuale River. Peddlers sell helium balloons and cotton candy. Clowns, magicians, and musicians entertain in the Los Arcos amphitheater.

There are also performances by *los voladores de Papantla,* the Papantla "flyers," near Los Arcos. Dressed in exquisite costumes of red-velveteen pants decorated with sequins, mirrors, embroidery, and fringe, five men climb a 98-foot pole. Four of them dive from the top of the platform as the leader "speaks" to them while balancing atop the pinnacle and playing a fife and drum. Held by a rope tied to one foot, the men wing around the pole exactly 13 times before landing on the ground. The total number of revolutions adds up to 52, a number of great ritual significance in the cosmology of the pre-Hispanic Mesoamericans. This traditional performance, native to Veracruz State, is held most weekend evenings at 7 PM and 8 PM in low season; in high season (December through April), it's every half hour from 7 PM to 10 PM. The exception is when cruise ships call (Tuesday through Thursday at this writing); performances are on the half hour from 9 AM to 1 PM in addition to the evening schedule.

Some of PV's most endearing art is en plein air. Stretching along the sea walk is a series of bronze sculptures that are constantly touched, photographed, and climbed on. These nonstop caresses give a bright bronze luster to strategic body parts of Neptune and the Nereid, a mermaid and her man. Higher up on its pedestal, Puerto Vallarta's well-known sea-horse icon retains a more traditional (and dignified) patina.

Rotunda on the Sea, a wacky grouping of chair-people by Alejandro Colunga, is a good spot to sit and watch the sea, although around sunset, people waiting their turn to be photographed here make it hard to linger.

The three mysterious pillow-headed ladder-climbing figures that compose *In Search of Reason,* by Sergio Bustamante, are just as otherworldly as the jewelry, painting, and statuettes sold in his Vallarta shops. Ramiz Barquet's *Nostalgia* is an in-situ ode to the artist's reunion with the love of his life.

Gary Thompson, owner of Galería Pacífico, leads public sculpture walking tours mid-November through mid-April. The fee- and reservation-free two-hour tours leave Tuesday at 9:30 AM from the north end of the malecón by the Hotel Rosita. The first stop is *Millennium,* and its creator, Mathis Lidice, gives a brief talk. Tours end at the gallery, where sculptor Ramiz Barquet answers questions about his three pieces on the tour and briefly presents clay modeling techniques.

✉ *Extending south from Calle 31 de Octubre to Los Arcos outdoor amphitheater and the Río Cuale.*

PUERTO VALLARTA
TOP ATTRACTIONS

La Iglesia de Nuestra Señora de Guadalupe

(A) The **Church of Our Lady of Guadalupe** is dedicated to the patron saint of Mexico and of Puerto Vallarta. The holy mother's image, by Ignacio Ramírez, is the centerpiece of the cathedral's slender marble altarpiece. The brick bell tower is topped by a lacy-looking crown that replicates the one worn by Carlota, short-lived empress of Mexico. The wrought-iron crown toppled during an earthquake that shook this area of the Pacific Coast in October 1995 but was soon replaced with a fiberglass version, supported, as was the original, by a squadron of stone angels. This was replaced with a newer and larger rendition in October 2009. ⊠ *Calle Hidalgo between Iturbide and Zaragoza, Centro* ☎ *No phone* ☉ *7:30 AM–8 PM daily.*

Museo Arqueológico

(B) Pre-Columbian figures and Indian artifacts are on display at the **Archaeological Museum.** There's a general explanation of Western Pacific cultures and shaft tombs and abbreviated but attractive exhibits of Aztatlán and Purépecha cultures and the Spanish conquest. ⊠ *Western tip of Isla Río Cuale, Centro* ☎ *No phone* ✉ *By donation* ☉ *Mon.–Sat. 10–6.*

Jardín Botánico de Puerto Vallarta

(C) On 20 acres of land 19 km (12 mi) south of town, the **Puerto Vallarta Botanical Gardens** features more than 3,000 species of plants. Set within the tropical dry forest at 1,300 feet above sea level, its trails lead to a stream where you can swim; palm, agave, and rose gardens; a tree fern grotto; an orchid house; and displays of Mexican wildflowers and carnivorous plants. There are free parking and a free guided tour daily at 1 PM December through Easter. The lovely, open-sided Hacienda de Oro

restaurant serves an array of starters as well as pizza and Mexican dishes. Beverages include wine and a full bar. Go to its Web site to arrange a four-hour birding (via ATV) or hiking tour, with lunch, for $85 per person. A taxi here will cost about $20, but for less than a dollar, you can take the "El Tuito" bus from the corner of Aguacate and Venustiano Carranza streets. Another tip: Slather on insect repellent before you go, and take some with you. This is the jungle, and *jejenes* (no-see-ums), mosquitoes, and other biting bugs can be counted on to attack. ⊠ *Carretera a Barra de Navidad Km 24, Las Juntas y Los Veranos* ☎ *322/223–6182* ⊕ *www.vallartabotanicalgardensac.org* 🖭 *$3* ⊙ *Mon.–Sat. 10–6.*

La Tobara

(D) Turtles sunning themselves on logs, crocodiles masquerading as logs, water-loving birds, and exotic orchids make the maze of green-brown canals that is

La Tobara an out-of-town must for nature lovers. Launches putter along these waterways from El Conchal Bridge, at the outskirts of San Blas, about a three-hour drive from Marina Vallarta, or from the nearby village of Matanchén. After cruising along for about 45 minutes—during which you'll have taken *way* too many photos of the mangrove roots that protrude from the water and the turtles—you arrive at spring-fed freshwater pools for which the area is named. You can hang out at the restaurant overlooking the pool or play Tarzan and Jane on the rope swing. Most folks take the optional trip to a crocodile farm on the way back, stretching a two-hour tour into three hours. ⊠ *El Conchal Bridge, entrance to/exit from San Blas, San Blas* ☎ *323/108–4174 (cell)* 🖭 *$9 per person; $28 for the whole boat* ⊙ *Daily 10–5.*

CRUISING TO PUERTO VALLARTA

Expanded and updated in 2007, PV's cruise-ship terminal berths three full-size ships at a time and is midway between Marina Vallarta and the Northern Hotel Zone, a 15-minute drive (barring traffic) from Old Vallarta. In 2008 about 275 ships called, bringing some 589,000 passengers who spent the day zinging along zip lines, riding horses into the hills, playing in the surf, or, in winter, sightseeing for humpbacks in Vallarta's bay.

Companies with cruises to the Pacific Coast include Carnival, Holland America, Norwegian, Princess, and Royal Caribbean. Most depart from Los Angeles (Long Beach) or San Diego and head to Los Cabos or Mazatlán, Puerto Vallarta, Manzanillo, Ixtapa/Zihuatanejo, and/or Acapulco; some trips originate in Vancouver or San Francisco.

Carnival. Carnival is known for its large-volume cruises and template approach to its ships, two factors that probably help keep fares accessible. Boats in its Mexican fleet have more than 1,000 staterooms; the newest ship, *Splendor,* was inaugurated in 2008. Seven-night trips out of Los Angeles hit Mazatlán, Los Cabos, and Puerto Vallarta. Las Vegas–style shows and passenger participation are the norm. ☎ *888/227–6482* ⊕ *www.carnival.com.*

Holland America Line. The venerable Holland America Line leaves from and returns to San Diego. Its 11-day Mexican Riviera cruise calls at Puerto Vallarta as well as Cabo San Lucas, Mazatlán, Acapulco, and Huatulco. ☎ *877/932–4259* ⊕ *www. hollandamerica.com.*

Norwegian Cruise Lines. Its tagline is "Whatever floats your boat," and Norwegian *is* known for its relatively freewheeling style and variety of activities and excursions. Six-day cruises are out of Los Angeles, with three nights at sea and full days in Los Cabos and PV. The seven-day trip adds a day in Mazatlán. ☎ *866/234–7350* ⊕ *www.ncl.com.*

Princess Cruises. Not so great for small children but good at keeping tweens, teens, and adults occupied, Princess strives to offer luxury at an affordable price. Its cruises may cost a little more than others, but you also get more for the money: large rooms, varied menus, and personalized service. The 10-day Riviera Mexico cruise aboard the *Sapphire Princess* starts in Los Angeles and hits Los Cabos, PV, and Mazatlán. Ten-day trips out of San Francisco add Acapulco and Ixtapa but don't stop at Mazatlán. ☎ *800/774–6237* ⊕ *www.princess.com.*

Royal Caribbean. Royal Caribbean's seven-night cruises originate in Los Angeles and stop in Los Cabos, Mazatlán, and PV. Ten-night cruises from San Diego add a stop in Acapulco as well as Ixtapa/Zihuatanejo, and 11-night cruises add the port of Manzanillo. Striving to appeal to a broad clientele, the line offers lots of activities and services as well as many shore excursions. ☎ *800/521–8611* ⊕ *www.royalcaribbean.com.*

GAY PUERTO VALLARTA

Puerto Vallarta is a gay old town. Men check each other out over drinks and suntan oil at the south end of Los Muertos beach, dangle from parachutes above the bay, buff themselves out at South Side gyms. Rainbow boys (and girls) spend a day sailing on vessels flying the multicolor flag of love and then dance until morning in one of the city's oversexed discos. Mexico's most popular gay destination draws crowds of "Dorothy's friends" from both sides of the Río Grande and from the Old World as well.

The Romantic Zone is the hub for rainbow bars and sophisticated, gay-friendly restaurants. Here, many foreigners have—after falling in love with Puerto Vallarta's beaches, jungly green mountains, and friendly people—relocated to PV to fulfill their ultimate fantasy in the form of bistro, bar, or B&B. International savvy (and backing) teamed up with Mexican sensibilities has produced a number of successful gay businesses.

Gay hotels offer entertainment that allows you to party on-site without having to worry about getting "home." In addition to gay properties such as Blue Chairs and Casa Cupula, hotels like Los Cuatro Vientos, in Centro, and Quinta María Cortez above Playa Conchas Chinas (⇨ Chapter 4) are gay-friendly.

■ TIP➜ Gay Guide Vallarta (⊕ www. gayguidevallarta.com) has lots of listings for long- and short-term condo rentals.

Clubbing may be the favorite pastime in the Romantic Zone, but there's more than one way to cruise Vallarta. Gay boat tours keep the libations flowing throughout the day, and horses head for the hills for bird's-eye views of the beach.

GET THE SCOOP

Gay Guide Vallarta (⊕ www.gayguidevallarta.com) is an excellent and occasionally opinionated source of info about gay-friendly and gay-owned hotels, restaurants, and nightlife.

THE BEACH SCENE

The undisputed yet unassuming king of daytime beach action is **Blue Chairs** (✉ South end of Los Muertos Beach, Col. E. Zapata ☎ 322/222–5040; 866/514–7969 in U.S. and Canada). Shaded by the bright azure umbrellas that distinguish the restaurant/bar/hotel, boys from the 'hood mingle with asphalt cowboys from the Midwest.

Waiters range from snarky queens to cherubic heteros. Next door, the green umbrellas blend with the blue; at this end of the beach, though, it's pretty much gay no matter what color the umbrellas. This is PV's most popular rainbow beach scene, a magnet for first-timers as well as those sneaking away from social obligations in Guadalajara.

SPORTS AND THE OUTDOORS

Cruises

Boana Hot Springs (✉ Boana Torre Malibu Condo-Hotel, Calle Amapas 325, Col. E. Zapata ☎ 322/222–0999 ⊕ www.boana. net) offers a twice-weekly romantic hot spring tour ($75). Included are transportation, a candlelight dinner, and open bar. In high season tours operate Tuesday and Friday, leaving at 4:45 PM and returning to PV at midnight. To hold a spot, make a deposit in person at Boana's office in Boana Torre Malibu, behind

Blue Chairs on Highway 200 just south of the Romantic Zone.

Diana's Gay Cruise (☎ *322/222–1510; 866/514–7969 in U.S. for reservations* ⊕ *www.dianastours.com*) is a booze-and-beach cruise (Thursdays and most Fridays also in high season) popular with lesbians and gays. Straights are also welcome, but minors are not. Go for the swimming, snorkeling, and lunch on the beach at Las Animas or another area beach, or for the unlimited national-brand beers and mixed drinks. Most of the time is spent on the boat. It's easiest to reserve tickets ($80) online using PayPal. Private tours are also available.

Health Clubs

On the South Side, gay-friendly **Acqua Day Spa & Gym** (✉ *Constitución 450, Col. E. Zapata* ☎ *322/223–5270*) has a sauna and steam room in addition to free weights and machines, massage, body treatments, and more. It's $10 per day and is closed Sunday.

Serious muscle men and women head for **Gold's Gym** (✉ *Calle Pablo Picasso s/n, Plaza Las Glorias, Zona Hotelera* ☎ *322/225–6671*) with aerobics, yoga, and Pilates as well as a sauna, steam, climbing wall, and hot tub. The $10-per-day ($28-per-week) price is reasonable, especially since it includes classes like yoga or Pilates. There's also free child care for toddlers to six year olds.

For women only, **Total Fitness Gym** (✉ *Calle Timón 1, at marina, Marina Vallarta* ☎ *322/221–0770*) is sparkly clean and has a sauna and lots of classes: yoga, Spinning, Latin rhythms, Zumba, aerobics, and Pilates. The daily fee is $13, including classes, or $30 per week. It's closed Sunday.

TOTAL RELAXATION

If you must break a sweat on your vacation, the best way is while experiencing a *temazcal*, an ancient Indian sweat lodge ceremony, at **Terra Noble** (✉ *Av. Tulipanes 595, Fracc. Lomas de Terra Noble* ☎ *322/223–0308* ⊕ *www.terranoble.com*). The spa also has therapeutic massage, body treatments, and facials.

Horseback Riding

Three-hour, $45 horseback adventures with **Boana Tours** (✉ *Torre Malibu, Carretera a Mismaloya* ☎ *322/222–0999* ⊕ *www.boana.net*) include one-way transportation to its ranch outside the city, a little more than an hour on the horse, a snack, and two drinks. You can take a swim in the river before returning on your own to PV. Most of the year there is just one daily afternoon tour at 2:15 PM.

WEDDINGS AND HONEYMOONS

Mexico is a growing wedding and honeymoon destination for Canadians and Americans. Many area hotels—from boutiques to internationally known brands—offer honeymoon packages and professional wedding planners. Although there's an obligatory civil ceremony that must accompany the Big Event, you can get married in a house of worship, on a beach, at a hotel chapel, or on a yacht or sailboat.

The Big Day

Choosing the Perfect Place. Puerto Vallarta—including resorts to the north along the Riviera Nayarit and south along the Costalegre—is one of Mexico's most popular wedding and honeymoon destinations. Many couples choose to marry on the beach, often at sunset because it's cooler and more comfortable for everyone; others chuck the whole weather conundrum and marry in an air-conditioned resort ballroom.

The luxury of enjoying your wedding and honeymoon in one place has a cost: You may find it hard to have some alone time with your sweetie with all your family and friends on hand. Consider booking an all-inclusive, which has plenty of meal options and activities to keep your guests busy. This will make it easier for them to respect your privacy and stick to mingling with you and your spouse at planned times. Among PV's best options for on-site, catered weddings are the Marriott CasaMagna, the Westin, the Villa Premiere, and Casa Velas. Le Kliff and El Dorado restaurants offer stunning views from their wedding-reception areas; Las Caletas offers unique beachfront weddings accessed by boat through Vallarta Adventures.

Wedding Attire. Some women choose a traditional full wedding gown with veil, but more popular and comfortable—especially for an outdoor wedding—is a simple sheath or a white cotton or linen dress that will breathe in the tropical heat. Some brides, of course, opt for even less formal attire: anything from a sundress to shorts or a bathing suit.

Weddings on the beach are best done barefoot, even when the bride wears a gown. Choose strappy sandals for a wedding or reception that's not on the sand, and forget the notion of stockings—it's usually too hot and humid. Whatever type gown you choose, it's best to both purchase and get any alterations done before leaving home. Buy a special garment bag and hand-carry your dress on the plane. Don't let this be the one time in your life that your luggage goes missing at great personal cost.

Time of Year. Planning according to the weather can be critical for a successful PV wedding. If you're getting married in your bathing suit, you might not mind some heat and humidity, but will your venue—and your future mother-in-law—hold up under a summer deluge? We recommend substituting the traditional June wedding that's so suitable for New England and Nova Scotia with one held between late November and February or March. April through mid-June is usually dry but extremely hot and humid. Summer rains begin to fall in mid-June. Sometimes this means a light sprinkle that reduces heat and humidity and freshens the trees; other times it means a torrential downpour that immediately floods the streets. Although hurricanes are rarer along the Pacific than the Caribbean, they can threaten September through early November. For an outdoor wedding, establish a detailed backup plan in case the weather lets you down.

Finding a Wedding Planner. Hiring a wedding planner will minimize stress for all but the simplest of ceremonies. A year or more in advance, the planner will, among other things, help choose the venue, recommend a florist, and arrange for a photographer and musicians. The most obvious place to find a wedding planner is at a resort hotel that becomes wedding central: providing accommodations for you and your guests, the wedding ceremony venue, and the restaurant or ballroom for the reception. But you can also hire an independent wedding coordinator; just google "Puerto Vallarta wedding" and you'll get tons of hits. Unless you're fluent in Spanish, make sure the person who will be arranging one of your life's milestones speaks and understands English well. Ask for references, and check them.

When interviewing a planner, talk about your budget, and ask about costs. Are there hourly fees or one fee for the whole event? How available will the consultant and her assistants be? Which vendors do they use and why? How long have they been in business? Request a list of the exact services they'll provide, and get a proposal in writing. If you don't feel this is the right person or agency for you, try someone else. Cost permitting, it's helpful to meet the planner in person.

Requirements. Getting a bona fide wedding planner will obviously facilitate completing the required paperwork and negotiating the legal requirements for marrying in Mexico. Blood work must be done upon your arrival, but not more than 14 days before the ceremony. All documents must be translated by an authorized translator from the destination, and it's important to send these documents certified mail to your wedding coordinator at least a month ahead of the wedding. You'll also need to submit an application for a marriage license as well as certified birth certificates (bring the original with you to PV, and send certified copies ahead of time). If either party is divorced or widowed, an official divorce decree or death certificate must be supplied. The bride, groom, and four witnesses will also need to present passports and tourist cards.

Jalisco State has additional requirements; for this reason some couples choose to have the civil ceremony in Nayarit State (Nuevo Vallarta or anywhere north of there) and then the "spiritual" ceremony in the location of their choice. Since church weddings aren't officially recognized in Mexico, even for citizens, a civil ceremony is required in any case, thus making your marriage valid in your home country as well. Another option is to be married (secretly?) in a civil ceremony in your own country and then hold the wedding event without worrying about all the red tape.

The Honeymoon

If you've chosen a resort wedding, you and many of the guests may be content to relax on-site after the bustle and stress of the wedding itself. Puerto Vallarta has a huge variety of accommodations, from name-brand hotels with spas and multiple swimming pools to three-bedroom B&Bs in the moderate price range. Many properties have special honeymoon packages that include champagne and strawberries on the wedding night, flowers in the room, spa treatments for the bride and attendants, or other sorts of pampering and earthly pleasures.

KIDS AND FAMILIES

What better way to bond with your kids than splashing in the pool or the sea, riding a horse into the hills, or zipping through the trees on a canopy tour? Puerto Vallarta may be short on sights, but it's long on outdoor activities like these. It also has a huge range of accommodation options: everything from B&Bs that leave lunch and dinner wide open for a family on the go to all-inclusive resorts where picky eaters can be easily indulged and kids of all ages can be kept engaged by activities or kids' clubs.

Places to Stay

Resorts: Except those that exclude children entirely, most of Vallarta's beach resorts cater to families and have children's programs. The Sol Meliá is great for little kids, as it offers lots of games and activities geared toward them; there's not so much of interest to teens here. The Marriott is kid-friendly, offering children's menus at most of its restaurants and kids' clubs for the 4-to-13 set. In addition to things like Ping-Pong, tennis, and volleyball, kids absolutely love liberating tiny turtle hatchlings into the sea during the summer/early fall turtle season.

At the high end of the price spectrum, Four Seasons has plenty for the kids to do, as well as golf and spa appointments for Mom and Dad. The protected, almost private beach here is great for the children, who also love floating on inner tubes in the ring-shaped swift-water swimming pool. The children's center, with loads of cool games and computer programs, keeps kids of all ages entertained.

South of Vallarta, Dreams is a great place for an all-inclusive family vacation, with movies on the beach and loads of activities for adults and children. Kids enjoy the secluded beach (parents needn't worry about them wandering off), the giant-screen TV on the beach for movies or ball games, and the treasure hunts and weekly overnight campouts.

Old Vallarta (El Centro and Colonia E. Zapata, aka Zona Romántica) consists mainly of moderate to budget hotels. Independent families are often drawn to such properties on or near Los Muertos Beach. Playa Los Arcos, for instance, is right on the sand; Eloisa, with its inexpensive studios (with kitchenettes) and suites, is a block from the bay.

Vacation Rentals: Apartments, condos, and villas are an excellent option for families. You can cook your own food (a big money saver), spread out, and set up a home away from home, which can make everyone feel more comfortable. If you decide to go the apartment- or condo-rental route, be sure to ask about the number and size of the swimming pools and whether outdoor spaces and barbecue areas are available.

Funky Yelapa, south of PV, has only a few hotels; most people rent homes—ranging from spartan to less spartan—via the Internet; www.yelapa.info has a wide range of rentals. **Boutique Villas** (☎ *322/209–1992 or 866/560–2281* ⊕ *www.boutiquevillas. com*) is an excellent resource for quality condos and villas in a variety of price ranges. Even in the winter (high) season, you can get a nice two-bedroom, two-bath condo for $150 a night. Add great locations, satellite TV in every bedroom, daily maid service, and the use of washer and dryer, and the value is obvious. You can even get your own cook who will do the shopping as well.

Beaches

Los Muertos Beach is a good bet for families who want access to snacks and water-sports rentals, and there are (usually) lifeguards here, too. Families favor the north end near Playas Olas Altas (the south end is the gay beach), but there's plenty of sand and sun for all. The all-inclusive resorts of Nuevo Vallarta rent water-sports equipment for use at a long, wide beach that continues all the way to Bucerías. The scene here is very laid-back, involving more lounging than anything else.

Water Activities

If you surf, or want to learn, Sayulita is a good option. There are also many good surfing beaches off the point at Punta Mita as well as around San Blas and Barra de Navidad.

Year-round you can catch glimpses of manta rays leaping from the water and dolphins riding the wakes of bay cruises. Winter sees whale-watching expeditions on which you can spot humpbacks and, occasionally, orcas.

Turtle season is summer through late fall; children love to take part in liberating the tiny hatchlings. Larger resort hotels on turtle-nesting beaches often encourage guests to participate in this, and wildlife operators offer turtle tours.

There's snorkeling (though sometimes lots of little jellyfish join you in the hot summer months) around Los Arcos just south of PV, at the Marieta Islands off Punta Mita, and at other beaches north and south. Divers haunt these spots, too, in addition to farther-away destinations.

PV's yachts and *pangas* (skiffs) are available for shore- or deep-water fishing excursions. Nuevo Vallarta has a much smaller fleet based at Paradise Village marina. In small towns like Mismaloya, Boca de Tomatlán, Rincón de Guayabitos, Sayulita, Tenacatita, and Barra de Navidad, you contract with local fishermen on or near the beach for angling expeditions.

Land Activities

Puerto Vallarta proper has a lovely botanical garden with a river in which kids can splash. In the hills behind town, you can go on horseback, mountain-bike, ATV, dune-buggy, or canopy-tour adventures. Golf courses range from private links at Punta Mita to fun and accessible courses in Nuevo Vallarta and Marina Vallarta. There are excellent courses to the south at El Tamarindo and Barra de Navidad.

After Dark

Nightly in high season musicians, clowns, and mimes perform at PV's Los Arcos amphitheater. Walk along the *malecón* en route, stopping to enjoy an ice cream, admire the sunset, or pose for pictures beside a sculpture.

Dinner shows often offer Mexican-theme buffets, mariachi music, and, sometimes, cowboys doing rope tricks. The pirate-theme vessel *Marigalante* has both day and evening cruises that kids love. PV has three modern movie theaters with English-language movies; note, though, that animated films or those rated "G" are usually dubbed in Spanish, as kids aren't fond of subtitles.

GREAT ITINERARIES

Each of these itineraries fills one day. Together they touch on some of PV's quintessential experiences, from shopping to getting outdoors to just relaxing at the best beaches and spas.

Romancing the Zone

Head south of downtown to the Zona Romántica for a day of excellent shopping and dining. Stop at Isla del Río Cuale for trinkets and T-shirts; have an island breakfast overlooking the stream at the River Cafe or an excellent lunch at Le Bistro, where the romantic, neo-Continental decor and monumental architecture produce a flood of endorphins.

■ TIP→ Most of the stores in the neighborhood will either ship your oversize prizes for you or expertly pack them and recommend reputable shipping companies.

Crossing the pedestrian bridge nearest the bay, drop nonshoppers at Los Muertos Beach. They can watch the fishermen on the small pier, lie in the sun, sit in the shade with a good book, or walk south to the rocky coves of **Conchas Chinas Beach,** which is good for snorkeling when the water is calm. Meanwhile, the shoppers head to **Calle Basilio Badillo** and surrounding streets for folk art, housewares, antiques, clothing, and accessories. End the day back at Los Muertos with dinner, drinks, and live music.

■ TIP→ Some of the musicians at beachfront restaurants work for the restaurant; others are freelancers. If a roving musician (or six) asks what you'd like to hear, find out the price of a song. Fifty pesos (a little more than $1) is typical.

Downtown Exploration

Puerto Vallarta hasn't much at all in the way of museums, but with a little legwork, you can get a bit of culture. Learn about the area's first inhabitants at the tiny but tidy **Museo Arqueológico** (closed Sunday), with info in English. From the museum, head downtown along the newest section of the **malecón,** which crosses the river. About four blocks north, check out the action in the main plaza and Los Arcos amphitheater. At the **Iglesia de Nuestra Señora de Guadalupe,** you can pay your respects to the patron saint of the city (and the country).

Strolling farther north along the malecón is like walking through a sculpture garden: Look for the statue of a boy riding a sea horse (it's become PV's trademark), and *La Nostalgia,* a statue of a seated couple, by noted PV artist Ramiz Barquet. Three figures climb a ladder extending into the air in Sergio Bustamante's *In Search of Reason.* One of the most elaborate sculptures is by Alejandro Colunga: *Rotunda del Mar* has more than a dozen fantastic figures—some with strange, alien appendages—seated on chairs and pedestals of varying heights.

A Day of Golf and Steam

Puerto Vallarta is one of Mexico's best golfing destinations. And what better way to top off a day of play than with a steam, soak, and massage? At the southern end of the Costalegre, Tamarindo has a great course (18 great holes) and a very good spa. The closest spas to the greens of Marina Vallarta and the Vista Vallarta are those at the Westin Regina and the CasaMagna Marriott, which has gorgeous new facilities. The El Tigre course is associated with the Paradise Village resort, whose reasonably priced spa is open also to those who golf at Mayan Palace, just up the road, and at Flamingos, at the far northern edge of Nuevo Vallarta.

■ TIP→ Ask your concierge (or look online) to find out how far ahead you can reserve,

and then try for the earliest possible tee time to beat the heat. If the course you choose doesn't have a club pool, you can have lunch and hang at the pool at the resorts suggested above or get a massage, facial, or other treatment (always reserve ahead).

A Different Resort Scene

If you've got wheels, explore a different sort of beach resort. After breakfast, grab beach togs, sunscreen, and other essentials for a day at a beach to the north of town. Before heading out, those with a sweet tooth should make a pit stop at PV's Pie in the Sky, which has excellent pie, chocolate, and other sugar fixes. (There's another Pie in the Sky in Bucerías, as well as a Los Chatos cake and ice cream shop.)

About an hour north of PV, join Mexican families on the beach at **Rincón de Guayabitos,** on attractive Jaltemba Bay. Play in the mild surf; walk the pretty, long beach; or take a ride in a glass-bottom boat to **El Islote,** an islet with a small restaurant and snorkeling opportunities. Vendors on Guayabitos beach sell grilled fish, sweet breads, and chilled coconuts and watermelon from their brightly colored stands.

On the way back south, stop in the small town of **San Francisco** (aka San Pancho) for dinner. You can't go wrong at La Ola Rica or the more sophisticated Cafe del Mar (brush the sand off your feet for that one). In high season and especially on weekend evenings, one of the two will probably have live music.

■ TIP→ Take a water taxi out for a look at El Islote, where with luck you might spot a whale between December and March.

LIZ + RICHARD

The affair between Richard Burton and Elizabeth Taylor ignited tourism to PV, which was an idyllic beach town when they first visited in 1963. Taylor tagged along when Burton starred in *The Night of the Iguana,* shot in and around Mismaloya beach. The fiery Welsh actor purchased Casa Kimberley (Calle Zaragoza, a few blocks behind the cathedral) for Liz's 32nd birthday and connected it to his home across the street with a pink-and-white "love bridge." Taylor owned the house for 26 years and left most of her possessions behind when she sold it. Casa Kimberley later became a B&B and is now part of Hacienda San Angel (*see Chapter 4, Where to Stay*).

SNAPSHOT OF PUERTO VALLARTA

Geography

Puerto Vallarta sits at the center point of C-shaped Banderas Bay. Spurs from the Sierra Cacoma run down to the sea, forming a landscape of numerous valleys. This highly fractured mountain range is just one of many within the Sierra Madre—which runs from the Rockies to South America. Sierra Cacoma sits at the juncture of several major systems that head south toward Oaxaca State. Forming a distinct but related system is the volcanic or transversal volcanic axis that runs east to west across the country—and the globe. Comprising part of the so-called Ring of Fire, this transverse chain includes some of the world's most active volcanoes. Volcán de Fuego, southeast of Puerto Vallarta in Colima State, and the giant Popocateptl, near the Gulf of Mexico, are active. Visible from PV are the more intimate Sierra Vallejo and the Sierra Cuale ranges, to the north and south, respectively.

Heading down to the sea from these highlands are a number of important rivers, including the Ameca and the Mascota, which join forces not far from the coast at a place called Las Juntas (The Joining). Now mostly dry, the Ameca forms the boundary between Jalisco and Nayarit states. The Cuale River empties into the ocean at Puerto Vallarta, dividing the city center in two. In addition to boasting many rivers, the area is blessed with seasonal and permanent streams and springs.

Banderas Bay, or Bahía de Banderas, is Mexico's largest bay, at 42 km (26 mi) tip to tip. The northern point, Punta Mita, is in Nayarit State. Towns at the southern extreme of the bay, at Cabo Corrientes (Cape Currents)—named for the frequently strong currents off its shore—are accessible only by boat or dirt roads.

The mountains backing the Costalegre are part of the Sierra Madre Occidental range. The hilly region of eroded plains has two main river systems: the San Nicolás and Cuitzmala.

Several hundred miles east of Banderas Bay, Guadalajara—capital of Jalisco State—occupies the west end of 5,400-foot Atemajac Valley, which is surrounded by mountains. Just south of Guadalajara, Lake Chapala is Mexico's largest natural lake.

Flora

The western flanks of the Sierra Madre and foothills leading down to the sea have tropical deciduous forest. At the higher levels are expanses of pine-oak forest. Many species of pines thrive in these woods, mixed in with *encinos* and *robles*, two different categories of oak. Walnut trees and *oyamel*, a type of fir, are the mainstays of the lower *arroyos*, or river basins.

Along the coast magnificent *huanacaxtle*, also called *parota* (in English, monkey pod or elephant ear tree), mingle with equally huge and impressive mango as well as kapok, cedar, tropical almond, tamarind, flamboyant, and willow. The brazilwood tree is resistant to insects and, therefore, ideal for making furniture. *Matapalo*, or strangler fig, are common in this landscape. As its name hints, these fast-growing trees embrace others in a death grip; once the matapalo is established, the host tree eventually dies.

Colima palms, known locally as *guaycoyul*, produce small round nuts smashed for oil or sometimes fed to domestic animals. Mango, avocado, citrus, and guava are found in the wild. Imported trees and bushes often seen surrounding homes and small farms include Indian laurel, bamboo, and bougainvillea.

The coastal fringe north of San Blas is surprisingly characterized by savannas. Guinea grass makes fine animal fodder for horses and cows. Lanky coconut trees line roads and beaches. Watery coconut "milk" is a refreshing drink, and the meat of the coconut, although high in saturated fat, can be eaten or used in many types of candy. Another drink, *agua de tuba,* is made from the heart of the palm; the trunk is used in certain types of construction. Mangroves in saltwater estuaries provide an ecosystem for crabs, crustaceans, and birds.

South of Banderas Bay, thorn forest predominates along the coastal strip, backed by tropical deciduous forest. Leguminous trees like the *tabachin,* with its bright orange flowers, have long, dangling seedpods used by indigenous people as rattles. Other prominent area residents are the acacias, hardy trees with fluffy puffballs of light yellow blooms. The dry forest is home to more than 1,100 species of cacti. The *nopal,* or prickly pear cactus, abounds; local people remove the spines and grill the cactus pads or use them in healthful salads. The fruit of the prickly pear, called *tuna,* is used to make a refreshing drink, *agua de tuna.*

Fauna

Hunting, deforestation, and the encroachment of humans have diminished many once-abundant species. In the mountains far from humankind, endangered margay, jaguar, and ocelot hunt their prey, which includes spider monkeys, deer, and peccaries. More commonly seen are skunks, raccoons, rabbits, and coyote. The coatimundi is an endearing little animal that lives in family groups, often near streambeds. Inquisitive and alert, they resemble tall, slender prairie dogs. Along with the tanklike, slow-moving armadillo, the sandy-brown coatimundi is among the animals you're most likely to spot without venturing too deep within the forest. Local people call the coatimundi both *tejón* and *pisote* and often keep them as pets.

Poisonous snakes include the Mexican rattlesnake and the fer-de-lance. Locals call the latter *cuatro narices* (four noses) because it appears to have four nostrils. It's also called *nauyaca;* the bite of this viper can be deadly. There are more than a dozen species of coral snakes with bands of black, yellow, and red in different patterns. False corals imitate this color scheme to fool their predators, but unless you're an expert, it's best to err on the side of caution.

The most famous of the migratory marine species is the humpback whale, here called *ballena jorobada,* or "hunchback" whale. These leviathans grow to 51 feet and weigh 40 to 50 tons; they travel in pods, feeding on krill and tiny fish. In a given year the females in area waters may be either mating or giving birth. During their annual migration of thousands of miles from the Bering Sea, the hardy creatures may lose some 10,000 pounds, or approximately 10% of their body weight. Hunted nearly to extinction in the 1900s, humpbacks remain an endangered species.

A few Bryde whales make their way to Banderas Bay and other protected waters near the end of the humpback season, as do some killer whales (orca) and false killer whales. Bottlenose, spinner, and pantropic spotted dolphins are present pretty much year-round. These acrobats love to bow surf just under the water's surface and to leap into the air. Another spectacular leaper is the velvety-black manta ray, which can grow to 30 feet

wide. Shy but lovely spotted eagle rays hover close to the ocean floor, where they feed on crustaceans and mollusks. Nutrient-rich Pacific waters provide sustenance for a wide range of other sea creatures. Among the most eye-catching are the graceful king angelfish and the iridescent bumphead parrotfish, striped Indo-Pacific sergeants and Moorish idols, and the funny-looking guinea fowl puffer and its close relative, the equally unusual black-blotched porcupine fish.

The varied landscape of Nayarit and Jalisco states provides a tapestry of habitats for some 350 species of birds. In the mangroves, standouts are the great blue heron, mangrove cuckoo, and vireo. Ocean and shorebirds include red-billed tropic birds as well as various species of heron, egret, gulls, brown and blue-footed boobies, and frigate birds. Military macaws patrol the thorn forests, and songbirds of all stripes live in the pine-oak forests. About 40% of the birds in the Costalegre region are migratory. Among the residents are the yellow-headed parrot and the Mexican wood nymph, both threatened species.

Environmental Issues

The biggest threat to the region is deforestation of the tropical dry forest. Slash-and-burn techniques are used to prepare virgin forest for agriculture and pasturing of animals. This practice is counterproductive, as the thin soil fails to produce after the mulch-producing trees and shrubs have been stripped.

The tropical dry forests (also called tropical thorn forest) are now being deforested due to the increasing tourism and human population. Controlled ecotourism offers a potential solution, although failed projects in the area have significantly altered or drained salt marshes and mangrove swamps.

The dry forest is an extremely important ecosystem. It represents one of the richest in Mexico and also one with the highest level of endemism (plant and animal species found nowhere else). Several species of hardwood trees, including the Pacific coast mahogany and Mexican kingwood, are being over-harvested for use in the building trade. The former is endangered and the latter, threatened.

South of Puerto Vallarta in the Costalegre are two adjacent forest reserves that together form the 32,617-acre Chamela–Cuixmala Biosphere Reserve. Co-owned and managed by nonprofit agencies, private companies, and Mexico's National University, UNAM, the reserve protects nine major vegetation types, including the tropical dry forest, tropical deciduous forest, and semi-deciduous forest. A riparian environment is associated with the north bank of the Cuixmala River. Within the reserve there are approximately 72 species considered at risk for extinction, including the American crocodile and several species of sea turtle.

Hojonay Biosphere Reserve was established by the Hojonay nonprofit organization to preserve the jaguar of the Sierra de Vallejo range and its habitat. The 157,060-acre reserve is in the foothills and mountains behind La Cruz de Huanacaxtle and San Francisco, in Nayarit State.

There are no tours or casual access to either reserve, which serve as buffers against development and a refuge for wildlife.

The People

The population of Puerto Vallarta is overwhelmingly of mestizo (mixed Native American and white/European) descent. According to the 2000 census, fewer than 1% of Jalisco residents speak an indigenous language. Compare that to nearby states: Michoacán with 3.6%; Guerrero with about 14%; and Oaxaca, where more than 33% of the inhabitants converse in a native language. Those indigenous people who do live in Jalisco State are small groups of Purépecha (also called Tarascans), in the south. The Purépecha were among the very few groups not conquered by the Aztec nation that controlled much of Mesoamerica at the time of the Spanish conquest.

Although not large in number, the indigenous groups most associated with Nayarit and Jalisco states are the Cora and their relatives, the Huichol. Isolated in mountain and valley hamlets and individual *rancherías* (tiny farms) deep in the Sierra Madre, both have to a large extent maintained their own customs and culture. According to the CDI (Comisión Nacional Para el Desarrollo de los Pueblos Indígenas, or National Commission for the Development of Native Peoples), there are about 24,390 Cora in Durango, Zacatecas, and Nayarit states, and some 43,929 Huichol, mainly in Nayarit, Jalisco, and Durango. Nearly 70% of the culturally related groups speak their native language.

No matter their background, you'll notice nearly all locals have a contagiously cheery outlook on life. There's an explanation for that: In 1947 a group of prominent vallartenses was returning along twisty mountain roads from an excursion to Mexico City. When the driver lost control and the open-sided bus plunged toward the abyss, death seemed certain. But a large rock halted the bus's progress, and Los Favorecidos (The Lucky Ones), as they came to be known, returned to Puerto Vallarta virtually unharmed. Their untrammeled gestures of thanks to the town's patron saint, the Virgin of Guadalupe, set the precedent for this animated religious procession. Today, all Puerto Vallartans consider themselves to be Los Favorecidos, and thus universally blessed—hence, the story goes, their optimism. For those of us fortunate enough to visit, taking home a bit of that spiritual magnetism can be the best souvenir.

The Magic of Mexico

To say that Mexico is a magical place means more than it's a place of great natural beauty and fabulous experiences. Cities like Catemaco, in Veracruz, have a reputation for their *brujos* and *brujas* (male and female witches, respectively) and herbal healers (*curanderos/curanderas*). But Mexicans use these services even in modern Mexico City and Guadalajara and in tourist towns like Puerto Vallarta. Some might resort to using a curandera to reverse *mal de ojo*, the evil eye, thought to be responsible for a range of unpleasant symptoms, circumstances, disease, or even death.

A *limpia*, or cleansing, is the traditional cure for the evil eye. The healer usually passes a raw chicken or turkey egg over the sufferer to draw out the bad spirit. Green plants like basil, or branches from certain trees can also be used, drawing the greenery over the head, front, and back to decontaminate the victim. Prayer is an essential ingredient.

Some cures are of a more practical nature. Mexican herbalists, like their colleagues around the world, use tree bark, nuts, berries, roots, and leaves to treat everything from dandruff to cancer. Epazote, or wormseed, is a distinctly flavored plant whose leaves are used in cooking. As its English name implies, its medicinal task is to treat parasites.

Most folk wisdom seems to draw from both fact and, if not fiction, at least superstition. Breezes and winds are thought to produce a host of negative reactions: from colds and cramps to far more drastic ailments like paralysis. Some people prefer sweating in a car or bus to rolling down the window and being hit by the wind, especially since mixing hot and cold is something else to be avoided. Even worldly athletes may refuse a cold drink after a hot run. Sudden shock is thought by some to cause lasting problems.

Although it doesn't take a leap of faith to believe that herbal remedies cure disease and Grandma's advice was right on, some of the stuff sold in shops is a bit "harder to swallow." It's difficult to imagine, for example, that the sky-blue potion in a pint-size bottle will bring you good luck, or the lilac-color one can stop people from gossiping about you. Those that double as floor polish seem especially suspect.

Whether magic and prophesy are real or imagined, they sometimes have concrete results. Conquistador Hernán Cortés arrived on the east coast of Mexico in 1519, which correlated to the year "One Reed" on the Aztec calendar. A few centuries prior to Cortés's arrival, the benevolent god-king Quetzalcoatl had, according to legend, departed the same coast on a raft of snakes, vowing to return in the year One Reed to reclaim his throne.

News of Cortés—a metal-wearing god-man accompanied by strange creatures (horses and dogs) and carrying lightning (cannons and firearms)—traveled quickly to the Aztec capital. Emperor Moctezuma was nervous about Quetzalcoatl's return and his reaction to the culture of war and sacrifice the Aztecs had created. In his desire to placate the returning god, Moctezuma ignored the advice of trusted counselors and opened the door for the destruction of the Aztec empire.

La Vida Loca

Living the good life in Mexico—specifically in and around Banderas Bay—seems to get easier year by year. Americans and Canadians are by far the biggest groups of expats. In addition to those who have relocated to make Mexico their home, many more foreigners have part-time retirement or vacation homes here. A two-bedroom property in a gated community by the sea begins at around $230,000. You could get more modest digs for less; at the upper end of the spectrum, the sky's the limit.

The sheer number of foreigners living in Puerto Vallarta facilitates adventures that were much more taxing a decade or two ago, like building a home or finding an English-speaking real estate agent or lawyer. Contractors and shopkeepers are used to dealing with gringos; most speak good to excellent English. The town is rich with English-language publications and opportunities for foreigners to meet up for events or volunteer work.

FESTIVALS AND EVENTS

January
El Día de los Santos Reyes (January 6) was the day of gift-giving in Latin America until Santa Claus invaded from the North. Although many families now give gifts on Christmas or Christmas Eve, Three Kings Day is still an important celebration. The children receive token "gifts of the Magi." *Atole* (a drink of finely ground rice or corn) or hot chocolate is served along with the *rosca de reyes,* a ring-shaped cake. The person whose portion contains a tiny baby Jesus figurine must host a follow-up party on Candlemass, February 2.

Held for the sixth time in 2010, the **Perrotón** (*Dog Show* ☎ 322/224–9966) has become an annual event. In addition to lectures, there are contests including ugliest dog, dog and owner who most resemble each other, most beautiful dog, and exhibitions of agility and obedience.

February
The four-day **Festival de Música San Pancho** (*Riviera Nayarit Tourism Board* ☎ 322/297–2516) is an amalgam of the area's best regional musicians; snowbirds also participate. The free jamboree is usually held in mid- to late February. The event has featured bluegrass, blues, jazz, funk, and standards in addition to cumbia and Mexican classics. Look for flyers around town. San Pancho is 50 minutes north of downtown Puerto Vallarta.

Charros (cowboys) from all over Mexico compete in the four-day **Campeonato Nacional Charro Vallarta** (*National Charro Championship* ☎ 322/ 429–7996 cell or 322/120–0678 cell) at Mojoneras. In addition to men's rope and riding tricks and the female competitors, there are mariachis, a parade, and exhibitions of charro-related art. Admission is $7–$12.

May
★ **Las Fiestas de Mayo** (*May Festivals* ☎ 322/223–2500) is a three-week fair with fireworks and regional crafts and foods that is more popular with locals than visitors. In Jalisco, no such festival would be complete without *charreadas* (rodeos). Restaurants lower their prices for two weeks at the beginning of low season during **Restaurant Week**, also known as the May Food Festival.

June
June 1 is **Día de la Marina** (☎ 322/224–2352). Like other Mexican ports, PV celebrates Navy Day with free boat rides (inquire at the Terminal Marítima or the XII Zona Naval Militar, just to the south). Watch colorfully decorated boats depart to make offerings to sailors lost at sea.

July and August
Barra de Navidad celebrates its patron saint, **San Antonio de Padua**, the week preceding July 13 with religious parades,

mass, street parties, and fireworks. **Cristo de los Brazos Caídos** is honored August 30–September 1 in much the same way as St. Anthony.

September

The **Celebration of Independence** is held on September 15 and 16, beginning on the evening of September 15 with the traditional *Grito de Dolores*. It translates as "Cry of Pain," but it also references the town of Dolores Hidalgo, where the famous cry for freedom was uttered by priest Miguel Hidalgo. Late in the evening on September 15 there are mariachis, speeches, and other demonstrations of national pride. On September 16, witness parades and charros on horseback through the main streets of town.

October

An annual event since 1996, **Old Town artWalk** (☎ 322/222–1982) showcases artwork at several dozen galleries. The galleries stay open late, sometimes offering an appetizer or snack, wine, beer, or soft drinks. Browse among the paintings, jewelry, ceramics, glass, and folk art while hobnobbing with some of PV's most respected artists. If you don't have a map, pick one up from one of the perennially participating galleries, which include Galería Arte Latinoamericano, Galería Corona, Galería 8 y Más, Galería Pacífico, Galería Uno, Galería Vallarta, Arte 550, and Galería de Ollas. This walk is held from 6 PM to 10 PM, from the last week of October until late April.

North of Nuevo Vallarta, Bucerías's **Mini Art Walk** (☎ 329/298–2506) is on Thursday nights from the last week of October until late April, 7–9 PM. Participating galleries are on Boulevard Lázaro Cárdenas around Calle Galeana.

November and December

Fodor's Choice ★ The **International Gourmet Festival** is one of PV's biggest events (⇨ *see "PV's Contemporary Cuisine Scene," Chapter 5*). Beginning in late November or early December, the public is invited to see movies of many genres, at reasonable prices, during the five-day **Vallarta Film Festival** (☎ 322/225–9251 or 322/224–1175 ⊕ *www.vallartafilmfestival.com*). Films and seminars are held at the Cinemark Plaza Caracol (✉ *Plaza Caracol, Zona Hotelera* ☎ 322/224–8927). Film-industry types come to hobnob and honor each other with awards for best director, picture, cinematographer, and actor. Mid-November through the end of April, three-hour **villa tours** (✉ *Calle Olas Altas 513* ☎ 322/222–5466 💷 *$35*) by the International Friendship Club get you inside the garden walls of some inspiring PV homes. English-speaking guides lead groups on air-conditioned buses Wednesday and Thursday. Tours depart at 10:30 AM. Lunch is included. The fee benefits local charities.

★ Puerto Vallarta's most important celebration of faith—and also one of the most elaborate spectacles of the year—is **Fiestas de la Virgen de Guadalupe** (☎ 322/223–2500 Ext. 232), designed to honor the Virgin of Guadalupe, the city's patron saint and the patroness of all Mexico. Exuberance fills the air as the end of November approaches and each participating business organizes its own procession. The most elaborate ones include allegorical floats and papier-mâché *matachines,* or giant dolls (for lack of a better phrase), and culminate in their own private mass. Groups snake down Calle Juárez from the north or the south, ending at the Cathedral in Old Vallarta.

Beaches

WORD OF MOUTH

"My friend and I and our young daughters spent an afternoon playing on the beach at Playa Mismoloya. My friend took the girls into the bathroom to wash up, and when she entered, she saw a lovely long tiled tub. Just as she was spraying water on them, a man came in, and in horrified Spanish managed to let her know the "tub" was actually a urinal. Needless to say, this has become a family legend."

—scdreamer

Throughout the region, from the Riviera Nayarit to the Costalegre, long, flat beaches invite walking, and reefs and offshore breaks draw divers, snorkelers, and surfers. In places, untouristy hideaways with little to distract you beyond waves lapping the shore may be accessible by land or by sea. Omnipresent seafood shanties are perfect vantage points for sunsets on the sand.

Although Pacific Mexico's beaches aren't the sugar-sand, crystal-water variety of the Caribbean, they're still lovely. The water here is relatively unpolluted, and the oft-mountainous backdrop is majestic.

PV sits at the center of horseshoe-shaped Bahía de Banderas (Banderas Bay), the second-largest bay in North America (after the Hudson). Exquisitely visible from cliff-side hotels and restaurants, the bay's scalloped coast holds myriad coves and small bays perfect for shelling, sunning, swimming, and engaging in more strenuous activities.

At Hotel Zone beaches and a few popular stretches of sand north and south of PV proper you can parasail, take boat rides, or jet-ski; some beaches lend themselves to kayaking, boogie boarding, or snorkeling. Foothills that race down to the sea are crowded with palms and cedars, and the jungle's blue-green canopy forms a highly textured background to the deep-blue ocean. Dozens of creeks and rivers follow the contours of these hills, creating estuaries, mangrove swamps, and other habitats.

South of Cabo Corrientes the mountains recede from the coast. Lovely yet lonely beaches and bays are fringed, as elsewhere in and around PV, by dry, tropical thorn forest with a variety of plants. Several species of whales cruise down in winter, and turtles spawn on the beaches from late summer into fall.

BEACH REGIONS

PUERTO VALLARTA

Paralleling the Romantic Zone, Playa los Muertos is PV's most popular beach, where restaurants and bars have music, vendors sell barbecued fish on a stick, and people cruise the boardwalk. Immediately north of Los Muertos is contiguous Olas Altas Beach. The beaches in the Hotel Zone and Marina Vallarta can be lively during holidays and high season but have less to recommend them the rest of the year; beach erosion is a problem here, and some of the MV hotels' beaches have little or no sand at high tide. At the south end of Banderas Bay are beautiful mountain-backed *playas* accessible only by boat.

NAYARIT

NUEVO VALLARTA

One wide, flat, sandy beach stretches from the mouth of the Ameca River north for miles, past the Nuevo Vallarta hotels (including the new developments at the north end, called Flamingos) and into the town of Bucerías. The generally calm water is good for swimming and, when conditions are right, bodysurfing or boogie boarding. Activities are geared to all-inclusive-hotel guests north of Paradise Village marina. Guys on the beach rent water-sports equipment, as do most of the hotels.

RIVIERA NAYARIT

From Nuevo Vallarta north into Nayarit State, rocky headlands sandwich stretches of sand. From Bucerías to Chacala and beyond to San Blas, beaches attract boogie boarders, beachcombers, and those who make their own fun. Although there are fewer services than in PV, the state government is investing heavily to develop the area. Surfing is big at Sayulita and Punta Mita (also called Punta *de* Mita), where some of the best spots are accessible only by boat. Guayabitos, with its nearby island, is a vacation mecca for Mexican families and a refuge for snowbirds from Canada and the northern United States. Off the main highway, long, sandy roads lead to more isolated beaches such as Destiladeras; however, many of these are unfortunately now being developed and as such are inaccessible to the public.

SOUTH OF PUERTO VALLARTA

South of PV the beaches constitute the domain of the independent traveler and the well-heeled recluse. High-end hotels on picturesque, rock-framed beaches arrange fishing and other pastimes. Other long, sandy beaches—many on large, semi-protected bays—are frequented by fishermen and local people relaxing at seafood shanties and allow shelling, snorkeling, fishing, and trips to nearby islands. Having a car is helpful for exploring multiple beaches, although local bus service is available.

GO FOR:	IN PV:	NORTH OR SOUTH OF PV:
Wildlife	Los Arcos; Playa Camarones (for whales in season); Marina Vallarta (for turtles in season)	Islas Marietas (Punta Mita); Playa Careyes and nearby beaches (for turtles in season)
Snorkeling	Los Arcos; Playa Conchas Chinas	Islas Marietas; Quimixto; Playa Mora
Walking or Jogging	Playa los Muertos; Playa Camarones	Nuevo Vallarta; Bucerías; Flamingos; La Manzanilla; Boca de Iguanas; Playa Tenacatita; Barra de Navidad, San Patricio–Melaque (Bahía de Navidad)
Calm, Swimmable Waters	Hotel pools; Conchas Chinas	Los Ayala, Rincón de Guayabitos (Bahía de Jaltemba); Playa Chalacatepec; Punta Perula; Boca de Iguanas; Tenacatita, San Patricio–Melaque
Surfing	Olas Altas (best April–September)	Punta Mita; Sayulita; Quimixto; Barra de Navidad
Eating/Drinking with Locals	Boca de Tomatlán; Playa Camarones (but not right on the beach)	Chacala; Rincón de Guayabitos (Bahía de Jaltembo); Punta Perula; Playa Tenacatita; Colimilla (Bahía de Navidad)

PUERTO VALLARTA

PV beaches are varied. Downtown's main beach, Los Muertos, is a fun scene, with shoulder-to-shoulder establishments for drinking and eating under the shade. There's year-round action, although water-sports equipment rentals may be available on weekends only during the rainy season. The itinerant vendors are present year-round, however, and can be annoying. Olas Altas Beach, which runs north from Los Muertos, has the same grainy brown sand but fewer vendors and services and sometimes waves big enough to surf or boogie. During vacation periods it's just as lively as Los Muertos Beach. North of the malecón and Hotel Rosita, more stretches of sand front minor hotels.

Hotel Zone beaches offer adults opportunities to play with aquatic toys, especially in high season. The sand here is often pocked with rocks, depending on the season and tides, and narrow in places. The beach at Marina Vallarta, between PV and Nuevo Vallarta, is swimmable but mainly uninspired except for the beach toys and hotels that offer refreshments. Again, sand here is lacking in front of some hotels, especially at high tide.

South of Vallarta proper are Conchas Chinas, a few smaller beaches, and Mismaloya. The wild beaches farther south (on the north side of Cabo Corrientes, from Las Animas to Yelapa) didn't have electricity until the 1970s or later. They tend to fill up with day-trippers between December and April but are well worth a visit.

Puerto Vallarta

- Playa Los Muertos
- Playa Olas Altas
- Playa las Glorias
- Puerto Vallarta
- Playa Camarones
- Playa los Tules
- Playa el Salado
- Marina Vallarta

0   4 mi
0   4 km

At Los Muertos as well as beaches in the Hotel Zone and Marina Vallarta, you can find Jet Skis, parasailing, and banana-boat rides in high season (December–April) and on weekends year-round.

GETTING HERE AND AROUND
You can readily access Downtown and Hotel Zone beaches from the street. Take a bus or a cab, or drive your car. There's coveted curbside parking, or you can pay by the hour at the Benito Juárez parking structure: it's just north of the Cuale River at the malecón and Calle Rodríguez, under Parque Lázaro Cárdenas, and across from Olas Altas Beach. The Hidalgo Street parking structure, near Playa Camarones a few blocks from the north end of the malecón, is another option.

BEACHES KEY	
🚤	Boat tours
⛺	Camping
🎣	Fishing
🏇	Horseback riding
🅿	Parking
🚻	Restroom
⛵	Sailing
🚿	Showers
🤿	Snorkel/Scuba
🏄	Surfing
🏊	Swimming

In Marina Vallarta the main public beach access (with on-street parking) is between the airport and Condominios Grand Bay. There's little to stop you from walking through the major hotels to the beaches, though, if you take a bus or cab to the area. There's also a paid parking lot between the Marival and Gran Velas hotels, by the Nuevo Vallarta tourism office.

DOWNTOWN PUERTO VALLARTA

Playa los Muertos. PV's original happenin' beach has nice bay views, and as action central, it's definitely PV's most engaging beach. Facing Vallarta's South Side (south of the Río Cuale), this flat beach hugs the Zona Romántica and runs about 1½ km (1 mi) south to a rocky point called El Púlpito. ■TIP→ **The steps (more than 100) at Calle Púlpito lead to a lookout with a great view of the beach and the bay.**

Joggers cruise the cement boardwalk early morning and after sunset; vendors stalk the beach nonstop, hawking kites, jewelry, and serapes as well as hair-braiding and alfresco massage. Their parade can range from entertaining (good bargainers can get excellent deals) to downright maddening. Bar-restaurants run the length of the beach; the bright blue umbrellas at the south end belong to Blue Chairs resort, the hub of PV's effervescent gay scene.

The surf ranges from mild to choppy with an undertow; the small waves crunching the shore usually discourage mindless paddling. Strapping young men occupy the lifeguard tower, but the service isn't consistent.

For shaded surf-side relaxation, grab a table under an umbrella at Playa Olas Altas.

Local people fish from the small pier at the foot of Calle Francisca Rodríguez or cast nets from waist-deep water near the beach's south end. Jet Skis zip around but stay out beyond the small breakers so aren't too distracting to swimmers and sunbathers. Guys on the beach offer banana-boat and parasailing rides. **Facilities:** Lifeguards, banana-boat rides, Jet Skis, parasailing; food concessions.

Playa Olas Altas. Its name means "high waves beach," but the only waves suitable for bodysurfing, boogie boarding, or, occasionally, surfing small waves are near the Cuale River, at the north end of this small beach. Although Olas Altas more often refers to the neighborhood of bars and businesses near the ocean south of the Río Cuale, it is also the name of a few blocks of sand between Daiquiri Dick's restaurant and the Río Cuale. It attracts fewer sunbathers than Los Muertos but is otherwise an extension of that beach and gets lively during holidays with sunbathers and impromptu snack stands and shaded tables on the sand. Facing Olas Altas Beach near Lázaro Cárdenas plaza are open-air stands selling beach accessories, small grocery stores, and beach-facing bar-restaurants. **Facilities:** Food concessions, parking (at Parque Lázaro Cárdenas).

BEACH OF THE DEAD

There are several versions of how Playa los Muertos got its name. One says that around the time it was founded, Indians attacked a mule train laden with silver and gold from the mountain towns, leaving the dead bodies of the muleteers on the beach. A version crediting pirates with the same deed seems more plausible. In 1935 anthropologist Dr. Isabel Kelly postulated that the place was an Indian cemetery.

Playa Camarones. The long, flat, brown sand of Shrimp Beach, favored by locals, parallels the malecón and the hotel Rosita as far north as the Buenaventura Hotel. It's always changing, perhaps rock-strewn in the morning and clear later when the tide goes out. In high (winter) season and holiday weekends, the beach has a lifeguard and water-sports concessions. Watch for whales in winter, too, from the P.V. Beach Club bar (whose owner has a penchant for impromptu karaoke sessions) or from the Barracuda Restaurant, next door. Although the waves are gentle, there are strange currents here, which should discourage all but strong swimmers. What you see here most often are small groups of men and boys surf casting. **Facilities:** Lifeguard (sometimes), banana-boat rides, Jet Skis, parasailing; food concessions, parking (at Parque Hidalgo).

NORTH OF DOWNTOWN

Zona Hotelera. The high-rise-backed Zona Hotelera beach goes by several monikers—mainly **Playa Las Glorias** but also **Playa Los Tules** around the Holiday Inn and Fiesta Americana hotels. Most people, however, just refer to each piece of beach by the hotel that it faces. Interrupted here and there by breakwaters, this fringe of gray-beige sand is generally flat but slopes down to the water. Winds and tides sometimes strew it with stones that make it less pleasant. Hit hard by Hurricane Kenna in 2002, the Sheraton, at the south end of the strip, had tons of sand deposited on its beach in 2005; it is, therefore, sandier than its neighbors, although still pocked with smooth, egg-size rocks. Some of the hotels, in particular Hotel Pelícanos and Canto del Sol, have no beach in front of their property; the water laps right at the hotel breakwater, even at low tide. **Facilities:** Banana-boat rides, Jet Skis, parasailing, snorkeling; food concessions.

Playa el Salado. At Marina Vallarta, Playa El Salado—facing the Grand Velas, Sol Meliá, Marriott, Mayan Palace, and Westin hotels—is sandy but in spots very narrow. Colorful in high season with parasailers and with windsurfers rented or lent at area hotels, these beaches are actually more fun when crowded than when solitary. During fine weather and on weekends, and daily during high season, you can rent Jet Skis and pack onto colorful banana boats for bouncy tours of 10 minutes or longer. Some hotels rent small sailboats, sailboards, and sea kayaks to guests and to nonguests. In late summer and early fall, there are opportunities to view turtle-protection activities. **Facilities:** Banana-boat rides, Jet Skis, kayaking, sailing, snorkeling; food concessions.

RIVIERA NAYARIT

At the northern end of Bahía de Banderas and farther into Nayarit State, to the north, are long, beautiful beaches fringed with tall trees or scrubby tropical forest. Only the most popular beaches like those of Nuevo Vallarta and Rincón de Guayabitos have much in the way of water-sports equipment rentals, but even the more-secluded ones have stands or small restaurants serving cold coconut water, soft drinks, beer, and grilled fish with tortillas.

Nuevo Vallarta to Punta Mita

GETTING HERE AND AROUND

In Nuevo Vallarta, park on the street or in the lot of the tourism office (40 pesos), between Gran Velas and Maribal hotels. Buses arrive here as well, but the all-inclusive hotels that predominate cater to guests only, so bring your own supplies. It's a cinch to install yourself anywhere on Bucerías's long beach, especially on the south side, where there's plenty of street-side parking. As most of the beaches north of here are off the main road, they are easiest to access by car (or taxi), although buses are frequent and drop passengers along the highway at the entrance to town.

A new road (rather, the improvement of an old, narrow dirt-and-gravel road) connects Punta Mita to Sayulita and, from there, rejoins Highway 200 to San Francisco and points to the north. However, if your destination is north of Punta Mita, there's no need to follow the coast road to the point. Simply bear right instead of left after Bucerías, continuing on Carretera 200.

NUEVO VALLARTA TO PUNTA MITA

Nuevo Vallarta. Several kilometers of pristine beach face the hotels of Playa Nuevo Vallarta. In the fall, a fenced-off turtle nesting area provides relief for the endangered ocean dwellers. Jet Skis whiz by, kids frolic in the roped-off water nearest the beach, and waiters attend to vacationers lounging in recliners in front of their respective hotels. The wide, flat, sandy stretch is perfect for long walks. In fact, you could walk all the way to Bucerías, some 8 km (5 mi) to the north. Most of the hotels here are all-inclusives, so guests generally move between their hotel pool, bar, restaurant, and the beach in front. All-inclusive programs mean that nonguests are barred from the bars and restaurants. **Facilities:** Banana-boat rides, Jet Skis, parasailing; lifeguards (seasonal), parking, toilets.

Flamingos. Between Nuevo Vallarta and Bucerías, Flamingos is a string of relatively new hotels facing the broad, brown-sand beach that is virtually identical to those of its neighbors to the north and south. Shacks on the sand rent water-sports equipment, while showers serve to clean up guests returning to their high-rise, mainly all-inclusive hotels. At the south end of the beach, driftwood and the occasional scurrying crab are more obvious than in the manicured areas by the hotels. As one approaches Nuevo Vallarta, elaborate homes begin to spring up like solitary mushrooms, inhabited by those who can afford and desire privacy. **Facilities:** Showers, boogie boards, banana-boat rides, Jet Skis, parasailing.

Bucerías. Eight kilometers (5 mi) north of Nuevo Vallarta, the substantial town of Bucerías attracts flocks of snowbirds, and this has encouraged the establishment of rental apartments and good restaurants. The surf is usually gentle enough for swimming, and a small shore break is sometimes suitable for body surfing. Beginning surfers occasionally arrive with their longboards. Backed by a fringe of beautiful coconut palms, the long beach is wide enough that it remains viable even at high tide. There are beautiful views of the arms of blue Banderas Bay to the north and south. The town is divided by an arroyo (dry river bed). On the north side, small shops face the main street, Avenida del Pacífico, while restaurants face the beach; many have tables on the sand. As the bay curves north toward La Cruz de Huanacaxtle, these businesses soon give way to small hotels, condo complexes, and single-family homes. If you have a car, parking is easiest south of the arroyo, where streets off the main beach access road, Avenida Lázaro Cárdenas, dead-end at the beach. From the south end of Bucerías you can walk all the way south to the Nayarit–Jalisco state line, created by the Ameca River. This walk of several hours takes you past the high-rise hotel developments at Flamingos and Nuevo Vallarta. **Facilities:** Food concessions.

> **BEACH BLANKET BOTHER**
>
> Although it might feel rude, it's culturally permissible to simply ignore itinerant vendors, especially if you're in the middle of a conversation. However, being blatantly impolite (i.e., shouting at the vendor to take a hike) *is* rude—no matter where you're from. A wide grin and a firm "*No, gracias*," with no further eye contact, is the best response—apart from "Yes, please, I'll take it," that is!

Playa La Manzanilla. On this crescent of soft, gold sand half a mile long, kids play in the shallow water while their parents float in the calm green water without a care. Cold drinks and so-so food are served at several seafood shacks on the sand. Protected by the Piedra Blanca headland to the north, the beach is at the northernmost edge of the town of La Cruz de Huanacaxtle. Named for a cross made of super-resilient wood (*huanacaxtle*, which translates to "ear pod," "elephant ear," or "monkey ear tree"), most people simply call the town "La Cruz." What was a rough little fishing village now has a 400-slip private marina aptly named Marina Riviera Nayarit at La Cruz (⊕ *www. marinarivieranayarit.com*). It was launched in 2008 as part of the Riviera Nayarit development plan. Like it or not, homey La Cruz is growing and becoming more sophisticated. **Facilities:** Beach umbrellas, boating, fishing, inner tubes; food concessions, parking.

Destiladeras. A few miles north of Piedra Blanca headland is a wide, 1½-km-long (1-mi-long) beach with powder-soft beige sand and some-times good waves for bodysurfers and boogie boarders. It's a pretty scene with the blue mountains to the north and south and the area's ubiquitous coconut palms framing views of the sky. On weekends and holidays, vendors prepare and sell yummy barbecue-blackened shrimp and fish kebabs, fresh fruit, and ceviche. Part of a new development called Nahui, Hotel Capella is under construction above the beach and, at this writing, was scheduled to open in 2011; a golf course was also in the planning stages. At the north end of the beach, **Punta el Burro** is a popular surf spot often accessed by boat from Punta Mita. **Facilities:** Food concessions, parking.

WATER-TOY PRICES

Prices for water toys in and around Vallarta are fairly consistent:

Jet Skis: $45–$50 per half hour (one or two riders)

Parasailing: $35–$40 for a 10-minute ride

Banana-boat rides: $12–$20 for a 10-minute ride (usually four-person minimum)

Hobie Cat or small sailboat: $35–$45 per hour

Kayak: $9–$15 per hour single; $15–$22 per hour double

Boogie Board: $5 per hour

El Anclote. The most accessible beach at Punta Mita and considered to be surf central is El Anclote, whose name means "the anchorage." Just a few minutes past the gated entrance to the tony Four Seasons and St. Regis hotels, the popular beach has a string of restaurants— once simple shacks but today of increasing sophistication and price. This is a primo spot for viewing a sunset. The surf is calmed by several rock jetties and is shallow for quite a way out, so it's a good spot for children and average to not-strong swimmers; however, the jetties have also robbed sand from the beach. There's a long, slow wave for beginning surfers; you can rent boards and take lessons from outfitters in town. Most of the jewelry and serape sellers and fishermen looking for customers have moved—or been moved—off the beach to more official digs in buildings along the same strip or facing the Four Seasons. Accessible from El Anclote (or the adjacent town of **Corral del Risco**), more than half a dozen great surf spots pump year-round; most are accessible only by boat. Punta Mita is the northernmost point of Banderas Bay, about 40 km (25 mi) north of Puerto Vallarta. **Facilities:** Fishing, snorkeling, surfing; food concessions, parking.

Islas Marietas. Snorkelers and divers favor the relatively clear waters and abundance of fish and coral on the bay side of the **Islas Marietas**, about a half hour offshore from El Anclote. In winter, especially January through March, these same islands are also a good place to spot orcas and humpback whales, which come to mate and give birth. Las Marietas is the destination for fishing, diving, and snorkeling; in addition, sea-life-viewing expeditions set out from El Anclote and Corral de Risco as well as from points up and down Banderas Bay. **Facilities:** None.

NORTH OF BANDERAS BAY

Real estate north of the bay began booming in the late '80s, although due to the worldwide recession, sales have tapered off and there are many FOR SALE signs on single-family homes and condos. Still, Mexicans continue to sell family holdings, jaded gringos build private homes,

and speculators from around the globe grab land on and off the beach. Changes notwithstanding, the Nayarit coast continues to enchant, with miles of lovely beaches bordered by arching headlands and hamlets drowsing in the tropical sun.

★ **Playa de Sayulita.** The increasingly popular town and beach of Sayulita is about 45 minutes north of PV on Carretera 200, just about 19 km (12 mi) north of Bucerías and 35 km (22 mi) north of the airport. Despite the growth, this small town is still laid-back and retains its surfer-friendly vibe. Fringed in lanky palms, Sayulita's curvaceous beach hugs the small bay. A decent shore break here is good for beginning or novice surfers; the left point break is more challenging. Skiffs on the beach have good rates for surfing or fishing safaris in area waters, and you can rent surfboards and snorkeling gear. **Facilities:** Fishing, snorkeling, surfing; food concessions, restrooms, showers.

★ **Playa de San Pancho.** Ten minutes north of Sayulita is the town of San Francisco, known to most people by its nickname, San Pancho. Its beach stretches between headlands to the north and south and is accessed at the end of the town's main road, Avenida Tercer Mundo. At the end of this road, on the beach, a couple of casual restaurants have shaded café tables on the sand where locals and visitors congregate. You'll sometimes see men fishing from shore with nets as you walk the 1½-km-long (1-mi-long) stretch of coarse beige sand. There's an undertow that should discourage less-experienced swimmers. A small reef break sometimes generates miniature waves for surfing (especially in September), but this isn't a surf spot. In fact the undertow and the waves, which are too big for family splashing and too small for surfing, have probably helped maintain the town's innocence—until now. Popular with a hip crowd, San Pancho has just a few hotels but a growing number of good restaurants. **Facilities:** Food concessions, showers, toilets.

Lo de Marcos. About 8 km (5 mi) north of San Pancho, Lo de Marcos is a humble town of quiet, wide streets. It fills up on weekends and holidays with Mexican families renting the bungalow-style motel rooms that predominate; a few RV parks on the beach attract long-term snowbirds. The town's main beach is flat and dark, but the sand is generally clean. There are small waves, not big enough for surfing but just right for splashing around. A small restaurant on the beach serves sodas, snacks, and the usual seafood suspects. Note that the once-popular playas **Las Minitas** and **Los Venados** are closed for private development. **Facilities:** Food concessions.

At popular Rincón de Guayabitos beach, you'll share umbrella space with locals and visitors alike.

Playa los Ayala. Playa los Ayala has a level beach, mild surf, and an excellent view of Isla del Coral, to which glass-bottom boats ferry passengers for about $7 (80 pesos) per person. There are small hotels and plenty of seaside palapas for shade and basic sustenance. On weekends, holidays, and in high season take a ride on a banana boat; most any time you can find a skiff owner to take you to Playa Frideritas or Playa del Toro, two pretty beaches for bathing that lie around the headland to the south and are accessible only by boat. You can walk, however, over the hill at the south end of the beach to a seafood restaurant on a small scallop of beach called Playa Frideras. **Facilities:** Banana-boat rides, boating; food concessions.

Rincón de Guayabitos. A little over a mile north of Ayala along the highway, Guayabitos bustles with legions of Mexican families on weekends and holidays; foreigners take up residence during the winter months. The main street, Avenida Nuevo Sol, has modest hotels, inexpensive restaurants, and scores of shops that all seem to sell the same cheap bathing suits and plastic beach toys. One block closer to the sea are more hotels along with some vacation homes right on the sand. Colorfully painted stands on the beach sell fresh chilled fruit and coconuts; others serve up fresh grilled fish on the cheap. This lovely beach bounded by headlands and the ocean is tranquil and perfectly suited for swimming. You can also arrange turtle and whale-watching excursions as well as boat rides to explore the coast or to Isla del Coral, just offshore. ■ TIP→ The boatmen who ferry passengers for a few hours' sunbathing on Isla del Coral may fail to mention that the restaurant there opens only in high season. Although there's usually a lady or two on the sand selling ceviche, bring

2

a picnic lunch just in case. **Facilities:** Boating, fishing, snorkeling; food concessions.

La Peñita. Contiguous with Guayabitos, at the north end of the bay, La Peñita has fewer hotels and a beach that's often abandoned save for a few fishermen. Its name means "little rock." The center for area business, La Peñita has banks, shoe stores, and ice cream shops; a typical market held each Thursday offers knock-off CDs, polyester clothing, and fresh fruits and vegetables. **Facilities:** None.

Boca de Naranjo. A couple of miles north of La Peñita, a dusty road leads to this long, secluded, sandy beach with excellent swimming. The rutted dirt road from the highway, although only about 4 km (2½ mi) long, takes almost a half hour to negotiate in most passenger cars. Enjoy great views of the coastline from one of nearly a dozen seafood shanties. Turtles nest here in August and September. There are rumors of a major development here in the near-ish future. **Facilities:** Restaurants.

Chacala. Some 30 km (19 mi) north of Rincón de Guayabitos, Chacala is another 9 km (5 mi) from the highway through exuberant vegetation. You can dine or drink at the handful of eateries right on the beach, take in the soft-scented sea air and the green-blue sea, or bodysurf and boogie board. Swimming is safest under the protective headland to the north of the cove; surfing is often very good, but you have to hire a boat to access the point break. The beach is long but rather narrow when the tide is in. At this writing, access to the beach was blocked by land that had been privatized for a major hotel project, but there was still beach access via the holistic retreat, Mar de Jade, near the south end of the bay. **Facilities:** Food concessions.

> ### TURTLE RESCUE
>
> In San Pancho, **Grupo Ecológico de la Costa Verde** (*Green Coast Ecological Group* ⊠ *Av. Latino América 102, San Pancho* ☎ *311/258–4100* ⊕ *www.project-tortuga.org*) works to save the olive ridley, leatherback, and eastern Pacific green turtles. Volunteers patrol beaches, collect eggs, maintain the nursery, tabulate data, and educate the public. (Apply any time during the year, via the Web site, for an assignment June through November.) Call or check their Web site to see if slide shows to raise awareness and funds are happening during your stay.

SOUTH OF PUERTO VALLARTA

While coastal Nayarit is jumping on the development bandwagon, the isolated beaches of Cabo Corriente and those of southern Jalisco—some surrounded by ecological reserves—continue to languish in peaceful abandon. Things here are still less formal, and aside from the super-posh resorts like El Careyes, El Tamarindo, and Las Alamandas, whose beaches are off-limits to nonguests, words like "laid-back" and "run-down" or "very basic" still apply, much to the delight of adventurous types.

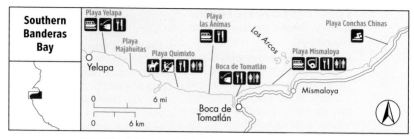

GETTING HERE AND AROUND

Catch a green bus to Conchas Chinas, Mismaloya, or Boca de Tomatlán from the southwest corner of Calle Basilio Badillo and Constitución in PV. Give the driver sufficient notice when you want to get off; pulling over along the narrow highway is challenging.

There are several ways to reach the beaches of southern Banderas Bay. Party boats (aka booze cruises) and privately chartered boats leave from Marina Vallarta's maritime terminal and generally hit Las Animas, Quimixto, Majahuitas, and/or Yelapa. You can also hire a water taxi from Boca de Tomatlán ($6 one way, usually on the hour 9 AM through noon and again in early afternoon), from the pier at Los Muertos ($20 round-trip, 11 AM and in high season at 10:15 and 11 AM), or from the tiny pier next to Hotel Rosita ($20 round-trip, 11:30 AM). ■TIP→ Note that weather and other variables can affect the water-taxi schedules.

For maximum time at the beach of your choice and minimum frustration, head out early and relax over a soda or coffee at Boca de Tomatlán as you wait for the next available skiff to depart. Catch the 4 PM taxi from Los Muertos to Yelapa only if you're planning to spend the night; it won't return until the next day. You can hire *pangas* (skiffs) at Boca, Mismaloya, or Los Muertos. The price depends on starting and ending points but runs about $35 per hour for up to eight passengers.

It's best to have your own car for exploring the Costalegre, as many beaches are a few kilometers—down rutted dirt roads—from the highway. However, if you want to hang out in the small but tourist-oriented towns of San Patricio–Melaque, Barra de Navidad, and La Manzanilla, you don't necessarily need wheels.

SOUTHERN BANDERAS BAY

★ **Playa Conchas Chinas.** Frequented mainly by visitors staying in the area, this beach has a series of rocky coves with crystalline water. Millions of tiny white shells, broken and polished by the waves, form the sand; rocks that resemble petrified cow pies jut into the sea, separating one patch of beach from the next. These individual coves are perfect for reclusive sunbathing and, when the surf is mild, for snorkeling around the rocks; bring your own equipment. It's accessible from Calle Santa Barbara, the continuation of the cobblestone coast road originating at the south end of Los Muertos Beach, and also from Carretera 200 near El Set restaurant. Swimming is best at the cove just north of La Playita de Lindo Mar, below the Hotel Conchas Chinas (where the beach ends), as there are fewer rocks in the water. You can walk—be it on the sand, over the rocks, or on paths or steps built for this purpose—from Playa Los Muertos all the way to Conchas Chinas. **Facilities:** None.

Playa Mismaloya. It was in this cove that *The Night of the Iguana* was made. Visitors from the '70s remember parking their vans on the sand and eating fish plucked from the sea for week after blissful week. Unfortunately, construction of the big, tan Hotel La Jolla de Mismaloya at the north end of the once-pristine bay has stolen its Shangri-La appeal, and to add insult to injury, in 2002, Hurricane Kenna stole much of the soft beige sand. Nonetheless, the place retains a certain cachet. It also has views of the famous cove from a couple of seafood restaurants on the south side of a wooden bridge over the mouth of the Río Mismaloya.

Sun-seekers kick back in wooden beach chairs, waiters serve up food and drink on the sand, massage techs offer their (so-so) services alfresco. Chico's Dive Shop sells dive packages and boat trips and rents snorkel gear, boogie boards ($10 for the day for either), and double sea kayaks ($20 per hour). Barceló La Jolla de Mismaloya has day passes for nonguests that are valid from 9 AM to 6 PM: $60 gets you use of facilities (pool, gym, game room, an hour of kayaking), plus food and drink. In the afternoons locals hang out at this beach, the kids playing in the sand while the moms wait for their men to return from fishing expeditions and touring gigs. The beach is about 13 km (8 mi) south of PV. The bus drops you on the highway, and it's a 200-yard walk from there down a dirt road to the beach. The tiny village of Mismaloya is on the east side of Carretera 200. **Facilities:** Boating, diving, kayaking, snorkeling; food concessions, toilets (Port-o-Potties on road to beach).

Boca de Tomatlán. This is the name of both a small village and a deep, V-shaped, rocky bay that lie at the mouth ("boca" means mouth) of the Río Horcones, about 5 km (3 mi) south of Mismaloya and 17 km (10½ mi) south of PV. Water taxis leave from Boca to the southern beaches; you can arrange snorkeling trips to Los Arcos. As far as most visitors are concerned, this is mainly the staging area for water taxis with nowhere else to hang out. However, this dramatic-looking bay fringed in palm trees does have a rustic appeal. Grocery stores sell chips, Cokes, and plastic water toys for tots; a handful of informal seaside cafés cluster at the water's edge. At very low tide only, it's possible for adventurers and cheapskates to walk south from Boca to Playa Las Animas (about 40 minutes) along a small path at waters' edge. You certainly don't want to be on this path, however, when the tide begins to come in, as the rocks behind it are steep and sharp. **Facilities:** Fishing; food concessions, toilets.

Playa las Ánimas. There's lots to do besides sunbathe at this beach and town 15 minutes south of Boca de Tomatlán. Framed in oak, coconut, and pink-flowering *amapa* trees, the brown-sand beach is named "The Souls" because pirate graves were reportedly located here many years ago. Along the 1-km-long (½-mi-long) beach are piles of smooth, strange rocks looking an awful lot like petrified elephant poo. Because of its very shallow waters, Las Animas is often referred to as *la playa de los niños* (children's beach), and it tends to fill up with families on

Grab a boat ride right off the beach at Boca de Tomatlán.

weekends and holidays. They come by water taxi or as part of half- or full-day bay cruises. Five or six seafood eateries line the sand; a few will lend their clients volleyballs to use on sand courts out front. You can also rent Jet Skis, ride a banana boat, or soar up into the sky behind a speedboat while dangling from a colorful parachute. **Facilities:** Banana-boat rides, boating, Jet Skis, parasailing; food concessions.

Quimixto. Between the sandy stretches of Las Ánimas and Majahuitas, and about 20 minutes by boat from Boca de Tomatlán, Quimixto has a narrow, rocky shoreline that attracts few bathers. Tour boats stop here, and their clients usually have a meal at one of the seafood eateries facing the beach. Horses by the dozens are standing by to take passengers to Quimixto Falls (about $13 round-trip). It's only slightly longer than the 25-minute ride to walk there. You can bathe at the base of the energetic falls; the pool is enclosed by sheer rock walls. Be careful of the current during the rainy season, when the water crashing into the pool tends to push swimmers toward the rock walls. Before proceeding to the falls, have a cool drink at the casual restaurant; consuming something is obligatory to gain access. During stormy weather or a full moon there's a fun, fast wave at Quimixto's reef, popular with surfers but, because of its inaccessibility, rarely crowded. **Facilities:** Horseback riding, surfing; food concessions, toilets.

Majahuitas. Between the beaches of Quimixto and Yelapa and about 35 minutes by boat from Boca de Tomatlán, this small beach is the playground of people on day tours and guests of the exclusive Majahuitas Resort. There are no services for the average José; the lounge chairs and toilets are for hotel guests only. Palm trees shade the white beach of broken, sea-buffed shells. The blue-green water is clear, and there's sometimes good snorkeling around the rocky shore. **Facilities:** None.

★ **Yelapa.** This secluded village and ½-km-long (¼-mi-long) beach is about an hour southeast of downtown PV and a half hour from Boca de Tomatlán—by boat, of course. A half-dozen seafood *enramadas* (thatch-roof huts) edge its fine, clean, grainy sand. Phones and electricity arrived in Yelapa around the turn of the 21st century. Believe it or not, it's the largest and most developed of the north Cabo Corrientes towns, with quite a few rustic rooms and houses for rent by the day, week, or month. That said, **bring all the money you'll need, as there's nothing as formal as a bank.**

The beach slopes down to the water, and small waves break right on the shore. In high season and during holidays, there are water-sports outfitters. From here you can hike 20 minutes into the jungle to see the small Cascada Cola del Caballo (Horse Tail Waterfall), with a pool at its base for swimming. (The falls are often dry near the end of the dry season, especially April–early June.) A more ambitious expedition of several hours brings you to less-visited, very beautiful Cascada del Catedral (Cathedral Falls). Beyond that, Yelapa is, for the most part, *tranquilisimo*: a place to just kick back in a beach chair and sip something cold. Seemingly right when you really need it, Cheggy or Agustina, the pie ladies, will show up with their homemade lime, coconut, or nut creations. **Facilities:** Boating, fishing, parasailing; food concessions.

SNORKELING SANCTUARY

Protected area Los Arcos is an offshore group of giant rocks rising some 65 feet above the water, making the area great for snorkeling and diving. For reasonable fees, local men along the road to Mismaloya Beach run diving, snorkeling, fishing, and boat trips here and as far north as Punta Mita and Las Marietas or the beach villages of Cabo Corrientes. Recommended for all of these trips is Mismaloya Divers (☎ 322/228–0020), with 23-foot skiffs and new, 75-horsepower, four-stroke motors. Restaurants and fishermen at Playa Mismaloya can also set you up.

CABO CORRIENTES

Just south of the end of Banderas Bay are the lovely beaches of pristine, wonderful Cabo Corrientes. These take an effort to visit, as well as a sturdy, high-clearance vehicle. Public transportation comes here and back once a day from the small town of El Tuito (40 km [25 mi] south of PV) along a partially paved but mainly rutted dirt-and-gravel road.

Playa Puntilla de Mayto. Thirty-eight kilometers (23 mi) down a passable road from El Tuito, this gorgeous beach is several miles long, embraced on either end by a rocky point. The sand is grainy but clean and slopes down to meet the rough to semirough surf. Despite the slope of the beach, this is a great place for a long walk or shore fishing. In late summer and fall there's a turtle camp where volunteers protect the eggs of the black and olive Ridley turtles that nest here. The Hotel de Mayto has rooms at modest prices and offers massage; next door, the friendly

CLOSE UP

Lingering in Yelapa

If you can't tear yourself away at the end of the day (or you miss the last water taxi), consider renting one of the locally run rustic accommodations near the beach. Modest but charming in a bohemian way, **Hotel La Lagunita** (☎ 322/209–5055 ⊕ www.hotel-lagunita.com) has rooms right over the water. Rustic superchic describes La Verana hotel (☎ 066/687–9358 ⊕ www.verana.com), a five-star property represented by Mexico Boutique Hotels. It doesn't accept walk-ins, however, and you need to make a large deposit in advance of your stay. You can arrange other accommodations by asking locals for referrals.

If you're lucky enough to be staying in Yelapa, there's plenty to do beyond the beach. Splash across the shallow lagoon or catch the water taxi to the main pier for a jungly walk past private homes and small shops; this is the Yelapa most folks never see. Turn right from the main pier, and walk to the point; turn left, and head up into the hills.

Check out the candlelit Club Yates disco on the south side of the estuary (Wednesday and Saturday nights during high season [December through Easter week] and holidays). Or ask around for birding adventures (⊕ www.birdinginyelapa.com), one of several yoga classes (especially ⊕ www.yogainyelapa.com, winter season only), or hire a local *pangero* (panga operator) for a trip to a secluded southern beach for swimming and a trek to a clandestine waterfall. For a simple meal in a tiny outdoor café, visit **El Manguito** (☎ 322/209–5061), just a few paces from the footbridge on the north side of the stream. Order shrimp, fish, lobster, beef, or just chips and salsa. It's open daily for breakfast, lunch, and dinner.

But the best part of staying in Yelapa is that after the booze cruises decamp and the water taxis put in for the night, you'll have the cool and groovy place to yourself.

folks of El Rinconcito have a small store and a few rooms to rent as well as four-wheelers and horses (200 pesos per hour for either). **Facilities:** ATVs, horseback riding, kayaking; food concessions.

Tehuamixtle. Just over 2 km (1 mi) from Mayto, Tehuamixtle is a sheltered cove with a few basic rooms to rent. The area is known for its oysters, which you can sample fresh from the sea at an open-air restaurant facing the fishing fleet. The surf here is very gentle and lacks currents, making it popular with local children. The pristine beach invites snorkeling and diving (bring your own equipment). Fishing boats bob at one end, below the restaurant; from here, the beach curves along in a sandy brown arch to a large green headland at the other end of the cove. Tehua, as locals call it, is about the same size as Mayto: 100 people. This fishing village has only had electricity since the turn of the 21st century. There's a beach road that connects Tehua with Cruz de Loreto, about 1½ hours to the south; otherwise go out through El Tuito. **Facilities:** Fishing; food concessions.

Villa del Mar. Four kilometers (2½ mi) beyond Tehuamixtle, Villa del Mar is a beautiful virgin beach on a broad sweep of bay. Several miles

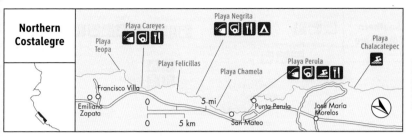

long, flat and sandy, it's great for long walks; turtles nest here in late summer and fall. At the south end of the beach, a huge estuary surrounded by coconut palms invites kayaking. The sandy streets in and around town and the beach are great for mountain biking, and local people will rent horses for a ride on the beach or into the countryside. **Facilities:** Horseback riding.

COSTALEGRE

Most people come to the Costalegre—dubbed "The Happy Coast" by Jalisco's tourism authorities—to stay at luxury accommodations on lovely, clean beaches: Las Alamandas, El Careyes, and El Tamarindo. Indeed, some of the nicest beaches with services are now the private domain of *gran turismo* (government-rated five-star-plus) hotels.

Other people head to southern Jalisco State without reservations to explore the coast at their leisure. There are still some delightful, pristine, and mainly isolated beaches along the Costalegre, most with few services aside from the ubiquitous seafood *enramadas* serving fish fillets and fresh ceviche. For lodging there are private homes to rent, condos, and unassuming hotels on or near the beach.

Whether you kick back at an elegant resort or explore the wild side, the area between Cabo Corrientes and Barra de Navidad, the latter at the southern extreme of Jalisco State, will undoubtedly delight.

GETTING HERE AND AROUND

It's optimum to explore the beaches of southern Jalisco by car, SUV, or camper. Fill up with gas at every opportunity, as gas stations are few. (If you do get into a bind, ask locals about any small stores that sell gas.) If you're in a rental car, reset the odometer and look for the kilometer signs at the side of the road. If you're driving a car marked in miles, not kilometers, the road signs are still useful, as many addresses are simply "Carretera 200" or "Carretera a Barra de Navidad" along with the marker number.

Buses leave from the **Central Camionero** (✉ *Carretera Puerto Vallarta—Tepic [Carretera 200], Km 9, Col. Las Mojoneras* ☎ *322/290–1009 or 322/290–0994*) in PV.

Playa Chalacatepec. A sylvan beach with no services lies down a rutted dirt road about 82 km (50 mi) south of El Tuito and 115 km (70 mi) south of PV. The road is negotiable only by high-clearance passenger cars and smallish RVs. The reward for 8 km (5 mi) of bone-jarring

Southern Costalegre

Playa Principal
Playa Coastecomate
Playa La Manzanilla
Playa Tenacatita
Playa Mora
Playa Melaque
Playa Majahua
Playa Boca de Iguanas
Playa Tamarindo
San Patricio Melaque
Barra de Navidadd
Jaluco
Emiliano Zapata
La Manzanilla
Tenacatita
Agua Caliente Viejo
0   5 mi
0   5 km

travel is a beautiful rocky point, Punta Chalacatepec, with a sweep of protected white-sand beach to the north that's perfect for swimming and bodysurfing. There's a fish camp here, so you may find some rather scraggly-looking dudes on this isolated beach. Admire the tidal pools at the point during low tide; take a walk along the open-ocean beach south of the point, where waves crash more dramatically, discouraging swimming. To get here, turn toward the beach at the town of José María Morelos (at Km 88). Just after 8 km (5 mi), leave the main road (which bears right) and head to the beach over a smaller track. From here it's less than 1½ km (1 mi) to the beach. At this writing, an airport was being built near the county seat, Tomatlán, and the beach was slated for hotels not yet named. **Facilities:** None.

Playa Perula. The handful of islands just off lovely Bahía de Chamela, about 131 km (81 mi) south of PV, protects the beaches from strong surf. The best place on the bay for swimming is wide, flat **Playa Perula** (turnoff at Km 76, then 3 km [2 mi] on dirt road), in the protective embrace of a cove just below the Punta Perula headland. Fishermen there take visitors out to snorkel around the islands (about $45 for up to 10 people) or to hunt for dorado, tuna, and mackerel (about $23 per hour for one to four people); restaurants on the soft beige sand sell the same as fresh fillets and ceviche. **Facilities:** Fishing, snorkeling; food concessions.

Playa Negrita. Also on Bahía de Chamela, this lovely beach is fringed in lanky coconut palms and backed by blue foothills. There are camping and RV accommodations and plenty of opportunities for shore fishing, swimming, and snorkeling. Almost every pretty beach in Mexico has its own humble restaurant; this one is no exception. **Facilities:** Fishing, snorkeling; camping facilities, food concessions.

Playa Careyes. About 11 km (6½ mi) south of Bahía Chamela, this beach is named for the *careyes* (hawksbill) turtles that lay eggs here. It's a lovely soft-sand beach framed by headlands. When the water's not too rough, snorkeling is good around the rocks, where you can also fish. There's a small restaurant at the north end of the beach, and often you can arrange to go out with a local fisherman (about $25 per hour). Water-loving birds can be spotted around the lagoon that forms at the south end of the bay. **Facilities:** Birding, fishing, snorkeling; food concessions.

Playa Teopa. Here, you can walk south from Playa Careyes along the dunes, although guards protect sea turtle nests by barring visitors during the summer and fall nesting seasons. A road from the highway at Km 49.5 gains access to Playa Teopa by car; ask the guard for permission

At Playa Melaque, it's a tough choice between hiring a laid-back fishing charter or sipping something refreshing at a grass-roofed beach hut.

to enter this way, as you'll need to pass through private property to gain access to the beach. **Facilities:** None.

★ **Playa Tenacatita.** Named for the bay on which it lies, Tenacatita is a lovely beach of soft sand about 34 km (20 mi) north of San Patricio–Melaque and 172 km (106 mi) south of PV. Dozens of identical seafood shacks line the shore; birds cruise the miles of beach, searching for their own fish. Waves crash against clumps of jagged rocks at the north end of the beach, which curves gracefully around to a headland. The water is sparkling blue. There's camping for RVs and tents at Punta Hermanos, where the water is calm and good for snorkeling, and local men offer fishing excursions ($50–$60 for one to four people) and tours of the mangroves ($27). **Of the string of restaurants on the beach, we recommend La Fiesta Mexicana. Facilities:** Fishing, snorkeling; camping facilities, food concessions.

★ **Playa Mora.** Near the north end of Playa Tenacatita, this pretty stretch of sand has a coral reef close to the beach, making it an excellent place to snorkel. Local fishermen take interested parties out on their boats, either fishing for tuna, dorado, or bonita or searching for wildlife such as dolphins and turtles. **Facilities:** Fishing, snorkeling; food concessions.

Playa Boca de Iguanas. South of Playa Mora on Tenacatita Bay, this beach (whose name means "Mouth of the Iguanas") of fine gray-blond sand is wide and flat, and it stretches for several kilometers. Gentle waves make it great for swimming, boogie boarding, and snorkeling, but beware the undertow. Some enthusiasts fish from shore. It's a great place for jogging or walking on the beach, as there's no slope. There are a couple of beach restaurants and an RV park here. The entrance is at Km 17. **Facilities:** Snorkeling; camping facilities, food concessions.

🕭 **Playa la Manzanilla.** This beautiful, 2-km-long (1-mi-long) beach is little more than a kilometer (half a mile) in from the highway, near the southern edge of Bahía de Tenacatita, 193 km (120 mi) south of PV and 25 km (15½ mi) north of Barra de Navidad (at Km 14). Informal hotels and restaurants are interspersed with small businesses and modest houses along the town's main street. Rocks dot the gray-gold sands and edge both ends of the wide beach; facing the sand are attractive, unpretentious vacation homes favoring a Venetian palate of ochre and brick red. The bay is calm. At the beach road's north end, gigantic, rubbery-looking crocodiles lie heaped together just out of harm's way in a mangrove swamp. The fishing here is excellent; boat owners on the beach can take you out for snapper, sea bass, and other *pescado* for $20–$25 an hour. **Facilities:** Fishing; food concessions.

Playa Melaque. Twenty-one kilometers (13 mi) south of La Manzanilla, Bahía de Navidad represents the end of the Costalegre at the border with Colima State. First up (from north to south) is **San Patricio–Melaque,** the coast's most populous town, with about 12,000 people. (It's actually two towns that have now met in the middle.) While parts of town look dilapidated or abandoned, its long, coarse-white-sand beach is beautiful and has gentle waves. Restaurants, small hotels, homes, and tall palms line the beach, which slopes down to the water. About 5 km (3½ mi) east of Barra de Navidad, which shares Navidad Bay, Melaque's beach curves around for several kilometers to end in a series of jagged rocks poking from the water. If you plop down in a seat under a shade umbrella its owner will soon show up. Pay about $5 and stay as long as you like. Fishermen here will take anglers out in search of dorado, tuna, wahoo, swordfish, mackerel, and others. ■TIP→ The best swimming and boogie boarding are about half the length of town, in front of El Dorado restaurant. **Facilities:** Banana-boat rides, boogie boarding, fishing, Jet Skis, kayaking, snorkeling, beach umbrellas.

Playa Principal (Barra de Navidad). Usually called just "Barra," this laid-back little town has sandy streets and a live-and-let-live demeanor. At any time but high tide you can walk between San Patricio and Barra, a distance of about 5 km (3½ mi). It's about 4½ km (3 mi) on the highway from one town to the other. Most of Barra is composed of two streets on a long sandbar. Calle Veracruz faces the vast lagoon and **Isla Navidad,** now home to the posh Gran Bay resort. Water taxis take folks to the Gran Bay's golf course or marina, or to the seafood restaurants of **Colimilla,** on the lagoon's opposite shore. Avenida Miguel de Legazpi faces Barra's sloping brown-sand beach and the ocean. These and connecting streets have small shops, simple but charming restaurants, and—like everywhere along Mexico's Pacific coast—a host of friendly townspeople. ■TIP→ Surfers look for swells near the jetty, where the sea enters the lagoon. **Facilities:** Boating, fishing; food concessions.

Adventure

WORD OF MOUTH

"We did the Yelapa and Majahuitas tour with Vallarta Adventures. We also did a jungle tour [with a different operator]. We enjoyed both."

—KVR

For the sheer variety of activities, Puerto Vallarta is one of the best adventure-vacation destinations on Mexico's Pacific coast. The water is warm and swimmable year-round, even downright bathlike July through November. The big blue bay attracts sea turtles, humpback whales, dolphins, and a growing number of snorkelers and divers. The fishing is excellent—from deep-sea angling for marlin and sailfish to trolling near shore for roosters and red snapper.

Banderas Bay and the beaches to the north and south have some surfable waves as well as plenty of calm bays and inlets for swimming and paddleboarding. Party boats and private yachts are great for accessing gorgeous and hard-to-reach beaches, primarily south of Vallarta along Cabo Corrientes.

The subtropical foothills are laced with streams and rivers that rush and tumble over rocks in the rainy season and dwindle but still impress at other times. Trails challenge mountain bikers and thrill dune buggy and ATV aficionados. Many family-owned ranches have horse-riding tours at reasonable prices—lasting from an hour or two to overnight forays into the Sierra Madre.

Most of the well-established tour operators are in Puerto Vallarta. North and south of town, activities are often arranged through hotels, though there are companies springing up to meet an increasing demand. Operators generally provide transportation from strategic pickup points, usually in downtown Puerto Vallarta, Marina Vallarta, Nuevo Vallarta, and sometimes in Conchas Chinas. To save traveling from one end of the bay to the other, try to choose an outfitter near your neck of the woods.

CRUISES

Daytime bay cruises generally begin with a quick jaunt to Los Arcos Underwater Preserve, off Mismaloya Beach. There's about a half hour for snorkeling or swimming—sometimes with legions of little jellyfish in addition to the turtles that feed on them. Cruises then proceed to Yelapa, Quimixto, or Playa las Animas, or to Islas Marietas for whale-watching (in winter), snorkeling, swimming, and lunch. Horseback riding is usually available at an additional cost (about $15).

There are plenty of tours available; our list contains some of the most popular and professional.

LOGISTICS

Buy your ticket from licensed vendors along the boardwalk at Los Muertos Beach, online, or through area tour operators. Prices are fluid; like car salespeople, the ticket sellers give discounts or jack up the price as the market allows. Full-day booze cruises cost about $40–$55 per person, including open bar, Continental breakfast, snacks, and snorkeling and/or kayaks. Two-hour sunset cruises with open bar cost about $25 per person. Dinner cruises cost $55–$85. Expect to pay a small port fee (15 pesos, a little more than $1) at the maritime pier; it is not included in the cost of the ticket.

OUTFITTERS

Cruceros Princesa. Full- and half-day trips take in the beaches of southern Bahía de Banderas with snorkeling, beach time, and lunch (on board or on the beach). The open bar features beer and a few brands of national spirits. Half-day cruises generally go to Los Arcos and either Las Animas or Las Caletas; full-day cruises access several different spots—such as Yelapa and either Majahuitas or Los Arcos, or Quimixto and Playa las Animas—as well as making jaunts to Islas Marietas for half-day whale-watching (in winter), snorkeling, swimming, and lunch. The boat *Sarape* heads to Los Arcos for 40 minutes of snorkeling and then continues to Las Animas and Quimixto; after beach time there's lunch aboard the boat on the return trip ($35). ⊠ *Terminal Marítima, Marina Vallarta* ☎ *322/224–4777* ⊕ *www.crucerosprincesa.com.mx*.

Cruceros Santamaría. Full-day tours head to Los Arcos, Las Animas, and Quimixto. You can also rent boats for large private parties. You can buy tickets from booth vendors; if you order by phone, staff will give you a confirmation number, but you still have to stand in line at the public marina, or *Terminal Marítima, where you pick up your ticket and pay the port fee.* ⊠ *Blvd. Francisco M. Ascencio, across from Sam's Club, Terminal Marítima, Marina Vallarta* ☎ *322/221–2511* ⊕ *www. crucerossantamaria.com*.

☺ A really-and-truly sailing vessel that has circumnavigated the world more than once, the ***Marigalante*** has a pirate crew that keeps things hopping for kids and teens with games, snorkeling, kayaking, or banana-boat rides during a seven-hour day cruise. The five-hour dinner cruise, with open bar, snacks, and pre-Hispanic show, is for adults only and has some bawdy pirate humor. Women who don't want to be "kidnapped" may prefer the day cruise or another operator. Both tours cost $85 for adults and about half that for kids under 12. Buy tickets online at a discount or from licensed vendors in town. The boat embarks from Terminal Marítima, across from Sam's Club on Boulevard Francisco M. Ascencio, in Marina Vallarta. ⊠ *Av. Politecnico Nacional 78 Int 304, Col. Educación* ☎ *322/223–0309 or 322/223–0875; 866/915–0361 from the U.S.; 866/954–5984 from Canada* ⊕ *www.marigalante.com.mx.*

★ **Vallarta Adventures.** Day or evening cruises are to Caletas Beach, the company's exclusive domain. Although the day cruise can accommodate 105 passengers, there's plenty of room to spread out: Boulder-bordered coves, sandy beaches, hammocks in the shade, and jungle trails ensure that you won't feel like a cow about to be branded "tourist." The Caletas by Day cruise includes snorkeling, kayaking, hiking, paella-making, and lunch (scuba or spa treatments available for additional fees). The Rhythms of the Night evening cruise includes dinner on the beach and a show at the amphitheater. Most folks love the show—men and women dressed as voluptuous natives do a modern dance to dramatic lighting and music. Tours cost $85 and $89, respectively. Kids under 7 aren't allowed on the nighttime tour. ⊠ *Paseo de las Palmas 39–A, Nuevo Vallarta* ☎ *322/297–1212; 888/303–2653 in U.S. and Canada* ⊠ *Edifício Marina Golf, Local 13-C, Calle Mástil, Marina Vallarta* ☎ *322/221–0657* ⊕ *www.vallarta-adventures.com.*

LAND SPORTS

ATV AND DUNE BUGGY TOURS

Increasingly, ATV, dune buggy, and jeep tours are heading for the hills around Puerto Vallarta. Most rides are to small communities, ranches, and rivers north, south, and east of town. Sharing a vehicle with a partner means a significant savings.

LOGISTICS
You need a valid driver's license and a major credit card. Wear light-weight long pants, sturdy shoes, bandanna (some operators provide one as a keepsake) and/or tight-fitting hat, sunglasses, and both sunscreen and mosquito repellent. In rainy season (July–October) it's hot and wet—ideal for splashing through puddles and streams; the rest of the year is cooler and dustier. In either season, prepare to get dirty. Three- to four-hour tours run $80–$120; full-day trips to San Sebastián cost about $165 for one rider or $175 for two.

OUTFITTERS
■ TIP➜ If you plan to gulp rather than sip on a tequila-tasting tour, please strongly consider riding two per ATV and designating one person as the day's driver. Doubling up is usually also the bargain rental option.

Adventure ATV Jungle Treks. This company leads daily three-hour ATV tours ($75 for one rider, $95 for two) that head into the hills behind Vallarta. The stop at Rancho Las Pilas includes a brief tequila-making tour and tasting, but lunch there is optional and not included in the price. A four-hour tour combines this ATV trek with a canopy tour through

Stereotypical "tourist" activity? Maybe—but riding an ATV down a beach is a good way to see more of the area than walking allows, and it's some serious fun.

River Canopy, along the Cuale River ($130 for one rider, $190 for two). ✉ *Calle Basilio Badillo 400, Col. E. Zapata* ☎ *322/223–0392.*

★ **Wild Vallarta.** Full- and half-day tours in Honda four-wheel ATVs and open-frame, five-speed "jungle buggies" with VW engines cost $80/$100 per day (single/double ATVs) to $110/$125 per day (dune buggy with or without lunch, respectively). The long and rugged ATV tour to San Sebastián, high in the Sierra Madre, requires some experience, but four-hour trips are fine for beginners. They offer a combined canopy and ATV tour ($140 for one, $215 for two people). ✉ *Manuel M. Dieguez 274–A, Col. E. Zapata* ☎ *322/222–8928* ⊕ *www.wildvallarta.com.*

CANOPY TOURS

Canopy tours are high-octane thrill rides during which you "fly" from treetop to treetop, securely fastened to a zip line. Despite the inherent danger of dangling from a cable hundreds of feet off the ground, the operators we list have excellent safety records. If you're brave, bring your camera to take photos while zipping along; just be sure the neck strap is long enough to leave your hands free.

LOGISTICS

Check with each operator regarding maximum weight (usually 250 pounds) and minimum ages for kids. ■ **TIP→ Don't take a tour when rain threatens.** A thunderstorm isn't the time to hang out near trees attached to metal cables, and rain makes the activity scary to say the least. Even during the rainy season, however, mornings and *early* afternoons are generally sunny.

MULTISPORT OPERATORS

Ecotours (☎ 322/223–3130 or 322/222–6606 ⊕ www.ecotoursvallarta.com). It's a downtown PV–based operator (with a second office at Marina Vallarta) whose offerings include hiking, diving, snorkeling, kayaking, birdwatching, whale-watching, and turtle tours.

Puerto Vallarta Tours. This company offers tours that are available from other area operators, but we recommend it for its excellent Web site, English-speaking operators and crew, and the convenience factor: through this one operator, you can book everything from canopy tours, ATVs, deep-sea fishing, and mountain biking to cruise tours, cultural tours, and bullfighting. ☎ 322/222–4935 or 01800/832–3632 in Mexico; 866/217–9704 or 866/464–6915 from U.S. or Canada ⊕ www.puertovallartatours.net.

Sociedad Cooperativa Corral del Risco (☎ 329/291–6298 ⊕ www.puntamitacharters.com). Local fishermen at Punta Mita (aka Punta de Mita) have formed this cooperative, which offers reasonably priced fishing trips, surfing, whale-watching excursions, and diving and snorkeling outings.

Tours Soltero (☎ 315/355–6777 ✉ raystoursmelaque@yahoo.com). Canadian expat Ray Calhoun and his wife Eva rent mountain bikes, snorkeling equipment, and boogie boards ($10 per day) and lead active tours from their base in San Patricio Melaque, a town next to Barra de Navidad south of PV. Typical excursions are snorkeling in Tenacatita with boogie boarding at Boca de Iguana, from 10 to 5 ($32), and a day trip to the state capital, Colima, which includes lunch and a stop at a typical hacienda-cum-museum ($60).

Vallarta Adventures (☎ 322/297–1212 in Nuevo Vallarta; 322/221–0657 in Marina Vallarta; 888/526–2238 from U.S. and Canada ⊕ www.vallarta-adventures.com). It's a well-respected operator with 20 years' experience, two offices, dozens of tours, and a staff of some 350. It's often used by high-end hotel concierges and cruise-ship activity directors for canopy tours, hiking, sailing, dinner-show cruises, Sierra Madre expeditions, and dolphin- and whale-watching cruises.

Rancho Mi Chaparrita. On his family ranch, Luis Verdin runs a 13-zip-line tour ($75) and horseback riding trips ($25 per hour). Or combine the two, accessing the ranch on Señor Verdin's lively, healthy horses via the beach and backcountry for a complete adventure ($95). The company rents boogie boards, surfboards, and paddleboards and give surfing lessons and four- to six-day surfing packages. They also offer snorkeling and whale- or wildlife-watching excursions around the Marietas Islands. ⊠ Manuel Rodriguez Sanchez 14, Sayulita ☎ 329/291–3112 ⊕ www.michaparrita.com.

Wildlife Connection (☎ 322/225–3621 ⊕ www.wildlifeconnection.com). Based in downtown PV, this Mexican-owned company does what its name implies: It connects you with wildlife (specifically birds, turtles, dolphins and whales) on seasonal trips. It also leads snorkeling and photography outings.

Both the young and the young at heart can zip through the nearby jungle on a tour with Canopy El Edén.

OUTFITTERS

★ **Canopy El Edén.** The daily trips to the spirited Mismaloya River and an adjacent restaurant are 3½-hour adventures ($81) that depart from the downtown office. You zip along 10 lines through the trees and above the river. To take full advantage of the lovely setting and good restaurant, take the first tour (departures are weekdays at 9, 10, 11, noon, 1:30, and 2:30—sometimes less frequently in low season), and bring your swimsuit. The schedule includes about an hour to spend at the river, spa, or restaurant. If you wish to stay longer and there's room, you can return to Vallarta with a later group; otherwise take a taxi or ask the restaurant staff for a lift to the highway, where buses frequently pass. ⊠ *Office: Plaza Romy, Calle I. Vallarta 228, Interior 1, Col. E. Zapata* ☎ *322/222–2516* ⊕ *www.canopyeleden.com.*

Fodor'sChoice **Canopy Tour de Los Veranos.** Los Veranos has the most zip lines (14), the ★ longest zip line (1,300 feet), and the highest zip line (500 feet off the ground). It also has the most impressive scenery, crossing the Río Los Horcones half a dozen times on several miles of cables. Departures are from the office, across from the Pemex station at the south side of Puerto Vallarta, every hour on the hour between 9 and 2 (arrive 15 minutes early), with reduced hours in low season (June through November). After your canopy tour, there's time to scale the climbing wall, play in the Horcones River, eat at the restaurant, or hang out at the bar overlooking the river, but check to make sure that a ride back to town is available. There are shuttles from Marina Vallarta and Nuevo Vallarta, and discounts for groups. ⊠ *Office: Calle Francisca Rodríguez*

336, Col. E. Zapata ☎ *322/223–0504; 877/563–4113 from U.S. and Canada* ⊕ *www.canopytours-vallarta.com.*

Rancho Mi Chaparrita. This family-owned company has a 13-line zip ($75) in Sayulita, on the owner's ranch. Add $20 and you can arrive on horseback for a complete adventure. ⊠ *Manuel Rodriguez Sanchez 14, Sayulita* ☎ *329/291–3112* ⊕ *www.michaparrita.com.*

Vallarta Adventures. Vallarta Adventures's canopy tour ($85) is the most convenient if you're staying in Nuevo Vallarta or Bucerías. You use gloved hands rather than a braking device to slow down or stop, and you must return to town right after the zip-line adventure, leaving no time for other activities. ⊠ *Paseo de las Palmas 39–A, Nuevo Vallarta* ☎ *322/297–1212; 888/526–2238 in U.S. and Canada* ⊠ *Edifício Marina Golf, Local 13–C, Calle Mástil, Marina Vallarta* ☎ *322/221–0657* ⊕ *www.vallarta-adventures.com.*

GOLF

"Not a bad mango in the bunch" is how one golf aficionado described Puerto Vallarta's courses. From the two courses at Four Seasons Punta Mita (prohibitively expensive for those not staying at the hotel) to the Gran Bay at Barra de Navidad, the region is a close second to Los Cabos in variety of play at a range of prices. Well-known designers are represented, including Jack Nicklaus and Tim Weiskopf.

LOGISTICS

Most of these courses offer first-class services including driving ranges and putting greens, lessons, clinics, pro shops, and clubhouses.

COURSES

PUERTO
VALLARTA
★

Marina Vallarta. Joe Finger designed this 18-hole course; the $129 greens fee includes practice balls, tax, and a shared cart. It's the area's second-oldest course and is closest and most convenient for golfers staying in the Hotel Zone, downtown Puerto Vallarta, and Marina Vallarta. Although it's very flat, it's far more challenging than it looks, with lots of water hazards. Speaking of hazards, the alligators have a way of blending into the scenery. They might surprise you, but they supposedly don't bite. Go to the course's Web site to find hotels participating in their "Stay and Play" golf packages. ⊠ *Paseo de la Marina s/n, Marina Vallarta* ☎ *322/221–0545 or 322/221–0073* ⊕ *www. marinavallartagolf.com.*

Vista Vallarta. Some of the best views in the area belong to the aptly named Vista Vallarta. There are 18 holes designed by Jack Nicklaus and another 18 by Tom Weiskopf. The greens fee for the course, which is a few miles northwest of the Marina Vallarta area, is $194. A shared cart and tax are included. ⊠ *Circuito Universidad 653, Col. San Nicolás* ☎ *322/290–0030 or 322/290–0040* ⊕ *www.vistavallartagolf.com.*

NUEVO
VALLARTA TO
BUCERÍAS

El Tigre. At the Paradise Village hotel and condo complex is this 18-hole course with 12 water features. The greens fee of $150 includes a shared cart, bottled water, practice balls, and cold towels, but not tax. Don't be surprised if you see a guy driving around with tiger cubs in his truck: the course's namesake and mascot is the passion of the club's director, Jesús

After Los Cabos, the Puerto Vallarta area has some of the most varied golf options in Mexico. The golfer on the left here is poised to sink a putt in Marina Vallarta.

Carmona Jiménez. El Tigre has a par-3 hole played entirely on an island. ⊠ *Paseo Paraíso 800, Nuevo Vallarta* ☎ *322/297–0773; 866/843–5951 from U.S.; 800/214–7758 from Canada* ⊕ *www.eltigregolf.com.*

★ **Four Seasons Punta Mita.** Nonguests are permitted to play the 195-acre, par-72, Jack Nicklaus–designed Pacífico course; however, they must pay the hotel's day use fee of 50% of the room rate (approximately $300 plus 28% tax and service charge), which covers use of a guest room and hotel facilities until dark. Reservations are essential. The greens fee is $262, including tax and the golf cart. The club's claim to fame is that it has perhaps the only natural island green in golf. Drive your cart to it at low tide; otherwise hop aboard a special amphibious vessel (weather permitting) to cross the water. There are seven other oceanfront links. Opened in 2009, the Bahía is another stunning 18-hole course. It has more undulating fairways and greens than the first course, but similarly spectacular ocean views—and high price tag. ⊠ *Punta Mita* ☎ *329/291–6000* ⊕ *www.fourseasons.com.*

Los Flamingos Country Club. Designed by Percy Clifford in 1978, PV's original course has been totally renovated. The 18-hole course in Los Flamingos development, at the northern extremity of Nuevo Vallarta, has new irrigation and sprinkler systems to maintain the rejuvenated greens. The high-season greens fee is $139, including a shared cart, tax, a bottle of water, and a bucket of balls. ⊠ *Carretera 200, Km 145, 12 km (8 mi) north of airport, Nuevo Vallarta* ☎ *329/296–5006* ⊕ *www. flamingosgolf.com.mx.*

Nayar Golf Course at Mayan Palace. Nine of the 18 holes at Mayan Palace have been completely redesigned by Jack Nicklaus. At this writing, renovations were getting the finishing touches, and the course should be open by press time; until they're finished golfers repeat play nine holes once ($80) or twice ($130). The full course was projected to run about $150. The fee includes cart, tax, use of practice range, and return transportation to hotel. Twilight fees (after 1 PM) are almost half that price, at $80 for 18 holes. ⊠ *Paseo de las Moras s/n, Fracc. Naútico Turístico, Nuevo Vallarta* ☎ *322/226–4000 Ext. 4600.*

COSTALEGRE **El Tamarindo**. About two hours south of Vallarta on the Costalegre is one

Fodor'sChoice of the area's best courses. At least six of the holes play along the ocean;

★ some are cliff-side holes with fabulous views, while others go right down to the beach. On a slow day, golfers are encouraged at tee time to have a swim or a picnic on the beach during their round, or to play a hole a second time if they wish. Designed by David Fleming, the breathtaking course is the playground of birds, deer, and other wildlife. It's an awesome feeling to nail the course's most challenging hole, the 9th: a par 3 with a small green surrounded by bunkers. The greens fee is $240, including cart and tax. Resort guests get priority for tee times; call up to a week ahead to check availability. ⊠ *Carretera Melaque–Puerto Vallarta, Carretera 200, Km 7.5, Cihuatlán* ☎ *315/351–5032 Ext. 113.*

Isla Navidad. It must have the best variety of play in the area, with three 9-hole courses of different terrain: mountain, lagoon, and ocean. Designed by Robert von Hagge, the course is beautifully sculpted, with lovely contours. Greens fees are $180 for 9 holes or $200 for 18, including driving-range practice and cart. ⊠ *Isla Navidad, Barra de Navidad* ☎ *314/337–9006* ⊕ *www.islanavidad.com.*

HORSEBACK RIDING

Most of the horseback-riding outfits are based on family ranches in the foothill towns of the Sierra like Las Palmas. Horses are permitted on the beach in smaller towns like Sayulita and San Francisco, but not in Vallarta proper, so expect to ride into the hills.

LOGISTICS

Outfitters pick you up either from the hotel or strategic locations north and south of town and return you to your hotel or to the pickup point. Short rides depart morning and afternoon, while longer rides are generally in the morning only, at least in winter, when the sun sets earlier.

Ask at the beachfront restaurants of tiny towns like Yelapa, Quimixto, and Las Animas, south of PV, to hook up with horses for treks into the jungle. Horses are generally well cared for; some are exceptionally fit and frolicky.

OUTFITTERS

Club de Polo Costa Careyes. Though the trail rides here are expensive at $100 for 45 minutes, you know you're getting an exceptional mount. Trips leave in early morning or around sunset. ⊠ *Km 53.5, Carretera 200, Carretera a Barra de Navidad, El Careyes* ☎ *315/351–0320* ⊕ *www.careyes.com.*

Cabalgatas, or horseback riding, is a wonderful way to get out into the countryside. These visitors are touring with guide company Rancho El Charro.

Rancho El Charro. Rancho Charro provides transportation to and from your hotel for rides to rivers and waterfalls. Choices include three-hour ($62), five-hour ($82, two different trails for average or experienced riders), and all-day rides ($120). ☎ *322/224–0114* ⊕ *www.ranchoelcharro.com.*

★ **Rancho Manolo.** The friendly folks at the family-owned property take you into the mountains they know so well. The usual tour is to El Edén, the restaurant-and-river property where the movie *Predator* was filmed. The three-hour trip (about an hour each way on horseback, with an additional hour for a meal, which is not included, or for splashing in the river) costs just $30—definitely a good deal. ✉ *Km 12, Carretera 200, at Mismaloya bridge, Mismaloya* ☎ *322/228–0018.*

Rancho Mi Chaparrita. This ranch has very nice, healthy horses willing to run (or walk, if you ask them politely). Ride on the beach, in the tropical forest, or a combination of the two for $25 an hour. There's a four-hour horse ride ($85) up to

ART ADVENTURE

The owners of **Galeria Arte 550** (see *Shopping chapter;* ☎ *322/222-7365* ⊕ www. yourcreativeawakening.com) offer unique tours combining art and adventure. Visits to the mountains and the botanical gardens, whale-watching trips, or other activities provide a springboard for journal drawing and artistic expression in clay, tile-decorating, or other media. Students can arrange their own accommodations or book a package, staying at the new B&B **House of Wind and Water** (see *Stay chapter*): lovely lodgings out in a neighborhood most tourists never see, along the Cuale River on the east side of Highway 200.

Monkey Mountain, with a short break at the top for photo ops and a stretch. ✉ *Manuel Rodriguez Sanchez 14, Sayulita* ☎ *329/291–3112* ⊕ *www.michaparrita.com.*

Rancho Ojo de Agua. The horses are part Mexican quarter horse and part Thoroughbred. According to proud owner Mari González, the stock comes from the Mexican cavalry. The family-owned business conducts sunset and half-day horseback rides (three to five hours, $56 and $68), the latter including lunch and time for a swim in a mountain stream. ✉ *Cerrada de Cardenal 227, Fracc. Aralias, Puerto Vallarta* ☎ *322/224–0607* ⊕ *www.ranchojodeagua.com.*

MOUNTAIN BIKING

Although the tropical climate makes it hot for biking, the Puerto Vallarta area is lovely and has challenging and varied terrain. Aim for the relatively cooler months of November through mid-April. A few operators lead rides up river valleys to Yelapa and from the old mining town of San Sebastian (reached via plane; included in price), high in the Sierra, back to Vallarta. It's about 45 km (28 mi) of twisty downhill.

In the rainy season, showers are mainly in the late afternoon and evening, so bike tours can take place year-round. In summer and fall rivers and waterfalls are voluptuous and breathtaking. A popular ending point for rides into the foothills, they offer a place to rest, rinse off (there's lots of mud), and have a snack or meal. In dry season, it's relatively cooler and less humid. The very best months for biking are December through February: the weather is coolest, and the vegetation, rivers, and waterfalls are still reasonably lush after the end of the rainy season in October.

LOGISTICS

Four- to five-hour rides average $35 to $45; Yelapa costs $110 and up. The ride down from San Sebastián, including one-way plane trip, goes for around $150. Rides of more than a half day include lunch, and all include helmet, gloves, and bikes.

OUTFITTERS

Eco Ride. A few streets behind Vallarta's cathedral, Eco Ride caters to intermediate and expert cyclists. Most rides start at the shop and go up the Río Cuale, passing some hamlets along single tracks and dirt roads. A few rides include time at local swimming holes; the Yelapa ride ($110) starts in El Tuito, about an hour south of PV (you get there by vehicle), and enjoys some magnificent scenery—with two 10-km (6-mi) uphills and a 20-km (12-mi) downhill—returns by boat after lunch on the beach. ✉ *Calle Miramar 382, Centro* ☎ *322/222–7912* ⊕ *www.ecoridemex.com.*

Vallarta Bikes. This family-operated, PV-based outfit has rides for beginner to advanced cyclists. A three- to four-hour beginner's ride to La Pileta ($35) is popular, as the departure point is near the town center and the destination a year-round swimming hole. This easy downhill ride includes lunch, as do all Vallarta Bikes' tours. The all-day, 35-km (22-mi) tour to Yelapa ($117) is more physical, but the reward is lunch overlooking

PICK-UP POLO

At **Club de Polo Costa Careyes** (✉ *Km 53.5, Carretera 200, Carretera a Barra de Navidad, El Careyes* ☎ *315/351–0320* ⊕ *www.careyes. com*) the cost is $80 per game per player and includes horse rental, polo pro, and greens fee. Spectators are welcome, too, at no charge, to watch the various games (generally held Tuesday, Wednesday, Friday, or Saturday at 4 PM) and tournaments. Both occur during the season: November through mid-April. Ask about packages including accommodations, clinics (mid-February through mid-March only), and lessons. **La Patrona Polo Club** (✉ *Ceilán 10, San Francisco* ☎ *311/258–4378 or 322/133–2601* ⊕ *www.polovallarta.com*) in Nayarit has matches on Saturday at 6 PM during the season (late November through June). You can watch from the on-site restaurant and enjoy entertainment and live jazz at the adjacent bar. You can also watch practice Tuesday and Thursday from the stands or the restaurant.

Yelapa's beautiful beach and returning by water taxi. ✉ *Francisco Villa 1442, Col. Los Sauces* ☎ *322/293–1142* ⊕ *www.vallartabikes.com.*

WATER SPORTS

FISHING

Sportfishing is excellent off Puerto Vallarta, and fisherfolk have landed monster marlin well over 500 pounds. Surf casting from shore nets snook, roosters, and jack crevalles. Hire a *panga* (skiff) to hunt for Spanish mackerel, sea bass, amberjack, snapper, bonito, and roosterfish on full- or half-day trips within the bay. Pangas can be hired in the traditional fishing villages of Mismaloya and Boca de Tomatlán, just south of town; in the Costalegre towns of La Manzanilla and Barra de Navidad; and in the north, at El Anclote and Nuevo Corral del Risco, Punta Mita.

Yachts are best for big-game fishing: yellowfin tuna; blue, striped, and black marlin; and dorado. Hire them for 4 to 10 hours, or overnight. Catch-and-release of billfish is encouraged. If you don't want to charter a boat, you can also join a party boat. Most sportfishing yachts are based at Marina Vallarta; only a few call home the marina at Paradise Village, in Nuevo Vallarta. The resort hotels of the Costalegre and Punta Mita arrange fishing excursions for their guests. Bass fishing at Cajón de Peña, about 1½ hours south of Vallarta, nets 10-pounders on a good day.

LOGISTICS

Most captains and crews are thoroughly bilingual, at least when it comes to boating and fishing.

LICENSES Licenses are required; however, a new set of regulations requires anglers to buy their fishing licenses ahead of time via a super-confusing Internet and bank-deposit system. Since boat owners are the ones (heavily) fined if there are unlicensed anglers aboard, you can leave it to the captain to make the necessary arrangements.

PRICES　Prices generally hover around $600–$650 for six hours, $600–$800 for eight hours, and $1,000–$1,200 for a 10-hour trip. A longer trip is recommended for chasing the big guys, as it takes you to prime fishing grounds like El Banco and Corbeteña. Pangas (skiffs) usually accommodate up to four clients and yachts, 4 to 10. Party boats start at $140 per person for an eight-hour day. Drinking water is generally included in the price; box lunches and beer or soda may be sold separately or included; sometimes it's BYOB. Pangas and superpangas, the latter with shade and a head of some sort, charge $175–$250 for four hours. You'll obviously save lots of money by going with the local guys in their often fast, but not luxurious, pangas.

OUTFITTERS

CharterDreams. Although most fisherfolk choose to leave around the smack of dawn, you set your own itinerary with this company. Excursions range from trips with one to three people for bass fishing to cruises with up to 12 people aboard luxury yachts. CharterDreams also offers whale-watching and private sailing, sightseeing, or snorkeling tours. ✉ *Marina Las Palmas II, Locales 1, Marina Vallarta* ☎ *322/221–0690* ⊕ *www.charterdreams.com.*

Gerardo Kosonoy. For fishing excursions in and around Barra de Navidad, at the southern end of the Costalegre, contact Sr. Kosonoy. He speaks excellent English and has low hourly rates. Alternatively, you can round up another fisherman with a panga from one of the two large fishing co-ops on the lagoon side of town. There's usually at least one representative hoping for clients at the water-taxi dock. Gerardo and his compadres charge 400 pesos (just shy of $30 at this writing) per hour for one to four passengers. There's a three-hour minimum. For fishing close to the shore, the price can be split among up to six anglers. ☎ *315/355–5739; 315/354–2251 cell* ✉ *hakuna-kosonoy@yahoo.com.*

★　**Fishing with Carolina.** This Canadian expat has been sending out anglers for 25 years. Party-boat fishing is $150. Charter your own four-passenger boat to fish in the bay; $400 covers a four-hour trip, or pay a bargain $600 for eight hours. To access the farthest locations, plan on 12 hours and about $1,000. ✉ *Terminal Marítima, Los Peines Pier Marina Vallarta* ☎ *322/224–7250* ⊕ *www.fishingwithcarolina.com.*

Mismaloya Divers. Do you remember the seductive-looking divers in *Night of the Iguana?* Well, their progeny might be among the local guys of this outfit. Panga trips here go for $175 for four hours, a bit more for longer trips. ✉ *Road to Mismaloya Beach, Mismaloya* ☎ *322/228–0020.*

Reel 1 In. This operation sells rods, reels, lures, and other fishing gear and offers full-day charters (one to four passengers) for $250 to $600, depending on the size of the boat. ✉ *Hotel Alondra, Suite 17, Calle Sinaloa 16, Barra de Navidad* ☎ *315/104–4951 cell or 360/402–3474 in U.S.* ⊕ *www.reel1in.com.*

Sociedad Cooperativa Corral del Risco. The families who run this co-op were forcibly relocated from their original town of Corral del Risco due to the development of luxurious digs like the Four Seasons. The guides may not speak English as fluently as the more polished PV operators, but they know the local waters, and the fees go directly to them and their families. Sportfishing for up to four people runs from about $200 for four hours in a smaller boat to $550 for a full-day charter in a superpanga to farther destinations like Corbeteña. ⊠ *Av. El Anclote 1, Manz. 17, Corral del Risco, Punta Mita* ☎ *329/291–6298* ⊕ *www.puntamitacharters. com.*

Vallarta Tour and Travel. Captain Peter Vines can accommodate eight fisherfolk with top-of-the-line equipment, including the latest electronics, sonar, radar, and two radios. Rates are reasonable (four hours $400, six hours $500, eight hours $600, 12 hours $800). Transportation from your hotel is included in the full-day bass-fishing expedition to Cajón de Peña; clients should call a couple weeks ahead to schedule this trip to make sure the bass are running. ⊠ *Marina Las Palmas II, Local 4, in front of Dock B, Marina Vallarta* ☎ *322/294–6240 cell; 877/301–2058 from U.S. and Canada.*

SEASONAL CATCHES

Sailfish and dorado are abundant practically year-round (though dorado drop out a bit in early summer and sailfish dip slightly in spring).

Winter: bonito, dorado, jack crevalle, sailfish, striped marlin, wahoo

Spring: amberjack, jack crevalle, grouper, mackerel, red snapper

Summer: grouper, roosterfish, yellowfin tuna

Fall: black marlin, blue marlin, sailfish, striped marlin, yellowfin tuna, wahoo

KAYAKING

Except on calm, glassy days, the open ocean is really too rough for enjoyable kayaking, and the few kayaking outfitters there are mainly offer this activity in combination with snorkeling, dolphin-watching, or boating excursions to area beaches. The best places for kayaking-and-birding combos are the mangroves, estuaries, large bays, and islands of the Costalegre, south of Puerto Vallarta.

LOGISTICS

Many of the larger beachfront hotels rent or loan sea kayaks to their guests. Double kayaks are easier on the arms than single kayaks. Since the wind usually picks up in the afternoon, morning is generally the best time to paddle. Stick to coves if you want to avoid energy-draining chop and big waves. Kayaks range from $10 to $15 an hour or $27 to $35 per day. All-inclusives like Dreams, just south of Puerto Vallarta, usually don't charge their guests for kayaks.

Ecotours. Ecotours, in downtown Vallarta, has kayaking tours from Boca de Tomatlán ($75). After paddling around a rocky point you end at tiny Playa Colomitos, where there's time for snorkeling and then a snack. You'll spend 1½ to 2 hours kayaking, and, though it's fun being on the water, the scenery isn't exactly breathtaking. ⊠ *Ignacio*

If the weather's nice, head out for a paddle; on calm days you can even leave protected coves for deeper waters.

L. Vallarta 243, Col. E. Zapata ☎ *322/223–3130 or 322/222–6606* ⊕ *www.ecotoursvallarta.com.*

SAILING

Although large Bahía de Banderas and towns to the north and south have lots of beautiful beaches to explore and wildlife to see, there are few sailing adventures for the public. Most boating companies don't want to rely on the wind to get to area beaches for the day's activities. The companies below are recommended for their true sailing skills and reliable vessels.

LOGISTICS

For insurance reasons, companies or individuals here don't rent bareboat (uncrewed) yachts even to seasoned sailors. Those who want to crew the ship themselves can do semi-bareboat charters, where the captain comes along but allows the clients to sail the boat.

OUTFITTERS

Casa Naval. Captain-owner Andre Schwartz has the *Symbiosis* (a comfortable 39-foot Beneteau Oceanis 390) for charters of four hours to several days. He charges $100 per hour for up to 10 passengers, with a discount of 10% for longer sails. ⊠ *El Faro de la Marina, Marina Vallarta* ☎ *322/100–4154 or 322/148–2203, both cell phones; 322/100–0154 for hard-of-hearing callers* ⊕ *www.casanaval.org.*

Dos Amantes. Easygoing owners Joe and Lori Lacey will tailor a day or overnight of sailing to their clients' wishes: giving sailing tips or sailing the boat themselves, providing gourmet food, snorkeling, and sunset-viewing opportunities, and most anything else. Costs are $600 to $900 for four-hour and full-day sails, respectively. ✉ *Marina Vallarta* ☎ *322/140–3171 cell, 322/140–3771 in U.S.* ⊕ *www.sailing-vallarta.com.*

Puerto Vallarta Tours. With this operator you can arrange day trips to Yelapa, Caletas, Quimixto, las Animas, or Los Arcos, or book private sailing charters. Prices for shared cruises range from $50 per person for a four-hour tour to Los Arcos to $80 for a full-day jaunt to Las Caletas, the latter including activities such as yoga, snorkeling, kayaking, and a cooking lesson. ☎ *322/222–4935; 866/701–3372 from U.S. and Canada* ⊕ *www.puertovallartatours.net.*

Vallarta Adventures. Different sorts of cruising adventures run anywhere from $55 per person for a Yelapa trip to $110 for the Sea Safari Eco Adventure—which includes horseback riding at Quimixto as well as lunch, horseback riding, and kayaking at remote Pizote, south of Yelapa. There are individual charters as well. ✉ *Paseo de las Palmas 39–A, Nuevo Vallarta* ☎ *322/297–1212; 888/303–2653 in U.S. and Canada* ✉ *Edificio Marina Golf, Local 13–C, Calle Mástil, Marina Vallarta* ☎ *322/221–0657* ⊕ *www.vallarta-adventures.com.*

SCUBA DIVING AND SNORKELING

The Pacific waters here aren't nearly as clear as those in the Caribbean, but they are warm and nutrient-rich, which means they attract a variety of sea creatures. Many of the resorts rent or loan snorkeling equipment and have introductory dive courses at their pools.

The underwater preserve surrounding Los Arcos, a rock formation off Playa Mismaloya, is a popular spot for diving and snorkeling. The rocky bay at Quimixto, about 32 km (20 mi) south of PV and accessible only by boat, is a good snorkeling spot. *Pangeros* based in Boca, Mismaloya, Yelapa and elsewhere can take you to spots off the tourist trail.

On the north side, Punta Mita has the Marietas Islands, with lava tubes and caves and at least 10 good places to snorkel and dive, including spots for advanced divers. El Morro Islands, with their big fish lurking in the underwater pinnacles and caves, are also suitable for experienced divers.

LOGISTICS

Although it's fine all year long, June through September is the very best time for snorkeling and diving. In summer, the water is at its warmest and calmest and visibility is at its best—80 to 120 feet on a good day. You can spot gigantic manta rays, several species of eel, sea turtles, and many species of colorful fish. In winter's less favorable conditions, some luck will yield orca and humpback whale sightings, an awesome experience.

OUTFITTERS

Chico's Dive Shop. This shop arranges PADI or NAUI certification, equipment rentals, and one- or two-tank dives. Trips to Los Arcos accommodate snorkelers ($40 per person) as well as those who want a one- or two-tank dive ($65 and $98, respectively). Book several days ahead for a night dive ($75 for one tank). From the Mismaloya shop, you

ANNUAL SPORTING EVENTS

MARCH
The winter season brings foreign vessels and lots of racing and boating activities, including the five-day **Banderas Bay Regatta** (☎ 322/297–2222 ⊕ www.banderasbayregatta.com; www.vallartayachtclub.com). There are cocktail parties, charity events, receptions, seminars, additional races, and boat parades as well as competitive races among boats designed for coastal and offshore cruising.

MAY
The five-day **Annual Sports Classic** (☎ 322/226–0404 Ext. 6038 [Veronica Alarcon at Sheraton Buganvilias] ⊕ www.puertovallarta.net/news/sports-classic-2008.php) invites amateurs, pros, and semipros to compete in basketball, soccer, and bowling; some years they also offer events in tennis and beach volleyball. Most events take place at the Agustin Flores Contreras Stadium, Los Arcos Amphitheater, or the beach in front of the Holiday Inn.

NOVEMBER
The **Puerto Vallarta International Half Marathon** (⊕ www.maratonvallarta.com), held in early November, gets bigger each year. There's a 5K run, too, and a big pasta dinner on the beach the day before the race.

The **International Puerto Vallarta Marlin & Sailfish Tournament** (☎ 322/225–5467 ⊕ www.fishvallarta.com) celebrated its 55th anniversary in 2010. The entry fee is nearly $4,000 per boat (up to four fishermen), but the prizes and prestige of winning are great. Categories are dorado (mahimahi), tuna, marlin, and sailfish, the last catch-and-release.

can also rent kayaks ($15 per hour). ⊠ *Paseo Díaz Ordáz 772, Centro* ☎ *322/222–1895*⊠ *Mismaloya Beach, in Barceló La Jolla de Mismaloya hotel, Mismaloya* ☎ *322/228–0248* ⊕ *www.chicos-diveshop.com.*

★ **Ecotours**. This authorized equipment dealer has English-speaking PADI dive masters. Two-tank dives run $82 to $90. All two-tank trips include lunch, refreshments, and gear. Snorkeling trips to the Marieta Islands, where you may spot dolphins and, in season, whales, cost $85 per person, including lunch overlooking the beach. Hotel pickup, boat ride, and snorkel gear are included in the price. ⊠ *Ignacio L. Vallarta 243, Col. E. Zapata* ☎ *322/223–3130 or 322/222–6606* ⊕ *www.ecotoursvallarta.com.*

★ **Sociedad Cooperativa Corral del Risco**. Tours with this co-op are a great deal if you have a group: two hours of snorkeling around the Marietas Islands, for up to eight people, costs just $95 on a one-motor boat, about $120 for the 2-motor vessel. This group represents local fishermen displaced when Punta Mita was developed by the Four Seasons and other associated establishments. ⊠ *Av. El Anclote 1, Manzana. 17, Corral del Risco* ☎ *329/291–6298* ⊕ *www.puntamitacharters.com.*

Vallarta Adventures. Vallarta Adventures accommodates nondivers (who can snorkel or kayak) as well as divers on trips that start at $90 ($105 for two tanks). It also has introductory dive classes for children and adults

($35) and open-water certification ($440). ⊠ *Paseo de las Palmas 39–A, Nuevo Vallarta* ☎ *322/297–1212; 888/303–2653 in U.S. and Canada* ⊠ *Edifício Marina Golf, Local 13–C, Calle Mástil, Marina Vallarta* ☎ *322/221–0657* ⊕ *www.vallarta-adventures.com.*

Vallarta Undersea. This operation offers PADI dive courses; runs dive trips; and sells, rents, and repairs dive equipment. It offers a couple of two-tank dives (at Majahuitas and Las Marietas) for $95; otherwise, it's $85 for a one-tank excursion to the usual dive sites, or $115 to El Morro or El Chimo. The office is in Marina Vallarta, and at this writing there were plans for a second office in La Cruz de Huanacaxtle. ⊠ *Calle Proa, Local 22, Marina Vallarta* ☎ *322/209–0025 or 322/209–0025* ⊕ *www.vallartaundersea.com.*

> ### WHEN TO CATCH A WAVE
>
> Locals have lots of folk wisdom about when to catch the best waves. Some say it's best right before a good rain, while others believe it's when the tide is moving toward an extreme high or low.

SURFING

The main surfing areas are in the north, in Nayarit State, and include Sayulita and Punta Mita, where there are nearly a dozen offshore breaks for intermediate and advanced surfers, some best accessed by boat. The best spots for beginners are shore breaks like those at El Anclote and Sayulita; in the south, Barra de Navidad is also appropriate for beginners.

LOGISTICS

SEASONS Waves are largest and most consistent between June and December; the water is also warmest during the rainy season (late June–October), averaging nearly 80°F (27°C) July through September.

PRICES Surfboard rentals start at $4 an hour or $18 a day. Surfing trips run around $45 per hour, usually with a three- or four-hour minimum. Shops sell rash guards (you usually don't need a full wet suit here), boogie boards, wax, and other necessities. For good info and links, check out ⊕ *www.surf-mexico.com.*

OUTFITTERS

Captain Pablo. At this outfitter on the beach at Sayulita you can rent equipment or take surfing lessons with Patricia: $30 should get you to your feet (board included). Surf tours, gear included, cost $180 for four hours (up to four surfers). ⊠ *Calle Las Gaviotas at beach, Sayulita* ☎ *329/291–2070 early morning and evenings only* ✉ *pandpsouthworth@hotmail.com.*

Sininen. Sininen rents surfboards ($5 per hour, $18 for the day) and paddleboards ($8/hour, $33 all day), gives lessons on both pieces of equipment, and sells surfboards and surf paraphernalia. Rent from the shop or head straight to its outpost a block away on the beach. ⊠ *Calle Delfín 4–S, Sayulita* ☎ *329/291–3186.*

Surf quality in Puerto Vallarta ranges from beginner-friendly to challenging.

Wildmex. Located right on the beach in Sayulita, Wildmex rents surfboards (as well as bicycles and kayaks) and gives surf lessons either at Sayulita or elsewhere around the bay, depending on conditions. (The Web site has a wave forecast feature that predicts wave height, wave period, and wind speed.) It offers four- and six-day surf packages and a weeklong surf camp; the latter includes accommodations, some meals, and airport transfer. The company also arranges horseback riding, fishing, yoga classes, and other activities. ✉ *The beach at Sayulita, Sayulita* ☎ *322/107–0601 cell or 322/100–7070 cell* ⊕ *www.wildmex.com.*

WILDLIFE-WATCHING

Banderas Bay and the contiguous coast and inland areas are blessed with abundant species of birds and beasties. Diverse habitats from riparian forests to nearby islands are home to a wide range of native and migratory birds, including about two dozen endemic species. Beyond birds, most of the wildlife spotting is marine: whales (December through end of March), dolphins, marine turtles, and giant manta rays, among many other species.

BIRD-WATCHING

Although there aren't many dedicated birding operators here, this region is perfect for the pastime. Vallarta has more than 350 species in a wide variety of habitats, including shoreline, rivers, marshes, lagoons, mangroves, and tropical and evergreen forests. In the mangroves, standouts are the great blue heron, mangrove cuckoo, and vireo. Ocean and shorebirds include brown and blue-footed boobies and red-billed tropic birds. Military macaws patrol the thorn forests, and songbirds of all stripes serenade the pine-oak forests at higher elevations.

LOGISTICS

Most people come on trips through birding clubs or organizations or hire a private birding guide. Outfitters charge $50–$60 for half-day tours and $100–$125 for full-day tours.

OUTFITTERS **Ecotours.** Ecotours runs three six-hour tours ($80 per person each) to different ecosystems, plus an overnight excursion to San Blas ($350). Bring plenty of insect repellent, especially in the rainy months. ⊠ *Ignacio L. Vallarta 243, Col. E. Zapata* ☎ *322/223–3130 or 322/222–6606* ⊕ *www.ecotoursvallarta.com.*

Wildlife Connection. Biologists lead a three-hour birding tour ($56) through a variety of different environments. ⊠ *Calle Francia 140, Dpto. 7, Col. Versalles, Puerto Vallarta* ☎ *322/225–3621* ⊕ *www.wildlifeconnection.com.*

Wings. It's a Tucson, Arizona–based operator that leads at least one weeklong tour each year to the mangroves and tropical forest around San Blas, Jalisco, and Colima. ☎ *520/320–9868; 888/293–6443 in U.S. and Canada* ⊕ *www.wingsbirds.com.*

DOLPHIN ENCOUNTERS

Many folks find the idea of captive dolphins disturbing; others cherish the opportunity to interact with these intelligent creatures that communicate through body language as well as an audible code we humans have yet to decipher. Decide whether you support the idea of captive-dolphin encounters, and act accordingly. Listed below are operators with captive dolphin programs as well as one that has an open-ocean encounter. As these gregarious mammals are fond of bow-surfing, most bay-tripping boats will encounter dolphins as they motor along, providing more opportunities to see dolphins as well as leaping manta rays and other sea life.

LOGISTICS

Dolphins are abundant in the bay year-round, though not 24/7. Dolphin encounters limit the number of humans per encounter and usually allow just two visits a day. Call before you arrive or early in your stay to book.

OUTFITTERS

★ **Dolphin and Sea Lion Discovery.** For both the Dolphin Encounter ($79) and the Dolphin Swim ($99) at Dolphin Discovery in the Sea Life Park you spend about 30 of the 45-minute experience in the water interacting with dolphins. In the Royal Dolphin Swim ($149), you still get only 30 minutes in the pool, but, with a higher ratio of cetaceans to humans, you get more face time. It's an expensive outing, and the memento photos really jack up the price (you're not allowed to take your own snaps, and they photograph each family member individually). To get the most bang for your buck, plan to spend the day at the water park. The entrance fee of $18/$14 for adults/kids to Aquaventures Park is included with dolphin program. ⊠ *Aquaventures Park, Carretera a*

DID YOU KNOW?

Many travelers chose to skip captive dolphin swims due to the practice's ethical implications. In Puerto Vallarta, alternative options include wild dolphin swims and boat-based dolphin-watching tours—both considered to have low impact on the dolphins and high impact on the participant.

Tepic, Km 155, Nuevo Vallarta ☎ *322/297–0724; 866/393–5158 in U.S.; 866/793–1905 in Canada* ⊕ *www.aquaventuras.com.*

☾ **Aquaventures Park.** Kids can plummet down one of 10 enormous water-slides, play on playground equipment, and indulge in junk food at the obligatory snack shops while their parents swim or relax around the pool. On the property are the dolphin and sea-lion discovery adventures. ⊠ *Carretera a Tepic, Km 155, Nuevo Vallarta* ☎ *322/297–0724* 🖃 *$18* ◷ *Tues.–Sun. 10–5.*

Wildlife Connection. This Mexican-owned company uses two-motor skiffs equipped with listening equipment to find pods of dolphins in the wild blue sea. You can then jump in the water to swim with these beautiful creatures in their own environment. The most common destination is around the Marietas Islands. The cost is $76 per person for a three- to four-hour tour, including travel time; tours are conducted April through December only. There's no guarantee, however, that the dolphins will stick around for the fun. There's also a combined tour searching for whales and dolphins, $80 a pop, December through March only. ⊠ *Calle Francia 140, Dpto. 7, Col. Versalles, Puerto Vallarta* ☎ *322/225–3621* ⊕ *www.wildlifeconnection.com.*

HIKING

The coastal fringe and the hills behind Vallarta—with streams and rivers heading down from the mountains—are beautiful areas for exploring, but few tour operators have hiking and walking trips. If you plan an impromptu exploration, it's best to take along a local familiar with the area.

LOGISTICS

Some of the biking tour operators (⇨ *Mountain Biking, above*) will lead hiking outings as well, if you ask.

OUTFITTERS

Ecotours. Its three-hour hike around El Nogalito River ($60) includes a pit stop at a rocky, waterfall-fed pool for a dip. En route to either you'll see a small number of birds, butterflies, and tropical plants. ⊠ *Ignacio L. Vallarta 243, Col. E. Zapata* ☎ *322/223–3130 or 322/222–6606* ⊕ *www.ecotoursvallarta.com.*

Vallarta Adventures. The outdoor adventure tour ($98) combines a speedboat ride and mule trek with rappelling, hiking, and a partial canopy tour. Although hikes are generally led by knowledgeable naturalists, the emphasis is on physical activity rather than flora and fauna sightings. Participants must be 10 or over and 250 pounds or under. ⊠ *Paseo de las Palmas 39–A, Nuevo Vallarta* ☎ *322/297–1212; 888/303–2653 from U.S. and Canada* ⊠ *Edifício Marina Golf, Local 13–C, Calle Mástil, Marina Vallarta* ☎ *322/221–0657* ⊕ *www.vallarta-adventures.com.*

Participating in a turtle-hatching tour (held from summer to late fall) will likely put you face to face with the adorable Lepidochelys olivacea, or olive ridley turtle, the smallest sea turtle species in the world.

TURTLE-WATCHING AND REPATRIATION

Mexico has seven of the world's eight sea turtle species. Three of those species live in and around Banderas Bay. The fastest growing and earliest to mature of the Pacific Coast turtles is the olive ridley, or *golfina*, which are more numerous than the Careyes and the even less frequently sighted leatherback. Researchers estimate there are 1 to 10 leatherbacks for every 1,000 olive ridleys in the Puerto Vallarta area.

After the female turtle creates a nest in the sand, the eggs incubate for approximately 60 days. The babies must bust out of eggs and earth on their own, and with luck they will head for the ocean under cover of night. Birds, crabs, and other wild animals are relentless predators. For every 1,000 baby turtles born, only 1 survives to adulthood. Fortunately the average nest holds several hundred eggs.

LOGISTICS

Tours run from summer through late fall. Wear shoes or sandals that are comfortable for walking in the sand. Bring a sweatshirt or light jacket, and plan to stay out late in the evening for most turtle repatriation programs, as that's when predators are less active. Most tours cost $46–$50 per person, last three to four hours, and combine educational programs with hands-on activities.

OUTFITTERS

Ecotours. Three-hour turtle tours August through mid-December cost $48. Depending on the time of year, you may walk the beach searching for females depositing their eggs in the sand and help remove these eggs for safekeeping. Whether or not you find egg-laying females, there are always little turtles for releasing to the wild at the end of the evening. Tours are Monday through Saturday. ✉ *Ignacio L. Vallarta 243, Col. E. Zapata* ☎ *322/223–3130 or 322/222–6606* ⊕ *www. ecotoursvallarta.com.*

Wildlife Connection. Trained biologists lead turtle repatriation programs. During the four-hour tours you'll drive ATVs to the beach to find and collect recently deposited eggs, if possible, and then blast over to Boca de Tomates Beach to liberate tiny turtles under the relative protection of darkness. ✉ *Calle Francia 140, Col. Versalles, Puerto Vallarta* ☎ *322/225–3621* ⊕ *www. wildlifeconnection.com.*

CAUTION

Several organizations, including Greenpeace, the Humane Society (U.S.), and the Whale and Dolphin Conservation Society, have spoken out against captive dolphin encounters, asserting that some water parks get dolphins from restricted areas and that the confined conditions at some parks put the dolphins' health at risk. Consider putting the $100-plus fee toward a snorkeling, whale-watching, or noncaptive dolphin encounter, where you can see marine life in its natural environment.

WHALE-WATCHING

Most of the boats on the bay, whether fishing boats or tour boats, also run whale-watching tours (December–mid-March). Some boats are equipped with hydrophones for listening to the whales' songs and carry trained marine biologists; others use the usual crew and simply look for signs of cetaceans. The species you're most likely to see are humpback and killer whales (a gray whale occasionally); false killer whales; and bottlenose, spinner, and pantropic spotted dolphins (yup, dolphins are whales, too!).

LOGISTICS

Whale-watching is only available December through March. Prime breeding grounds are around the Marietas Islands. The larger boats leave from Marina Vallarta, but you can hire fishermen in villages like Corral del Risco, Mismaloya, Boca de Tomatlán, Yelapa, Las Animas, Barra de Navidad, and Tenacatita for less formal, more intimate trips. The larger boats are more likely to have radio equipment useful for communicating with others about the location of whale pods. Some outfitters offer a discount if you sign up online.

OUTFITTERS

Ecotours. After a brief lecture about cetacean ecosystems, you'll board a boat equipped with hydrophones at Punta Mita for a three-hour tour. Tours are daily in season (mid-December to mid-March) and cost $75. ✉ *Ignacio L. Vallarta 243, Col. E. Zapata* ☎ *322/223–3130 or 322/222–6606* ⊕ *www.ecotoursvallarta.com.*

Sociedad Cooperativa Corral del Risco. Two hours of whale-watching or snorkeling around the Marietas Islands, for up to 10 people, costs $114. Anyone older than 6 but younger than 60 also pays $2 for a wristband allowing entrance to the Marietas, a national aquatic park. You search until whales are spotted, and then have a half-hour of viewing time before returning to dry land. ✉ *Av. El Anclote 1, Manz. 17, Corral del Risco* ☎ *329/291–6298* ⊕ *www.puntamitacharters.com.*

Vallarta Adventures. Professional guides assist you in spotting dolphins and whales on several different types of cruises to sites on and around Banderas Bay. Sailing trips for seeking cetaceans are also an option ($89). ✉ *Paseo de las Palmas 39–A, Nuevo Vallarta* ☎ *322/297–1212; 888/303–2653 in U.S. and Canada* ✉ *Edifício Marina Golf, Local 13–C, Calle Mástil, Marina Vallarta* ☎ *322/221–0657* ⊕ *www.vallarta-adventures.com.*

Wildlife Connection. The company gives whale-watching tours in season for $76. Its professional biologists are dedicated to educating the public about area wildlife. ✉ *Calle Francia 140, Col. Versalles, Puerto Vallarta* ☎ *322/225–3621* ⊕ *www.wildlifeconnection.com.*

Where to Stay

WORD OF MOUTH

"Having a small child, a kitchen is a plus. We have rented places from a studio directly on the ocean, a 1 bedroom in town, and a 2 bedroom in the hotel zone. The offerings are endless. You really don't need an AI. The restaurants are part of the experience."

—rpowell

WHERE TO STAY PLANNER

Lodging Strategy

Where should I stay? With hundreds of Puerto Vallarta hotels, it may seem like a daunting question. But fret not—we've done most of the legwork. The selections here represent the best this city has to offer—from the best budget digs to the sleekest designer resorts. Scan "Best Bets" on the following pages for top recommendations by price and experience. Or find a review quickly in the listings—search by neighborhood, then alphabetically. Happy hunting!

Need a Reservation?

Hotel reservations are an absolute necessity when planning your trip to Puerto Vallarta—although rooms are easier to come by these days. Competition for clients also means properties undergo frequent improvements, especially late September through mid-November, so when booking ask about any renovations, lest you get a room within earshot of construction, or find your hotel is temporarily without commonplace amenities such as swimming pool or spa.

⚠ **Overbooking is a common practice, so get confirmation in writing via fax or e-mail.**

Services

Most resort hotels have air-conditioning, cable TV, one or more restaurants, room service, and in-room irons and ironing boards. Many have voice mail, coffeemakers, and hair dryers. Ethernet or Wi-Fi Internet service is common in guest rooms; if not, there's likely a guest computer or three in a common area. Most hotels above the budget or moderate price level have fitness facilities, alternatively, visit a nearby sports club or gym (there are many). Some hotels are entirely smoke-free, meaning even smoking outdoors is frowned upon or prohibited.

Can I Drink the Water?

Most of the fancier hotels have reverse osmosis or other water filtration systems. It's fine for brushing your teeth, but play it safe by drinking bottled water (there might be leaks that let groundwater in). Note that the bottled water might cost extra, although there's usually a notice if it's not free. Buy a few bottles at the corner grocery instead.

Chain Hotels

Tried-and-true chains may have excellent rates and can be good last-minute options. **Holiday Inn/Intercontinental Group** (☎ 800/465–4329 in U.S., 01800/000–0404 in Mexico ⊕ www.holiday-inn.com). **Marriott** (☎ 888/236–2427 in U.S. and Canada, 01800/900–8800 in Mexico ⊕ www.marriott.com). **Sheraton** (☎ 800/325–3535 in U.S. ⊕ www.starwood.com/sheraton). **Westin** (☎ 800/937–8461 ⊕ www.starwoodhotels.com/westin).

Boutique Hotels

México Boutique Hotels (☎ 322/221–2277; 01800/508–7923 in Mexico; 800/728–9098 in U.S. or Canada ⊕ www.mexicoboutiquehotels.com) is a private company that represents 45 intimate properties selected for their setting, cuisine, service, and overall allure.

Apartments and Villas

When shared by two couples, a spacious villa can save you a bundle on upscale lodging and on meals. Villas often come with stereo systems, DVD players, a pool, maid service, and air-conditioning. Prices range from $100 to $1,000 per night, with 20% to 40% discounts off-season.

One good resource is **Cochran Real Estate** (☎ 322/228-0419 in PV ⊕ www.buyeragentmexico.com). **Hideaways International** (☎ 603/430-4433; 800/843-4433 in U.S. ⊕ www.hideaways.com) requires a membership fee. **Villas and Apartments Abroad** (☎ 212/213-6435; 800/433-3020 in U.S. ⊕ www.vaanyc.com) offers mainly larger accommodations (sleeping six or more) in Puerto Vallarta and Punta Mita. **Villas International** (☎ 415/499-9490; 800/221-2260 in U.S. ⊕ www.villasintl.com) has (pricey) villas and apartments in and around Vallarta. Online rental agency **VRBO** (⊕ www.vrbo.com) has numerous listings in PV, Riviera Nayarit, and Costalegre.

Pricing

We list high-season prices, before meals or other amenities. Low-season rates usually drop 20%–30%. We always list available facilities, but not whether they cost extra.

Less expensive hotels include tax in the quote. Most higher-priced resorts add 18% tax on top of the quoted rate; some add a 5%–10% service charge. Moderately priced hotels swing both ways. Tax and/or tips are often included with all-inclusive plans.

■ TIP→ An all-inclusive (AI) might make you reluctant to spend money elsewhere. So you don't miss out on area restaurants and activities, stay at more modest digs for part of your trip, and go AI for a day or two. Some AI hotels also have day passes ($60–$90).

WHAT IT COSTS IN U.S. DOLLARS

	¢	$	$$	$$$	$$$$
Hotels	under $60	$60–$120	$121–$180	$181–$250	over $250

For a standard room in high season, generally excluding taxes and service charges.

In This Chapter

Meal Plans

AI: All-Inclusive; including all meals, drinks, and most activities. **BP:** Breakfast Plan; full breakfast. **CP:** Continental Plan; Continental breakfast. **EP:** European Plan; without meals. **FAP:** Full American Plan; breakfast, lunch, and dinner. **MAP:** Modified American Plan; breakfast and dinner.

Using the Maps

You'll see mapping symbols and coordinates (⊹ 3:F2) after property names or reviews; these locate the property on the appropriate map. The number after the ⊹ symbol indicates which map; the letter and number after the colon indicate the property's location on that map's grid.

BEST BETS FOR PUERTO VALLARTA LODGING

Fodor's offers a selective listing of lodging experiences at every price range. Here, we've compiled our top recommendations by price and experience. The very best properties are designated in the listings with the Fodor's Choice logo.

Fodor's Choice ★

Casa Obelisco, p. 127

Dreams Puerto Vallarta Resort & Spa, p. 111

El Careyes Beach Resort, p. 133

El Tamarindo Beach & Golf Resort, p. 133

Hacienda Alemana Frankfurt, p. 95

Hotel des Artistes, p. 124

Hotel Posada de Roger, p. 96

Playa Los Arcos Beach Resort & Spa, p. 97

Quinta Maria Cortez, p. 112

Villa Amor, p. 128

By Price

¢

Hotel Posada de Roger, p. 96

Hotel Sarabi, p. 138

Marco's Place Suites & Villas, p. 120

$

Casa Dulce Vida, p. 101

Hotel Eloísa, p. 96

Los Cuatro Vientos, p. 103

Playa Los Arcos Beach Resort & Spa, p. 97

Villa Amor, p. 128

$$

Buenaventura Grand Hotel & Spa, p. 101

Casa Cúpula, p. 108

Hacienda Alemana Frankfurt, p. 95

Haramara Retreat, p. 128

Presidente InterContinental Puerto Vallarta Resort, p. 112

Quinta Maria Cortez, p. 112

$$$

CasaMagna Marriott Puerto Vallarta Resort & Spa, p. 105

Casa Obelisco, p. 127

Punta Serena Villas & Spa, p. 135

$$$$

Dreams Puerto Vallarta Resort & Spa, p. 111

El Careyes Beach Resort, p. 133

El Tamarindo Beach & Golf Resort, p. 133

Four Seasons Resort, Punta Mita, p. 124

Hotel des Artistes, p. 124

Hotel St. Regis Punta Mita, p. 125

By Experience

BEST BEACH

El Careyes Beach Resort, p. 133

Hotel Blue Chairs, p. 95

Hotel des Artistes, p. 124

Las Villitas Tenacatita, p. 135

Playa los Arcos Beach Resort & Spa, p. 97

Presidente InterContinental Puerto Vallarta Resort, p. 112

Quinta Maria Cortez, p. 112

BEST SPA

CasaMagna Marriott Puerto Vallarta Resort & Spa, p. 105

Four Seasons Resort, Punta Mita, p. 124

Paradise Village Beach Resort & Spa, p. 121

GREEN FOCUS

Four Seasons Resort, Punta Mita, p. 124

Haramara Retreat, p. 128

Hotelito Desconocido Sanctuary Reserve & Spa, p. 134

House of Wind and Water, p. 102

MOST KID-FRIENDLY

Dreams Puerto Vallarta Resort & Spa, p. 111

Four Seasons Resort, Punta Mita, p. 124

Meliá Puerto Vallarta All Inclusive Beach Resort, p. 105

Paradise Village Beach Resort & Spa, p. 121

BEST FOR SUNSETS

Hacienda San Angel, p. 102

Hotel Blue Chairs, p. 95

Hotel des Artistes, p. 124

Hotel Playa Conchas Chinas, p. 111

Hotel St. Regis Punta Mita, p. 125

Punta Serena Villas & Spa, p. 135

WHERE SHOULD I STAY?

	NEIGHBORHOOD VIBE	PROS	CONS
Zona Romántica	Older, modest hotels with low price and proximity to the beach. Varied restaurants, cafés, and gay bars buzz well into the night.	Action central; walking distance to bars, shops, restaurants, and beaches north and south. Buses to other zones.	Few hotels offer parking; mostly modest hotels only with few amenities; many older hotels could use renovation.
Centro and Environs	Colorful Old Vallarta, with a few interesting hotels in the hills with excellent bay views. More shops and restaurants than hotels.	Central location. Plenty of nightlife, buses, and taxis. Cruising the boardwalk is fun day or night.	Noisy traffic from old buses squeezing through narrow streets. Dearth of parking spaces. Less lively at night than Zona Romántica.
Marina Vallarta	Luxury high-rise hotels near the marina, facing the beach. Good for walking, casual biking, and jogging, but no city scene.	Close to marina's yacht harbor with boats, restaurant-bars, and shops. Near airport and golf courses.	Pricey hotels only; cab ride to most everywhere except marina; lacks local character; narrow to nonexistent beach in front of many hotels.
Nayarit— Around Banderas Bay (Bucerias, La Cruz de Huanacaxtle, Nuevo Vallarta, Punta Mita)	Away from more touristy Vallarta, but near enough for excursions are the all-inclusive-focused Nuevo Vallarta, easy-going Bucerías, rustic La Cruz, and luxurious Punta Mita.	Less hustle and hype than Puerto Vallarta; small-town vibe (Nuevo Vallarta excepted); good for walking; safe and friendly; excellent beaches.	Expensive cab and long bus rides from Vallarta; fewer nightlife, restaurant, and shopping options; each town has narrow range of accommodations.
Nayarit—North of Banderas Bay (San Francisco, Sayulita, Rincon de Guayabitos)	Beachy, pleasant, youth and family-oriented, these Riviera Nayarit towns attract self-sufficient travelers looking for R&R by the sea.	Pretty beaches; expanding tourist infrastructure; moderately priced lodgings and restaurants; easy-going appeal for laid-back singles, couples, and families.	Long ways from airport; fairly long walk to main highway; carless travelers must rely on taxis (expensive when used routinely) or less-than-pristine local buses.
South Along Banderas Bay	Smaller resorts and condos nestled in hills of towering tropical vegetation; most overlook the sea and are some distance apart. Friendly gay scene.	Beautiful views; close proximity to Zona Romántica, Mismaloya, and attractions to the south. Uncrowded villages; perfect for a tranquil escape.	Isolated from immediate action, proximity to nearest bars and restaurants varies depending on hotel location. Carless guests have long walks ahead of them.
Costalegre	Mix of deluxe hideaways for the rich and famous with small beach towns sporting basic lodgings, vacation rentals, and miles of glorious beaches.	Uncrowded beaches, fewer beach vendors, unadorned Mexico (except for the luxury spots). Long, flat, sandy, palm-fringed beaches; plenty of local color.	Fewer amenities, low-key nightlife. The area is challenging to explore without a car as it's far from transportation hubs.

4

Centered in the middle of a large bay, Bahía de Banderas, Puerto Vallarta is the traditional hub for area beach hotels. Look for smaller budget hotels downtown, and oceanfront high-rise hotels to the north in the Hotel Zone (Zona Hotelera), Marina Vallarta, and Nuevo Vallarta. Even farther north, Riviera Nayarit is where to go for unique B&Bs, boutique hotels, and some truly luxurious villas.

Having reached critical mass, Puerto Vallarta's hotel scene is more about upgrading than building new properties. In the Centro and Zona Romántica neighborhoods, expect refurbished budget and moderately priced hotels (with the exception of luxury property Hacienda San Angel). Continue north into Zona Hotelera for condos, time-shares, and high-rises.

Areas directly to the north and south of the city continue to add vacation properties. Just north of town in Nuevo Vallarta, look for the new condo-hotel Taheima Wellness Resort & Spa. South of town in Costalegre, the boutique ecoluxe oasis Hotelito Desconocido has reopened after two years of renovation with an extensive new holistic spa.

The most development is occurring in Riviera Nayarit, where the 100 mi of coastline between San Blas and Nuevo Vallarta are experiencing a building boom. Once the private playground of surfers and beachgoers seeking waves and long stretches of solitary sand, many popular beaches are now becoming resort destinations. Playa Destiladeras, between La Cruz de Huanacaxtle and Punta Mita, is home to the new Fairmont Rancho Banderas—an upscale family-focused resort of one-, two-, and three-bedroom villas. The area is also home to the 2,100-acre Litubú development that is set to have two golf courses, the new La Tranquila resort, private homes, a beach club, and public shopping and dining.

No matter what you're looking for—from cliff-side condos with beach access to small inns with trails leading into the jungle, from enormous pools with swim-up bars to private plunge pools—almost any hospitality wish can be fulfilled here.

At Hacienda Alemana, guests can choose to dine alfresco.

PUERTO VALLARTA

ZONA ROMÁNTICA

The Romantic Zone, AKA Colonia Emiliano Zapata, is PV's party central. Gay and straight bars are interspersed with diminutive boutiques and restaurants. Los Muertos and Amapas beaches face the fray, a convenient place to party, eat, and drink. Moderately priced hotels overlook the sand, with budget options a few blocks away. New parking structures provide parking, as most hotels here do not. Taxis and buses make exploring surrounding areas a snap.

$$ ▦ **Casa Andrea**. One- and two-bedroom apartments in this spiffy property are truly homey. Each has a different floor plan—some have larger kitchens, but all of them are fully equipped. All also have air-conditioning, ceiling fans, and dark-wood beams that contrast with white ceilings and walls. Use the hotel's computers to check your e-mail, or curl up with a book or watch a video in the library. Coffee and pastries are served each morning on the garden patio, where guests (many of them return visitors) sit and chat. The location, a few blocks from Los Arcos and the malecón, is a real plus. With some exceptions, high-season bookings are by the week. Expect some homely but sweet rescued dogs to be wandering about. **Pros:** free Wi-Fi; great location in Zona Romántica; homey feel; good value. **Cons:** often fully booked; no credit cards accepted. ⊠ *Calle Francisca Rodríguez 174, Col. E. Zapata* ☎ *322/222–1213* ⊕ *www.casa-andrea.com* ⇱ *11 apartments* ⚭ *In-room: a/c, no phone,*

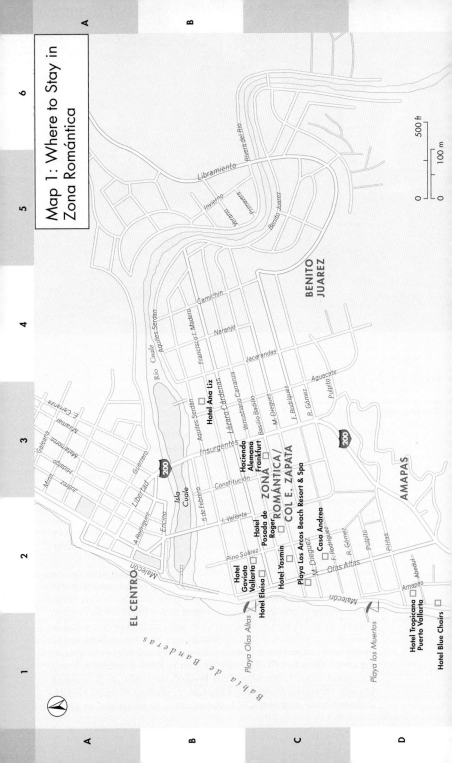

Map 1: Where to Stay in Zona Romántica

Bahía de Banderas

Río Cuale

Isla Cuale

EL CENTRO

BENITO JUAREZ

AMAPAS

ZONA ROMÁNTICA/
COL E. ZAPATA

Playa Olas Altas

Playa los Muertos

Malecón

Malecón

Hotel Ana liz

Hacienda Alemana Frankfurt

Hotel Posada de Roger

Hotel Gaviota Vallarta

Hotel Eloisa

Hotel Yasmin

Playa Los Arcos Beach Resort & Spa

Casa Andrea

Hotel Tropicana Puerto Vallarta

Hotel Blue Chairs

Mina
Juárez
Galeana
Matamoros
Hidalgo
Miramar
E. Carranza
Guerrero
A. Rodríguez
Libertad
Encino
5 de febrero
J. Vallarta
Pino Suárez
Constitución
Insurgentes
Aquiles Serdán
Lázaro Cárdenas
Francisco I. Madera
Venustiano Carranza
Basilio Badillo
M. Dieguez
F. Rodríguez
R. Gómez
Olas Altas
M. Dieguez
F. Rodríguez
R. Gómez
Pulpito
Pilitas
Amapas
Abedul
Aguacate
Pulpito
Jacarandas
Naranjo
Camichin
Benito Juarez
Rivera del Rio
Libramiento
Invierno
Primavera
Verano

500 ft
100 m
0

200
200

kitchen, no TV, Wi-Fi. In-hotel: bar, pool, gym, laundry facilities, Internet terminal 🚫 *No credit cards* ⏹️ *CP* ✠ *2:C2.*

$$ 🛏️ **Hacienda Alemana Frankfurt.** Rooms here have king-size beds, 32-inch

Fodor's Choice TVs, and double-pane windows to keep out noise. The decor and furnish-

★ ings are original, modern, and warm—poured-cement floors, fine wood furniture, marble sink surrounds. Regular rooms are spacious; even more spacious are the three-room suites, which are also a steal in low season and well-priced year-round. On the large patio is a *biergarten* and the hotel's restaurant, Café Frankfurt, which is well worth a meal or two. Although this is a comfortable, classy place to stay, it's better suited to self-sufficient guests, as there's no front-desk staff. A la carte breakfast at Langostino's Restaurant, facing Los Muertos Beach, is included. The free bottled water in your room's pint-sized fridge is replenished daily; guests pay for the beer or soft drinks stocked there. **Pros:** excellent on-site German restaurant; free access to gym, sauna, and steam room (off-site); DVDs and iPod stations upon request; great for couples. **Cons:** no real reception staff, so no one around when restaurant closed; possible noise from *biergarten.* ✉️ *Calle Basilio Badillo 378, Col. E. Zapata* ☎ *322/222–2071* 🌐 *www.haciendaalemana.com* 🛏️ *10 rooms* ♿ *In-room: a/c, safe, kitchen (some), refrigerator, Wi-Fi. In-hotel: restaurant, gym, parking (free), some pets allowed* 🚫 *MC, V* ⏹️ *CP* ✠ *1:C3.*

¢ 🛏️ **Hotel Ana Liz.** Those who prefer to spend their vacation cash on eating out and shopping might consider this spotlessly clean, bright, motel-like budget hotel a few blocks south of the Cuale River. Two floors of rooms face each other across an outdoor corridor and have tiny bathrooms but reasonably comfortable beds. Ask for a room away from the noisy street. Backpacking Europeans often stay at this extremely plain place when they come to town; they're likely drawn by the substantial discounts for monthly stays. You can rent a television for about $4 per day, but you'll get local channels only. **Pros:** best bargain in town for dedicated budget travelers; walking distance to beach, Puerto Vallarta eateries, and mini-grocery stores; near Internet cafés and taco stands. **Cons:** zero frills; no TV. ✉️ *Francisco I. Madero 429, Col. E. Zapata* ☎ *322/222–1757* 🛏️ *23 rooms* ♿ *In-room: a/c, no phone* 🚫 *No credit cards* ⏹️ *EP* ✠ *1:B3.*

$$ 🛏️ **Hotel Blue Chairs.** In the past two years, previously tired rooms have been revived; they are still modest but now have flat screen TVs, twin lamps on bedside tables, antique-white furnishings, and pretty paint jobs. Still, the mostly gay clientele stays here not for the rooms but for all that Blue Chairs offers as a social destination. Drag and strip shows, theme nights, events, parties, booze cruises, and beach cruising all begin—and often end—right here. It's worth the difference in price to upgrade from an interior room to a partial- or full-ocean view room with a larger balcony. **Pros:** a great place to enjoy nonstop evening activities; right on the gay beach; concierge service; significant low-season and online discounts. **Cons:** few amenities; lackadaisical service by beachside waiters; slow elevators. ✉️ *Almendro 4 at malecón, Los Muertos Beach, Col. E. Zapata* ☎ *322/222–5040; 888/302–3662 in U.S.; 866/403–8497 in Canada* 🌐 *www.hotelbluechairs.com* 🛏️ *24 rooms, 16 suites* ♿ *In-room: a/c, kitchen (some), refrigerator (some). In-hotel: 2 restaurants, bars, pool* 🚫 *AE, MC, V* ⏹️ *EP* ✠ *1:D2.*

4

$ 🛏 **Hotel Eloísa.** A block from the beach and overlooking Lázaro Cárdenas Park, this hotel has more of a downtown feel rather than a beachy one. Rooms are plain but clean, and there's a great city-and-mountain view from the rooftop, which has a pool and party area. Studios have small kitchenettes in one corner; suites have larger kitchens, separate bedrooms, and two quiet air-conditioners. Units with great views (nos. 511–514) cost the same as those without, so ask for one *con vista panorámica* (with a panoramic view) at check-in; they won't guarantee these ahead of time. The cheapest rooms have no TV or air-conditioning. **Pros:** snug studios overlook park; large pool on roof. **Cons:** no parking; mainly older a/c units. ✉ *Lázaro Cárdenas 179, Col. E. Zapata* 🕾 *322/222–6465 or 322/222–0286* ⊕ *www.hoteleloisa.com* 🛏 *63 rooms, 6 studios, 8 suites* 🛆 *In-room: a/c (some), no phone, kitchen (some), refrigerator (some). In-hotel: 2 pools* ⊟ *MC, V* ⊺⊙⊦*EP* ✛ *1:C2.*

$ 🛏 **Hotel Gaviota Vallarta.** Simple rooms in this six-story low-rise have somewhat battered colonial-style furnishings; some have tiny balconies but only a few on the top floors have a partial ocean view. The small figure-eight pool in the middle of the courtyard is exposed but still refreshes. Choose air-conditioning and cable TV or fan only, without the *tele,* to save about $25 per night. The two-bedroom apartments are poorly designed and have stiff Mexican furnishings. For the same price you can get two standard rooms, although without the kitchen facilities. JB Golden Age nightclub next door provides Latin and pop music throughout the week (it's live on weekends and canned otherwise) for a small cover charge, usually $4–$8 per person. **Pros:** moderately priced rooms a block from the beach; choice of a/c or not; 5% cash discount; salsa club next door. **Cons:** poor pool placement; unattractive furnishings; no Internet; very small parking lot not open during high season. ✉ *Francisco I. Madero 176, Col. E. Zapata* 🕾 *322/222–1500 or 322/222–5518* ⊕ *www.hotelgaviota.com* 🛏 *84 rooms* 🛆 *In-room: a/c (some), no phone, kitchen (some), refrigerator (some). In-hotel: restaurant, bar, pool, parking (free)* ⊟ *MC, V* ⊺⊙⊦*EP* ✛ *1:C2.*

¢   🛏 **Hotel Posada de Roger.** If you hang around the pool or the small shared balcony overlooking the street and the bay beyond, it's not hard to get to know the other guests—many of them savvy budget travelers from Europe and Canada. Rooms are spare and vaultlike—some are downright dark. Fredy's Tucan, indoor-outdoor bar-restaurant (no dinner; $) is popular with locals—mainly for breakfast. The hotel is in a part of the Zona Romántica known for its restaurants and shops; Playa los Muertos is a few blocks away. **Pros:** great location; tinkling fountain and quiet courtyard; good bar-restaurant; free Wi-Fi. **Cons:** no in-room safes; cramped rooms; get-what-you-pay-for beds. ✉ *Calle Basilio Badillo 237, Col. E. Zapata* 🕾 *322/222–0836 or 322/222–0639* ⊕ *www.hotelposadaderoger. com* 🛏 *47 rooms* 🛆 *In-room: a/c, Wi-Fi (some). In-hotel: restaurant, bar, pool, Wi-Fi, parking (free)* ⊟ *AE, MC, V* ⊺⊙⊦*EP* ✛ *1:C2.*

Fodor'sChoice
★

$ 🛏 **Hotel Tropicana Puerto Vallarta.** This is a reasonably priced, well-landscaped, bright white hotel at the south end of Playa Los Muertos. Superior rooms don't cost much more than standards, and although they have more or less the same amenities, they're in a newer wing and most have better views. Suites have no separate living area but are larger than other rooms and have several different areas for sitting or playing cards, as well as a four-burner stove, blender, and fridge. The most economical rooms come without a/c, TV, or a beach view. **Pros:** great beach access; great Zona Romántica location; nice pool and landscaping. **Cons:** no bathtubs; no Internet access; wristbands required for all guests; furnishings and paint need upgrading. ⊠ *Calle Amapas 214, Col. E. Zapata* ☎ *322/226–9696* ⊕ *www.hoteltropicana.com* ⤴ *148 rooms, 12 suites* ☖ *In-room: a/c (some), no TV (some). In-hotel: restaurant, bar, pool, beachfront, parking (free)* ═ *MC, V* ⭐| *EP* ✛ *1:D2.*

¢ 🖼 **Hotel Yasmín.** Two-story and L-shaped, this budget baby has no pool, but it's just a block from the beach and joined at the hip to Café de Olla, a popular Mexican restaurant. It's also near Parque Lázaro Cárdenas, with underground parking, and dozens of bars, restaurants, and boutiques. Small, ho-hum rooms have low ceilings, firm beds, and open closets but also floor fans and cable TV: not a bad deal for the price. About four bucks more buys you a/c, so go ahead and splurge. The front-desk staff can sometimes be brusque, but that doesn't really diminish the experience. **Pros:** very inexpensive; close to Zona Romántica action; pleasant courtyard garden with café, tables, and chaise longues. **Cons:** dark rooms; low ceilings; no pool. ⊠ *Calle Basilio Badillo, Col. E. Zapata* ☎ *322/222–0087* ⤴ *27 rooms* ☖ *In-room: a/c (some), no phone* ═ *No credit cards* ⭐| *EP* ✛ *1:C2.*

$ 🖼 **Playa Los Arcos Beach Resort & Spa.** This hotel is recommended for its
Fodor's Choice location: right on the beach and in the midst of Zona Romántica's restau-
★ rants, bars, and shops. Though the price is right, some longtime visitors
🕑 report that quality has slipped in recent years. Still, yellow trumpet vines and lacy palms draped in tiny white lights enliven the pool and the bar-restaurant, which has music nightly and a Mexican fiesta on Saturday evening. Some rooms are larger than others and have a balcony with plastic lounge chairs; balcony rooms are the same price as those without, so ask for a balcony when booking. **Pros:** great Zona Romántica location; nightly entertainment with theme-cuisine buffet. **Cons:** small bathrooms; some rooms have tired furnishings; tour-group noise in high season. ⊠ *Av. Olas Altas 380, Col. E. Zapata* ☎ *322/222–0583; 800/648–2403 in U.S.; 888/729–9590 in Canada; 01800/327–7700 toll-free in Mexico* ⊕ *www. playalosarcos.com* ⤴ *158 rooms, 13 suites* ☖ *In-room: a/c, safe (some), kitchen (some), refrigerator (some). In-hotel: restaurant, bar, pool, spa, beachfront, parking (free)* ═ *AE, MC, V* ⭐| *AI, EP* ✛ *1:C2.*

CENTRO AND ENVIRONS

At the north end of downtown, moderately priced and four- to five-star hotels stretch north from the boardwalk along a manicured (and seasonally rocky) beach. A sunset stroll on the malecón is easily accessible from these hotels, as are bustling downtown's activities, galleries, shops, and restaurants. North of the Cuale River, el Centro has fewer hotels than the Zona Romántica, which is just across the bridge and easy walking distance. The exception is the city center's only luxury hotel, Hacienda San Angel, which is situated just far enough away from Zona Romántica for the walk to be noteable (but still not prohibitive).

HOTELS AT A GLANCE:
PUERTO VALLARTA AND RIVIERA NAYARIT

Hotel	Worth Noting	Cost (*Includes Tax)	Rooms	Restaurants	On the Beach	Pools	Spa	Golf Course	Tennis Courts	Health Club/ Gym	Children's Programs	Location
PUERTO VALLARTA: ZONA ROMANTICA												
Casa Andrea	homey apartments	$720/week	11									Col. E. Zapata
Hacienda Alemana Frankfurt	modern and comfortable	$136	10	1						yes		Col. E. Zapata
Hotel Ana Liz	bare-bones; great location	$27*	23									Col. E. Zapata
Hotel Blue Chairs	gay scene central	$100–$130	40	2	yes	1						Col. E. Zapata
Hotel Eloísa	request a free view	$55–$70	74			2						Col. E. Zapata
Hotel Gaviota Vallarta	a block from the beach	$60–$85	84	1		1						Col. E. Zapata
Hotel Posada de Roger	best budget digs; varied crowd	$55	47	1		1						Col. E. Zapata
Hotel Tropicana Puerto Vallarta	modest beachfront digs	$77*	160	1	yes	1						Col. E. Zapata
Hotel Yasmín	budget rooms w/ cable	$47–51*	27									Col. E. Zapata
Playa Los Arcos Beach Resort & Spa	fab city-beach location	$110	171	1	yes	1	yes					Col. E. Zapata
PUERTO VALLARTA: CENTRO AND ENVIRONS												
Buenaventura Grand Hotel & Spa	fun for couples and families	$153	234	3	yes	2	yes					Col. 5 de Diciembre
Casa Dulce Vida	spacious apartments	$70–$130	6			1						Centro
Fiesta Americana Hotel & Resort	amazing palapa	$180–$200	291	3	yes	1				yes	4–12	Zona Hotelera Norte
Hacienda San Angel	only $$$$ downtown; elegant	$485–$745	21	1		3						Col. El Cerro
Hotel Rosita	north end of malecón	$92–$134	115	1	yes	1						Col. 5 de Diciembre
House of Wind and Water	Artists' haven outside tourist zone	$75*	5									Col. Paso del Guayabo
Los Cuatro Vientos	Old Puerto Vallarta spirit;	$69*	14	1		1						Centro
Sheraton Buganvilias Resort	large but reliable	$199–$219	600	4	yes	2	yes		2	yes	4–12	Zona Hotelera Norte
PUERTO VALLARTA: MARINA VALLARTA												
CasaMagna Marriott Puerto Vallarta	something for everyone	$219	433	4	yes	2	yes			yes	4–12	Marina Vallarta
Meliá Puerto Vallarta All Inclusive	great for younger kids	$295*	221	6	yes	1			2	yes	0–11	Marina Vallarta
Velas Vallarta Suite Resort	all suites; lots of comforts	$390	339	2	yes	2	yes		3	yes	4–12	Marina Vallarta
Westin Resort & Spa, Puerto Vallarta	great architecture	$249	280	2	yes	3	yes		3	yes	4–12	Marina Vallarta

RIVIERA NAYARIT: AROUND BANDERAS BAY

		Price	Rooms								Ages	Location
Casa de Mita	excellent eats included	$485	8	1	yes	1	yes		1	yes		Punta Mita
Decameron All-Inclusive Hotel & Resort	bargain, all-inclusive	$136*	620	7	yes	7	yes		3	yes		Bucerías
Fairmont Rancho Banderas												
Four Seasons Resort, Punta Mita	excellent spa, golf	$595	168	3	yes	4	yes	yes	4	yes	5–12	Punta Mita
Grand Velas All Suites & Spa Resort	sleek majesty	$620	267	4	yes	4	yes	yes	1	yes	4–12	Nuevo Vallarta
Hotel Carmelitas	new rooms near the beach	$45*	12									Bucerías
Hotel des Artistes	Charming apartments at the beach	$390	12	2	yes	2	yes		2	yes		Punta Mita
Hotel Palmeras	large pool; block from beach	$80*	21	1	yes	1			1			Bucerías
Hotel St. Regis Punta Mita	Classy nouveau Mexican	$632	119	3	yes	3	yes	yes	3	yes		Punta Mita
La Tranquila												
Marco's Place Suites & Villas	basic but comfortable	$50*	18	1	yes	1			1			Bucerías
Marival Resort and Suites	lots to do; all-inclusive	$226	495	6	yes	4	yes		4	yes	4–11	Nuevo Vallarta
Paradise Village Beach Resort & Spa	great value for families	$145	702	4	yes	2	yes	yes	2	yes	4–11	Nuevo Vallarta
Taheima Wellness Resort & Spa								yes				
Villa Bella	tranquil, intimate	$180	6	1	yes	1	yes		1			La Cruz de Huanacaxtle

RIVIERA NAYARIT: NORTH OF BANDERAS BAY

		Price	Rooms								Ages	Location
Casa Obelisco	great breakfasts	$200*	4	1		1			1			San Francisco
Costa Azul	lots of sports and activities	$169*	26	1	yes	1			1			San Francisco
Haramara Retreat	Yoga-inspired natural haven	$170	15	1	yes				1			Sayulita
Villa Amor	terrific views	$110	33	1	yes				1			Sayulita
Villas Buena Vida	good swimming beach	$74	45	1	yes	2			2			Rincón de Guayabitos

RIVIERA NAYARIT: SOUTH ALONG BANDERAS BAY

		Price	Rooms								Ages	Location
Barceló La Jolla de Mismaloya	all suites; lots to do	$369*	317	5	yes	4	yes		1	yes	5–12	Mismaloya
Casa Cúpula	gay friendly, oasis of chic	$165–$295	14	1		1	yes			yes		Col. Amapas
Casa Iguana All-Suites Hotel	all suites; full kitchens	$110	52	1		1	yes			yes		Mismaloya
Dreams Puerto Vallarta Resort & Spa	elaborate theme nights	$372*	337	6	yes	3	yes	yes	2	yes	3–12	Zona Hotelera Sur
Hotel Playa Conchas Chinas	great beach	$110*	23	1	yes	1				yes		Conchas Chinas

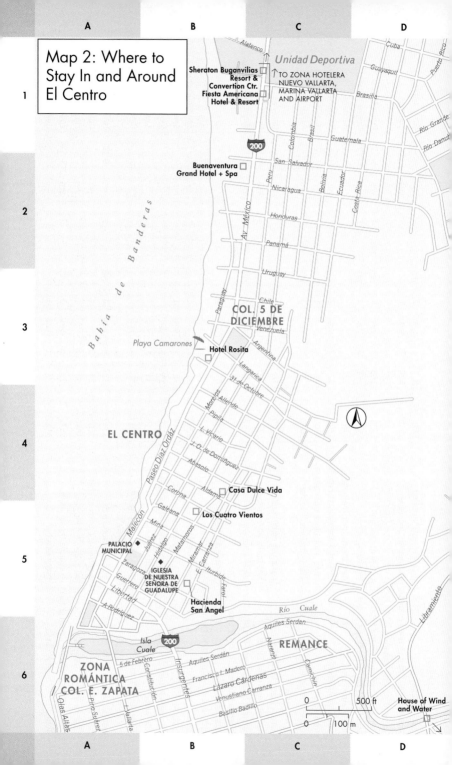

Map 2: Where to Stay In and Around El Centro

A   B   C   D

1

Sheraton Buganvilias □
Resort &
Convertion Ctr.
Fiesta Americana
Hotel & Resort

Unidad Deportiva

↑ TO ZONA HOTELERA
NUEVO VALLARTA,
MARINA VALLARTA
AND AIRPORT

Cuba
Guayaquil
Puerta Rica
Brasilia
Río Grande
Río Danut

200

Buenaventura □
Grand Hotel + Spa

San Salvador
Nicaragua

Colombia
Brasil
Guatemala
Perú
Bolivia
Ecuador
Costa Rica

Av. México

2

Bahía de Banderas

Honduras
Panamá
Uruguay

COL. 5 DE
DICIEMBRE

Chile
Venezuela

Paraguay

3

Playa Camarones   Hotel Rosita
□

Langarica
31 de Octubre
Argentina

EL CENTRO

31 de Octubre
M. Allende
Morelos
Pipila
L. Vicario
J. O. de Domínguez
Abasolo

4

Paseo Díaz Ordáz

Corona
Altamira   Casa Dulce Vida
Galeana
□ Los Cuatro Vientos

5

PALACIO ◆
MUNICIPAL

Malecón
Mina
Juárez
Hidalgo
Zaragoza
IGLESIA
DE NUESTRA
SEÑORA DE
GUADALUPE
Guerrero
Libertad
A. Rodríguez

Matamoros
Miramar
E. Carranza
Libramiento

□
Hacienda
San Ángel

Río   Cuale

Aquiles Serdán

6

Isla
Cuale

200

ZONA
ROMÁNTICA
/ COL. E. ZAPATA

5 de Febrero
Constitución
Insurgentes
Aquiles Serdán
Francisco I. Madero
Lázaro Cárdenas
Venustiano Carranza
Basilio Badillo
Naranjo
Cardenche

REMANCE

0   500 ft
0   100 m

House of Wind
and Water

Olas Altas
Pino Suárez
Vallarta

A   B   C   D

$$ ⛱ **Buenaventura Grand Hotel & Spa**. The location on downtown's north-
☾ ern edge is just a few blocks from the malecón, shops, hotels, and
restaurants. The beach has gentle waves, but with brown sand and
rocks. Views up and down the bay are great; it attracts more fisher-
men and people walking or jogging than bathers. There's a lively pool
scene; the adults-only area, a shallow pool with submerged chaise
longues facing the sea, is a big part of the draw. Rooms are cheerful,
with wood furniture, bright white linens, and tastefully subdued accent
colors. Ocean-facing balconies are tiny, and if you sit, you can't see a
thing. Still, the sum of the whole makes up for any deficiencies, and
the all-inclusive rate is a good deal, especially for families. **Pros:** great
place to socialize; good breakfast buffet; concierge service; five-minute
walk to the malecón and downtown. **Cons:** balconies are small, no
parking; fee to use next-door gym. ⊠ *Av. México 1301, Col. 5 de Dici-
embre* ☎ *322/226–7000; 888/859–9439 in U.S. and Canada* ⊕ *www.
hotelbuenaventura.com.mx* ⇱ *216 rooms, 18 suites* ⚒ *In-room: a/c,
Wi-Fi. In-hotel: 3 restaurants, room service, bars, pools, spa, beach-
front, water sports, laundry service, Internet, Wi-Fi hotspot* ☰ *AE,
MC, V* ⏣ *AI, EP* ✛ *2:B2.*

$ ⛱ **Casa Dulce Vida**. Hidden four blocks off the busy malecón, this '60s-
era villa has apartments of various sizes filled with modern Mexican
art and comfortable, if well-worn, furniture. All apartments have
well-equipped kitchens, and in the last few years the management has
brought in new mattresses and bedding and some other important room
amenities. A few rooms have ocean-view terraces; the largest has three
bedrooms, two baths, and a separate dining room. There's a red-tile
pool and tropical gardens. In high season the property accepts only
weeklong bookings. **Pros:** home-away-from-home feel; great value; lush
landscaping and ocean breezes; friendly staff helps book tours; solid
Wi-Fi in all rooms. **Cons:** booked for weeks and months at a time in
high season; some rooms better than others. ⊠ *Calle Aldama 295, El
Centro* ☎ *322/222–1008* ⊕ *www.dulcevida.com* ⇱ *6 suites* ⚒ *In-room:
a/c (some), no phone, kitchen, refrigerator, no TV, Wi-Fi. In-hotel: pool,
Wi-Fi hotspot* ☰ *No credit cards* ⏣ *EP* ✛ *2:B4.*

$$$ ⛱ **Fiesta Americana Hotel & Resort**. The dramatically designed terra-cotta
building rises above a deep-blue pool that flows beside palm oases; a
seven-story palapa (which provides natural air-conditioning) covers the
elegant lobby—paved in patterned tile and stone—and a large round
bar. The ocean-view rooms have a modern pink and terra-cotta color
scheme, beige marble floors, balconies, and tile baths with powerful
showers. The beach is small but bustles with activity and equipment
rentals, and the breakwater forms a sheltered nook that's nice for swimming. It's in the Northern Hotel Zone, about halfway between the
Marina Vallarta complex and downtown Puerto Vallarta. **Pros:** across
from Plaza Caracol, with its shops, grocery store, and Cineplex; lots
of on-site shops, 24-hour room service. **Cons:** no ocean view from
second and third floors; hotel is a cab or bus ride from most restaurants. ⊠ *Blvd. Francisco M. Ascencio, Km 2.5, Zona Hotelera Norte*
☎ *322/226–2100; 800/343–7821 in U.S.* ⊕ *www.fiestaamericana.com*
⇱ *288 rooms, 3 suites* ⚒ *In-room: a/c, safe, Internet, Wi-Fi. In-hotel:*

3 restaurants, room service, bars, pool, gym, beachfront, children's programs (ages 4–12), laundry service, Wi-Fi hotspot, parking (free) ⊟AE, DC, MC, V ¶◎| EP ⊹ 2:C1.

$$$$ 🖫 **Hacienda San Angel.** Each room is unique and elegant at this pricey boutique hotel in the hills five blocks above the malecón. Public spaces also exude wealth and privilege: 16th- through 19th-century antiques are placed throughout, water pours from fonts into Talavera-tile-lined basins, mammoth tables grace open dining areas. The Celestial Room has a wondrous view of Bahía de Banderas and the cathedral's tower from its open-air, thatch-roof living room. You can call Canada or the United States for free and enjoy live music with complimentary cocktails in the early evening. There are fabulous views of the bay from the new second-floor restaurant, Hacienda San Angel Gourmet, which serves international food beginning at 6 PM. Non-guests are welcome by previous reservation. **Pros:** the most elegant lodging in downtown Puerto Vallarta; concierge service; excellent bay views; reasonably priced airport transfers. **Cons:** short but steep walk from the malecón; 5% service fee (in addition to taxes) plus 10% fee for using a credit card; three-night minimum; fewer amenities than hotels of comparable price point. ⊠ *Calle Miramar 336, at Iturbide, Centro* ☎ *322/222–2692; 877/815–6594* ⊕ *www.haciendasanangel.com* ☞ *21 rooms* △ *In-room: a/c, safe, DVD. In-hotel: restaurant, pools, laundry service, Internet, Wi-Fi hotspot, no kids under 16* ⊟ *AE, MC, V* ¶◎| *CP* ⊹ *2:B5.*

$ 🖫 **Hotel Rosita.** What started as a sleepy 12-room hostelry—one of Puerto Vallarta's very first—is now a busy 115-room downtown hotel. It's still a viable budget option, mainly recommended for its location on the north end of the malecón. Rooms are very basic; expect white-tile floors and fabrics with floral prints. The cheapest quarters have no air-conditioning. Request a room facing the water, as much for the view as for the natural light; rooms facing the street are dark, making them feel cramped. **Pros:** old-fashioned value near downtown; Sunday brunch buffet under $10. **Cons:** no bathtub; older floors and furnishings; so-so beach; Wi-Fi in lobby only. ⊠ *Paseo Díaz Ordáz 901, Col. 5 de Diciembre* ☎ *322/223–2000* ⊕ *www.hotelrosita.com* ☞ *115 rooms* △ *In-room: a/c (some). In-hotel: restaurant, bar, pool, laundry service, Wi-Fi hotspot* ⊟ *AE, MC, V* ¶◎| *EP* ⊹ *2:B3.*

$ 🖫 **House of Wind and Water.** Some elements are traditional, like the brick archways, tile floors, and fine woodwork. But most of the design elements at this cozy B&B are the creations or acquisitions of the artist-owners: large format paintings, whimsical bathrooms with hand-painted sinks and exposed copper tubing, and estate-sale furnishings. Guest-room balconies, the dining room, and plunge pool on the garden terrace overlook an amazing hillside of wild tropical plants and the Cuale River. Although not in downtown Vallarta, this property is a breath of fresh air for those who don't mind being a cab, bus, or car ride away from the action. Fully filtered fresh spring water from the mountain flows from all the faucets and showerheads, and the owners compost, use water-saving appliances and other ecologically minded practices. The hotel is the venue for courses that combine Vallarta experiences (like whale-watching, snorkeling, or trips to the mountains or botanical gardens) with artistic creations in cloth, ceramic tiles, or other media. **Pros:** in a real Mexican neighborhood by the Cuale River; gorgeous views of jungle-clad hillside; ecoconscious owners. **Cons:** at end of long, rather steep dirt driveway; no a/c; no shopping or nightlife in immediate area. ⊠ *Calle Azucena 1109, Paseo del Guayabo* ☎ *322/140–4866 cell* ⊕ *www.houseofwindandwater.com* ⟿ *5 rooms* ⚹ *In-room: no a/c, no phone, refrigerator (some), Wi-Fi. In-hotel: restaurant (breakfast only or dinner with previous reservation), laundry service, Wi-Fi hotspot, no kids under 6* ⊟ *Credit cards through PayPal only* ¶⊙¶ *CP* ✛ *2:D6.*

$ ⊡ **Los Cuatro Vientos.** This Old Vallarta original opened in 1955, and some folks have been coming here forever. That explains why most of the guests and staff seem like old friends. The Chez Elena restaurant, the unadorned rooftop bar, and the best rooms have nice views of the bay and of the city's red rooftops. Come to rub shoulders with Europeans and others who appreciate a bargain and a bit of history. Rooms are plain and without amenities, yet the traditional brick ceilings give a homey feel and the El Centro location a few blocks behind the hustle of downtown streets around the malecón provides a feel of Vallarta in less frenetic times. **Pros:** downtown location overlooking the bay; deep, grottolike pool; free Wi-Fi. **Cons:** short but steep walk or drive from downtown; no lounge area around pool; no a/c; some rooms up multiple flights of stairs. ⊠ *Calle Matamoros 520, El Centro* ☎ *322/222–0161* ⊕ *www.cuatrovientos.com* ⟿ *14 rooms* ⚹ *In-room: no a/c, no phone, no TV, Wi-Fi (some). In-hotel: restaurant, room service, bar, pool* ⊟ *MC, V* ¶⊙¶ *CP* ✛ *2:B5.*

$$$ ⊡ **Sheraton Buganvilias Resort & Convention Center.** Juan Carlos Name (pronounced NAH-may), a disciple of modern-minimalist Mexican architect Luis Barragán, designed this looming high-rise near the Hotel Zone's south end and within walking distance of downtown. It's reliable, anonymous, and geared toward conventioneers and other groups. Rooms have a perky, bright, white-and-cherry-red color scheme and very snug and comfortable beds with pillow-top mattresses and downy duvets. This is the closest of the major Zona Hotelera Norte hotels to downtown Puerto Vallarta. **Pros:** excellent Sunday champagne brunch; concierge service; AAA and AARP discounts. **Cons:** slow elevators; so-so beach; faces busy and rather unattractive boulevard. ⊠ *Blvd. Francisco M. Ascencio 999, Zona Hotelera Norte* ☎ *322/226–0404; 800/325–3535* ⊕ *www.sheratonvallarta.com* ⟿ *480 rooms, 120 suites* ⚹ *In-room: a/c, safe, kitchen (some), Internet, Wi-Fi (some). In-hotel: 4 restaurants, room service, bars, tennis courts, pools, gym, spa, beachfront, water sports, children's programs (ages 4–12), laundry service, Internet, parking (free)* ⊟ *AE, MC, V* ¶⊙¶ *EP, CP* ✛ *2:C1.*

MARINA VALLARTA

Although its newness relative to the rest of Puerto Vallarta makes it feel a little homogenous, this small enclave of luxury hotels gives off a quiet, subdued vibe that more than makes up for it. This is the closest of the PV subdivisions to the airport. The Marriott, Westin, and other brand names face a narrow beach that pales in comparison to the properties' sparkling swimming pools and high-end spas. Offering all-inclusive as

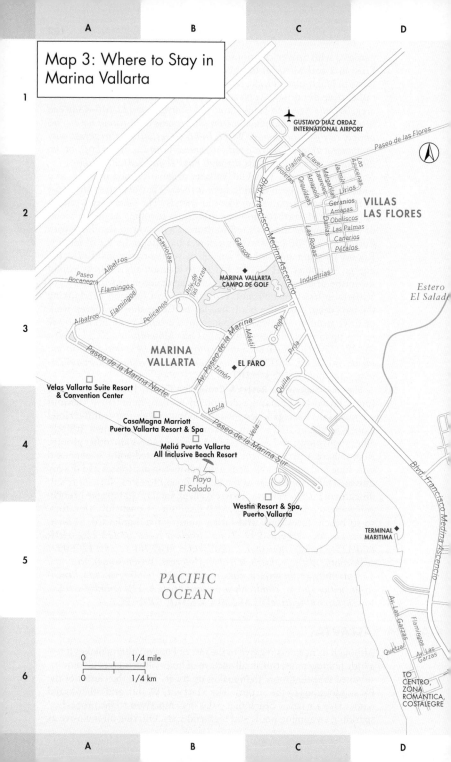

Map 3: Where to Stay in Marina Vallarta

GUSTAVO DÍAZ ORDAZ
INTERNATIONAL AIRPORT

Paseo de las Flores

**VILLAS
LAS FLORES**

Gladiola
Clavel
Violetas
Jazmín
Las
Azucenas
Margaritas
Amapola
Laureles
Orquídeas
Lirios
Geranios
Amapas
Obeliscos
Dalias
Las Palmas
Las Rosas
Canarios
Pétalos

Gansos

Paseo
Bocanegra

Albatros

Gaviotas

Flamingos

Flamingos

Prv. de
las Garzas

MARINA VALLARTA
CAMPO DE GOLF

Industrias

*Estero
El Salado*

Albatros

Pelícanos

Av. Paseo de la Marina

Mástil

Popa

Proa

**MARINA
VALLARTA**

Paseo de la Marina Norte

Tirmón

◆ EL FARO

Quilla

□ Velas Vallarta Suite Resort
& Convention Center

Ancla

Paseo de la Marina Sur

Vela

Blvd. Francisco Medina Ascencio

□ CasaMagna Marriott
Puerto Vallarta Resort & Spa

□ Meliá Puerto Vallarta
All Inclusive Beach Resort

*Playa
El Salado*

Westin Resort & Spa,
Puerto Vallarta

TERMINAL ◆
MARÍTIMA

*PACIFIC
OCEAN*

Av. Las Garzas

Flamingos

Av. Las Garzas

Quetzal

TO
CENTRO,
ZONA
ROMÁNTICA,
COSTALEGRE

| 0 | 1/4 mile |
| 0 | 1/4 km |

Blvd. Francisco Medina Ascencio

TENNIS, ANYONE?

Public tennis courts are few and far between in Vallarta, although most hotels have courts for guests. Here are two options for public courts:

Of the public tennis complexes, **Club de Tenis Canto del Sol** (⊠ *Hotel Canto del Sol, Local 18, Planta Baja, Blvd. Francisco M. Ascencio Zona Hotelera* ☎ *322/226–0123*) is the largest, with four clay and four asphalt courts; all but two are lighted. Private lessons are $35 per hour, including racquet; court rental is $13 per hour, $20 per hour for night play. Club hours are 7 AM to 10

PM (7–4 on Sunday); fees give you access to showers, but there are no lockers. The **Holiday Inn** (⊠ *Blvd. Francisco M. Ascencio, Km 3.5, Zona Hotelera Norte* ☎ *322/226–1700 Ext. 1792*) has two asphalt courts rented out at $8 per hour; it's twice that for four players; another $2 to rent the racquets, and an additional $4 per hour (per court, not per person) at night. Hours are 8 AM–8 PM daily, and you can usually make arrangements to come at 7 AM or to stay later to finish a game or set. A pro gives private lessons ($22 per hour). Reservations are essential.

well as EP accommodations, these high-rise hotels are near a beautiful if low-key private marina (faced with shops, bars, and eateries) and the Marina Vallarta Golf Course.

$$$ ☐ **CasaMagna Marriott Puerto Vallarta Resort & Spa.** The CasaMagna is ☺ hushed and stately in some places, lively and casual in others. Here's a classy property that nonetheless welcomes children. All of the restaurants—including a sleek Asian restaurant serving Thai, sushi, and teppanyaki and a large, pleasant sports bar—have kids' menus. The meandering grounds boast a large infinity pool as well as gardens of indigenous plants. Rooms have an upbeat, classy decor; each has a balcony, and most have an ocean view. Access to the excellent spa facilities is included with the purchase of any spa service. **Pros:** lovely spa; great concierge service; good Japanese restaurant. **Cons:** unimpressive beach; no business center or Internet terminals for guests. ⊠ *Paseo de la Marina 455, Marina Vallarta* ☎ *322/226–0000; 888/236–2427 in U.S. and Canada* ⊕ *www.casamagnapuertovallarta.com* ⮣ *404 rooms, 29 suites* ⚭ *In-room: a/c, safe, Wi-Fi. In-hotel: 4 restaurants, room service, bars, pools, gym, spa, beachfront, children's programs (ages 4–12), laundry service, Wi-Fi hotspot, parking (free)* ⊟ *AE, DC, MC, V* ⥁|⊙|*EP* ✛ *3:B4.*

$$$$ ☐ **Meliá Puerto Vallarta All Inclusive Beach Resort.** The sprawling, all-inclu- ☺ sive Meliá, on the beach and close to the golf course, is popular with families. The breezy lobby houses an eclectic collection of Mexican art and memorabilia. The plazas beyond have still more artwork as well as garden areas, fountains, ponds, and bits of whimsy such as a supersize chessboard with plastic pieces as big as a toddler. There's a huge pool, an outdoor theater with nightly shows, and elaborate children's programs and amenities—including a climbing wall and a batting cage. Rooms are quiet havens in subdued blues, creams, and sands. Considering it's an all-inclusive, prices are very reasonable. **Pros:** lots of activities for small children; giant pool; concierge service; free Wi-Fi; two children under 5

free. **Cons:** small beach diminishes further at high tide; lots of children. ⊠ *Paseo de la Marina Sur 7, Marina Vallarta* ☎ *322/226–3000; 888/956–3542 in U.S.* ⊕ *www.solmelia.com* ⋑ *217 rooms, 4 suites* ⌂ *In-room: a/c, safe, refrigerator, Wi-Fi (some). In-hotel: 6 restaurants, bars, tennis courts, pool, gym, beachfront, children's programs (ages 4 months–11 years), laundry service, Internet, Wi-Fi hotspot, parking (free)* ⊟ *AE, MC, V* ⊗ *AI* ⊕ *3:B4.*

$$$$ ⌂ **Velas Vallarta Suite Resort & Convention Center.** Silky sheets and cozy down duvets, multiple ceiling fans, and large flat-screen TVs are a few of the creature comforts that set Velas apart from the rest. Each large living area has two comfortably wide built-in couches in colorful prints and a round dining table. Huichol cross-stitch tapestries and modern Mexican art decorate the walls. Studios and one-, two-, and three-bedroom suites have the same amenities except that the studios don't have balconies or beach views. Tall palms, pink bougainvillea, and wild ginger with brilliant red plumes surround the three enormous pools. This is a perfect destination for those who want to relax on-site, as the hotel offers tennis clinics, arts and crafts, theme nights, and lots of other activities. **Pros:** large suites; yoga; Spanish classes and other activities; pillow menu; special deals allowing kids to stay free are sometimes available. **Cons:** small spa; zealous time-share salespeople; high price point. ⊠ *Av. Costera s/n LH2, Marina Vallarta* ☎ *322/226–9500 or 866/847–4609* ⊕ *www.velasvallarta.com* ⋑ *339 suites* ⌂ *In-room: a/c, safe, kitchen, refrigerator, Wi-Fi. In-hotel: 2 restaurants, room service, bars, tennis courts, pools, gym, spa, beachfront, children's programs (ages 4–12), laundry service, Internet, Wi-Fi hotspot, parking (free)* ⊟ *AE, MC, V* ⊗ *AI* ⊕ *3:A3.*

$$$$ ⌂ **Westin Resort & Spa, Puerto Vallarta.** Hot pink! Electric yellow! Color aside, the Westin's buildings evoke ancient temples and are about as mammoth in size. There's not a bad sightline anywhere, whether you're gazing out to the leafy courtyard or down an orange-tile, brightly painted corridor lined with Mexican art. The jarring echoes here are tempered by the rush of an enormous water feature. In the spacious, balconied rooms concrete-and-stone floors massage bare feet, and top-of-the-line mattresses with soft duvets make for heavenly siestas. Guest quarters above the sixth floor have ocean views; those below face the 600 palm trees surrounding four beautiful pools. **Pros:** fabulous beds and pillows; impressive architecture and landscaping; attentive but not overzealous staff; concierge service. **Cons:** small beach; no ocean views from lower floors. ⊠ *Paseo de la Marina Sur 205, Marina Vallarta* ☎ *322/226–1100; 800/228–3000 in U.S. and Canada* ⊕ *www.starwoodhotels.com* ⋑ *266 rooms, 14 suites* ⌂ *In-room: a/c, safe, Wi-Fi. In-hotel: 2 restaurants, room service, bars, tennis courts, pools, gym, spa, beachfront, children's programs (ages 4–12), laundry service, Internet, Wi-Fi hotspot, parking (free), some pets allowed* ⊟ *AE, DC, MC, V* ⊗ *BP* ⊕ *3:C4.*

STAYING WITH KIDS

Puerto Vallarta is an excellent destination for children. Miles of beaches keep kids busy in the sand and the sea, and activities like horseback riding, canopy tours, boating expeditions, and wildlife spotting keep tots and teens entertained. Area hotels, also, cater to kids. Most five-star beach resorts have children's pools and supervised programs that give adults the leisure time they crave.

Among those hotels with the most expansive children's programs is the all-inclusive Sol Meliá. Trained personnel run day-care programs for children as young as four months at no additional cost. Flinstone-theme play equipment and multiple activities entertain children ages 5 to 11 in the Bam Bam Club. At the nationally owned **Crown Paradise Club Vallarta** (⊕ *www.crownparadise. com*), family rooms here have kid-size bunk beds and trundle beds in their own area with a TV. At this all-inclusive, there's room service from a special kids' menu; soaps and amenities are Disney themed. Babies and toddlers are offered care and activities at Baby Paradise; bigger kids play on their own playground and engage in sand-castle building, soccer, and dancing, among other activities, or splash in the pirate-theme water park. Teens are offered organized sports like water polo and beach volleyball.

The **Mayan Resorts' Kids Club** (⊕ *www.mayanresorts.com*), with locations in Puerto Vallarta and Nuevo Vallarta, has an especially engaging kids' program featuring cooking and dance lessons, water polo and bowling competitions, and environmental programs. Two nights a week, programs extend into the evenings with costumed pirate shenanigans and treasure hunts and beach campouts.

As for resorts, "upscale" sometimes translates as couples-oriented, but the Four Seasons Resort, Punta Mita is all about families. Kids (and parents) love floating on the lazy river. the children's activity center is the envy of parents who sneak in to play foosball, table air hockey, or their favorite computer games, or attempt to keep up with the steps of the Dance Machine. Younger children dig the tree house and playground; a youthful concierge for teens organizes football games, bonfires on the beach, and dances, among other activities. Kids' club employees meet families at check-in with gift bags, and in-room amenities include bottle-warmers, strollers, and high chairs. There are also T-shirts and fun toiletries for children. These services carry no extra fee; babysitters are available at an hourly rate.

SOUTH ALONG BANDERAS BAY

South of the Zona Romántica and above Los Muertos and Amapas beaches is a mix of gay hotels, pretty villas, and other vacation rentals (like individual homes and condo complexes). As the coast stretches south, more isolated beaches like Conchas Chinas and Mismaloya are home to small, individual hotels as well as five-star beauties like Dreams and the InterContinental. Although removed from the action (and traffic) of PV's other hotel areas, these accommodations offer relatively easy access to Zona Romantica and el Centro via taxis and public buses.

$$$$ Barceló La Jolla de Mismaloya. Guests consistently give this hotel high marks. Each of the classy suites here has an elegant feel, with a brown-and-taupe color scheme and an ample terrace with a table and four chairs. Separate sitting rooms have a second flat-screen TV, and there's even a pillow menu. The pools are surrounded by spacious patios, so there's plenty of room to find the perfect spot in the sun or the shade, whether you're on your honeymoon or with the kids. Given the elegance of the place, it's a shame to have to wear the usual wristbands required of All Inclusive guests. **Pros:** recently redecorated and remodeled; concierge service; lots of on-site dining and activity options. **Cons:** beach is small, least expensive rooms don't have ocean views; no bathtubs. ⊠ *Zona Hotelera Sur, Km 11.5, Box 158B, Mismaloya* ☎ *322/226–0660; 800/227–2356* ⊕ *www.barcelo.com* ↗ *317 suites* ♿ *In-room: a/c, safe, Wi-Fi. In-hotel: 5 restaurants, room service, bars, tennis court, pools, gym, spa, beachfront, diving, water sports, bicycles, children's programs (ages 5–12), laundry service, Internet, Wi-Fi hotspot, parking (free)* ▤ *MC, V* ⦿ *AI* ✛ *4:C6.*

WORD OF MOUTH

"We enjoyed our stay at Westin.... It does feel very airy almost anywhere, and the property with its four huge meandering pools and palm trees is very inviting and lovely. The views from our deluxe ocean-view room were fabulous. Things aren't on Caribbean time here; the service was very good. You'll find a much bigger expanse of beach at the Marriott, a few blocks down, but we didn't come to Puerto Vallarta just for the beach." —Stephie

$$ Casa Cúpula. This popular, up-to-date boutique hotel is located a 10-minute walk from the beach and the Zona Romántica, catering largely to a gay and lesbian clientele. Most guest rooms have terraces with wonderful views of the sea and the surrounding neighborhood. Suites have kitchenettes, washer-dryers, separate living and sleeping quarters, and a home-theater system. All the rooms are classy, restrained, and individually decorated. The airy, shared dining room–lounge is comfortable and welcoming; the rooftop terrace with infinity dipping pool is lovely. The property is open year-round, but repairs and maintenance take place August and September and can get noisy. **Pros:** airport transfers via Cadillac Escalade; concierge service; free Wi-Fi; oh-so-comfy beds and pillows. **Cons:** challenging location up a hill, though not a far walk to attractions. ⊠ *Callejón de la Igualdad 129, Col. Amapas* ☎ *322/223–2484; 866/352–2511* ⊕ *www.casacupula.com* ↗ *14 rooms, 6 suites* ♿ *In-room: a/c, safe, kitchen (some), refrigerator, DVD, Wi-Fi. In-hotel: restaurant, room service, bar, pool, gym, laundry service, some pets allowed, no kids under 18* ▤ *AE, MC, V* ⦿ *CP* ✛ *4:C5.*

$$ Casa Iguana All-Suites Hotel. Palms and plants edge the walkways that line the swimming pool and goldfish ponds; balconies look down on this idyllic garden scene. Suites have full kitchens, shower-only baths, and tropical-style furniture in a muted palette. The hotel is on a cobblestone street off the highway; if you don't want to hoof it into Puerto Vallarta, take one of the local buses that pass by every 10 or 15 minutes. The beach is a five-minute walk away, on the other side of the highway; and the village of Mismaloya, with wandering chickens and sometimes pigs,

Dreams Puerto Vallarta Resort & Spa

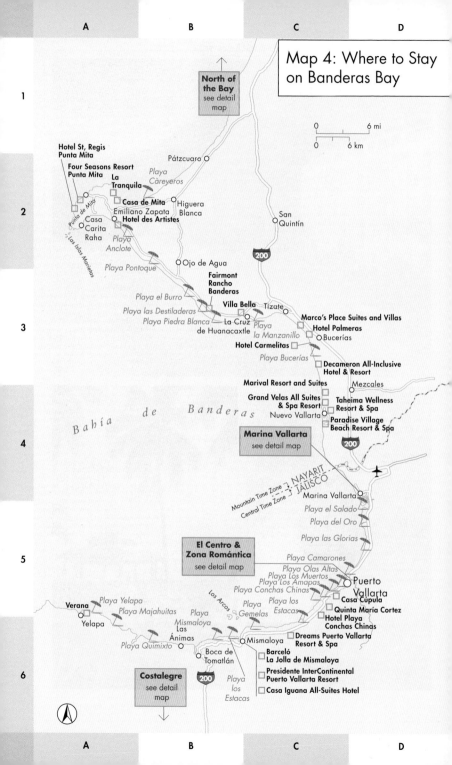

Map 4: Where to Stay on Banderas Bay

A   **B**   **C**   **D**

1

North of the Bay
see detail map

0   6 mi
0   6 km

2

Hotel St. Regis Punta Mita
Four Seasons Resort Punta Mita
La Tranquila
Pátzcuaro
Playa Càreyeros
Casa de Mita
Higuera Blanca
Emiliano Zapata
Hotel des Artistes
Casa Carita Raha
Punta de Mita
a Las Islas Marietas
Playa Anclote
San Quintín
I-200

Playa Pontoque

Ojo de Agua

Fairmont Rancho Banderas
Playa el Burro
Villa Bella
Playa las Destiladeras
Tizate
Playa Piedra Blanca
La Cruz de Huanacaxtle
Playa la Manzanillo
Marco's Place Suites and Villas
Hotel Palmeras
Bucerías
Hotel Carmelitas

3

Playa Bucerías
Decameron All-Inclusive Hotel & Resort

Marival Resort and Suites
Mezcales
Grand Velas All Suites & Spa Resort
Taheima Wellness Resort & Spa
Bahía   *de*   *Banderas*
Nuevo Vallarta
Paradise Village Beach Resort & Spa

Marina Vallarta
see detail map

4

I-200

Mountain Time Zone   NAYARIT
Central Time Zone   JALISCO
Marina Vallarta
Playa el Salado
Playa del Oro

El Centro & Zona Romántica
see detail map

Playa las Glorias

Playa Camarones

5

Playa Olas Altas
Playa Los Muertos
Playa Los Amapas
Puerto Vallarta
Verana
Playa Yelapa
Casa Cúpula
Playa Majahuitas
Playa Conchas Chinas
Quinta María Cortez
Yelapa
Playa Mismaloya
Las Ánimas
Playa los Estacas
Hotel Playa Conchas Chinas
Playa Gemelas
Los Arcos
Playa Quimixto
Dreams Puerto Vallarta Resort & Spa
Mismaloya

6

Boca de Tomatlán
Barceló La Jolla de Mismaloya
Presidente InterContinental Puerto Vallarta Resort
Playa los Estacas
Casa Iguana All-Suites Hotel
I-200

Costalegre
see detail map

A   **B**   **C**   **D**

is within squealing distance. The stylish Boca Bento Latin Bar & Grill is on-site; if you eat too much, you can always sign up for the hotel's six-week "Slenderize" program. **Pros:** experience village life not far from Puerto Vallarta's bars and restaurants; on-site grocery; FAP meals at Boca Bento gourmet restaurant. **Cons:** tiny gym; a cab or bus ride from nightlife, restaurants, and shops; not on beach. ⊠ *Av. 5 de Mayo 455, Mismaloya* ☎ *322/228–0186* ⊕ *www.casaiguanahotel.com* ⊃ *49 2-bedroom suites, 3 3-bedroom suites* ⚬ *In-room: a/c, kitchen, refrigerator, Wi-Fi. In-hotel: restaurant, room service, bar, pools, gym, spa, Internet, Wi-Fi hotspot, parking (free)* ⊟ *AE, MC, V* ¡⊙¡ *EP, FAP* ✚ *4:C6.*

$$$$ ⊞ **Dreams Puerto Vallarta Resort & Spa.** The dramatic view of the gorgeous, rock-edged beach is just one reason that this all-inclusive is special. Theme nights go a bit beyond the usual Mexican fiestas: You'll find salsa dancing classes, reggae nights, and movies on the beach. Instead of buffet restaurants there are six à la carte eateries, including seafood, Mexican, international, and an adults-only Italian dinner restaurant. All of the charming suites have excellent views, but only the newer ones have balconies, some with a hot tub. There are tons of activities for both kids and adults, and no wristbands (required at most All-Inclusives to identify guests) to clash with your resort-casual clothes. **Pros:** gorgeous private beach; 24-hour concierge service; easy drive or bus to downtown Puerto Vallarta; weekly campout for kids. **Cons:** no-reservation restaurant system means waiting to eat during busiest seasons; standard rooms don't have balconies. ⊠ *Carretera a Barra de Navidad (Carretera 200), Km 3.5, at Playa Las Estacas, Zona Hotelera Sur* ☎ *322/226–5000; 866/237–3267 in U.S. and Canada* ⊕ *www.dreamsresorts.com* ⊃ *337 suites* ⚬ *In-room: a/c, safe, refrigerator, DVD, Wi-Fi. In-hotel: 6 restaurants, room service, bars, tennis courts, pools, gym, spa, beachfront, water sports, bicycles, children's programs (ages 3–12), Internet, laundry service, parking (free)* ⊟ *AE, D, DC, MC, V* ¡⊙¡ *AI* ✚ *4:C6.*

Fodor's Choice
★

$ ⊞ **Hotel Playa Conchas Chinas.** Studios here have functional kitchenettes, basic cookware, and somewhat thin mattresses on wood-frame beds. Each has a small tiled tub as well as a shower. The real pluses of this plain-Jane hotel are the balconies with spectacular beach views and the location above rocky, picturesque Conchas Chinas Beach. Guests love the sound of the crashing waves at night, and most can ignore the tired furnishings because of the super location and the popular restaurant overlooking the beach below. It's about a 25-minute walk from downtown Puerto Vallarta along the sand. Lots of stairs make it a poor choice for people with mobility problems. **Pros:** excellent view of rock-framed Conchas Chinas Beach; good weekend breakfast buffet at nonaffiliated restaurant overlooking the beach; few bothersome vendors on the beach; friendly staff. **Cons:** some units smell funky; worn-out furnishings; long trip into Puerto Vallarta. ⊠ *Carretera a Barra de Navidad (Carretera 200), Km 2.5, Conchas Chinas* ☎ *322/221–5763 or 322/221–5230* ⊕ *www.conchaschinas.com* ⊃ *21 rooms, 2 suites* ⚬ *In-room: a/c, safe, kitchen, refrigerator. In-hotel: restaurant, bar, pool, beachfront, Wi-Fi hotspot, parking (free)* ⊟ *AE, MC, V* ¡⊙¡ *EP* ✚ *4:C5.*

$$ ⬚ **Presidente InterContinental Puerto Vallarta Resort.** This property has an enviable location above a beautiful aqua-toned cove. Rooms are classy, with a minimalist look, white-tiled floors, and citrus-hued fabrics. You'll be asked to choose from among four experiences (Joy of Life, Renewal, Romance, and Peace of Mind) that involve changing the scents, music, stones, flowers, and certain amenities in your room to set the desired tone. An additional, an optional resort fee of around $15 per room provides guests with DVD movies from the library, access to the tennis court and gym, in-room Wi-Fi, and the kids' club. **Pros:** lovely bay great for swimming; 24-hour concierge and business center; resort package same price as what most upscale hotels charge for Wi-Fi alone, but with more privileges. **Cons:** small gym and spa. ⊠ *Carretera a Barra de Navidad (Carratera 200), Km 8.6, Mismaloya* ☎ *322/228–0191, 888/424–6835* ⊕ *www.acquaesencia.com* ⇗ *97 rooms, 23 suites* ☖ *In-room: a/c, safe, DVD, Wi-Fi. In-hotel: 3 restaurants, room service, bars, tennis court, pool, gym, spa, beachfront, diving, laundry service, Internet, Wi-Fi hotspot, parking (free)* ⊟ *AE, MC, V* ⧪❘❙❘❙ *EP, AI* ✛ *4:C6.*

$$ ⬚ **Quinta Maria Cortez.** This B&B has soul. Its seven levels ramble up a
Fodor'sChoice steep hill at Playa Conchas Chinas, about a 20-minute walk along the
★ sand to the Zona Romántica (or a short hop in a bus or taxi). Rooms are furnished with antiques and local art; most have kitchenettes or full kitchens, along with balconies. Other draws are the efficient and welcoming staff, the fortifying breakfast (cooked to order) served on a palapa-covered patio, the nearly private beach below, and the views from the rooftop sundeck. It's popular and has few rooms, so make reservations early. Minimum stays are three nights in winter and on major holidays. **Pros:** intimate, personable digs; close to Puerto Vallarta; above lovely Conchas Chinas Beach. **Cons:** small property; frequently booked solid. ⊠ *Calle Sagitario 126, Playa Conchas Chinas* ☎ *322/221–5317; 888/640–8100 reservations* ⊕ *www.quinta-maria.com* ⇗ *7 rooms, 3 villas* ☖ *In-room: a/c (some), safe, kitchen (some), refrigerator, no TV. In-hotel: pool, beachfront, Internet, Wi-Fi hotspot, no kids under 18* ⊟ *AE, MC, V* ⧪❘❙❘❙ *BP* ✛ *4:C3.*

$$$$ ⬚ **Verana.** Understated luxury and an open-to-nature building design describe this eight-suite boutique property located in a jungle about an hour south of Vallarta. Built into the hillside overlooking lovely Yelapa Bay, Verana is sleek and contemporary yet surrounded by nature and built of locally available materials. Each of the freestanding suites has a different view and feel; several have outdoor showers and all are warm, inviting, and romantic. All have ceiling fan but just a few have air-conditioning. Three meals a day plus tax and transportation are included in the price. Horses can be rented for treks into the jungle, and there are casual and atmospheric local "dive" restaurants for those who want to rub shoulders with hoi polloi—both locals and Yelapa's dedicated foreign and ex-pat population. **Pros:** simple luxury; no electronic distractions; Watsu massage and yoga classes; Wi-Fi keeps guests in reasonable contact with the world. **Cons:** accessible to Puerto Vallarta only by boat; five- to seven-night minimum; depending on season; steep hike up from boat dock (ask for mule if needed). ⊠ *Playa de Yelapa,*

Domicilio Conocido (30-minute boat ride west from Boca de Tomat-lan), Playa de Yelapa ☎ 322/222–0878 ⊕ www.verana.com ⤴ 8 rooms ⚲ In-room: no a/c (some), no phone, no TV, Wi-Fi (some). In-hotel: restaurant, room service, bar, pool, spa, diving, water sports, laundry service, Wi-Fi hotspot, no kids under 16 ⊟ AE, MC, V ⊗ Closed June 8–Oct. ⦿ EP, FAP ✛ 4:A5.

RIVIERA NAYARIT

AROUND BANDERAS BAY

Perfect for travelers who like to stay put, the Riviera Nayarit is add-ing five-star accommodations on previously undeveloped beaches like Litibú and Playa Destiladeras. In Bucerías, traffic-free streets and a gor-geous sandy beach lure older snowbirds. The same crowd tends toward less-built-up La Cruz, with its upscale marina but few hotels. At the northern end of Banderas Bay, exclusive Punta Mita has über-expensive villas and hotels as well as a few modest digs for avid surfers. Closest to PV, Nuevo Vallarta offers all-inclusive high-rise hotels where—despite the fact that there's just one main road—it's easy to get disoriented in the winding side streets.

BUCERÍAS

$$ 🖵 **Decameron All-Inclusive Hotel & Resort**. This high-volume hotel is at the south end of long and lovely Bucerías Beach and has manicured grounds and a pool for each of its six buildings. Rooms are plain and not particularly modern, with laminate bathroom counters and cheap doors. But that's a small price to pay for the excellent beachfront loca-tion and astoundingly low all-inclusive price. Rooms in the older sec-tion have the best views, since they were built along the water; rooms on the other side of the road have the benefit of being adults-only and are almost brand new. Besides location, the only real distinction between one room and another is whether the room has a king or two double beds. The median age of the clientele here is around 50 years old. **Pros:** excellent deal for all-inclusive (room-only and air pack-ages, too); long beach great for walking or jogging; Spanish classes, yoga classes, and dance lessons plus many other activities. **Cons:** only a few Internet stations for hundreds of guests; only one of six build-ings has an elevator. ⊠ *Calle Lázaro Cárdenas 150, Bucerías, Nayarit* ☎ *329/298–0226; 01800/011–1111* ⊕ *www.decameron.com* ⤴ *620 rooms* ⚲ *In-room: a/c, safe, Internet. In-hotel: 7 restaurants, bars, tennis courts, pools, gym, bicycles, Internet, parking (free)* ⊟ *MC, V* ⦿ *AI* ✛ *4:C3.*

¢ 🖵 **Hotel Carmelitas**. In the heart of Bucerías, this small budget hotel is as unassuming as can be, only a few years old, and well maintained. Nicely decorated rooms with matching furniture of wrought iron and wood, and cheerful artwork face an L-shaped corridor. All rooms are the same, with one full bed and small, clean, brightly tiled bathrooms with shower only. A periwinkle-and-mauve color scheme brightens the corridor; rooms at the back face a wider corridor with plastic tables

Continued on page 120

SPAAAHH

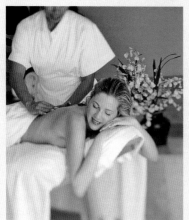

The trend of luxury spas in Mexico, and particularly in vacation hot spots like Puerto Vallarta, shows no signs of slowing. From elegant resort spas scented with essence of orange and bergamot to Aztec-inspired day spas, each has its own personality and signature treatments. Competition keeps creativity high, with an ever-changing menu of new treatments, many using native products like sage, chocolate, aloe vera, and even tequila.

All of the spas listed here are open to nonguests, but reservations are essential. Guests of the hotel may get discounts. Spa customers can sometimes use other facilities at a resort, such as the restaurant, beach, pool, or gym. Ask when you book. Prices are generally on par with those of resort spas worldwide, but some deals are to be had, if you go with the less-expensive but still high-quality spas we lists. Or scout out hotel-spa packages and specials.

Resort/ Spa name	Body Treatments	Facials	Seaside Treatments	Treatments For Two	Fitness Day Pass	Hot Tub	Temazcal
Casa Magna Marriott	$75–$135	$105–$145	yes	yes	yes	yes	no
Four Seasons	$140–$255	$100–$230	yes	yes	yes	yes	yes
Terra Noble	$65	$65	no	yes	yes	yes	yes
Paradise Village	$75–$170	$46–$134	yes	no	$12–$19	no	no
Grand Velas	$80–$200	$135–$311	yes	yes	$40	yes	no
Tahéima	$100–$250	$90–$230	no	yes	yes	yes	yes

(top) Four Seasons

TOP SPOTS

OHTLI SPA, CASAMAGNA MARRIOTT

APUANE SPA, FOUR SEASONS PUNTA MITA

The modern yet organic-looking Ohtli spa and its high-tech gym offer 22,000 square feet of elegant pampering. You can relax before or between treatments in the lounge, with a glass of water infused with love in the form of pink quartz crystals and messages of love in 13 languages. Come early to load up on this liquid love and to enjoy the cold pool, steam, sauna, and other elements of the separate men's and women's spa facilities.

Huichol art and interior gardens maintain a spiritual and nature-oriented mood. Many of the treatments use local ingredients. The signature exfoliation treatment contains agave, cornmeal, and sea salt.

BODY TREATMENTS & SERVICES: Exfoliation (9 kinds); wraps (8 kinds); massage (10 kinds).

BEAUTY TREATMENTS: Facials (6 kinds); manicure; pedicure; waxing; children's treatments.

PRICES: Body treatments $75–$135; facials $105–$145; hair $25–$95; **manicure or pedicure** $30–$72; **waxing** $18–$60.

PACKAGES: Mother and daughter ice cream pedicure; other seasonal packages.

CasaMagna Marriott Puerto Vallarta, Paseo de la Marina 5, Marina Vallarta. ☎ *322/226-0079* ⊕ *www.marriott.com* ▭ *AE, DC, MC, V.*

Professional service is the hallmark of this exclusive spa. An inspirational experience is the Ha Waye healing waters treatment: a four-handed massage under a soothing Vichy bath complemented by aromatherapy.

Treatments are among the most expensive in the area, but everything is top drawer. Native products are used almost exclusively; the Hakali massage, for example, employs catus pulque, which is applied to the skin using fresh cactus paddles.

BODY TREATMENTS & SERVICES: Exfoliation massage (18 types); Vichy hydrotherapy; wraps and scrubs (12 types).

BEAUTY TREATMENTS: Facials (7 types); manicure; pedicure; hair/scalp treatment.

PRICES: Body treatments $140–$265; **facials** $100–$230; **hair** $95–$145; **manicure/pedicure** $65–$95; **waxing** $27–$88.

PACKAGES: Couples treatments such as Like Water for Chocolate—a chocolate scrub and facial; a hot-stone massage; and servings of fruit, chocolate fondue, and champagne.

Punta de Mita, Bahía de Banderas. ☎ *329/291-6000* ⊕ *www.fourseasons. com/puntamita.* ▭ *AE, DC, MC, V.*

TERRA NOBLE

Your cares begin to melt away as soon as you enter the rustic, garden-sur-rounded property of this day-spa aerie overlooking Banderas Bay. Familiar and unpretentious, Terra Noble is more accessible pricewise than some of the area's more elegant spas. After-treatment teas are served on an outdoor patio with a great sea view. Two-hour temazcal sweat lodge rituals cleanse on three levels: physically, mentally, and spiritually. Groups can take advantage of the clay and painting classes. Note that although credit cards are not accepted, you can reserve and pay online in advance using PayPal.

BODY TREATMENTS: Reflexology; massage (5 types); several wraps and scrubs; temazcal sweat lodge; yoga/meditation.

BEAUTY TREATMENTS: Facials.

PRICES: Body treatments and facials $65.

PACKAGES: A few economical packages such as the Stress Recovery (a sea-salt body scrub, a massage, and a facial), for $145.

Av. Tulipanes 595, at Fracc. Lomas de Terra Noble, Col. 5 de Diciembre. ☎ 322/223-3530 ⊕ www.terranoble.com. ⊟ AE, MC, V (through PayPal only).

PALENQUE SPA, PARADISE VILLAGE

On a peninsula between the beach and marina, this modern Maya temple of glass and marble is a cool, sweet-smelling oasis with separate wings for men and women; each is equipped with private hydrotherapy tubs, whirlpools, saunas, and steam rooms. The coed gym has state-of-the-art equipment and views of the ocean, plus studio classes and an indoor lap pool.

The reasonably priced therapy selections are extensive, from an anti-cellulite seaweed wrap to milk baths with honey, amaranth, and orange oil or the aromatherapy massage, employing clove, sage, bergamot, and other essential oils.

BODY TREATMENTS: Aromatherapy; facials; exfoliation; hot-stone massage; hydrotherapy; wraps, scrubs, and body treatments (10 types); reflexology; shiatsu.

BEAUTY TREATMENTS: Facials (8 types); manicure, pedicure.

PRICES: Body treatments $75–$170; facials $46–$134; manicure/pedicure $46–$72; hair $39–$101; waxing $19–$69.

PACKAGES: A wide variety that allow switching treatments in an equivalent price bracket. The basic plan combines three 50-minute treatments.

Paseo de los Cocoteros 1 Nuevo Vallarta. ☎ 322/226-6770 ⊕ www.paradisevillage.com. ⊟ AE, MC, V.

TOP SPOTS

GRAN VELAS	TAHÉIMA

The spa at Nuevo Vallarta's most elegant all-inclusive resort has dramatic architectural lines and plenty of marble, stone, teak, and tile. The 16,500-square-foot facility has 20 treatment rooms and ample steam, sauna, and whirlpools. Lounge in the comfortable chaises near the "plunge lagoon" (with warm and cold pools).

Highlights of the extensive treatments menu are the chocolate, gold, or avocado wraps; Thai massage; cinnamon-sage foot scrub; and the challenging buttocks sculpt-lift. There's even a kids spa menu. Adjoining the spa is an impressive fitness facility.

BODY TREATMENTS: Reflexology; massage (18 types); shiatsu; Vichy shower; exfoliation; wraps, scrubs, baths, and body treatments (32 types).

BEAUTY TREATMENTS: Facials (ages 12+); manicure/pedicure; hair care; waxing; makeup.

PRICES: Body treatments: $80–$200; **facials:** $135–$311; **manicure/pedicure:** $25–$100; **hair care:** $35–$110; **waxing:** $23–$63; **makeup:** $85.

PACKAGES: Happy Bride, Just for Men, and Detox Ritual packages, plus 10% discount for three or more treatments; otherwise, no packages.

Av. de los Cocoteros 98 Sur, Nuevo Vallarta. ☎ *322/226–8000* ⊕ *www.grandvelas.com.* ⊟ *AE, MC, V.*

Tahéima's spa facilities overlook the lagoons and mountains of Nuevo Vallarta. Holistic is taken beyond Mexico-inspired treatments like temazcal to include Zen archery, tai chi, chi gong, and labyrinth meditation. More passive options are lymphatic drainage, "nerve mobilization," and aromatherapy in addition to traditional menu items like Swedish massage. Treatments for men include facials.

A rooftop lounge makes fresh fruit drinks perfect for between treatments, or head to the indoor pool, steamroom, sauna, whirlpool, or men's or women's lounge.

BODY TREATMENTS: massage (9 types); shiatsu; Reiki; exfoliation; reflexology; temazcal.

BEAUTY TREATMENTS: Facials (5 kinds); manicure/pedicure; hair care; waxing

PRICES: Body treatments $100–$250; facials $90–$230; **manicure/pedicure** $40–$70; **hair care** $45–$120; **waxing** $20–$80

PACKAGES: All-Inclusive Passport program provides resort guests with one 60-min. massage per day; access to the sauna, steam room, whirlpool, and men's or women's lounge; and 25% off beauty treatments.

Paseo de las Garzas Lote 272-A, Nuevo Vallarta. ☎ *322/297–2255* ⊕ *www.taheima.com* ⊟ *MC, V.*

GLOSSARY

acupuncture. Painless Chinese medicine during which needles are inserted into key spots on the body to restore the flow of *qi* and allow the body to heal itself.

aromatherapy. Massage and other treatments using plant-derived essential oils intended to relax the skin's connective tissues and stimulate the flow of lymph fluid.

ayurveda. A traditional Indean medical practice that uses oils, massage, herbs, and diet and lifestyle modification to restore balance to the body.

body brushing. Dry brushing of the skin to remove dead cells and stimulate circulation.

body polish. Use of scrubs, loofahs, and other exfoliants to remove dead skin cells.

hot-stone massage. Massage using smooth stones heated in water and applied to the skin with pressure or strokes or simply rested on the body.

hydrotherapy. Underwater massage, alternating hot and cold showers, and other water-oriented treatments.

reflexology. Massage on the pressure points of feet, hands, and ears.

reiki. A Japanese healing method involving universal life energy, the laying on of hands, and mental and spiritual balancing. It's intended to relieve acute emotional and physical conditions. Also called radiance technique.

salt glow. Rubbing the body with coarse salt to remove dead skin.

shiatsu. Japanese massage that uses pressure applied with fingers, hands, elbows, and feet.

shirodhara. Ayurvedic massage in which warm herbalized oil is trickled onto the center of the forehead, then gently rubbed into the hair and scalp.

sports massage. A deep-tissue massage to relieve muscle tension and residual pain from workouts.

Swedish massage. Stroking, kneading, and tapping to relax muscles. It was devised at the University of Stockholm in the 19th century by Per Henrik Ling.

Swiss shower. A multijet bath that alternates hot and cold water, often used after mud wraps and other body treatments.

temazcal. Maya meditation in a sauna heated with volcanic rocks.

THE TEMAZCAL TRADITION

Increasingly popular at Mexico spas is the traditional sweat lodge, or *temazcal*. Herb-scented water sizzles on heated lava rocks, filling the intimate space with purifying steam. Rituals blend indigenous and New Age practices, attempting to stimulate you emotionally, spiritually, and physically. For the sake of others, it's best to take a temazcal only if you're committed to the ceremony, or at least open-minded, and not claustrophobic.

Thai massage. Deep-tissue massage and passive stretching to ease stiff, tense, or short muscles.

thalassotherapy. Water-based treatments that incorporate seawater, seaweed and algae.

Vichy shower. Treatment in which a person lies on a cushioned, waterproof mat and is showered by overhead water jets.

Watsu. A blend of shiatsu and deep-tissue massage with gentle stretches—all conducted in a warm pool.

and chairs. The single-story hotel is one block from the beach. All rooms are no-smoking. Although they advertise the two-bedroom suite ($120), with a king bed and two doubles, for a family of six, the space is pretty tight. **Pros:** low price; close to beach; quiet residential neighborhood. **Cons:** no views; no amenities. ⊠ *Francisco I. Madero 19, Bucerías* ☎ *329/298–0024* ⤳ *12 rooms* ⚐ *In-room: a/c. In-hotel:* ⊟ *No credit cards* ⑪ *EP* ✛ *4:C3.*

$ 🛏 **Hotel Palmeras.** A block from the beach, in an area with lots of good restaurants, "The Palms" has two floors of rooms surrounding a large, clean, rectangular pool. Guests can use the barbecue grill and eat or socialize at umbrella-shaded café tables or plastic loungers with cushions around the pool. Rooms and suites are either in the original, street-facing unit or the newer, ocean-facing building. They vary in configuration and price, but most rooms have a full kitchen; at the very least each has a three-quarter-size refrigerator, microwave, coffeemaker, and toaster. Some units have room for a family, with two separate sleeping quarters and kitchen, but no patio or private balcony. The two suites have ocean views and large, private patios. **Pros:** free Wi-Fi; inexpensive older rooms for bargain hunters; newer rooms have patios and ocean view; rooftop deck with views of red tile roofs, beach, and lacy palm trees; good deals on weekly and monthly rentals; rent the penthouse for a month for less than $10 per night. **Cons:** some rooms have odd layout; no parking. ⊠ *Lázaro Cárdenas 35, Bucerías, Nayarit* ☎ *329/298– 1288; 647/722–4139 in U.S.* ⊕ *www.hotelpalmeras.com* ⤳ *21 rooms* ⚐ *In-room: a/c, no phone, kitchen (some), refrigerator (some), Wi-Fi. In-hotel: pool, no-smoking rooms* ⊟ *MC, V* ⑪ *EP* ✛ *4:C3.*

¢   🛏 **Marco's Place Suites & Villas.** Despite its name, this property is a three-story motel. Rooms are small (and baths are tiny) but are cheery and bright with rather hard beds with polyester bedspreads. Sit on chaise longues around the pool or at café tables outside the first-floor rooms. The property is a block from the beach, which is one of its biggest assets, and on the north side of town near shops and restaurants. **Pros:** several different outdoor spaces for reading or relaxing; even least expensive room has kitchenette. **Cons:** uninspired decor; street parking only; cash only. ⊠ *Calle Juventino Espinoza 6–A, Bucerías, Nayarit* ☎ *329/298–0865* ⊕ *www.marcosplacevillas.com* ⤳ *15 rooms, 3 suites* ⚐ *In-room: a/c, kitchen, refrigerator. In-hotel: pool* ⊟ *No credit cards* ⑪ *EP* ✛ *4:C3.*

LA CRUZ DE HUANACAXTLE

$$$ 🛏 **Villa Bella.** Tropical plants give character to this intimate property where the owner gives her personal attention to guests. The homey hotel is on a hill above quiet La Cruz de Huanacaxtle, just north of Bucerías. Choose a garden-view or ocean-facing suite; several have a terrace overlooking the coast, and a large dining area/kitchen and living room. A big breakfast is served in the open-air dining room; the adjacent common area has a computer with Internet access and DVD and CD players. The small swimming pool overlooks a jungly hillside and beyond, the marina, and the town of Huanacaxtle. **Pros:** free airport pickup before 6 PM with at least three-night stay; lap pool; free cocktail (or two) Monday through Saturday afternoons; large breakfast with Mexican

specialties. **Cons:** up a steep road (best for those with a car); little night-life in area; rooms have lots of knickknacks; three-night minimum stay in high season. ⊠ *Calle del Monte Calvario 12, La Cruz de Huanacax-tle, Nayarit* ☎ *329/295–5161; 329/295–5154; 877/273–6244 toll-free in U.S.; 877/513–1662 toll-free in Canada ⊕ www.villabella-lacruz.com* ⤳ *2 rooms, 4 suites* ⚐ *In-room: a/c (some), no phone, kitchen (some), no TV (some). In-hotel: restaurant, bar, pool, Internet, Wi-Fi hotspot* ⊟ *MC, V* |◯| *BP* ✦ *4:B3.*

NUEVO VALLARTA

$$$$ ⊞ **Grand Velas All Suites & Spa Resort.** In scale and majesty, the public areas of this property outshine all other Nuevo Vallarta all-inclusive resorts. Ceilings soar overhead, and the structure and furnishings are simultaneously minimalist and modern yet earthy, incorporating stucco, rock, polished teak, and gleaming ecru marble. The spa is excellent, and the views—with the garden-shrouded pool in the foreground and the beach beyond—are striking. Rooms are sleek, with elegant furnish-ings and appointments. The high price entitles you to top-of-the-line spirits in minibars and restaurants. **Pros:** exceptionally beautiful rooms and public spaces; lovely spa; extremely long beach great for walk-ing. **Cons:** Nuevo Vallarta location is far from Puerto Vallarta (but 10 minutes by car from Bucerías); at more than $600 per night, you think they'd kick in free Wi-Fi. ⊠ *Paseo de los Cocoteros 98 Sur, Nuevo Val-larta* ☎ *322/226–8000; 888/261–8436 in U.S. and Canada ⊕ www. grandvelas.com* ⤳ *267 1-, 2-, and 3-bedroom suites* ⚐ *In-room: a/c, safe, DVD, Wi-Fi. In-hotel: 4 restaurants, room service, bars, tennis court, pools, gym, spa, beachfront, children's programs (ages 4–12), laundry service, Internet, Wi-Fi hotspot, parking (free), some pets allowed* ⊟ *AE, MC, V* |◯| *AI* ✦ *4:C4.*

$$$ ⊞ **Marival Resort and Suites.** Come here if you're looking for an all-inclu-sive bargain that includes a wealth of activities. On the one hand, rooms have strong air-conditioning and amenities like hair dryers, irons, and ironing boards; on the other, rooms also have small tubs, cheap doors, and uninspired modern decor. There's an extra charge, inexplicably, for the use of in-room safes. Only a few units have ocean views, but there are plenty of individual palapas and lounge chairs at the beach. If you go to bed early, avoid the Club building, with a downstairs karaoke bar that goes on until midnight. **Pros:** value-priced; immaculately kept grounds; premium booze brands. **Cons:** most rooms have no tub or an uncomfortable square tub; musty smell in some rooms; cheap fin-ishing touches like plastic chairs and fake plants. ⊠ *Paseo Cocoteros s/n at Blvd. Nuevo Vallarta, Nuevo Vallarta* ☎ *322/226–8200 ⊕ www. gomarival.com* ⤳ *373 rooms, 122 suites* ⚐ *In-room: a/c, Wi-Fi. In-hotel: 6 restaurants, room service, bars, tennis courts, pools, gym, spa, beachfront, bicycles, children's programs (ages 4–11), Internet, Wi-Fi hotspot, parking (free)* ⊟ *MC, V* |◯| *AI* ✦ *4:C4.*

$$ ⊞ **Paradise Village Beach Resort & Spa.** This Nuevo Vallarta hotel and
☺ time-share property is perfect for families, with lots of activities geared to children. Many people love it, although the property's dedication to time-share guests makes some hotel guests feel short-shrifted. Most suites have balconies with either marina or ocean views. Furnishings are

Quinta Maria Cortez

Hotel des Artistes

attractive as well as functional, with pretty cane sofa beds in a sooth-ing palette and well-equipped kitchens. Locals like to visit the clean, well-organized spa, which smells divine and is noted for its massages and facials. The beach here is tranquil enough for swimming, although some small waves are suitable for bodysurfing. **Pros:** reasonably priced spa; can walk all the way to Bucerías on the beach; fully loaded kitchen in all suites; efficient a/c units; wide range of accommodations. **Cons:** big cats caged in depressing zoo; Internet room for time-share guests only; time-share oriented; guests must bring cable for Internet access. ⊠ *Paseo de los Cocoteros 1, Nuevo Vallarta, Nayarit* ☎ *322/226–6770; 866/334–6080* ⊕ *www.paradisevillage.com* ☞ *702 suites* ♿ *In-room: a/c, safe, kitchen, refrigerator, Internet. In-hotel: 5 restaurants, room service, bars, golf course, tennis courts, pools, gym, spas, beachfront, children's programs (ages 4–11), Wi-Fi hotspot, parking (free)* ⊟ *AE, MC, V* ⦿ *EP, AI* ✛ *4:C4.*

$$$ ⊞ **Taheima Wellness Resort & Spa.** Nuevo Vallarta's unusual new condo-hotel was inaugurated in 2010. The residence resort, which is geared toward couples, sells "learning vacations" and offers courses in every-thing from Mexican history to natural hormone replacement and stress-reduction techniques. The Wellness Spa offers treatments like aro-matherapy, lymphatic drainage, and "nerve mobilization" as well as the more traditional Swedish massage. Guest rooms have a contemporary, white-on-white theme. Studios have kitchenettes; all of the larger suites have full size kitchen. Ground-floor suites have private plunge pools; some rooms have hydro-massage bathtubs. In keeping with the wellness theme, the entire property is non-smoking. **Pros:** pillow menu; in-suite washer/dryer; stainless steel dishwasher and major appliances; 24-hour room service; free shuttle to nearby locations. **Cons:** possible noise from ongoing construction; two blocks from the beach. ⊠ *Paseo de las Garzas Lote 272–A, Nuevo Vallarta* ☎ *322/297–2255* ⊕ *www.taheima. com* ☞ *400 2-bedroom suites* ♿ *In-room: a/c, safe, kitchen, refrigera-tor, Wi-Fi. In-hotel: 2 restaurants, room service, bar, golf course, ten-nis courts, pool, gym, spa, laundry facilities, laundry service, Internet terminal, Wi-Fi hotspot, parking (free)* ⊟ *MC, V* ⦿ *AI* ✛ *4:C4.*

PUNTA MITA

$$$$ ⊞ **Casa de Mita.** Architect-owner Marc Lindskog has created a nook of nonchalant elegance, with updated country furnishings of wicker, leather, and wood; rock-floor showers without curtains or doors; and cheerful Pacific Coast architectural details. Mosquito netting lends romance to cozy, quilt-covered beds. Waves crashing onshore, their sound somehow magnified, create white noise that lulls you to sleep. In the morning, settle into a cushy chaise on your private patio to watch seabirds swim; at night watch the sunset behind Punta Mita. These simple pleasures make this hideaway a winner. It doesn't hurt that the food is truly delicious, the bar is well stocked with international labels, and it's all included in the room price. **Pros:** delicious food; nearly private beach; concierge service; free international phone calls. **Cons:** little nightlife in vicinity; three-night minimum stay; strict cancellation policy. ⊠ *Playa Careyeros, Punta Mita, Nayarit* ☎ *329/298–4114 or 866/740–7999* ⊕ *www.casademita.com* ☞ *6 rooms, 2 suites* ♿ *In-room:*

a/c, no phone, safe, refrigerator, no TV, Wi-Fi (some). In-hotel: restaurant, bar, pool, spa, beachfront, water sports, Internet, Wi-Fi hotspot ▭ *AE, MC, V* ❑❍ *AI* ✛ *4:A2.*

$$$$ ▦ **Fairmont Rancho Banderas.** Long the playground of surfers and those seeking solitary beaches, Destiladeras Beach, in the Punta de Mita area, is now being developed with several time shares and hotels. Located on a cliff above the beach or right on the beach, Fairmont Rancho Banderas's rooms have ocean or garden views; the attractive pool spills down several levels to end above the sand, where palm-thatch "umbrellas" shade chaise longues. Even the smallest villa has a full kitchen (although most only have a two-burner electric stove and no oven), private bedroom, and huge balcony with patio furniture and a day bed for an afternoon siesta. **Pros:** well-equipped kitchens; rooms have stereo; iPod deck and DVD players, plasma TV. **Cons:** 10 AM checkout; one restaurant only; car, bus, or taxi ride from restaurants and nightlife. ⊠ *Carretera a Punta de Mita, Km 8.3, Playa Destiladeras 63732* ☎ *329/291–7000* ⊕ *www. ranchobanderas.com* ↪ *48 1-, 2-, and 3-bedroom suites, 1 penthouse villa* ⌂ *In-room: a/c, safe, kitchen, refrigerator, DVD, Wi-Fi. In-hotel: restaurant, room service, bar, pool, gym, spa, beachfront, water sports, laundry facilities, laundry service, Internet terminal, Wi-Fi hotspot, parking (free)* ▭ *AE, MC, V* ❑❍ *EP* ✛ *4:B3.*

$$$$ ▦ **Four Seasons Resort, Punta Mita.** The hotel and its fabulous spa perch
☺ above a lovely beach at the northern extreme of Bahía de Banderas, about 45 minutes from the Puerto Vallarta airport and an hour north of downtown Puerto Vallarta. Spacious rooms occupy Mexican-style casitas of one, two, and three stories. Each room has elegant yet earthy furnishings and a private terrace or balcony—many with a sweeping sea view. The Jack Nicklaus–designed championship golf course has a challenging, optional 19th island hole; a second course opened in 2009. The gym is first-rate, and a good variety of sporting and beach equipment is on hand. Just offshore, the Marietas Islands are great for snorkeling, diving, whale-watching, and fishing. This is the place for indulging golf and spa fantasies or just using the luxurious, top-notch facilities. It's a great spot for kids, too, with fantastic beaches, a doughnut-shaped pool with current where you can float in inner tubes, and an excellent kids' playroom with Internet and lots of cool games. **Pros:** beautiful beach; concierge service; yoga on the point; excellent spa; private yacht for charter. **Cons:** staff trained to be overly solicitous (you'll be saying "hola" a lot); very expensive spa treatments; not all rooms have ocean view. ⊠ *Bahía de Banderas, Punta Mita, Nayarit* ☎ *329/291–6019; 800/819–5053 in U.S. and Canada* ⊕ *www.fshr.com/ puntamita* ↪ *141 rooms, 27 suites* ⌂ *In-room: a/c, safe, refrigerator, DVD, Internet, Wi-Fi. In-hotel: 3 restaurants, room service, bars, golf courses, tennis courts, pools, gym, spa, beachfront, water sports, children's programs (ages 5–12), laundry service, Internet, Wi-Fi hotspot, parking (free)* ▭ *AE, MC, V* ❑❍ *BP, EP* ✛ *4:A2.*

$$$$ ▦ **Hotel des Artistes.** Located at the north end of Punta de Mita, this
Fodor'sChoice three-story condo-hotel offers charming two- and three-bedroom apart-
★ ments. Situated just beyond the string of El Anclote's beach-facing restaurants, it isn't part of the walled, über-priced Punta Mita compound

that houses the Four Seasons and St. Regis. Individually decorated by their owners, each apartment has a full-size washer and dryer as well as a generous balcony or patio overlooking the sand and the sea. The smallest apartment is 1,200 square feet. Large kitchens have stainless-steel sinks and faucets, granite countertops with plenty of prep room, and white marble floors. Non-guests can join the gym (with access to the separate men's and women's steam, sauna, and hot tub) by the day, week, month, or year. The innovative (if expensive) cuisine at the adjoining Café des Artistes del Mar provides a nice change of pace from the more traditional seafood restaurants that line the street. **Pros:** lots of amenities for a small condo-hotel; 20 minutes from fun, funky Sayulita; multiple a/c units. **Cons:** valet parking only; owner-decorated apartments leave design open to their whims. ⊠ *Av. El Anclote 5, Punta de Mita* ☎ *329/291–5005* ⊕ *www.hoteldesartistes.net* ↪ *12 2- and 3-bedroom suites* △ *In-room: a/c, safe, kitchen, refrigerator, DVD, Wi-Fi. In-hotel: 2 restaurants, room service, bar, 2 pools, gym, spa, beachfront, water sports, laundry facilities, laundry service, Wi-Fi hotspot, some pets allowed* ☰ *AE, MC, V* ⌶⍥ *CP* ✛ *4:A2.*

$$$$ ⌶ **Hotel St. Regis Punta Mita.** The first St. Regis in Mexico (there's now a lovely sister property in Mexico City), this Starwood group member boasts a nouveau Mexican architectural style combining geometric simplicity with the warmth of giant palapa roofs and other natural elements. Sleek white tubs, simple outdoor showers, and flat-screen TVs maintain the spare look of the overall design, but room decor is simultaneously cheerful, light, and charming. Separate adults-only pools and restaurants make the space welcoming for couples seeking quiet and or romance as well as for families with tots in tow. Punta Mita's two golf courses flank the property, which is a boon for golfers; the beach is pretty and private but rocky and not suitable for swimming. When reserving, request a partial-ocean-view room, as it's the same price as a garden-view room. **Pros:** 80% of rooms have at least partial beach views; personal butlers perform services for all guests; faces Las Marietas Islands; impressive guest-to-employee ratio. **Cons:** rocky beach means no kayaking, swimming, or other water sports; three-night minimum stay (seven nights in high season). ⊠ *Carretara 200, Km. 19.5, Lote H4, Punta de Mita* ☎ *329/291–5830* ⊕ *www.stregis.com/ puntamita* ↪ *99 rooms, 20 suites* △ *In-room: a/c, safe, kitchen (some), refrigerator (some), Internet, Wi-Fi. In-hotel: 3 restaurants, room service, bars, 2 golf courses, tennis courts, 3 pools, gym, spa, beachfront, laundry service, Internet terminal, Wi-Fi hotspot, parking (free)* ☰ *AE, MC, V* ⌶⍥ *EP* ✛ *4:A2.*

$$$$ ⌶ **La Tranquila.** The government-and-private-invested Litibú in Punta Mita project got off to a rocky start when the world economy tanked in 2008. Some Litibú projects are now nearing completion, including "The Tranquil" condo hotels, spread over many acres. Interiors are masculine and contemporary, with a muted color scheme. There are seven swimming pools, each with attached bar and snacking opportunities. Families are welcomed, and there are plenty of *chapoteaderos*, or "kiddie pools." If you're a golfer, ask for a room closest to the new, 18-hole Greg Norman course. By the end of 2011, 140 new suites are scheduled to be completed.

Pros: luxurious apartments; spacious grounds; variety of dining options. **Cons:** possible construction noise from ongoing building; lack of real town nearby; expensive. ✉ *Carretera a Punta Mita Km 2, Playa Litibú, Punta de Mita* ☎ *800/628–9857* ⊕ *www.latranquilaresorts.com* ⬎ *169 apartments, from studios to 3-bedroom units* ⚮ *In-room: a/c, safe, kitchen, refrigerator, Wi-Fi. In-hotel: 7 restaurants, room service, bars, golf course, tennis court, 7 pools, gym, spa, beachfront, water sports, laundry service, Internet terminal, Wi-Fi hotspot, parking (free), some pets allowed* ▬ *AE, MC, V* ⦿*EP* ✛ *4:A2.*

NORTH OF BANDERAS BAY

Although distinctive in flavor, both San Francisco (aka San Pancho) and Sayulita attract youthful, laid-back travelers and offer mid-range and modest hotels, plus vacation rentals. San Francisco offers a real community feel, with wide-gridlike streets, family homes with character, and a plain but pretty beach. Surfers head for smaller, hipper Sayulita, with a pretty bay and a variety of nearby beaches. On beautiful Jaltemba Bay, Rincon de Guayabitos caters to middle-class Mexican families (and snowbirds in the winter), with moderately priced hotels and small restaurants offering mainly Mexican and seafood. Each town lies on the beach about a mile off the coast highway.

$$$ **Casa Obelisco.** The vibe is warm and romantic, the cozy-chic rooms—
Fodor's Choice endowed with original paintings, folk art, and super-comfortable king
★ beds with pillow-top mattresses and mosquito nets—are perfect for spooning and honeymooning. Ambition here means drinks by the pool, walks on the beach, and trips into town or down to Sayulita (5 km [3 mi] south). Each ocean-facing patio (some private, some shared) has either a hammock or table with *equipale* (pigskin) chairs. American owners provide opinions and information about the area. Breakfasts are varied and expansive. Kahlua, the well-behaved doodle dog, is a boon to pet-starved guests. **Pros:** attentive hosts; bountiful, varied breakfasts; newer construction. **Cons:** down long, bumpy cobblestone road from town; street parking only. ✉ *Calle Palmas 115, Fracc. Costa Azul, San Francisco Nayarit* ☎ *311/258–4315* ⊕ *www. casaobelisco.com* ⬎ *4 rooms* ⚮ *In-room: a/c, no phone, no TV. In-hotel: bar, pool, no kids under 16* ▬ *No credit cards* ⊗ *Closed July– Sept.* ⦿*BP* ✛ *5:B3.*

$$ **Costa Azul.** What makes this place
⟲ attractive are the many activities

OM AWAY FROM HOME

Via Yoga (⊕ www.viayoga.com), based in Seattle, Washington, offers six-night packages at Villa Amor that include twice-daily yoga and Pilates classes. **Haramara Retreat** (☎ 329/291–3558 ⊕ www.haramararetreat.com), just south of Sayulita, caters to yoga groups (including vegetarian cuisine) and offers private yoga lessons in two wood-floored pavilions with ocean views. At Yelapa's **Yoga in Yelapa** (⊕ www. yogainyelapa.com), Judith Roth teaches beginning through advanced students at her studio overlooking the bay; she can combine practice with birding, chanting, and other esoteric disciplines.

offered: horseback riding, kayaking, hiking, surfing (with lessons), and excursions to the Marietas Islands or La Tobara mangroves near San Blas. The all-inclusive plan, which includes activities, can be arranged through the U.S. office in San Clemente, California, but not in Mexico. But since San Pancho has a number of excellent restaurants, the European Plan is recommended. The sandy beach faces the open ocean, but the staff discourages guests from swimming there. Officially there's no Wi-Fi in guest rooms, but those closest to the restaurant may get access. **Pros:** great place to bond with kids of all ages; lots of planned outdoor activities and tours. **Cons:** mediocre food; some guests have complained of disorganized and unhelpful staff members; stringent cancellation policy. ⊠ *Calle Amapas at Calle Las Palmas, Fracc. Costa Azul, San Francisco, Nayarit* ☎ *311/258–4000; 800/365–7613 toll-free in U.S.* ⊕ *www.costaazul.com* ⇨ *18 rooms, 5 suites, 3 villas* ♻ *In-room: a/c, no phone, kitchen (some), refrigerator (some), no TV. In-hotel: restaurant, bars, pool, beachfront, water sports, laundry service, Wi-Fi hotspot, parking (free)* ⊟ *MC, V* ⦿| *EP, FAP* ⊕ *5:B3.*

$$ ⊞ **Haramara Retreat.** Mind-blowing views and acres of trees are yours, as well as blissful breezes off the Pacific Ocean, at this oasis of tranquility just south of Sayulita. Originally a retreat for yoga groups only, Haramara—which means "Grandmother Sea" in the Huichol language—is now open to individual travelers. With its own private beach and several large pergolas for meditation, Haramara is a wonderful venue for a rejuvenating vacation away from phones, television, and (gasp!) cyberspace. Included in the price are three healthful meals at the ocean-view restaurant, which specializes in vegetarian cuisine but offers seafood as well. Vegans and those with food allergies or other dietary requirements are accommodated. Expert body workers give several types of massage, and private yoga lessons are available, as are surfing lessons and surf safaris. A packed dirt path lead up and down the hilly, 12-acre property to thatch-roofed bungalows that open to the sea breezes. The showers also are open-sided so you can admire the views as you bathe. Comfortable beds are surrounded by mosquito netting; hardwood floors, bamboo siding, and thatch roofs complete the Robinson Crusoe feel of the place. **Pros:** wonderful views; tranquil setting on a huge, tree-studded property; gifted body workers and yoga teachers. **Cons:** no Wi-Fi access; cab ride from Sayulita; limited cell phone coverage. ⊠ *Off paved road from Sayulita to Punta de Mita, about 2½ km (1½ mi) off Carretera 200, Playa Escondida* ☎ *329/291–3558* ⊕ *www.haramararetreat.com* ⇨ *15 bungalows, 1 dorm-style room* ♻ *In-room: no a/c, no phone, no TV. In-hotel: restaurant, beachfront, laundry service, parking (free), no kids under 7* ⊟ *MC, V* ⦿| *FAP* ⊕ *5:B3.*

$ ⊞ **Villa Amor.** What began as a hilltop home has slowly become an amalgam of unusual, rustic, but luxurious suites with indoor and outdoor living spaces. The higher up your room, the more beautiful the view of Sayulita's coast. The trade-off for such beauty? A long walk up a seemingly endless staircase and the dearth of room phones make contacting the front desk frustrating. Accommodations, managed by different owners, range from basic to honeymoon suites with terraces and plunge pools. Details like recessed color-glass light fixtures, Talavera sinks in

Fodor's Choice
★

bathrooms, brick ceilings, wrought-iron table lamps, art in wall niches, and colorful cement floors add a lot of class. The property overlooks a rocky cove where you can fish from shore; a beautiful sandy beach is a few minutes' walk. The staff lends out kayaks, boogie boards, and snorkeling gear. **Pros:** nice location across bay from Sayulita's main beach; staff arranges tours, transportation, and tee times; charming and unique lodgings at reasonable prices. **Cons:** tons of stairs; no phones or Wi-Fi in guest rooms; open-to-the-elements rooms can have creepy crawlies. ⊠ *Playa Sayulita, Sayulita, Nayarit* ☎ *329/291–3010* ⊕ *www. villaamor.com* ⬇ *33 villas* △ *In-room: a/c (some), no phone, kitchen (some), refrigerator, no TV. In-hotel: restaurant, bar, water sports, bicycles, laundry service* ▭ *MC, V* ⦿ *EP* ✛ *5:B4.*

$ ⊟ **Villas Buena Vida.** On beautiful Rincón de Guayabitos Beach, this property has three-story units, breeze-ruffled palms, and manicured walkways. Four guests are allowed in even the smallest rooms (which have two double beds and run-of-the-mill hotel furnishings), making this a deal for bargain hunters. Guayabitos is a Mexican resort town that's recently begun attracting snowbirds and travelers looking for less touristy digs. The bay has calm surf that's good for swimming; a long, flat beach embraced by twin headlands (great for walking); and boat trips to the quiet coves and solitary beaches along Jaltemba Bay. Be prepared for the staff to count every spoon and spatula when you check in and out. **Pros:** beautiful bay-side location; 5% cash discount. **Cons:** uninspired furnishings; unreliable Internet access in rooms via Wi-Fi. ⊠ *Retorno Laureles 2, Rincón de Guayabitos, Nayarit* ☎ *327/274–0231* ⊕ *www.villasbuenavida.com* ⬇ *36 rooms, 9 suites* △ *In-room: a/c, kitchen, refrigerator. In-hotel: restaurant, pools, laundry facilities* ▭ *MC, V* ⦿ *EP* ✛ *5:C3.*

COSTALEGRE

LA MANZANILLA AND POINTS NORTH

More developed for tourism than neighboring towns on gorgeous Tenacatita Bay, La Manzanilla springs to life in the winter months, when previously shuttered galleries and restaurants open. Mexican families visit in the rainy months of students' summer vacations. The vibe is earthy and organic; streets are sandy and traffic-free. Miles of gorgeous beaches beckon, and those travelers with a car or a penchant for bus travel can explore miles of similarly natural and charming Costalegre beaches even farther north toward San Mateo, Punta Perula, and beyond.

$$ ⊟ **Coconuts by the Sea.** A friendly couple of American expats own and run this charming cliff-top hideaway with a drop-dead-gorgeous view of the ocean and Boca de Iguana Beach below. The furniture is stylish, and homey touches like lamps and fish-theme wall decorations make the snug apartments just right for holing up. The two apartments upstairs, with thatched roofs and kitchen and living room open to the elements, are not usually available in summer due to the rain; the rest of the year they're highly coveted. One has an outdoor shower with a view. **Pros:** homey apartments; great sea views; very nice beaches

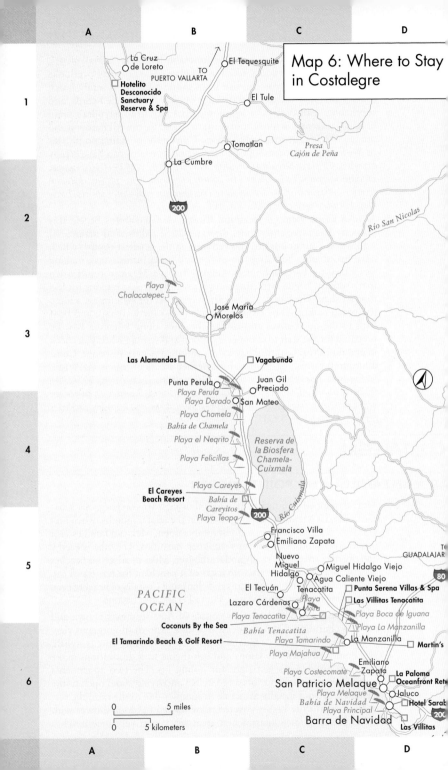

HOTELS AT A GLANCE: COSTALEGRE

Hotel	Worth Noting	Cost (*Includes Tax)	Rooms	Restaurants	On the Beach	Pools	Spa	Golf Course	Tennis Courts	Health Club/Gym	Children's Programs	Location
Coconuts by the Sea	fab beach views	$125*	4		yes	1						Bahía Tenacatita
El Careyes Beach Resort	impeccable decor	$268	55	1	yes	1	yes		2	yes		Careyes
El Tamarindo Beach & Golf Resort	stunning good taste	$875	32	1	yes	1	yes	yes	1	yes		Cihuatlán
Hotel Sarabi	cheap and cheerful	$28–$32	21									Barra de Navidad
Hotelito Desconocido Sanctuary Reserve & Spa												
La Paloma Oceanfront Retreat	well-equipped studios	$700–850/week	13		yes	1						San Patricio-Melaque
Las Alamandas	ultra-exclusive	$448	14	1	yes	1	yes		1	yes		Quemaro, C
Las Villitas	well situated	$56*	8		yes							Barra de Navidad
Las Villitas Tenacatita	lovely bay	$56–98*	25		yes	1						Bahía Tenacatita
Punta Serena Villas & Spa	adults-only oasis	$240*	24	1	yes	1	yes			yes		Bahía Tenacatita
Vagabundo	far from crowds	$47	21			1						Punta Perula

El Careyes Beach Resort

El Tamarindo Beach & Golf Resort

on Tenacatita Bay. **Cons:** its few rooms make last-minute reservations unlikely; long downhill walk to the beach; car is almost a must unless you're staying put; to pay by credit card, must use PayPal in advance. ⊠ *Playa Boca de Iguanas, 6 Dolphin Way, Bahía Tenacatita, Jalisco* ✛ *195 km (121 mi) south of Puerto Vallarta, 21 km (13 mi) north of Barra de Navidad* ☎ *315/100–8899 cell; 949/945–7465 in U.S. or Canada* ⊕ *www.coconutsbythesea. com* ⇆ *4 rooms* ♿ *In-room: a/c, no phone, kitchen, refrigerator, Wi-Fi. In-hotel: pool, parking (free)* ☰ *AE, MC, V (through PayPal only)* ⦿| *EP* ✛ *6:C5.*

$$$$ 🏨 **El Careyes Beach Resort.** On a gorgeous bay framed by flowering veg-
Fodor's Choice   etation, El Careyes is a boldly painted village of a resort. Guest rooms
★   have large windows and private patios or balconies; suites have outdoor hot tubs. Colorful furnishings and artwork create a sophisticated Mexican palette. The full-service spa has fine European beauty and body treatments; a deli sells fine wines, prosciutto, and other necessities of the good life. A full range of water-sports equipment awaits you at the beach, and there are dune buggies and kayaks, too. There are more dining options in the area than at other Costalegre resorts, making a rental car a plus. It's a short walk to pretty Playa Rosa and a short drive to Bahía Tenacatita. **Pros:** large spa menu; unique architecture; on a beautiful cove. **Cons:** business center has one computer only for guests to check e-mail; only one on-site restaurant; 5% service charge. ⊠ *Carretera a Barra de Navidad (Carretera 200), Km 53.5, Costa Careyes, Jalisco* ✛ *161 km (100 mi) south of Puerto Vallarta, 55 km (34 mi) north of Barra de Navidad* ☎ *315/351–0000* ⊕ *www.elcareyesresort. com* ⇆ *22 rooms, 29 suites, 3 multi-bedroom casitas* ♿ *In-room: a/c, safe, kitchen (some), refrigerator (some), DVD. In-hotel: restaurant, room service, bar, tennis courts, pool, gym, spa, beachfront, water sports, bicycles, laundry service, Internet, Wi-Fi hotspot, parking (free)* ☰ *AE, MC, V* ⦿| *EP* ✛ *6:B4.*

$$$$ 🏨 **El Tamarindo Beach & Golf Resort.** More than 2,000 acres of ecological
Fodor's Choice   reserve and jungle surround this magical resort along 16 km (10 mi)
★   of private coast. The architecture fuses Mediterranean-style elements with local building materials; world-renowned Ricardo Legorreta was one of the architects. Many villas have an outdoor living room. All have dark-wood floors; king-size beds; wet bars; ample bathrooms; and patios with plunge pools, hammocks, and chaise longues. Sofas are upholstered in rich textured fabrics. At night the staff lights hundreds of candles around the villas to create a truly enchanting setting. The golf course is excellent. **Pros:** concierge service; individual plunge pools; CD and DVD players in each room; yoga and Pilates classes (in high season). **Cons:** 10% service fee on top of 18% sales and hotel taxes; prohibitively expensive for most people; no Wi-Fi in rooms; only one shared computer for checking e-mails. ⊠ *Carretera Melaque–Puerto Vallarta (Carretera 200), Km 7.5, Cihuatlán, Jalisco* ✛ *204 km (127*

4

mi) south of Puerto Vallarta, 12 km (7 mi) north of Barra de Navidad ☎ *315/351–5031; 01800/823–3037 toll-free in Mexico; 866/717–4316 from U.S. or Canada* ⊕ *www.eltamarindoresort.com* ⇨ *29 villas, 3 4-bedroom houses* ☐ *In-room: a/c, safe, DVD. In-hotel: restaurant, room service, bar, golf course, tennis court, pool, gym, spa, beachfront, diving, water sports, bicycles, laundry service, Internet, Wi-Fi hotspot, parking (free)* ☐ *AE, MC, V* ❑ *EP* ✛ *6:C6.*

$$$$ ⬚ **Hotelito Desconocido Sanctuary Reserve & Spa.** A two-year renovation, during which time the resort was closed, has resulted in a more sedate, less whimsical decor that, like the original Hotelito, includes elements of hardwood, bamboo,

> ### TURTLE RESCUE
>
> Releasing tiny turtles into the sea, done in the evening when there are fewer predators, is a real thrill for kids, and for many adults as well. The Westin, **CasaMagna Marriott Puerto Vallarta,** Fiesta Americana, Velas Vallarta, and Dreams Resort in Puerto Vallarta as well as Las Alamandas and El Tamarindo on the Costalegre have marine turtle conservation programs. They employ biologists to collect eggs from nests on nearby beaches, incubate them in protected sand pits, and help guests repatriate them into the wild blue sea.

and palm-thatch designed by a group of young *tapatios* (artisans from Guadalajara). It's far from rustic, however: witness 600-thread-count sheets, Jacuzzi tubs, expansive furnished terraces, and private docks with personal canoes; the smallest palafito (house on wooden stilts) is more than 1,000 square feet. There are private butlers, too. The property is lit by torches, lanterns, candles, and low-wattage lamps. On a long stretch of beach, this isolated hotel is an idyllic escape for its discerning, high-end clientele. An integral part of the concept is health and self-improvement. Programs range from the 5-day "mom-to-be" to the 21-day "love the way you look" program; organic fruits and veggies make their way from the property's garden to guests' table, along with fish and seafood. **Pros:** isolated, unique, and charming; holistic spa with aromatherapy, yoga, and many other services; concierge service. **Cons:** rustic-chic it is, affordable it isn't; isolated. ⊠ *Playón de Mismaloya s/n, Cruz de Loreto* ✛ *97 km (60 mi) south of Puerto Vallarta, 119 km (74 mi) north of Barra de Navidad* ☎ *800/851–1143* ⊕ *www.hotelito.com* ⇨ *27 suites, 3 villas* ☐ *In-room: a/c (some), no phone, no TV. In-hotel: 2 restaurants, bar, pool, gym, spa, beachfront, water sports, bicycles, Internet terminal, parking (free)* ☐ *AE, MC, V* ❑ *EP, FAP* ✛ *6:A1.*

$$$$ ⬚ **Las Alamandas.** Personal service and exclusivity lure movie stars and royalty to this low-key resort in a thorn-forest preserve about 1½ hours from both Puerto Vallarta and Manzanillo. Suites are filled with folk art; their indoor-outdoor living rooms have modern furnishings with deliciously nubby fabrics in bright, bold colors and Guatemalan-cloth throw pillows. Request a TV, DVD player, and movie from the library for an evening in; there's little else to do at night. There's lots more to do in the daytime, however, including picnics anywhere on the property and boat rides on the Río San Nicolás. There's a 10% service charge and a two-night minimum; the average stay is seven nights.

Pros: stargazing from rooftop bar; stunning yet cozy architecture; one-hour horseback ride and use of bicycles; boogie boards included; concierge service. **Cons:** open-style bungalows not pleasant in rainy season, with mosquitoes and high humidity; not close to any restaurants or nightlife; riptides. ⊠ *Carretera 200, Km 85, Quemaro* ✛ *83 km (52 mi) south of Puerto Vallarta, 133 km (83 mi) north of Barra de Navidad* ☎ *322/285–5500 or 888/882–9616* ⊕ *www.lasalamandas. com* ⌐ *14 suites* ⌂ *In-room: a/c, refrigerator, DVD. In-hotel: restaurant, room service, bars, tennis court, pool, gym, spa, beachfront, water sports, bicycles, laundry service, Internet, parking (free)* ▭ *AE, MC, V* ⦿*EP, FAP* ✛ *6:B3.*

$ ⌂ **Las Villitas Tenacatita.** Las Villitas is a wonderful place to kick back on one of Pacific Mexico's most beautiful bays: Tenacatita. Each of the compact bungalows has a bathroom with tub rather than just a shower, a small sitting room with two single beds that double as couches, kitchenette, and a separate bedroom with a king-size bed. Standard rooms have no tub or kitchen but are nearly half the price. Both types are cheerfully painted and have large glass doors that make it easy to take in the beach views. You can borrow a kayak for a jaunt into the bay or use the volleyball or multisport fields on the beach. Ask for discounts on stays Monday through Thursday in low season. **Pros:** right on the beach; beautiful bay; doors and windows are screened. **Cons:** little nightlife nearby; no TV; no a/c; no Internet. ⊠ *Playa Tenacatita, Calle Bahía de Tenacatita 376, Bahía Tenacatita, Jalisco* ✛ *183 km (114 mi) south of Puerto Vallarta, 37 km (23 mi) north of Barra de Navidad* ☎ *315/355–5354; 01800/980–7060 toll-free in Mexico* ⊕ *www. lasvillitas.com.mx* ⌐ *5 rooms, 10 bungalows* ⌂ *In-room: no a/c, no phone, kitchen (some), refrigerator (some). In-hotel: pool, beachfront* ▭ *No credit cards* ⦿*EP* ✛ *6:C5.*

$$$ ⌂ **Punta Serena Villas & Spa.** Guests come from New York and Italy to this adults-only oasis of calm. Perched on a beautiful headland, "Point Serene" enjoys balmy breezes and life-changing views from the infinity hot tub. The hot tub, the beach far below, and pool are clothing optional. Spa treatments are inventive: Roses and red wine promote moisturizing; carotene and honey contribute to a glowing tan; and the Mayan Wrap connects you herbally to the glowing god within. Shamans leads a temazcal (ritual healing steam ceremony) twice weekly, and activities like horseback riding, tennis (three courts), and nonmotorized water sports at the adjacent Blue Bay hotel are included in the price. Additionally, rooms have lovely furnishings and decor and shared or private terraces, some with fab beach views. **Pros:** gorgeous views; intriguing spa treatments; complimentary horseback ride and mangrove cruise. **Cons:** isolated; limited menu; cobblestone walkways and hills make walking difficult for some folks. ⊠ *Carretera Barra de Navidad– Puerto Vallarta (Carretera 200), Km 20, Tenacatita, Jalisco* ✛ *196 km (122 mi) south of Puerto Vallarta, 20 km (12 mi) north of Barra de Navidad* ☎ *315/351–5020* ⊕ *www.puntaserena.com* ⌐ *12 rooms, 12 suites* ⌂ *In-room: a/c, safe, Internet, Wi-Fi. In-hotel: restaurant, bar, pool, gym, spa, beachfront, water sports, laundry service, Internet, Wi-Fi, parking (free), no kids under 21* ▭ *AE, MC, V* ⦿*AI* ✛ *6:C5.*

4

Buying a Time-Share

In Puerto Vallarta, time-share salespeople are as unavoidable as death and taxes, and almost as dreaded. Although a slim minority of people actually enjoy going to one- to four-hour time-share presentations to get the freebies that range from a bottle of $12 Kahlúa to rounds of golf, car rentals, meals, and shows, most folks find the experience incredibly annoying. For some it even casts a pall over their whole vacation.

The bottom line is, if the sharks smell interest, you're dead in the water. Time-share salespeople occupy tiny booths up and down main streets where tourists and cruise passengers walk. In general, while *vallartenses* are friendly, they don't accost you on the street to start a conversation. Those who do are selling something. Likewise, anyone calling you *amigo* is probably selling. The best solution is to walk by without responding, or say "No thanks" or "I'm not interested" as you continue walking. When they yell after you, don't feel compelled to explain yourself.

Some sly methods of avoidance that have worked for others are telling the tout that you're out of a job but dead interested in attending a presentation. They'll usually back off immediately. Or explaining confidentially that the person you're with is not your spouse. Time-share people are primarily interested in married couples—married to each other, that is! But our advice is still to practice the art of total detachment with a polite rejection and then ignore the salesperson altogether if he or she persists.

Even some very nice hotels allow salespeople in their lobbies disguised as the Welcome Wagon or information gurus. Ask the concierge for the scoop on area activities, and avoid the so-called "information desk."

Time-share salespeople often pressure guests to attend time-share presentations, guilt-tripping them ("My family relies on the commissions I get," for example) or offering discounts on the hotel room and services. The latter are sometimes difficult to redeem and cost more time than they're worth. And although it may be the salesperson's livelihood, remember that this is your vacation, and you have every right to use the time as you wish.

But if you do return to Puerto Vallarta frequently, a time-share might make sense. Here are some tips for navigating the treacherous waters:

■ Cruise the Internet before your vacation. Check out resale time-shares in the area, which makes it easier to determine the value of what's offered.

■ Worthwhile time-shares come with the option of trading for a room in another destination. Ask what other resorts are available.

■ Time-share salespeople get great commissions and are very good at their jobs. Be brave, be strong, and sign on the dotted line only if it's what you really want. Remember there are plenty of good vacation deals out there that require no long-term commitment.

■ Buyer's remorse? If you buy a time-share and want to back out, be aware that most contracts have a five-day "cooling-off period." Ask to see this in writing before you sign the contract; then you can get a full refund if you change your mind.

¢ 🏨 **Vagabundo.** Chamela Bay, 79 km (49 mi) south of Puerto Vallarta, is an excellent place off the gringo trail for swimming, fishing, or exploring nearby islands. Simple rooms surround a swimming pool in this motel-like, quiet, two-story hotel a block from the beach at Punta Pérula. "Bungalows" have separate bedrooms and well-equipped kitchen-dining areas; the latter don't win any beauty contests but do have a table with four chairs, stove, refrigerator, and cooking and serving utensils. The hotel owner speaks excellent English. **Pros:** beautiful Chamela Bay within walking distance; well-stocked kitchenettes. **Cons:** no Internet service; on the highway, not the beach; little charm. ⊠ *Calle Independencia 100, Chamela Bay, Punta Pérula, Jalisco* ✛ *79 km (49 mi) south of Puerto Vallarta, 137 km (85 mi) north of Barra de Navidad* ☎ *315/333–9736* ⤳ *16 rooms, 5 bungalows* ☝ *In-room: a/c, kitchen (some), refrigerator (some), Wi-Fi (some). In-hotel: pool, laundry service* ⊟ *No credit cards* ⊗ *EP* ✛ *6:B3.*

SAN PATRICIO–MELAQUE

San Patricio–Melaque is actually two towns that have met in the middle. Slightly more bustling than nearby Barra, its tourist-related shops and restaurants are interspersed among those catering to the needs its 12,000 residents. Visitors tend to be older and stay longer than those in Barra, which can be reached via a 5-km (3.5-mi) walk along the beach. Modest hotels and reasonably priced vacation rentals predominate.

$$ 🏨 **La Paloma Oceanfront Retreat.** Rates are reasonable considering that the small studio apartments have everything home does. Spacious kitchens come with juicers, blenders, toasters, and coffeemakers in addition to stove and refrigerator; microwaves are available upon request. Four of the units face the long, beautiful bay and sandy beach (where the waves are often good for boogie boarding). You can walk on the beach all the way to Barra de Navidad. Each room is configured differently, but all are bright and cheerful, with private patios and paintings by the owner (she gives lessons in high season). There's a large pool and patio facing the ocean. In high season, there's a one-week minimum stay. **Pros:** beside a beautiful bay; long beach perfect for walking and jogging. **Cons:** one-week minimum stay in high season; pay cash or bank deposit only. ⊠ *Av. Las Cabañas 13, San Patricio–Melaque* ✛ *6 km (4 mi) north of Barra de Navidad* ☎ *315/355–5345* ⊕ *www.lapalomamexico.com* ⤳ *13 studio apartments* ☝ *In-room: a/c, no phone, kitchen, refrigerator, DVD (some), Wi-Fi (some). In-hotel: pool, Internet terminal, Wi-Fi hotspot, parking (free)* ⊟ *Cash only* ⊗ *CP* ✛ *6:D6.*

BARRA DE NAVIDAD

With its two main sandy streets on a skinny sandbar separating Christmas Bay and the open ocean, this casual little town is about three hours south of Vallarta at the southern extreme of Jalisco state. Easy to navigate on foot, Barra is within striking distance of many beautiful beaches which can be visited by car, taxi, or public bus. Hotels are mainly basic, with the exception of the luxurious and snooty Grand Bay Hotel, across the channel.

¢ ⛊ **Hotel Sarabi.** The snug little rooms a block from the beach are indeed a bargain. Those with kitchenettes are still very affordable and have white-tile breakfast bar, four-burner stove, small refrigerator, and plenty of utensils. There's very little difference in the nightly rate between these and those that have air-conditioning but not a kitchenette. For the best deal, opt for a room with a fan only. Two floors of rooms face the small parking lot. Most always on the premises, the owner runs a tight ship and makes sure rooms are clean and well tended. For the cheap price, it's a super bargain. There's Wi-Fi in the sitting room–library and in some of the guest rooms. **Pros:** owner managed; clean and tidy; close to the beach; well priced. **Cons:** no telephone; no Internet station. ⊠ *Av. Veracruz 196, Centro, Barra de Navidad* ☎ *315/355–8223* ⊕ *www. hotelsarabi.com* ↘ *16 rooms, 5 bungalows* ⚒ *In-room: a/c (some), no phone, kitchen (some), refrigerator (some), Wi-Fi (some). In-hotel: parking (free)* ⊟ *No credit cards* ⫾◎⫾ *EP* ✢ *6:D6.*

$ ⛊ **Las Villitas.** Aside from the luxurious and costly Grand Bay Isla Navidad and the behemoth Hotel Alondra, Barra de Navidad has only basic hotels with few rooms, and most aren't a particularly good value compared to similar hotels elsewhere. This hotel with a domed brick ceiling, comfortable beds, and remote-control air-conditioning is among the best choices. The two largest rooms have two twin beds as well as a king, plus a DVD player and a mini-refrigerator. **Pros:** well situated near mom-and-pop groceries and restaurants; right on the beach; discounts Tuesday–Thursday and for six-night stay. **Cons:** basic rooms; no credit cards accepted; no room phones. ⊠ *Calle López de Legazpi 127, Barra de Navidad, Jalisco* ☎ *315/355–5354; 01800/980–7060 toll-free in Mexico* ⊕ *www.lasvillitas.com.mx* ↘ *8 rooms* ⚒ *In-room: a/c, no phone, refrigerator (some), DVD (some), Wi-Fi. In-hotel: beachfront, Wi-Fi hotspot* ⊟ *No credit cards* ⫾◎⫾ *EP* ✢ *6:D6.*

Where to Eat

WORD OF MOUTH

"So many great restaurants, it's difficult, literally hundreds. Be aware that many restaurants here serve TexMex. Real Mexican food can be found at the taco stands and the really economical places. Try El Arrayan for more upscale Mexican."

—cabron

WHERE TO EAT PLANNER

Eating Out Strategy

Where should we eat? With hundreds of PV-area eateries competing for your attention, it may seem like a daunting question. But fret not—we've eaten our way around town on your behalf. The selections here represent the best this destination has to offer—from tacos at street-side stands to five-star haute cuisine. Search "Best Bets" for top recommendations by price, cuisine, and experience. Or find a review quickly in the alphabetical listings.

Orientation

You'll see mapping symbols and coordinates (✛ 3:F2) after property names or reviews; these locate the property on the appropriate map in this chapter. The number after the ✛ symbol indicates which map; the letter and number after the colon indicate the property's location on that map's grid.

Mealtimes

Upon rising, locals start with coffee and *pan dulce* (sweet breads) for *desayuno* (breakfast) at the area's coffee shops and small restaurants. Schedule permitting, Mexicans love to eat a hearty *almuerzo*, or full breakfast, at about 10. The day's main meal, *comida*, is typically between 2 and 5 PM, consisting of soup and/or salad, bread or tortillas, a main dish, side dishes, and dessert. *Cena* (dinner) is lighter; many people just have milk or hot chocolate and a sweet roll or tamales between 8 and 9 PM.

That said, PV is tourist-friendly, and most eateries accommodate travelers with breakfast all day and main meals served from noon until late in the evening. Restaurants have long hours in PV, though seafood shacks on the beach may close by late afternoon or sunset. Outside the resort areas, restaurants may close at 7 or 8 PM. The state of Nayarit is on Mountain Standard Time (an hour earlier than PV), but most restaurants from Punta de Mita south follow Central Time (as in PV). If in doubt, call to confirm what time zone is observed. Unless otherwise noted, restaurants in this guide are open daily for lunch and dinner.

Prices

Avoid paying for water; instead ask for *un vaso con agua* or *agua de garrafón*—either should net you a glass of purified water from the jugs for cooking and rinsing vegetables. Most restaurants offer lunch deals with special menus at great prices. (At more traditional restaurants the lunch menu may not be available before 1 or 1:30 PM.) Some small or casual restaurants accept only cash.

WHAT IT COSTS IN U.S. DOLLARS				
¢	$	$$	$$$	$$$$
RESTAURANTS under $6	$6–$12	$13–$19	$20–$25	over $25

Restaurant prices are for a median main course for the principal meal, usually dinner, excluding tax and service.

Children

Though it's unusual to see children in the dining rooms of Puerto Vallarta's upscale restaurants, dining with youngsters here does not have to mean culinary exile. Many of the restaurants reviewed in this chapter are excellent choices for families and are marked with a ducky symbol ☾.

Reservations

It's possible to get a same-day reservation if your timing's flexible. With a bit of luck it's possible to just show up for dinner, even at the nicest places; go early (6 PM) or late (after 9 PM) and politely inquire about any last-minute vacancies or cancellations. Occasionally, an eatery may ask you to call the day before your scheduled meal to reconfirm; don't forget, or you could lose out. You'll find that except small mom-and-pop establishments, many places provide valet parking at dinner for reasonable rates (often around $2–$3, plus tip).

Tipping and Taxes

In most restaurants, tip the waiter 10%–15%. (To figure out a 10% tip, move the decimal point one place to the left on your total; add half that for 15%.) Some restaurants include a service charge, so only tip more if service has been exceptional. Tip at least $1 per drink at the bar. Never tip the maître d' unless you're out to impress your guests or expect to pay another visit soon. Even in the tonier restaurants, tax is typically already factored in to the cost of individual menu items.

What to Wear

Dining out in Puerto Vallarta tends to be a casual affair—even at some of the more expensive restaurants you're likely to see customers in dressy shorts or jeans. It's extremely rare for PV restaurants to actually require a jacket and tie, but all of the city's more formal establishments appreciate a gentleman who dons a jacket. Let your good judgment be your guide.

In This Chapter

Smoking

The law forbids smoking in enclosed areas, including bars. However, smoking might be still be allowed, especially if there is an outdoor patio. Call ahead to find out a restaurant's policy.

Beer and Spirits

Jalisco is far and away Mexico's most important tequila-producing state, and its green-agave cousin, *raicilla*, is gaining in popularity (though still hard to find). Mexican beers range from light like Corona and Sol to medium-bodied and golden like Pacífico and Bohemia; great darks include Negra Modelo and Indio.

BEST BETS FOR PUERTO VALLARTA DINING

With hundreds of restaurants to choose from, how will you decide where to eat? Fodor's writers and editors have selected their favorite restaurants by price, cuisine, and experience in the Best Bets lists *below*. You can also search by neighborhood—just peruse the following pages to find specific details about a restaurant in the full reviews later in the chapter.

Fodor's Choice ★

Café des Artistes Bistro Gourmet, p. 154
ChocoBanana, p. 173
Daiquiri Dick's, p. 149
El Arrayán, p. 157
El Brujo, p. 167
Frascati, p. 168
La Coleguita, pp. 163, 169
La Ola Rica, p. 172
La Taquiza, p. 163
Trio, p. 161
Vista Grill, p. 153

Best by Price

¢

The Coffee Cup, p. 161
Fredy's Tucan, p. 151
La Taquiza, p. 163

$

ChocoBanana, p. 173
El Brujo, p. 167
La Coleguita, pp. 163, 169

La Playa, p. 171
Mamá Rosa, p. 159
Mariscos 8 Tostadas, p. 159

$$

Archie's Wok, p. 149
Cafe del Mar, p. 171
Frascati, p. 168
La Ola Rica, p. 172

$$$

Barcelona Tapas, p. 154
Daiquiri Dick's, p. 149
El Arrayán, p. 157
La Piazzetta, p. 152

$$$$

Café des Artistes Bistro Gourmet, p. 154
Mark's Bar & Grill, p. 167
Porto Bello, p. 165
Trio, p. 161
Vista Grill, p. 153

Best by Cuisine

AMERICAN

ChocoBanana, p. 173
The Coffee Cup, p. 161
Thierry's Prime Steakhouse, p. 165

CLASSIC MEXICAN

El Arrayán, p. 157

CONTEMPORARY MEXICAN

Los Xitomates, p. 159
Mestizo, p. 160

EUROPEAN

Café des Artistes Bistro Gourmet, p. 154

INTERNATIONAL

Daiquiri Dick's, p. 149
Trio, p. 161

ITALIAN

Frascati, p. 168
La Piazzetta, p. 152

SEAFOOD

El Brujo, p. 167
Langostinos, p. 152
Mariscos 8 Tostadas, p. 159
Mariscos Tino's, p. 170

Best by Experience

BRUNCH

Mamá Rosa, p. 159

CHILD-FRIENDLY

ChocoBanana, p. 173
La Playa, p. 171
Memo's Pancake House, p. 153
Thierry's Prime Steakhouse, p. 165

GREAT VIEW

Hacienda San Angel Gourmet, p. 158
Ikuai, p. 168
Vista Grill, p. 153

LIVE MUSIC WITH DINNER

La Palapa, p. 152

MOST ROMANTIC

Cafe del Mar, p. 171
Café des Artistes Bistro Gourmet, p. 154
Hacienda San Angel Gourmet, p. 158

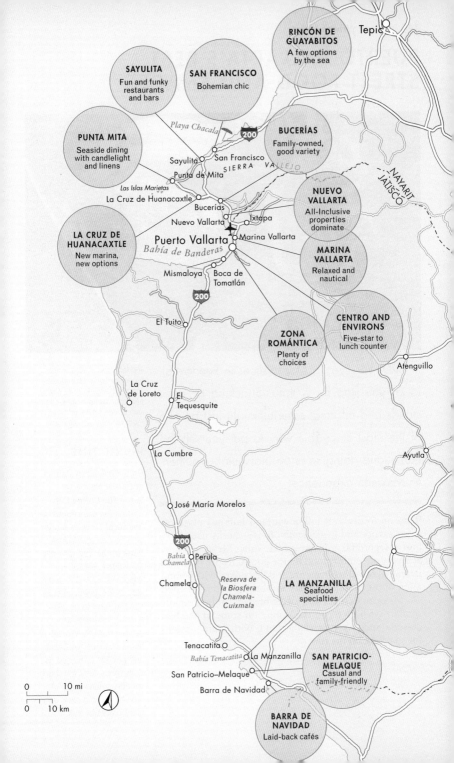

PUERTO VALLARTA'S BEST STREET FOOD AND SNACKS

In New York you go for a slice; in Puerto Vallarta, you stop for a taco. Snacking at street stands and informal eateries might just be one of the most enjoyable way to get yourself fed here—and doing so is an indisputably authentic Mexican experience.

Top left: stop at least once for a beachside taco plate. Top right: helado to go? Sí, por favor. Bottom right: cheap snacks don't have to mean a meal without presentation.

Read on to discover unknown (and famous) places to enjoy savory and hygienic *antojitos*—snacks like tacos, burritos, gorditas, and quesadillas—that Mexicans enjoy as a sort of comfort food on the go. Many are fried and fattening, but other items are griddle-cooked with a minimum of oil, and quesadillas and burritos aren't fried at all. Mexican desserts and sweet breads can be insipidly similar; we'll give you the skinny on some of the best desserts and sweet snacks around, with a few options for snacking on the run.

PICNIC TIME

Grab a box lunch starting at 6 AM at Marina Vallarta's **The Coffee Cup** (✉ *Condominios Puesto del Sol, Local 14-A, at marina* ☎ *322/221-2517*). At **A Page in the Sun** (✉ *Calle Olas Altas 399, Col. E. Zapata* ☎ *322/222-3608*), stop in for American-style comfort food to go, like a turkey and avocado sandwich. At Puerto Vallarta's Los Muertos Beach and bayside at Rincón de Guayabitos, look for beach vendors selling coconut bread, fish on a stick, and giant pieces of fruit.

PV'S BEST STREET FOOD AND SNACKS

Nothing says "Pacific Coast Mexico" like a shrimp taco or a fish burrito, but other "street foods" are equally popular. Step up to these taco carts or tiny storefronts to get a taste of authentic Puerto Vallarta.

In downtown Vallarta, locals love the quesadillas, shredded beef burritos, and tacos at **Tutifruti** (✉ *Allende 200, Centro* ☎ *322/222–1068, closed Sun.*), where you can also get a sandwich, burger, or fruit smoothie. Carmen Porras, owner of El Arrayán, highly recommends **Tacos Chuy** (✉ *Aquiles Serdán near Ignacio L. Vallarta, Col. E. Zapata*), whose owner worked at the Mexico City storefront where *tacos al pastor* (shredded pork tacos), the house specialty, were invented.

If it's seafood tacos you crave, you can't do better than **Mariscos Cisneros** (✉ *Calle Aguacate 271, Col. E. Zapata* ☎ *322/223–3569*), where tasty salsas accompany shrimp-stuffed quesadillas and fat burritos of smoked marlin, octopus, or the catch of the day. From the Hotel Zone, wander a bit to sample authentic Mexico City–style street snacks at **Dona Salúd** (✉ *Berlín 122, Col. Versalles*). Sample quesadillas with mushrooms, *rajas* (sautéed mild peppers), or *gorditas de maiz con piloncillo* (stuffed corn cakes made with brown sugar-laced corn).

In Marina Vallarta, an upscale place to go for snacks and beer is **Tacos & Beer** (✉ *Av. Paseo de la Marina Sur s/n, across from Hotel Mayan Palace* ☎ *322/209–0909*), which sells pizza as well. As you continue north, Bucerías's **Tacos Linda** (✉ *Av. Lázaro Cárdenas s/n at Abasolo,Bucerías* ☎ No phone) occupies a small patio surrounded by hurricane fencing. Watch a telenovela on the overhead TV as you wait for savory meat tacos and other snacks on huge, just-made tortillas. North of Banderas Bay, in little San Pancho (aka San Francisco), the multitudes rave about the fish and shrimp tacos at **Baja Takeria** (✉ Av. Tercer Mundo 70).

SWEET STUFF

The locally owned bakery **Los Chatos** (✉ *Francisco Villa 359, Col. Olímpico* ☎ *322/223–0485,* ⊕ *www.loschatos.com*) sells cakes, tarts, and house-made gelato. For a fresh-fruit water, frozen fruit bar, or ice cream cone, stop in at a **Michoacán** or **Holanda** ice cream shop.

In Sayulita, **Panino's** (✉ *Delfines 1, Sayulita,* ☎ *322/103–3723*) produces good brownies, croissants, and other baked goods. On Bucerías's South Side, a dedicated following snaps up the cinnamon rolls at **Sweet Things Bake Shop** (✉ *Lázaro Cárdenas 64* ☎ *322/278–6960*).

In the Old Town at **Paris Café** (✉ Pino Suarez 158, *Col. E. Zapata* ☎ *322/222–8472*), a gruff and eccentric Frenchman who bakes bare-chested is PV's version of Seinfeld's "soup Nazi." Grab a mini-cheesecake, crunchy chocolate cookie, or soft-center brownie at **Pie in the Sky** (✉ *Lázaro Cárdenas 247, Col. E. Zapata,* ☎ *322/223–8183* ⊕ *www. pieinthesky.com.mx*).

5

PUERTO VALLARTA'S CONTEMPORARY CUISINE SCENE

Outside Mexico City, Puerto Vallarta probably has the most highly distilled concentration of gourmet restaurants in the country. Nowhere is the competition as fierce for vacationers' discretionary dining dollars.

Top left: dine in the open air under Le Kliff's giant palapa. Top right: chefs use the latest techniques. Bottom right: seafood is a popular local ingredient.

Because there are so many inexpensive food options, it's easy to save up to splurge on a truly fabulous meal. Along with the area's famous tequilas and its less-known cousin, raicilla, these wonderful meals may be accompanied by mariachi bands, soothing trios, and magical vistas of the mountains and sea.

To get the most punch for their peso, foodies come in May for the two-week "Restaurant Week" or visit during November's International Gourmet Festival, when dozens of guest chefs bring new recipes and ideas from around the globe. The highest concentration of gourmet restaurants is in Old PV, but as the Riviera Nayarit grows in sophistication, so do the possibilities for fine dining there. In addition to the exclusive restaurants of Punta Mita's Four Seasons and St. Regis resorts, Nayarit State's gourmet stars are San Pancho, Sayulita, and Bucerías.

INTERNATIONAL GOURMET FESTIVAL

Puerto Vallarta's annual gourmet festival (⊕ *www. festivalgourmet.com*) has brought international attention since 1994. During the 10-day food fling each November, chefs from around the world bring new twists on timeless classics. Events include classes and seminars, and restaurants and guest chefs create special menus with wine pairings. Attendees can sample food from otherwise inaccessible restaurants of all-inclusive hotels.

FOOD WITH A VIEW

One thing that sets PV apart from other beach destinations is its magnificent views. Restaurants perched on steep seaside hills provide drop-dead-gorgeous bay views. **Vista Grill** (✉ *Púlpito 377, Col. E. Zapata* ☎ *322/222–3570*) has a large patio with stunning bay views. **Hacienda San Angel** (✉ *Miramar 336, Centro* ☎ *322/222–2692*) has old-fashioned, elegant charm (reservations recommended). South of PV proper, excellent views of the gray-blue mountains beyond the bay are seen from **Blanca Blue** (✉ *Carreterra a Barra, Km 7.5, Playa Garzas Blancas* ☎ *322/176–0700 cell*), which excels at both decor and drinks. You'll find the best views at a series of open-air patios under a huge palapa roof at **Le Kliff** (✉ *Carretera a Barra, Km 17.5* ☎ *322/228–0666*), south of PV. A view of the Nayarit mountains backing the yacht harbor is best from **Ikuri** (✉ *Calle Marlín 39–A* ☎ *329/295–5526 Ext. 106*), at La Cruz's new Marina Riviera Nayarit.

RAICILLA: NEW KID ON THE BLOCK

Traditionally sold in resealed Coca Cola bottles or little plastic jugs, *raicilla*—the cousin of tequila—is becoming fashionable and more accessible. Bartender Cesar Valencia describes the green agave liquor as having a "stronger, smokier, and somewhat burnt aftertaste" compared to tequila. Double-distilled white or aged (*blanco* or *reposado*, respectively) varieties of raicilla can be sipped straight up or in margaritas at Puerto Vallarta's **La Casa del Tequila** (✉ *Calle Morelos 589* ☎ *322/222–2000*).

En route to El Tuito—center of production and distribution of raicilla, about an hour south of PV—**Blanca Blue** (✉ *Carr. a Barra Km. 7.5, Playa Garzas Blancas* ☎ *322/176–0700 cell*) makes a well-received raicilla martini. To learn about the raicilla distillation process, visit **Hacienda El Divisadero** (✉ *Camino Tuito–Chacala, Km 9, El Tuito* ☎ *322/225–2171* ⊕ *www.haciendaeldivisadero.com*).

RESTAURANT WEEK

Puerto Vallarta works its collective tail off during the December to Easter high season. When *vallartenses* can finally take a breath—and then give a collective sigh of relief—they reward themselves with **Restaurant Week** (⊕ *www.virtualvallarta. com/restaurantweek*): super-reasonably priced nights out at the destination's best restaurants. Despite its name, this upscale feeding frenzy lasts two weeks at the end of May. For less money than a Manhattan cab ride you can nosh on seafood, Japanese, Italian, or gourmet Mexican fare. Each of almost 40 participating restaurants offers prix-fixe meals with choices among appetizers, entrées, and desserts for either 179 or 299 pesos.

By Jane
Onstott

First-time travelers come for the sun and sea, but it's PV's wonderful restaurants that create legions of long-term fans. You can pay L.A. prices for perfectly decorated plates but also get fresh-caught fish and hot-off-the-griddle tortillas for scandalously little dough. Enjoy a 300-degree bay view from a cliff-top aerie or bury your toes in the sand, dressed up or completely casual. It's the destination's great variety of venues and cuisine that keeps returning foodies blissfully content.

During the past 30 years, immigrant chefs have expanded the culinary horizons beyond seafood and Mexican fare. You'll find everything from haute cuisine to fish kebabs. Some of the most rewarding culinary experiences are found outside of fancy restaurants and familiar chain eateries at the street-side tacos stalls and neighborhood *fondas,* humble spots serving bowls of chile-laced pozole and seafood-heavy Mexican comfort food.

The trend of the day is restaurant-lounges. Ten years ago, DeSantos (co-owned by the drummer of the Mexican rock band Maná) was the first to combine dining and dancing in a hip new way, with its noisy, ground-floor bar-restaurant and pulsing dance club above. Today DeSantos, Ztai, Mandala, and other lounges provide places to party with the locals beyond their cool and chill dining rooms.

For those who prefer dining alfresco (and wearing flip-flops) to the glamour scene, almost every popular beach has a *palapa* shanty or two selling fish fillets and snacks, sodas, and beer. Some offer the Pacific Coast specialty *pescado sarandeado* (butterflied red snapper rubbed with salt and spices and grilled over a wood fire) or the devilishly simple (and fiery hot) dish *aguachile,* a ceviche salad. The catch of the day may vary, but the white plastic tables and chairs in the sand are permanent fixtures.

RESTAURANT REVIEWS

Listed alphabetically within neighborhoods.

PUERTO VALLARTA

ZONA ROMÁNTICA

Many excellent restaurants are packed into the tourist-heavy neighborhood. As throughout Vallarta, they are mainly casual places where a sundress or a pair of slacks is about as dressed up as most people get. Seafood and Mexican fare are the specialties at taco stands and at the restaurants facing Los Muertos beach. Pizza joints and Italian eateries are also popular, and there are plenty of places for dessert and coffee, too.

$$
ASIAN
✗ **Archie's Wok.** Dishes at this extremely popular pan-Asian restaurant include Thai garlic shrimp, *pancit* (Filipino stir-fry with pasta), and Singapore-style (lightly battered) crispy fish. There are also several vegetarian dishes. The spinach and watercress salad with feta, pecans, and a hibiscus dressing is healthful, refreshing, and perfect for a late lunch (the restaurant opens only after 2 PM). Ceilings are high, and the decor is Asian tropical: dark wood, lacy potted palms, and Indonesian étagères. Thursday through Saturday from 7:30 to 10:30 PM, the soothing harp music of well-known local musician D'Rachel is the perfect accompaniment to your meal. ⊠ *Calle Francisca Rodríguez 130, Col. E. Zapata* ☎ *322/222–0411* ⌲ *Reservations not accepted* ▭ *MC, V* ☉ *Closed Sun. and Sept.* ⊕ *1:C2.*

$
CLASSIC
MEXICAN
✗ **Café de Olla.** Repeat visitors swear by the enchiladas and carne asadas at this earthy restaurant. It's also one of the few places in town where you can get a margarita made of *raicilla* (green-agave firewater as opposed to tequila, which comes from the blue agave) when available. A large tree extends from the dining-room floor through the roof, local artwork adorns the walls, and salsa music often plays in the background. Note that as soon as Café de Olla opens for the season, it fills up and seems to stay full: You may need to wait for a table, especially at breakfast and dinner. If you give up waiting, the taco shop next door is very good. ⊠ *Calle Basilio Badillo 168–A, Col. E. Zapata* ☎ *322/223–1626* ⌲ *Reservations not accepted* ▭ *No credit cards* ☉ *Closed Tues. and Sept. 15–Oct. 15* ⊕ *1:C2.*

$$$
INTERNATIONAL
Fodor's Choice
★
✗ **Daiquiri Dick's.** Locals come over and over for breakfast (the homemade orange-almond granola is great), visitors for the good service and consistent Mexican and world cuisine. The lunch-dinner menu has fabulous appetizers, including superb lobster or shrimp tacos with a drizzle of béchamel sauce and perfect, tangy jumbo-shrimp wontons. On the menu since the restaurant opened almost 30 years ago is Pescado Vallarta, or grilled fish on a stick. The tortilla soup is popular, too. Start with a signature daiquiri; move on to the extensive wine list. The open patio dining room frames a view of Playa Los Muertos, creating a beautiful, simple scene to enjoy while you sip that drink. ⊠ *Av. Olas Altas 314, Col. E. Zapata* ☎ *322/222–0566* ⊕ *www.ddpv.com* ▭ *MC, V* ☉ *Closed Sept. and Tues. May–Aug.* ⊕ *1:C2.*

5

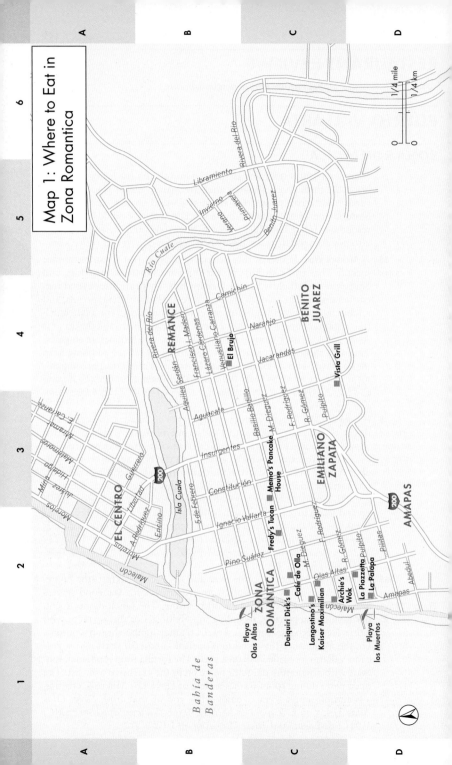

Map 1: Where to Eat in Zona Romantica

Bahía de Banderas

EL CENTRO

ZONA ROMANTICA

REMANCE

BENITO JUAREZ

EMILIANO ZAPATA

AMAPAS

Playa Olas Altas

Playa los Muertos

El Brujo

Vista Grill

Fredy's Tucan

Memo's Pancake House

Daiquiri Dick's

Café de Olla

Langostino's

Kaiser Maximilian

Archie's Wok

La Piazzetta

La Palapa

1/4 mile
1/4 km

Daiquiri Dick's is a casual yet quality favorite in Zona Romántica.

$ **✕ El Brujo.** It's on a noisy street corner, but the seriously good food and
CLASSIC generous portions mean that this is still an expat favorite. The *molca-*
MEXICAN *jete*—a sizzling black pot of tender flank steak, grilled green onion, and
soft white cheese in a delicious homemade sauce of dried red peppers—
is served with a big plate of guacamole, refried beans, and made-at-
the-moment corn or flour tortillas. Try the breaded scallops, stuffed
fish with shrimp and creamy *huitlacoche* (black corn fungus) sauce,
or a grilled skirt steak with mushrooms and bell peppers bathed in
tomato sauce. If you're into simpler fare, the unadorned grilled fish fillet is fresh and delicious, too. ✉ *Venustiano Carranza 510, at Naranjo,
Col. Remance* 🕿 *322/223–2036* ⚒ *Reservations not accepted* 🖃 *MC,
V* ⊘ *Closed 2 wks in late Sept.–early Oct.* ✛ *1:B4.*

¢ **✕ Fredy's Tucan.** Even in low season Fredy's, next door to the Hotel de
CAFÉ Roger, is packed full of Mexican families, gringo friends, and local businesspeople. Your mug of coffee will be refilled without having to beg;
service is brisk, professional, and friendly. Breakfast is the meal of choice,
with pancakes and waffles, Mexican specialties, omelets, and eggs Bene-
dict with thick slices of ham. The lunch menu is abbreviated but offers
plenty of choices for those who enjoy soups, salads, burgers, nachos, and
quesadillas. Eat on the pretty covered patio or inside, where big plate-
glass windows let you keep an eye on busy Calle Basilio Badillo. You can
get a fruit smoothie or a stiff drink from the bar. It closes just before 3
PM. ✉ *Calle Basilio Badillo 245, Col. E. Zapata* 🕿 *322/223–0778* ⚒ *Reservations not accepted* 🖃 *No credit cards* ⊘ *No dinner* ✛ *1:C2.*

$$ **✕ Kaiser Maximilian.** Viennese entrées dominate the menu, which is modi-
EUROPEAN fied each year when the restaurant participates in PV's culinary festival.
One favorite is herb-crusted rack of lamb served with horseradish and

pureed vegetables au gratin; another is venison medallions in chestnut sauce served with braised white cabbage and steamed vegetables. The adjacent café (open 8 AM–midnight) has sandwiches, excellent desserts, and 20 specialty coffees—all of which are also available at the main restaurant. To avoid the stream of street peddlers off the patio, eat in the charming, European-style dining room, where handsome black-and-white-clad servers look right at home amid dark-wood framed mirrors, brightly polished brass, and lace café curtains. ⊠ *Av. Olas Altas 380, Col. E. Zapata* ☎ *322/223–0760* ⊟ *AE, MC, V* ☺ *Closed Sun.* ✦ *1:C2.*

$$$$
INTERNATIONAL

✕ **La Palapa**. This large, welcoming, thatched-roof eatery is open to the breezes of Playa Los Muertos and filled with wicker-covered chandeliers, art-glass fixtures, and lazily rotating ceiling fans. The menu meanders among international dishes with modern presentation: roasted stuffed chicken breast, pork loin, seared yellowfin tuna drizzled in cacao sauce. The seafood enchilada plate is divine. It's pricey, but the beachfront location and, in the evening, the low lights and Latin jazz combo (8 to 11 PM nightly) keep people coming back. Breakfast here (daily after 8 AM) is popular with locals as well as visitors. This is the sister property to Vista Grill, which has great views of the bay from the hills above town. ⊠ *Calle Púlpito 103, Playa Los Muertos, Col. E. Zapata* ☎ *322/222–5225* ⊕ *www.lapalapapv.com* ⊟ *AE, D, MC, V* ✦ *1:D2.*

$$
ITALIAN

✕ **La Piazzetta**. Locals come for the Naples-style pizza, cooked in a brick oven and with a crust that's not too thick, not too thin. There's also great pasta and a good variety of entrées, like salmon with caviar, and lemon and broccoli with fettuccine in cream sauce served piping hot. For appetizers try the tomato-topped bruschetta toasts or steamed mussels with lemon, parsley, and butter. Most folks sit on the large patio; there's also an intimate dining room. The personal attention of the owner, Mimmo Lorusso, guarantees repeat business. It's open 4 PM to midnight. A new location has opened in the residential district behind Costco and the northern hotel zone. ⊠ *Calle Rodolfo Gómez 143 at Av. Olas Altas, Col. E. Zapata* ☎ *322/222–0650* ⊕ *www.lapiazzettapv.com* ⊟ *MC, V* ☺ *Closed Sun. No lunch* ✦ *1:D2.*

$
SEAFOOD

✕ **Langostino's**. Right on the beach just north of the pier at Playa Los Muertos, Langostino's is a great place to start the day with a heaping helping of Mexican rock, cranked up to a respectable volume. For lunch or dinner, the house favorite at this professional and pleasant place is surf and turf (called *mar y tierra*), and the three seafood combos are a good value. The kids can play on the beach while you linger over coffee or suds. ⊠ *Calle Manuel M. Dieguez, at Los Muertos Beach, Col. E. Zapata* ☎ *322/222–0894* ⊟ *Closed Aug. 20 through Sept.* ⊟ *No credit cards* ✦ *1:C2.*

FOOD GLOSSARY

Here are some of the dishes you're likely to find on area menus or in our reviews below. *Buen provecho!*

arrachera: skirt steak.

carne asada: thin cut of flank or tenderloin, grilled or broiled and usually served with grilled onions, beans, rice, and guacamole.

carnitas: bites of steamed, fried pork served with tortillas and a variety of condiments.

chilaquiles: pieces of corn tortillas fried and served with red or green sauce; good ones are crispy, not soggy, and topped with chopped onions and *queso cotija*, a crumbly white cheese.

chile en nogada: a green poblano chili stuffed with a semi-sweet meat mixture and topped with walnut sauce and pomegranate seeds; as Mexico's national dish—the green chili, white sauce, and red seeds

reflect the nation's flag—it is often served in September in honor of Independence Day.

chile relleno: batter-fried green chili (usually mild) stuffed with cheese, seafood, or a sweet meat mixture; served in a mild red sauce. Some health-conscious restaurants make them without batter.

menudo: tripe stew.

pozole: a rich pork- or chicken-based soup studded with hominy (corn kernels) and served alongside a plate of condiments including raw onions, chilies, radishes, cilantro, oregano, sliced cabbage, and tostadas.

tostada: a crispy fried tortilla topped with beans and/or meat, cheese, and finely chopped lettuce or cabbage. May also describe the corn tortilla, which is served with foods like ceviche and pozole.

¢ ✕ **Memo's Pancake House.** Your child will most certainly find something

AMERICAN he or she likes on this Pancake House menu. There are 12 kinds of

🐣 pancakes—including the "Oh Henry," with chocolate bits and peanut butter—and eight kinds of waffles. Other breakfast items include *machaca* (shredded beef) burritos, *chilaquiles*, and eggs Florentine, but these tend to be perfunctory; pancakes and waffles are your best bet. The large dining room bursts with local families on weekends and homesick travelers. It can get noisy, and service tends to slip when Memo is out of town. The draped back patio is pretty, but it's like a greenhouse when the day heats up. The restaurant shuts down at 2 PM. ⊠ *Calle Basilio Badillo 289, Col. E. Zapata* ☎ *322/222–6272* ⏴ *Reservations not accepted* 🟰 *No credit cards* ⊗ *No dinner* ✛ *1:C3.*

$$$ ✕ **Vista Grill.** Sensational views of the sunset and sparkling city-light

INTERNATIONAL panoramas after dark make this one of the best restaurants in PV for

Fodor'sChoice a celebratory toast—of life, love, or the perfect vacation. Dedicated

★ observers can spot whales spouting offshore almost any day during the winter months. An army of attentive waiters brings baskets of delicious, buttery rolls and whisks away plates. Try the stellar crab-and-sea-bass cakes, lobster tacos, or sashimi with truffle-and-soy vinaigrette and avocado coulis. The chef adds new dishes every very weeks; the barman stocks top-of-the-line spirits, and there is a large wine cellar representing several continents. ⊠ *Calle Púlpito 377, near Calle Aguacate, Col. Alta Vista* ☎ *322/222–3570* ⊕ *www.vistagrill.com* ⊟ *MC, V* ⊗ *No lunch* ⊹ *1:C4.*

CENTRO AND ENVIRONS

Comprising the malecón (seawalk) and the half dozen blocks behind it, El Centro has mostly moderately priced hotels—but plenty of upscale restaurants. Parking is limited mainly to streetside; many of the better restaurants offer valet parking. Café des Artistes, Trio, Los Xitomates, and others offer a variety of cuisines and elegant yet casual dining—which is what Puerto Vallarta diners demand. At the other end of the spectrum, downtown PV has a great assortment of bargain eateries, including those offering tacos (in street stands and sit-down restaurants) and diners catering to locals with excellent prices on changing daily specials.

$$$
SPANISH
✕ **Barcelona Tapas.** One of the few places in town with both good food and an excellent bay view, Barcelona Tapas has traditional Spanish tapas like garlicky roasted potatoes, spicy garlic shrimp, and grilled mushrooms. In addition to traditional paella, there's also a seafood-only version. To start you off, attentive waiters bring a free appetizer and delicious homemade bread. The "chef's surprise" six-course tasting menu lets you try soup, salad, and dessert as well as hot and cold tapas. The restaurant is air-conditioned in summer; the rest of the year the windows are taken off to let the breezes in. You pay for that patio view by having to walk up a few dozen stairs. ⊠ *Calle Matamoros at 31 de Octubre, Centro* ☎ *322/222–0510* ⊕ *www.barcelonatapas. net* ⋟ *Reservations essential* ⊟ *AE* ⊹ *2:C4.*

$$$
INTERNATIONAL
Fodor's Choice
★
✕ **Café des Artistes Bistro Gourmet.** Several sleek dining spaces make up the original, downtown restaurant Café des Artistes; the most beautiful and romantic is the courtyard garden with modern sculpture. The main restaurant achieves a contemporary Casablanca feel with glass raindrops and tranquil music. In either area, choose an appetizer, entrée, and dessert from the three-course bistro menu. We recommend the creamy soup of smoked chipotle chilies followed by a fresh fillet of fish cooked in one of several Mexican styles, and finishing with the crème brûlée. Also within these walls, Thierry Blouet's Cocina de Autor (closed Sunday and in September) is a limited-seating restaurant pairing four- to six-course tasting menus with or without wines. Decor is restrained, with a waterfall garden behind plate glass taking center stage. In these restaurants, drinks add significantly to the price of the meal. Many diners end the night at the clubby cigar bar or Constantini Wine Bar, which offers some 50 vintages by the glass as well as distilled spirits, appetizers, and live music most nights of the week. ⊠ *Av. Guadalupe Sánchez*

> ### NATURAL THIRST-BUSTER
>
> The guy on the malecón with a giant gourd and a handful of plastic cups is selling *agua de tuba,* a refreshing, pleasant, yet innocuous drink made from the heart of the coconut palm. It's stored in a gourd container called a *huaje* and served garnished with chopped walnuts and apples.

For a delicious meal with an open-air feel, try Café des Artistes del Mar.

740, Centro ☎ 322/222–3229 ⊕ www.cafedesartistes.com ▭ AE, MC, V ⊗ No lunch ✛ 2:C4.

$$

CLASSIC MEXICAN

✕ **Chez Elena.** Frequented in its heyday by Hollywood luminaries and the who's who of PV, this downtown restaurant still has a loyal following. The casual patio ambience is simple, but the wholesome food is satisfying, and the portions are generous. House specialties include fajitas and Yucatan-style pork. Elena's is also known for an eclectic signature dish, the Indonesian *sate mixto*, skewers of meat and chicken spiced with peanut sauce, as well as its killer handcrafted margaritas and its flaming coffee drinks. ✉ *Calle Matamoros 520, Centro* ☎ *322/222–0161* ▭ *MC, V* ⊗ *Closed June–Sept. No lunch* ✛ *2:B5.*

¢

CLASSIC MEXICAN

✕ **Comedor de Sra. Heladia.** Here you can glimpse the real Old Vallarta. A short but steep walk up from the malecón is this neighborhood dining room, which serves construction workers and locals. It's in a typical one-story Vallarta house of whitewashed brick with a red-tile roof and a burnished-cement floor. The lady of the house serves breakfast from 8 to 11 AM and a limited later meal of two or three entrées, served between 1 and 5 PM. Choices like meatballs in tomato sauce, pork chops, or pig's feet are usually accompanied by rice, beans, homemade salsa, and a basket of hot tortillas. There's no menu, and you'll need to communicate in basic Spanish. ✉ *Calle Aldama at Calle Matamoros, Centro* ☎ *322/223–9612* ♠ *Reservations not accepted* ▭ *No credit cards* ⊗ *Closed Sun. No dinner* ✛ *2:B5.*

$$

MODERN MEXICAN

✕ **El Andariego.** A few blocks past the north end of the malecón is this lively Mexican restaurant. Paintings of the city brighten the walls; at night the lighting is subdued and the mood is family-oriented. Many of the traditional breakfasts are the stick-to-your ribs variety. Lunch

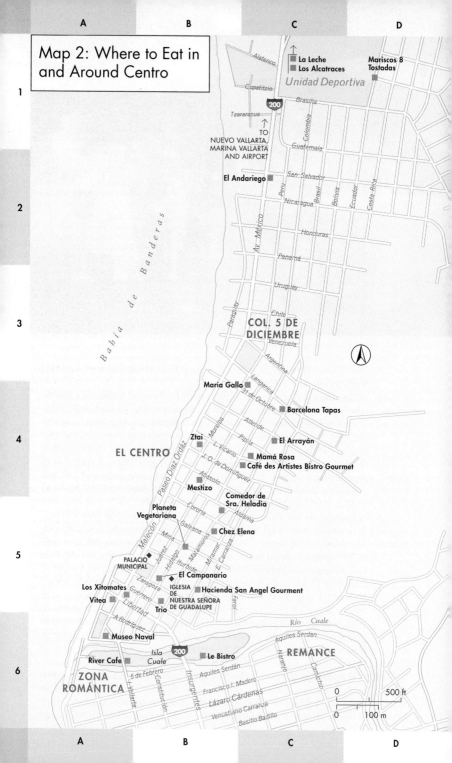

Map 2: Where to Eat in and Around Centro

La Leche
Los Alcatraces

Mariscos 8 Tostadas

Unidad Deportiva

TO
NUEVO VALLARTA,
MARINA VALLARTA
AND AIRPORT

El Andariego

COL. 5 DE DICIEMBRE

Bahía de Banderas

Maria Gallo

Barcelona Tapas

Ztai

El Arrayán

EL CENTRO

Mamá Rosa

Café des Artistes Bistro Gourmet

Mestizo

Comedor de Sra. Heladia

Planeta Vegetariana

Chez Elena

PALACIO MUNICIPAL

El Campanario

Los Xitomates

IGLESIA DE NUESTRA SEÑORA DE GUADALUPE

Hacienda San Angel Gourment

Vitea

Trio

Museo Naval

Río Cuale

REMANCE

River Cafe

Isla Cuale

Le Bistro

ZONA ROMÁNTICA

0   500 ft
0   100 m

Streets
Alatenco, Cupatitzio, Tzararacua, Brasilia, Colombia, Guatemala, San Salvador, Peru, Nicaragua, Brasil, Bolivia, Ecuador, Costa Rica, Honduras, Panamá, Uruguay, Pantopia, Chile, Venezuela, Argentina, Langarica, 31 de Octubre, Allende, Morelos, Pípila, L. Vicario, J. O. de Domínguez, Paseo Díaz Ordáz, Abasolo, Corona, Aldama, Galeana, Mina, Hidalgo, Iturbide, Matamoros, Miramar, E. Carranza, Juárez, Zaragoza, Guerrero, Libertad, A. Rodríguez, Ferol, Malecón, Aquiles Serdán, Naranjo, Camichín, 5 de Febrero, Constitución, V. Vallarta, Insurgentes, Francisco I. Madero, Lázaro Cárdenas, Venustiano Carranza, Basilio Badillo

The dedicated staff at El Arrayan make traditional Mexican dishes seem exotic.

and dinner menus are different, but the cost is about the same. Expect numerous salads, pasta dishes, a good variety of chicken and beef dishes, and seafood and lobster prepared to your taste. Enjoy live music (electric guitar versions of "Proud Mary," or mariachi music) nightly, usually between 6 and 10 PM. There's free wireless Internet in both restaurant and bar. ⊠ *Av. México 1358, at El Salvador, Col. 5 de Diciembre* ☎ *322/222–0916* ⊕ *www.elandariego.com.mx* ⊟ *MC, V* ✛ *2:C2.*

$$
CLASSIC
MEXICAN
Fodor's Choice
★

✕ **El Arrayán.** The oilcloth table covers, enameled tin plates, exposed rafters, and red roof tiles of this patio-restaurant conjure up nostalgia for the quaint Mexican home of less frenetic times. Here you can find the things *Abuelita* (Grandma) still loves to cook, with a few subtle variations. Highlights of classic Mexican dishes from around the country are rib-eye steak served with traditional cactus-pad salad, duck *carnitas* in a glaze of smoky chili and orange, and *cochinita pibil,* a dish from the Yucatan Peninsula of tender pork cooked in a banana leaf and served with black beans and fried plantain. For dessert try caramel flan or a light tamarind-flavored ice. It's a bit pricey for Mexican comfort food, but it has a very dedicated fan club. ⊠ *Calle Allende 344, at Calle Miramar, Centro* ☎ *322/222–7195* ⊕ *www.elarrayan.com.mx* ⊟ *MC, V* ☾ *Closed Tues. No lunch* ✛ *2:C4.*

¢
CLASSIC
MEXICAN

✕ **El Campanario.** Fans swirl the air, doors are open to the street, and cheerful oilcloths cover wooden tables at this no-frills spot across from the cathedral. Egg dishes and chilaquiles are served 9 AM to 11 AM, and an inexpensive daily lunch menu is served 2 PM to 5 PM. For around $5, you get soup, a main dish, a drink, homemade tortillas, and dessert. Office workers come in for takeout or drift in between 6 PM and 10 PM for tacos, *tortas* (Mexican-style sandwiches on crispy white rolls), or pozole. A recipe for the last is given—along with a positive dining review—in a framed *Los Angeles Times* article from the 1980s. ⊠ *Calle Hidalgo 339, Centro* ☎ *322/223–1509* ▤ *No credit cards* ⊘ *Closed Sun. and 5–6* PM ✛ *2:B5.*

$$$$ ✕ **Hacienda San Angel Gourmet.** Even non-mariachi fans are bewitched
INTERNATIONAL by the harmonious musical meanderings of the 12-piece, stunningly uniformed, brass-and-string band that serenades diners most nights from the second-floor terrace overlooking Banderas Bay and the velvet hills of Puerto Vallarta. Ivy climbs blond, hacienda-style columns, and chandeliers bathe in a romantic light the second-floor dining room of this stunningly restored boutique hotel-restaurant. The chef has a restrained hand when it comes to salt and spices; recipes are straightforward yet not bland or boring. Recommended is the red snapper with polenta, tender filet mignon, or *cabrería* (a choice cut of beef on the bone) served on a bed of mashed potatoes and sautéed spinach. You might start with delicately battered and fried calamari served in a cone of crisp nori; for dessert indulge in an ice cream sundae, coconut crème brûlée, or peach crepes. ⊠ *Calle Miramar 336, Centro* ☎ *322/222–2692* ⊕ *www.haciendasanangel.com* ⌂ *Reservations essential* ▤ *AE, MC, V* ⊘ *No lunch* ✛ *2:B3.*

$$$$ ✕ **La Leche.** If chef Alfonso Cadena weren't so cool (he looks like a
INTERNATIONAL refined, former rock star because he is one!), then La Leche's main dining room, an all-white rotunda lined with shelves of milk cans, could come off as gimmicky. But each night as Cadena personally presents a different menu on a chalkboard, his "blank canvas" dining space becomes the perfect backdrop for a unique meal. For instance, a delicate seafood bisque, unveiled in whimsical ceramic tureens, might precede an exquisite mahimahi in a citrus reduction that provides the perfect balance of sweet and sour, rich and refreshing. Servers are attentive and friendly, but there is ample time between courses, so be prepared for an enjoyable but lengthy evening. Reservations aren't required but are a good idea. ⊠ *Blvd. Francisco M. Ascencio, Km 2.5, next to Hotel Fiesta Americana, Zona Hotelera Norte* ☎ *322/293–0900* ⊕ *www. lalecherestaurant.com* ▤ *AE, MC, V* ⊘ *No lunch* ✛ *2:C1.*

$$$ ✕ **Le Bistro.** Start off with a classic tortilla soup or a combo appetizer
INTERNATIONAL plate of guacamole, quesadillas, and nachos before moving on to one of the Mexican or international main dishes: crab enchiladas, chicken-and-squash-blossom crepes, duck with blackberry sauce, or red snapper with red-pepper-studded crust and tequila-lime sauce. The romantic and exotic-looking restaurant is draped in ferns and tropical plants and overlooks the Cuale River; carved-stone columns, zebra chairs, and wicker settees are among the sophisticated touches. Breakfast is no longer served. ⊠ *Isla Río Cuale 16–A* ☎ *322/225–9945* ⊕ *www.lebistro. mx* ▤ *AE, MC, V* ⊘ *Closed Sun. and mid-Aug.–Sept.* ✛ *2:B6.*

$ ✕ **Los Alcatraces.** For a breakfast of chilaquiles that are crisp, not soggy,
CLASSIC come to "The Calla Lilies." *Café de olla,* real Mexican coffee simmered
MEXICAN with cinnamon and *panela* (unrefined brown sugar), is served in a keep-warm carafe; crumbly white cheese is delivered from a ranch in the nearby hills. All meals are economical, especially the combo plate: a quesadilla, chiles rellenos, skirt steak, rice, beans, and a taco. Weekdays, a fixed-price

lunch for under $5 consists of soup, main dish, beans, and a fruit drink. This is a good, authentic-Mexican option for people staying in the Hotel Zone, although adjectives like "charming" and "picturesque" do not apply. ⊠ *Blvd. Francisco M. Ascencio 1808, Col. Olímpica* ☎ 322/222–1182 ▭ *No credit cards* ⊗ *No dinner weekends* ✛ *2:C1.*

$ ✕ **Los Xitomates.** A snug and homey space just a block off the malecón in
MODERN Old PV, this restaurant is named "Red Tomatoes." It was purchased in
MEXICAN 2007 by Javier Fernández Somellera, who first entered its kitchen as a guest chef during PV's Gourmet Festival. Originally from Guadalajara, Somellera studied at Paris's Cordon Bleu and has worked in Seattle, Mexico City, and London restaurants to refine his techniques. Most of the inventive menu—everything from appetizers to entrées—is worth trying, from the seared tuna starter to the tortilla soup to the main courses like Torreón-style steak grilled with green onions and cactus pads or the fresh sea bass with green tomato sauce. There's sometimes a ball game on TV at the intimate bar at the back; tiny tables for two overlook the street on the small second-floor balcony. ⊠ *Calle Morelos 601, Centro* ☎ 3222/222–9434 ⊕ *www.losxitomates.com.mx* ▭ *MC, V* ⊗ *No lunch* ✛ *2:A5.*

$ ✕ **Mamá Rosa.** Locals return over and over for the expansive breakfast
MODERN buffet (served until 2 PM, but freshest before noon) and, in the evening,
MEXICAN for budget gourmet meals. Recommended main dishes include the nut-crusted salmon served on a bed of asparagus and thin sliced potatoes, shrimp medallions in pineapple and chipotle chili sauce, lamb meatballs in red wine sauce, and Mamá Rosa special chicken, stuffed with chorizo and spinach on a bed of beans. Ingredients are reassuringly recognizable but uniquely combined. Presentation is also a work of art, proving that a beautifully designed dish isn't the sole province of restaurants with high prices and small portions. The setting is pleasant but not fancy; upper and lower patios are surrounded by plenty of plants. ⊠ *Calle Leona Vicario 269, Centro* ☎ 322/222–4010 ⊕ *www. mamarosavallarta.com* ▭ *MC, V* ⊗ *Closed Mon. No lunch, no dinner May–mid-Oct.* ✛ *2:C4.*

$$$ ✕ **Maria Gallo.** By day it offers nifty *comida corrida*: set-priced, three-
MEXICAN course menus that change daily. For about five bucks you get a pitcher of freshly made *aqua fresca*, a starter (usually soup or salad), and a choice of half a dozen main courses. Chef-owner Memo Wulff studied at San Francisco's California Culinary Institute, and although his dishes are Mexican, they are not quite business as usual. Recent dishes included calamari in a spicy red sauce (*al diablo*, which means "to the devil"), char-grilled *carne asada*, and pork shank burritos, most served with rice, a puddle of refried black beans, and your choice of rolls or tortillas. After 7 PM the menu switches to *antojitos*: tacos, tostadas, flautas, and other snacking dishes. The ambience is casual, the music is lively and Latino, and the walls are decorated with handmade art projects. ⊠ *Calle Morelos 558, Centro* ☎ 322/223–1193 ▭ *No credit cards* ⊗ *Closed Sun.* ✛ *2:C3.*

$ ✕ **Mariscos 8 Tostadas.** The original Mariscos 8 Tostadas (the other is in
SEAFOOD Marina Vallarta) is located behind Blockbuster Video in the Hotel Zone. It features full seafood plates alongside its ceviches, tacos, and appetizers. The odd menu translations at these restaurants are a clear indication that

the clientele is local. For instance, the tuna sashimi appears as *atún fresco con salsa rasurada*, or "tuna cut thick with shaved sauce." The tuna *is* thicker than that in U.S. sushi houses and is served in a shallow dish with soy sauce, micro-thin cucumber slices, sesame seeds, green onions, chili powder, and lime. The ceviche couldn't be fresher, and portions are more than generous. ✉ *Calle Río Guayaquil 413, at Calle Ecuador, Col. Versalles (Zona Hotelera)* ☎ *322/222–7691* 🚫 *No credit cards* ⊘ *Closed 2 wks in Sept. No dinner* ✛ *2:D1.*

> ## TACO PRIMER
>
> In this region's informal eateries, a taco is generally a diminutive corn tortilla heated on an oiled grill filled with meat, shrimp, or batter-fried fish. If your server asks "*¿Preparadita?*" he or she is asking if you want it with cilantro and onions. Add-your-own condiments are *salsa mexicana* (chopped raw onions, tomatoes, and green chilies), liquidy guacamole made with green *tomatillos* (small green tomatoes), and pickled jalapeño peppers. Some restaurants also feature garnishes of chopped nopal cactus.

$$$
MODERN
MEXICAN ✕ **Mestizo.** Vegetarians can dive into squash-blossom soup, a house salad with goat-cheese croutons, and the tangy coconut-mango-ginger salad. Omnivores feast on grilled goat with cactus, chicken with *huitlacoche* (corn fungus), beef medallions, or red snapper fillet with mild poblano-pepper cream sauce. Traditional ingredients dominate the individual recipes, but they are produced with a lighter touch as well as attention to detail that makes the dishes almost too pretty to devour. The garden setting, under a spreading *arrayán* tree at a restored old home, couldn't be more charming or imbue a more authentic ambience. And the *danzón* music reminiscent of Old Mexico music salons only adds to the New World experience. ✉ *Calle Abasolo 233, Centro* ☎ *322/222–1333* ⊕ *www.mestizovallarta.com* 🚫 *AE, MC, V* ⊘ *Closed Sun. and May–Oct. No lunch* ✛ *2:B4.*

$
VEGETARIAN
🔄 ✕ **Planeta Vegetariana.** Those who stumble upon this hogless heaven can "pig out" on tasty, meatless *carne asada* and a selection of main dishes that changes daily. Choose from at least three healthful yet unexciting main dishes, plus beans, several types of rice, and a soup at this unassuming buffet-only place. Though the selection of overdressed salads is good, the greens tend to be wilted or soggy. A healthful fruit drink, coffee, or tea, and dessert are included in the reasonable price. Eggs are not used; items containing milk products are labeled as such. ✉ *Iturbide 270, Centro* ☎ *322/222–3073* 🚫 *No credit cards* ✛ *2:B5.*

$$$
INTERNATIONAL ✕ **River Cafe.** At night, candles flicker at white-skirted tables with comfortable cushioned chairs, and tiny white lights sparkle in palm trees surrounding the multilevel terrace. This riverside restaurant is recommended for breakfast and for the evening ambience. Attentive waiters serve such international dishes as seafood fettuccine and vegetarian crepes; the wild-mushroom soup and fried calamari with aioli sauce are especially recommended. If you're not into a romantic dinner, belly up to the intimate bar for a drink and—Friday and Saturday evenings—live jazz. (In high season there's live music of various genres nightly.) Breakfast is served daily after 8 AM. ✉ *Isla Río Cuale, Local 4, Centro* ☎ *322/223–0788* ⊕ *www.rivercafe.com.mx* 🚫 *AE, MC, V* ✛ *2:A6.*

$$$ ✕ **Trio.** Conviviality, hominess, and dedication on the parts of chef-own-
INTERNATIONAL ers Bernhard Güth and Ulf Henriksson have made Trio one of Puerto
Fodor's Choice Vallarta's best restaurants—hands down. Fans marvel at the kitchen's
★ ability to deliver perfect meal after perfect meal. Popular demand guar-
antees rack of lamb with fresh mint and, for dessert, the warm chocolate
cake. The kitchen often stays open until nearly midnight, and dur-
ing high season the restaurant opens the back patio, second floor, and
rooftop terrace. Waiters are professional yet unpretentious; either the
sommelier or the maître d' can help you with the wine. But the main
reason to dine here is the consistently fabulous food, which is also a
great value. ⊠ *Calle Guerrero 264, Centro* ☎ *322/222–2196* ▭ *AE,
MC, V* ☉ *No lunch* ✛ *2:B5.*

$$ ✕ **Vitea.** When chefs Bernhard Güth and Ulf Henriksson, of Trio, needed
FRENCH a challenge, they cooked up this delightful seaside bistro. So what if
your legs bump your partner's at the small tables? This will only make it
easier to sneak bites from her plate. The decor of the open, casual venue
is as fresh as the food. Appetizers include the smoked salmon roll with
crème fraîche, or choose from the selection of "small plates" like the
spicy shrimp tempura or the garlic-chili manicotti. Alternately, make a
meal of the bistro's soups, sandwiches, and salads. It's a nice place for
breakfast overlooking the malecón. ⊠ *Libertad 2, north of Cuale River
on the malecón, Centro* ☎ *322/222–8703* ▭ *MC, V* ⊕ *www.viteapv.com*
☉ *Closed 1 wk in late Sept.* ✛ *2:A5.*

$$$ ✕ **Ztai.** Lounge music emanates from the cool, dark, modern interior
INTERNATIONAL and into the appealingly spare outdoor garden shaded by bamboo and
fig trees. The food is quite good, and portions are large. Try the fresh
and oh-so-lightly-fried calamari, the fruity shrimp ceviche, duck tacos,
or the tender filet mignon. Asian flavors spice up the seafood recipes,
while the meat dishes lean toward Continental cuisine. After dinner you
can recline with a cocktail on one of the beds, sofas, or bar stools of
Ztai's upstairs lounge. ⊠ *Calle Morelos 737, Centro* ☎ *322/222–0364*
⊕ *www.ztai.com* ▭ *AE, MC, V* ☉ *No lunch* ✛ *2:B4.*

MARINA VALLARTA

Many of Marina Vallarta's restaurants face the boats at this area's main
attraction: the yacht harbor. Interspersed with shops and storefronts
selling fishing charters and canopy tours, the restaurant scene is easy to
negotiate, with no busy boulevards or rushing traffic. After their meals
diners can take a spin around the marina or look at the shops here or
at Plaza Neptuno, which abuts it. It's also an easy walk to the Hotel
Zone facing the beach, where international brand-name hotels offer
their own fine-dining opportunities.

¢ ✕ **The Coffee Cup.** Early-risers and those heading off on fishing char-
CAFÉ ters will appreciate the daily 5 AM opening time, and closing time isn't
until 10 PM. The café, which is filled with wonderful art for sale, has
fruit smoothies, coffee in many manifestations, and tasty frappes with
Oreo cookie bits or frosting-topped carrot cake. Have a breakfast bagel
(served all day), a wrap, or a generously filled deli sandwich on a kaiser

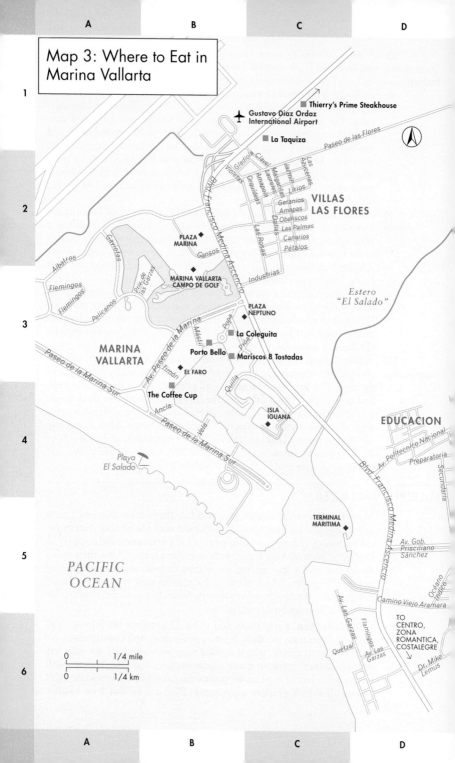

Map 3: Where to Eat in Marina Vallarta

Thierry's Prime Steakhouse

Gustavo Díaz Ordaz
International Airport

La Taquiza

Paseo de las Flores

VILLAS LAS FLORES

Gladiolas
Clavel
Margaritas
Laureles
Amapas
Orquídeas
Violetas
Jazmín
Lirios
Las Azucenas

Geranios
Amapas
Dalias
Obeliscos
Las Palmas
Canarios
Pétalos

Gansos

Industrias

PLAZA MARINA

Albatros

Flemingos

Flemingos

Gaviotas

Pelicanos

Pico de las Garzas

MARINA VALLARTA CAMPO DE GOLF

Las Rosas

Estero "El Salado"

PLAZA NEPTUNO

Popa

La Coleguita

Porto Bello

Mástil

Proa

MARINA VALLARTA

Av. Paseo de la Marina

Paseo de la Marina

Mariscos 8 Tostadas

Timón

EL FARO

The Coffee Cup

Quilla

Ancla

Vela

Paseo de la Marina Sur

Paseo de la Marina Sur

ISLA IGUANA

EDUCACION

Av. Politécnico Nacional

Preparatoria

Secundaria

Playa El Salado

TERMINAL MARITIMA

Bhvd. Francisco Medina Ascencio

Av. Gob. Priciliano Sánchez

Océano Índico

PACIFIC OCEAN

Camino Viejo Aramara

TO CENTRO, ZONA ROMANTICA, COSTALEGRE

Av. Las Garzas

Flamingos

Quetzal

Av. Las Garzas

Dr. Mike Lemus

0   1/4 mile
0   1/4 km

roll (perhaps the roast beef with horseradish, the honey-roasted turkey, or pastrami). Box lunches to go include sandwich, chips, two soft drinks or waters, dessert, and a trail-mix bar. Restaurant patrons can use the inexpensive Internet phone to call the United States or Canada, check e-mail at one of three computers, or sit all day with their laptops to take advantage of the free Wi-Fi. ⊠ *Condominios Puesto del Sol, Local 14–A, at marina, Marina Vallarta* ☎ *322/221–2517* ▭ *MC, V* ✛ *3:B4.*

$ ✕ **La Coleguita.** Just what you needed in the middle of the day: free
MEXICAN tequila shots. Waiters at this super-popular family- and businessperson-oriented restaurant bring a generous serving of tequila to your table soon after you arrive, along with a small bowl of shrimp broth to open the appetite and a basket of crispy tostadas with a few types of fresh salsas. But what really impresses the crowds are the enormous platters of shrimp (breaded, spicy, or sautéed in garlic) served with a small salad and a big scoop of rice. You can order a whole red snapper or a generous fish fillet as well. The ambience at this patio restaurant facing the boats and the marina is casual and festive; the crowd hums with contentment while other restaurants nearby seemingly have been drained of clientele. It's open from 1 PM to 8 PM. ⊠ *Calle Popa s/n, Condominios Marina del Rey, Local 17, Marina Vallarta* ☎ *322/108–9726* ▭ *No credit cards* ▭ *Closed Tues.* ✛ *3:B3.*

¢ ✕ **La Taquiza.** Here's a tip: Stop by this locals den on your way to the
CLASSIC airport (it's just across the street), and get food to go. Hertz, National,
MEXICAN and other rental-car storefronts surround this bright and shiny hole-
Fodor's Choice in-the-wall. You can order food, drop off your rental car, and then
★ get a shuttle to the airport. Or eat in at the brightly polished green Formica tables (with matching chairs). Included in the filling lunch specials, which change daily, are the tasty lime drink (or barley drink or whatever's freshly made that moment), pinto bean soup, and choice of several main dishes. Most dishes are served in or on old-fashioned red pottery plates, bowls, and mugs. By about 5 PM, after breakfast and lunch specials are served, it's strictly tacos, *huaraches* (cornmeal patties topped with meats and condiments), and other grilled meat items called *antojitos.* ⊠ *Blvd. Francisco M. Ascencio 4594, Col. Villa Las Flores* ☎ *322/209–1138* ▭ *No credit cards* ☉ *Closed Sun.* ✛ *3:C1.*

$ ✕ **Mariscos 8 Tostadas.** The odd menu translations at these restaurants
SEAFOOD are a clear indication that the clientele is local. For instance, the tuna sashimi appears as *atún fresco con salsa rasurada,* or "tuna cut thick with shaved sauce." The tuna *is* thicker than that in U.S. sushi houses and is served in a shallow dish with soy sauce, micro-thin cucumber slices, sesame seeds, green onions, chili powder, and lime. The ceviche couldn't be fresher, and portions are more than generous. The most popular venue on the marina is always jammed, yet the waitstaff is efficient and friendly, the music plenty loud and tuned to Bob Marley or perhaps Frank Sinatra. There's a small storefront subsidiary in the parking lot at Plaza Marina; the original venue, behind Blockbuster Video in the Hotel Zone, has full seafood plates alongside its ceviches, tacos, and appetizers. ⊠ *Calle Quilla at Calle Proa, Local 28–29, Marina Vallarta* ☎ *322/209–1508* ▭ *No credit cards* ☉ *No dinner* ✛ *3:B3.*

5

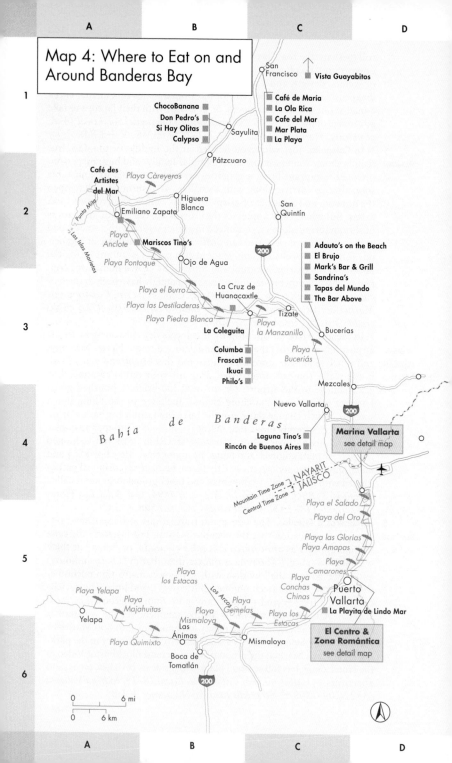

Map 4: Where to Eat on and Around Banderas Bay

San Francisco

Vista Guayabitos

ChocoBanana
Don Pedro's
Si Hay Olitas
Calypso

Sayulita

Café de María
La Ola Rica
Cafe del Mar
Mar Plata
La Playa

Pátzcuaro

Café des Artistes del Mar

Playa Càreyeros

Higuera Blanca

Emiliano Zapata

San Quintín

Punta Mita

Playa Anclote

Las Islas Marietas

Mariscos Tino's

Playa Pontoque

Ojo de Agua

200

Adauto's on the Beach
El Brujo
Mark's Bar & Grill
Sandrina's
Tapas del Mundo
The Bar Above

Playa el Burro

La Cruz de Huanacaxtle

Playa las Destiladeras

Playa Piedra Blanca

Tizate

Playa la Manzanillo

Bucerías

La Coleguita

Columba
Frascati
Ikuai
Philo's

Playa Bucerías

Mezcales

Nuevo Vallarta

200

Bahía   de   Banderas

Marina Vallarta
see detail map

Laguna Tino's
Rincón de Buenos Aires

Mountain Time Zone — NAYARIT
Central Time Zone — JALISCO

Playa el Salado

Playa del Oro

Playa las Glorias
Playa Amapas

Playa los Estacas

Playa Camarones

Playa Yelapa

Playa Majahuitas

Yelapa

Playa Conchas Chinas

Playa Mismaloya

Las Ánimas

Playa Gemelas

Los Arcos

Playa los Estacas

Puerto Vallarta

La Playita de Lindo Mar

El Centro & Zona Romántica
see detail map

Playa Quimixto

Boca de Tomatlán

Mismaloya

200

0   6 mi
0   6 km

$$$
ITALIAN
✕ **Porto Bello.** Yachties, locals, and other return visitors attest that everything on the menu here is good—start with mixed antipasto or fried calamari, and then move on to the signature fusilli with artichokes, olives, and lemons or the sautéed fresh fish with spinach and arugula sauce. And if you're not satisfied, the kitchen will give you something else without quibbling. Undoubtedly that's what makes Marina Vallarta's veteran restaurant one of its most popular. The dining room is diminutive and air-conditioned; the patio overlooking the marina is more elegant, with a chiffon ceiling drape and white ceiling fans. Since there are no lunch specials and the Italian menu is the same at dinner, most folks come in the evening. ⊠ *Condominiums Marina del Sol, Local 7, Marina Vallarta* ☎ *322/221–0003* ⊕ *www.portobellovallarta.com* ▭ *AE, MC, V* ✛ *3:B3.*

$$$
STEAKHOUSE
✕ **Thierry's Prime Steakhouse.** "The emphasis here is on comfort food . . . the type of things I cook for myself at home," says chef-owner Thierry Blouet, who also owns the elegant French restaurant Café des Artistes. Prime rib (the beef is from Texas) and short ribs are the specialties, outshining the rib eye, New York cut, and other carnivorous entrées. Side dishes include lightly dressed salads, the not-to-be-missed green beans or asparagus (whichever looks best at the market), parboiled and grilled to perfection, then doctored with kosher salt and finely chopped nuts. Appetizers include the delicious octopus served on steamed sliced potatoes drizzled with olive oil and dusted with herbs and ground chile piquín. Despite the scale and minimalist decor—walls are painted matte black, low-wattage bulbs dangle from high ceilings, and the walls are nearly devoid of artwork—the space feels comfortable and warm. It's not just for tourists. Mavens with kids take a break from shopping expeditions while businessmen talk turkey in oversize, pick leatherette booths. If parents want to linger over decaf and guava-mango mousse, their kids can paint on a giant cow sculpture or watch videos in the supervised basement playroom. ⊠ *Blvd. Francisco M. Ascencio 2485, Peninsula Mall, Zona Hotelera Norte* ☎ *322/221–1212* ⊕ *www.thierrysprime.com* ▭ *AE, MC, V* ✛ *3:C1.*

SOUTH OF BANDERAS BAY

South of the Zona Romántica, condos, private homes, and hotels line the coast road or perch above the beach. Accessible by boat, beach towns like Las Animas, Quimixto, and Yelapa attract mainly day-trippers who enjoy the tropical beach scene and accept the limited and unoriginal menus of fish, ceviche, or grilled chicken or steak. Yelapa, with its dedicated cadre of seasonal (late fall—winter—early spring) foreign residents, has a broader selection of restaurants above the beach.

$$
INTERNATIONAL
✕ **La Playita de Lindo Mar.** Open to the ocean air, the wood-and-palm-front restaurant looks right at home on Conchas Chinas Beach. And there are wonderful views of waves crashing on or lapping at the shore. Enjoy breakfast or an expansive, inexpensive weekend brunch buffet (it runs 8 AM to 1 PM; come before 11 in the morning for the freshest food). Select from crepes, frittatas, omelets, and *huevos Felix* (eggs scrambled with fried corn tortillas, served with a grilled cactus pad,

beans, and grilled serrano chilies). Lunch and dinner choices include crispy crab tacos, grilled burgers and chicken, shrimp enchiladas with spinach, and much, much more. If you're driving, look for the sign for *Hotel Lindo Mar* on the coast highway; you can park in the small lot near the beach or in the hotel lot and take the elevator down to the beach. ⊠ *Carretera a Barra de Navidad, Km. 2.5, Playa Conchas Chinas, at Hotel Lindo Mar* ☎ *322/221–5511* ⊕ *www.lindomarresort. com* ▭ *MC, V* ⊹ *4:C5.*

RIVIERA NAYARIT

AROUND BANDERAS BAY

Nuevo Vallarta is an all-inclusive destination and therefore has few dining options outside the hotels. To the north, Bucerías has many fine restaurants—some sophisticated, others family-friendly and inexpensive, as well as a few good Italian and French bistros. On the north side of town, a string of beach-facing restaurants offer fresh seafood in a variety of presentations, from regional dishes like *pescado sarandeado* (salt-and-herb-rubbed whole fish cooked over a wood fire) to fresh fillet of fish grilled with plenty of garlic. With its new marina, La Cruz de Huanacaxtle has a small but growing number of good restaurants. At the northern tip of the bay, Punta de Mita offers seafood restaurants facing the sand along with fine dining at the Four Seasons and St. Regis hotels, where reservations for non-guests are strictly required.

BUCERÍAS

$$$

SEAFOOD

✕ **Adauto's on the Beach.** As you walk along the main street, facing the beach on the north side of Bucerías's dry riverbed, waiters from the various seafood establishments will call you "friend" (or more likely "amigo") and try to coax you into their establishments. One of the longest running and most reliable is this one at the south end of the group, just past the main square and dry riverbed. Sit in the street-side dining room facing the sea if you want ceiling fans to swirl the air, or down below on the beach if you're content with a sultry blast of warm, salty air. Watch the pelicans dive for their supper as you munch on fish fillets or shrimp dishes prepared a half dozen different ways, or *pescado sarandeado* (whole fish grilled over a wood fire). ⊠ *Av. del Pacífico 11–A, Bucerias* ☎ *329/298–2790* ⊗ *Closed Mon.* ▭ *MC, V* ⊹ *4:C3.*

$

DESSERT

✕ **The Bar Above.** This little place above Tapas del Mundo defies categorization. It's a martini bar without a bar that also serves varied desserts—the owners prefer a setting that encourages people to come converse with friends rather than hang out like barflies. Order from the day's offerings, maybe molten chocolate soufflé (the signature dish), the cardamom-laced bread pudding, or a charred pineapple bourbon shortcake. Lights are dim, the music is romantic, and there's an eagle's view of the ocean from the rooftop nest. ⊠ *Corner of Av. Mexico and Av. Hidalgo, 2 blocks north of central plaza, Bucerías* ☎ *329/298–1194* ▭ *No credit cards* ⊗ *Closed Sun. and June–Oct. No lunch* ⊹ *4:C3.*

$

CLASSIC
MEXICAN

Fodor's Choice

★

✕ **El Brujo.** This newer Bucerías branch of El Brujo is located right on the beach but with the same food and generous portions of the original location in Puerto Vallarta. The *molcajete*—a sizzling black pot of tender flank steak, grilled green onion, and soft white cheese in a delicious homemade sauce of dried red peppers—is served with a big plate of guacamole, refried beans,

and made-at-the-moment corn or flour tortillas. Try the breaded scallops, stuffed fish with shrimp and creamy *huitlacoche* (black corn fungus) sauce, or a grilled skirt steak with mushrooms and bell peppers bathed in tomato sauce. If you're into simpler fare, the unadorned grilled fish fillet is fresh and delicious, too. ✉ *Av. del Pacífico 202-A, Bucerías* ☎ *329/298–0406* ⚠ *Reservations not accepted* ▭ *MC, V* ☉ *Closed 2 wks late Sept.–early Oct.* ✚ *4:C3.*

$$$

INTERNATIONAL

✕ **Mark's Bar & Grill.** You can dine alone at the polished black-granite bar without feeling too lonely, or catch an important ball game. But seemingly a world away from the bar and (muted) TV is the charming restaurant known for its delightful decor and international cuisine. Both can be appreciated on the back patio, open to the stars, or in the softly lit dining room. Menu standouts include the homemade pizza, the salads, and the macadamia-crusted fresh fish fillets with Thai curry. The lamb is flown in from New Zealand; shrimp comes from San Blas; and the black Angus beef is from Monterrey. Mixed organic lettuces, chives, and basil come from the lady down the street. The restaurant is elegant yet warm and inviting, with a golden glow over everything and, sometimes, roving musicians. More than a dozen wines are offered by the glass. ✉ *Lázaro Cárdenas 56, Bucerías* ☎ *329/298–0303* ⊕ *www. marksbucerias.com* ▭ *MC, V* ☉ *No lunch* ✚ *4:C3.*

$$

MEDITERRANEAN

☺

✕ **Sandrina's.** The walls of this veteran, Canadian-owned restaurant and locals' favorite are covered in colorful paintings: portraits and tropical scenes and still lifes. Columns are adorned with bright broken-tile mosaics. The restaurant opens after 3 PM; it's very pleasant to dine on the back patio at night amid dozens of candles and tiny lights. The menu varies in accomplishment as well as cuisine: On our last visit we sampled tasty lentil soup and a nicely grilled hamburger as well as dry hummus and uninspired tzatziki. There are plenty of other choices, including pizza, salads, pasta dishes, and such Mediterranean fare as chicken souvlaki and Greek-style chicken. Order a liqueur-laced coffee or dessert from the bakery counter. The café at the front has great espresso but is open in high season only, usually December through Easter. ✉ *Av. Lázaro Cárdenas 33, Bucerías* ☎ *329/298–0273* ⊕ *www.sandrinas.com* ▭ *MC, V* ☉ *No lunch. Closed Tues. and 2 wks in Sept.* ✚ *4:C3.*

$

INTERNATIONAL

✕ **Tapas del Mundo.** Here, worldly recipes of this and that are served in small plates perfect for sharing. Sit at the long, U-shaped bar around the open kitchen or at a second table behind it. The cooks, who look like unassuming local girls wearing shorts and T-shirts, produce wonderful daily special dishes with ingredients found fresh that day as well as the restaurant's standards, like shrimp with guajillo chilies served with homemade tortillas, goat cheese with herbs (a small portion), Anaheim chilies stuffed with goat cheese, or Oriental beef strips. Better order a second dish of the delightful breaded green olives—you'll be fighting over them. The owner's one-man stand-up routine can be entertaining or a bit overbearing, depending on your mood. The Bar Above, upstairs, sells desserts, coffee, and mixed drinks. ⊠ *Corner of Av. Mexico and Av. Hidalgo, 2 blocks north of central plaza, Bucerías* ☎ *329/298–1194* ▭ *No credit cards* ☉ *Closed June–Sept. No lunch* ✛ *4:C3.*

LA CRUZ DE HUANACAXTLE

$ ✕ **Columba.** Yearn for manta ray stew? Crave fresh tuna balls? Simply
SEAFOOD   must have shark soup? The recipes here are geared to the local palate; if you're an adventurous eater with a hankering for fresh, strangely prepared (a lot of things are minced beyond recognition) seafood dishes, give Columba a try. It's on the road to the fishermen's beach in Cruz de Huanacaxtle. As a backup plan, have an appetizer here, and then head for one of the other picks in Bucerías or La Cruz. This restaurant closes at 6:30 or 7 PM and serves only beer and sodas as beverages. It has the least expensive lobster around. ⊠ *Calle Marlin 14, at Calle Coral, La Cruz de Huanacaxtle* ☎ *329/295–5055* ▭ *No credit cards* ☉ *Closed Mon.* ✛ *4:C3.*

$$ ✕ **Frascati.** La Cruz is slowly becoming more sophisticated (okay, *gentri-*
ITALIAN   *fied*), and Frascati combines the Old World and the New: It's friendly
Fodor's Choice   and intimate while simultaneously sophisticated. The ambience is mel-
★   low and earthy yet upscale. Wicker-basket light fixtures provide a moody feeling; you get a small but powerful light with which to read the menu. Background music slides between house, electronic, and aerobics-class boom-boom. Choose your pasta (several are house-made) and then one of 12 toppings, including traditionals (such as Bolognese, pesto, four cheeses, and pomodore) or something chef-inspired like the Arturito, a sauce of fresh tomatoes, cream, chicken, and basil. The mixed seafood combo, served in an oversize martini glass, is delish. In addition to lightly battered and deep-fried denizens of the deep, the appetizer comes with batter-fried julienne zucchini and crispy fried parsley. ⊠ *Av. Langosta 10, at Av. Coral, La Cruz de Huanacaxtle* ☎ *329/295–6185* ⊕ *www.frascatilacruz.com* ▭ *AE, MC, V* ☉ *No lunch* ✛ *4:C3.*

$$$ ✕ **Ikuai.** Service is leisurely at the new restaurant in La Cruz's beautiful,
INTERNATIONAL   new yacht club. Luckily, lovely views of the open ocean, the green-blue Nayarit mountains, and the boats in the million-dollar private marina provide an excellent diversion while you wait. The international menu of breakfast, lunch, and dinner items has some Mexican specialties as well. Choose a standard dish like spaghetti carbonara or ricotta and spinach-stuffed ravioli *al pomodoro* (in tomato sauce) or something more exotic. There's pork in a sauce of red fruits, cacao, and coffee, for example, as well as a chilled shrimp curry and watermelon soup, and mango-studded ceviche. The coffee, served in a large ceramic mug, is hot and strong. The restaurant's odd name means "place to eat" in the Huichol language. ⊠ *Calle Marlin 39–A, La Cruz de Huanacaxtle*

☎ *329/295–5526 Ext. 106* ⊕ *www. marinarivieranayarit.com* ═ *MC, V* ☾ *No dinner Sun.–Mon.* ✛ *4:C3.*

$ ✕ **La Coleguita.** This restaurant, an offshoot of the Marina Vallarta original, is on the highway just north of La Cruz de Huanacaxtle, across the road from the entrance to La Manzanilla beach. Waiters bring a generous serving of free tequila to your table soon after you arrive, along with a small bowl of shrimp broth to open the appetite and a basket of crispy tostadas with a few types of fresh salsas. But what really impresses the crowds are the enormous platters of shrimp (breaded, spicy, or sautéed in garlic) served with a small salad and a big scoop of rice. You can order a whole red snapper or a generous fish fillet as well. It's open from 1 PM to 8 PM. ✉ *Carretera Punta de Mita, Km 4, across from the entrance to La Manzanilla beach, La Cruz de Huanacaxtle* ☎ *322/108–9725* ═ *No credit cards* ☾ *Closed Tues.* ✛ *4:B3.*

CLASSIC MEXICAN

Fodor's Choice ★

TACO NIGHTS

Friday through Sunday nights in La Cruz de Huanacaxtle are Taco Nights (6 to 10 or 11 PM). At the home of the Díaz Gómez family (Calle Huachinango, two blocks north of traffic circle), locals and travelers socialize over delicious carne asada tacos or quesadillas with freshly made flour or corn tortillas, excellent homemade salsas, and homemade flan for dessert. Bring your own beer or indulge in rich, cinnamon-kissed *horchata,* a drink made from ground rice, or refreshingly tangy *agua de jamaica,* made from hibiscus flowers.

5

$ ✕ **Philo's.** Ambitious Philo's does it all. It's a fun bar with live rock-country-oldies music Thursday–Saturday after 8:30 PM; a meeting place for local fund-raisers and events; and a community center with a computer, Spanish classes, and a pool table. And if you were wondering, the food is good, too. Options include pizza, sandwiches, burgers, and barbecued chicken and ribs. Philo's special pizza has goat cheese, sun-dried tomatoes, onion, and pineapple—and it delivers (including to boats in the Riviera Nayarit Marina). It's open for breakfast, lunch, and dinner in high season, otherwise dinner only. ✉ *Calle Delfín 16, La Cruz de Huanacaxtle* ☎ *329/295–5068* ⊕ *www.philoslacruz.com* ═ *MC, V* ☾ *May–Oct. closed Sun.–Mon., no lunch.; from Nov.–Apr., closed on Mon.* ✛ *4:C3.*

AMERICAN

NUEVO VALLARTA

$$ ✕ **Laguna Tino's.** Vine-covered trees poke through the roof of the breeze-blessed, covered outdoor eatery overlooking a placid lagoon. The Carvajal family has worked hard to make this Nuevo Vallarta restaurant a local favorite. Tino's is full even midweek, mainly with groups of friends or businesspeople leisurely discussing deals. A multitude of solicitous, efficient waiters proffer green-lipped mussels meunière; shrimp in béchamel-almond sauce with mushrooms, spinach, and bacon; and the regional specialty, fish *sarandeado* (rubbed with herbs and cooked over a wood fire). For something simpler, try shrimp or marlin tacos, or the grilled catch of the day. ✉ *Blvd. Nayarit 393, Nuevo Vallarta* ☎ *322/297–0221* ═ *MC, V* ✛ *4:C4.*

SEAFOOD

$$$ ✕ **Rincón de Buenos Aires.** Restaurants are a hard sell in all-inclusive-dominated Nuevo Vallarta. This one has managed to survive (it was formerly called La Porteña). The setting, an L-shaped covered patio with kids'

ARGENTINE

play equipment in the center, is Mexican, but the food is pure Argentine flavor. Every cut of meat is grilled over mesquite, from the steaks to Angus prime rib. The adventurous yet tasty *chinculinas* (tender tripe appetizers) and chorizo turnovers certainly are authentic. Rice, veggies, and other sides must be ordered separately. Italian dishes and a few non-Argentine things like salmon and chicken dishes are also available. Come for a late lunch (it opens only after 2 PM) or dinner. ⊠ *Blvd. Nayarit 25, Nuevo Vallarta* ✦ *Between highway to Bucerías and El Tigre golf course* ☎ *322/297–4950* ⊟ *AE, MC, V* ☉ *Closed Mon.* ✦ *4:C4.*

PUNTA DE MITA

$$$
INTERNATIONAL

✕ **Café des Artistes del Mar.** A more casual and beachy interpretation of the downtown Puerto Vallarta brand faces the water at the north end of Playa El Anclote. If you sit on the dark-stained deck, you'll have the best view of the ocean, Marietas Islands, and the left arm of Banderas Bay. Portions are petite, but the five-course tasting menu still manages to stuff one silly. Representative courses include a delicious beet-and-goat-cheese appetizer; spinach salad with poached pear and Gorgonzola cheese; salmon carpaccio with lemony scallops tartare; a deliciously tender short rib with pineapple chutney; and, for dessert, vanilla ice cream with mango foam. The soundtrack is sexy Brazilian and other ethnic-tinted jazz, the waitstaff is attentive, and the views are divine. It is attached to the condo-hotel Hotel des Artistes, although separately owned and managed. ⊠ *Av. El Anclote 5, Punta de Mita* ☎ *329/291–5415* ⊕ *www.cafedesartistes.com* ⊟ *MC, V* ☉ *Closed Mon.* ✦ *4:A2.*

$$
SEAFOOD

✕ **Mariscos Tino's.** This casual, open-air branch of Tino's is set on a beach and is hugely popular with locals and tourists alike. Tino's is full even midweek, mainly with groups of friends or businesspeople leisurely discussing deals. The seafood is excellent: Try the ceviche-like *aguachile*, shrimp marinated with lime, tomatoes, chili, onions, cilantro, and cucumber. Don't miss the fish *sarandeado*, a regional specialty of snapper or sea bass rubbed with citrus and herbs and cooked over a wood fire. For non-seafood fans, the chicken fajitas and rib-eye steak are great options. ⊠ *Av. El Anclote 64, El Anclote, Punta Mita* ☎ *329/291–6473* ⊕ *www.tinosvallarta.com* ⊟ *MC, V* ✦ *4:A2.*

NORTH OF BANDERAS BAY

As developers, vacationers, and retirees flock to the area north of Banderas Bay, its restaurants grow in number and sophistication. The exception is Rincón de Guayabitos, designed more for national tourism, where restaurants compete in number if not variety of cuisine or sophistication. Small San Francisco (aka San Pancho) has a number of stylish restaurants as well as a handful of excellent taco and burrito joints. Just a few minutes south, beachy Sayulita caters to surfers on a budget with lots of economical eateries, but also offers enough moderately priced restaurants serving international food to keep its multinational visitors happy.

SAN FRANCISCO

$ × **La Playa.** The owners of La Ola
CLASSIC Rica, just up the street, have opened
MEXICAN this more casual lunch spot right
☕ on the sand of San Pancho's beach,
squeezed between twin headlands.
Sit at a table near the full bar (which
specializes in mojitos) or settle into
a chaise longue closer to the water's
edge. Choose a roast beef or chipotle chicken sandwich, fish-and-chips
(with crunchy wedge-cut fries and
fresh mahimahi), a couple of fish
tacos, or a shrimp tostada. Lively
tropical tunes and lacy coconut
palms complete the idyllic picture.
You can walk off your meal along
the beach or sleep it off on your
plastic, umbrella-shaded chaise.
Behind the restaurant are several

TIME IS OF THE ESSENCE

The state of Nayarit (Nuevo Vallarta and points north, i.e., la
Riviera Nayarit) is in the Mountain
Standard Time zone, while Jalisco
(Marina Vallarta to Barra de Navidad) is on Central Standard Time.
But because tourism in Bucerías
and Nuevo Vallarta has always
been linked to that of Puerto
Vallarta, many Nayarit businesses
run on Jalisco time. When making
dinner reservations or checking
restaurant hours, ask whether
the place runs on *hora de Jalisco*
(Jalisco time) or *hora de Nayarit.*

snug, second-story bungalows with kitchenette for rent. ⊠ *On the beach,
San Francisco* ☎ *311/258–4381* ▭ *No credit cards* ⊙ *Closed Mon. No
dinner* ✛ *4:C1.*

$$ × **Cafe del Mar.** Chefs Eugene of Singapore and Amandine, a Belgian-
INTERNATIONAL Mexican, artfully blend Asian, Mediterranean, and Mexican cuisines
to create a simple but sophisticated menu emphasizing seafood and
chicken dishes. Try the sashimi of the day, Vietnamese spring rolls,
smoked salmon linguini, or green curry chicken with jasmine rice. The
setting itself is open and seductive in an earthy-chic, minimalist, Marin
County sort of way. This is not the place for carnivores (no red meat),
but the kitchen does creative things with fish, shrimp, and chicken
dishes with a light, modern, and Asian touch. Tiny white lights and
soft music accompany individual tables under a bower of purple and
red flowering vines. There's usually a guitarist serenading during Friday
dinner; the restaurant is open for lunch as well. Save room for a coconut
rice dessert with flambéed tropical fruit. ⊠ *Av. China 9, at Calle Asia,
San Francisco* ☎ *311/258–4251* ▭ *No credit cards* ⊙ *Closed Wed. and
Aug.–Sept.* ✛ *4:C1.*

$ × **Café de María.** There are three distinct menus for breakfast, lunch,
CAFÉ and dinner. In the morning order one of an army of different omelets,
a smoothie, or an attractively presented fruit bowl with yogurt. The
lunch menu lunges among the classics: BLTs and burgers, roast beef
sandwiches, spaghetti, and four different salads. Coffee and a scoop
of excellent Blue Bell ice cream or slice of carrot cake are also options.
At dinnertime choose a reasonably priced rib-eye steak, shrimp in
mango or chipotle chili sauce, or a fish fillet. Bathrooms are clean and
pleasant. The two rooms of this renovated former home overlook the
street just a few blocks from the beach. ⊠ *Av. Tercer Mundo at Calle
América Latina, San Francisco* ☎ *311/258–4439* ▭ *No credit cards*

La Ola Rica has a delightfully homey feel.

🕐 *Closed Wed., no dinner Tues. (all year); closed Sept.–mid-Oct. No dinner June–Aug.* ✛ 4:C1.

$$
INTERNATIONAL
Fodor's Choice
★

✕ **La Ola Rica.** One of San Pancho's first upscale restaurants, "The Delicious Wave," has still got it goin'. Small, medium-crust, wood-fired pizzas are just right for an appetizer (we recommend the Brie pizza with caramelized onions) or, with a soup or salad, as a delicious dinner for one. Another good appetizer is the fresh white cheese round served with warm tomato sauce and fresh basil. The margaritas are lovely, and wine by the glass is a generous portion. All of the doe-eyed, wasp-waisted waitresses are relatives of the locally born and raised co-owner, Triny. Eat to the beat of a jazz-dominated sound track: overlooking the street on the covered patio or inside the home-cum-restaurant, artfully decorated with eclectic paintings, photographs of Old Mexico, and saints in niches. Summer hours vary each season, depending on tourist traffic; it's best to call during the off-season to double-check days and hours open. ✉ *Av. Tercer Mundo s/n, San Francisco* ☎ *311/258–4123* 🖶 *MC, V* 🕐 *Closed Sun.; no lunch. Closed Sat.–Wed. June–July. Closed Aug.–Oct.* ✛ 4:C1.

$$$$
CONTINENTAL

✕ **Mar Plata.** Decor is nonchalant yet sophisticated and so, come to think of it, is the waitstaff. Impressive second-story digs have views of the sea as well as a celestial seasoning of stars on the ceiling in the form of tin lamps from Guadalajara. Dark-blue and deep terra-cotta walls juxtapose nicely; the huge space is saved from looking industrial by innovative installations and fixtures. Heavy old wood doors are transformed to tabletops, chairs are mismatched, and floors are poured of untreated cement. Co-owner and chef Amadine Darmstaedter's recipes wed traditional Argentine meats with updated Continental cuisine in a happy transcontinental marriage. Portions are smallish, and entrées exclude sides. There's live music Sunday and occasional flamenco shows or tango classes. ⊠ *Calle de Palmas 130, Col. Costa Azul, San Francisco* ☎ *311/258–4424* ⊕ *www.marplata.com.mx* ⊟ *MC, V* ⊙ *Closed Mon. and June–Sept. No lunch* ✛ *4:C1.*

SAYULITA

$$ ✕ **Calypso.** This second-story restaurant overlooks the town plaza from
ECLECTIC beneath an enormous palapa roof. Locals rave about the deep-fried calamari served with spicy cocktail and tangy tartar sauces; it's an appetizer that's large enough for several people to share. Portions in general are very generous. There are good pasta dishes, including the house special with basil and sun-dried tomatoes. The Cobb salad has tons of blue cheese; the Caesar and Chinese-chicken salads are also highly recommended. Really you can get everything from a burger and fries to fajitas, enchiladas, or shrimp scampi with fettuccini. The menu is varied and the food reasonably priced. You can pay by credit card only if the bill totals 250 pesos or more. ⊠ *Av. Revolución 44, across from plaza, Sayulita* ☎ *329/291–3704* ⊟ *MC, V* ⊙ *No lunch* ✛ *4:B1.*

$ ✕ **ChocoBanana.** One of Sayulita's pioneer restaurants has really gotten
AMERICAN spiffy, adding tile mosaic accents and generally beautifying its terrace
Fodor's Choice restaurant. The Wi-Fi doesn't hurt, either. BLTs and burgers, omelets and
★ bagels, chicken with rice, and chai tea are some of what you'll find here.
Ⓒ They also have a good selection of vegetarian dishes. Service isn't fast, in keeping with laid-back Sayulita's surfer attitude. This perennial favorite catercorner from the main square is almost always full of people eating and loafing; there's a kids' menu for the truly young. It closes at 6 PM (2 PM on Sunday). ⊠ *Calle Revolución at Calle Delfín, on plaza, Sayulita* ☎ *329/291–3051* ⊟ *No credit cards* ⊙ *No dinner Sun.* ✛ *4:B1.*

$$ ✕ **Don Pedro's.** Sayulita institution Don Pedro's has wonderful pizzas
INTERNATIONAL baked in a wood-fire oven, prepared by European-trained chef and co-owner Nicholas Parrillo. Also on the menu are consistently reliable seafood dishes, yummy Niçoise salad, and tapenade. The mesquite-grilled filet mignon is just about the best around; it comes with baby vegetables, mashed potatoes, and pita bread. The pretty second-floor dining room, with the better view, is open when the bottom floor fills up, usually during the high season (November to May). During high season they also have dance classes and dancing to Latin tunes, currently on Monday, and live flamenco guitar on Thursday. This is a good spot for breakfast, too, after 8 AM. ⊠ *Calle Marlin 2, at beach, Sayulita* ☎ *329/291–3090* ⊕ *www.donpedros.com* ⊟ *MC, V* ⊙ *Closed Sept.* ✛ *4:B1.*

$ ✕ **Si Hay Olitas.** This simply decorated, open-front restaurant near tiny
CLASSIC Sayulita's main plaza is the one most often recommended by locals
MEXICAN for dependable Mexican and American fare. Order a giant burrito,
Ⓒ

Sayulita's ChocoBanana has become so much more than just vaguely suggestive banana treats.

vegetarian platter, burger, grilled chicken, or a seafood combo. There's a little of everything to choose from, and it's open for breakfast. The setting is casual, and the menu has plenty of things that children will like. ✉ *Av. Revolución 33, Sayulita* ☎ *329/291–3203* ▭ *No credit cards* ✛ *4:B1.*

RINCON DE GUAYABITOS

$$
CLASSIC
MEXICAN

✕ **Vista Guayabitos.** Portions are large, and the cooking seems to have improved with time, although the main reason to visit is the lovely views of a solitary beach, uninhabited Coral Island, and the beaches of Rincón de Guayabitos. The hawk's-eye ocean view is especially wonderful around sunset. Order a full Mexican meal or just a shrimp or fish taco and a beer or cocktail. Changing daily specials like ribs, mashed potatoes, and corn on the cob, with a glass of wine or beer, are filling if unimaginative. Shrimp is prepared in a handful of ways; for kids there are hamburgers (or shrimp burgers) and fries or quesadillas. Food service begins at noon, although the stated opening time is 11:30 AM. ✉ *Carretera a Los Ayala, Km 1.5, Rincón de Guayabitos* ☎ *327/274–2589* ⊕ *www.vistaguayabitos.com* ▭ *MC, V* ✛ *4:C1.*

> ### KNOW YOUR TORTILLAS
>
> In Mexico, most tortillas are made of milled cornmeal. They are flattened into thin disks, griddle cooked, and served with just about every dish. Flour tortillas are a specialty of northern Mexico and are typically offered only with certain dishes, like *queso fundido* (cheese fondue).

COSTALEGRE

BARRA DE NAVIDAD

Barra de Navidad is a funky little town catering to lovers of casual Mexico. Its restaurants are similarly informal, offering smoothies and homemade muffins and banana bread or other generally healthful, unsophisticated fare. Beach- and lagoon-facing restaurants offer up similar menus featuring grilled mahimahi served with rice and veggies. Across its lagoon, seaside shanties are the place to go for an afternoon idyll of sand, sea, ceviche, and cold beer.

$$ ✕ **Ambar Del Mare.** A French chef from Provence brings a welcome addition to Barra's circumspect culinary scene, along with good thin-crust pizzas, escargots, crepes, and other tasty French and Italian fare. Of the many pasta dishes, the lasagna, cannelloni, and ravioli use pasta made from scratch. The restaurant's compact size and good tunes, along with the small bar in the middle and the few tables looking out over the beach, give it a bistro feel. ⊠ *Calle López de Legazpi 158, by Hotel Alondra, Barra de Navidad* ☎ *315/355–8169* ▭ *No credit cards* ⊗ *Closed May–Nov. No lunch.*

CONTINENTAL

¢ ✕ **Casa de la Abuela.** The amiable and service-oriented owner makes this one of the town's top choices for breakfast, snacks, or a light lunch. Service isn't particularly swift, but while you wait for your meal you can enjoy listening to an eclectic selection of Latin and American rock and jazz on the great sound system. Take your time as you sip cappuccino and munch on the assortment of delightful, authentically Mexican homemade cookies that comes with it. Refills of the good American-style coffee are given ungrudgingly. Besides smoothies, fresh juices, omelets, chilaquiles, and other breakfast food, Miguel and his family serve snacks like guacamole and chips, and burgers and fries for lunch. ⊠ *Av. Miguel López de Legazpi 150, Barra de Navidad* ☎ *No phone* ▭ *No credit cards* ⊗ *Closed Mon. No dinner.*

AMERICAN

LA MANZANILLA

La Manzanilla and other beachfront towns on Bahías Tenacatita and Chamela have dozens of seaside *ramadas*: palm-frond-covered eateries under which white plastic tables and chairs face the water. Offerings range from enchiladas and chiles rellenos to ceviche and the local dish aguachile which, like ceviche, is seafood (usually shrimp) "cooked" in lime juice and seasoned with very hot peppers. While still not terribly cosmopolitan, La Manzanilla offers the widest selection of eateries.

$ ✕ **Martin's.** This second-floor, palapa-roof restaurant is the most reliable in town for food and good cheer, and for hours of operation, too, as it's open year-round. There are Mexican- and American-style breakfasts, fajitas and shrimp for lunch and dinner, and sporadic serenades. This is as much a place for socializing as for eating; at the bar you can quaff champagne, cognac, martinis, or wine. There's usually live jazz, flamenco, or Latin music from 8 PM to midnight on Monday in high sea-

CLASSIC
MEXICAN

son. ⊠ *Calle Playa Blanco 70, La Manzanilla* ☎ *315/351–5106* ▭ *No credit cards* ⊘ *Closed Tues. Apr.–mid-Dec., and Sept. 19–Oct. 1.*

SAN PATRICIO–MELAQUE

Like neighboring Barra de Navidad, San Patricio–Melaque faces Christmas Bay (Bahía de Navidad) and has plenty of seafood eateries facing the sand. (Those who want to burn a few calories can walk along the beach to eat at Barra's restaurants . . . or vice versa.) Surrounding the square are informal taco and sandwich shops as well as storefronts selling ice cream and groceries, which could be purchased for a picnic under one of the palm-thatch shade umbrellas for rent on the beach. A few more sophisticated and international restaurants, such as Canadian-owned Maya, enliven the dining scene during the winter season.

¢   ✕ **Cenaduría Flor Morena**. Some folks say the enchiladas here are the best
MEXICAN   they've ever eaten. And others call this place a "local institution." Everyone pretty much agrees that this hole-in-the-wall with scarred tables and walls is the best place around to get good, inexpensive pozole, tamales, and tacos. Facing the main square, it's a small, one-room restaurant surrounded by pharmacies, ice cream shops, and mom-and-pop grocery stores. As its name implies, it's a place to eat dinner. ⊠ *Facing main plaza below Catscan bar, San Patricio–Melaque* ☎ *No phone* ▭ *No credit cards* ⊘ *Closed Mon.–Tues. No lunch.*

$ ✕ **El Dorado**. This is the best place in town for seafood; the ocean view
SEAFOOD   from under the tall, peaked palapa roof isn't bad either. In addition to the garlic-and-oil fish fillets and breaded shrimp, there's grilled chicken with baked potato, beef tips with rice and beans, soups, quesadillas, steak, great guacamole, and fries. It's open all day (8 AM until 10 PM) and serves everyone from white-collar business types to families and friends meeting for lunch to tourists cleaned up for an evening out. Popular with local families, business people, and travelers, it's a simple and unadorned but large restaurant facing Christmas Bay. After your meal, kick your shoes off and take a walk on the beach. ⊠ *Calle Gómez Farias 1, San Patricio–Melaque* ☎ *315/355–5239* ▭ *MC, V.*

$$ ✕ **Maya**. Two Canadian women have teamed up to bring sophistication
INTERNATIONAL   to San Patricio–Melaque's dining scene. East meets West in contemporary dishes such as tequila-lime prawns and corn, and Gouda-cheese fritters with a smoked jalapeño aioli. Favorite entrées include Szechuan prawns and prosciutto-wrapped chicken. The hours of operation are complex and subject to change; it's best to check the Web site or confirm by phone. There's often live music including jazz or blues. ⊠ *Calle Alvaro Obregón 1, Villa Obregón, San Patricio–Melaque* ☎ *315/102–0775 cell* ⊕ *www.restaurantmaya.com* ▭ *No credit cards* ⊘ *Closed Sun.–Mon. and mid-May–Oct. No lunch.*

Shopping

WORD OF MOUTH

"Get street maps and just take a walk around, it's an easy town to explore on your own. Lots of galleries, shops (both tourist and local), arts and crafts, tile factory, etc."

—suze

It's hard to decide which is more satisfying: shopping in Puerto Vallarta, or feasting at its glorious restaurants. There are enough of both to keep a bon vivant busy for weeks. But while gourmands return home with enlarged waistlines, gluttonous shoppers need an extra suitcase for the material booty they bring home.

Puerto Vallarta's highest concentration of shops and restaurants shares the same prime real estate: Old Vallarta. But as construction of hotels, time-shares, condos, and private mansions marches implacably north up the bay, new specialty stores and gourmet groceries follow the gravy train. To the south, the Costalegre is made up primarily of modest seaside towns and self-contained luxury resorts, and shopping opportunities are rare.

More than a half-dozen malls line "the airport road," Boulevard Francisco M. Ascencio, which connects downtown with the Hotel Zone and Marina Vallarta. There you'll find folk art, resort clothing, and home furnishing stores amid supermarkets, and in some cases bars, movie theaters, and banks.

A 15% value added tax (locally called IVA, officially the *impuesto al valor agregado*) is levied on most larger purchases. (Note that it's often included in the price, and it's usually disregarded entirely by market vendors.) As a foreign visitor, you can reclaim this 15% by filling out paperwork at a kiosk in the Puerto Vallarta airport and other major airports around the country. That said, most visitors find the system tedious and unrewarding and avoid it altogether. You must make purchases at approved stores and businesses, and your merchandise must total $115 or more. Even if you plan to pay with cash or a debit card, you must present a credit card at the time of purchase and obtain a receipt and an official refund form from the merchant. Tax paid on meals and lodgings won't be refunded.

SMART SOUVENIRS

ARTS AND CRAFTS

Puerto Vallarta is an arts and crafts paradise, particularly if you're fond of ceramics, masks, fine art, and Huichol folk art. Indeed, there are several shops in and around Puerto Vallarta that specialize in or carry a good selection of Huichol works, including Galería Tanana, Peyote People, the Huichol Collection, and Hikuri. A few shops sell stunning pieces of Huichol beaded jewelry (⇨ *"The Art of the Huichol," below)*. You'll also find stylish clothing and better-than-average bathing suits; vivid handwoven and embroidered textiles from Oaxaca and Chiapas; and comfortable, family-size hammocks from Yucatán State. Handmade or silk-screened, blank greeting cards make inexpensive and lovely framed prints.

GLASS AND PEWTER

Glassblowing and pewter were introduced by the Spanish. A wide range of decorative and utilitarian pewter items are produced in the area. The glassware selection includes distinctive deep-blue goblets and chunky, emerald-green-rimmed drinking glasses. All are excellent buys, although breakable and heavy to ship.

JEWELRY

Many PV shop owners travel extensively during the summer months to procure silver jewelry from Taxco, north of Acapulco *(for more information ⇨ see "One Man's Metal").*

POTTERY

After Guadalajara and its satellite towns Tlaquepaque and Tonalá—which produce ceramics made using patterns and colors hundreds of years old—Puerto Vallarta is the best place in the region to buy pottery, and at reasonable prices. PV shops also sell Talavera (regular or tin-glazed majolica) pottery from Puebla and Tlaxcala.

UNUSUAL GIFTS

For less-than-obvious souvenirs, go traditional and consider a *molinillo*, a carved wooden beater for frothing hot chocolate; you can find these at street vendors or traditional markets for about $1.50. A set of 10 or so *tiras de papel* (string of colored tissue-paper flags) in a gift shop will set you back only about $2. Handmade huaraches, or traditional sandals, are hard to break in (get them wet and let them dry on your feet), but they last for years.

6

TIPS AND TRICKS

Better deals are often given to cash customers—even though credit cards are nearly always accepted—because stores must pay a commission to the credit-card companies. You may have to pay an additional 5% or more on credit-card purchases. U.S. dollars are almost universally accepted, although most shops pay a lower exchange rate than a bank (or ATM) or *casa de cambio* (money exchange).

Bargaining is expected in markets and by beach vendors, who may ask as much as two or three times their bottom line. Occasionally an itinerant vendor will ask for the real value of the item, putting the energetic haggler into the awkward position of offering far too little. One vendor says he asks *norteamericanos* "for twice the asking price, since they always want to haggle." The trick is to know an item's true worth by comparison shopping. It's not common to bargain for already inexpensive trinkets like key chains or quartz-and-bead necklaces or bracelets.

Shop early. Though prices in shops are fixed, smaller shops may be willing to bargain if they're really keen to make a sale. Anyone even slightly superstitious considers the first sale of the day to be good luck, an auspicious start to the day. If your purchase would get the seller's day started on the right foot, you might just get a super deal.

> **WALKING AND GAWKING**
>
> On Wednesday evenings during high season (November–April), the PV art community hosts Old Town artWalk (⇨ *Chapter 1*). Participating galleries welcome lookie-loos as well as serious browsers between 6 PM and 10 PM; most provide at least a cocktail. Look for signs in the windows of participating galleries, or pick up a map at any of them ahead of time. There's a smaller version in Bucerías on Thursday evenings at a few galleries on Avenida Lázaro Cárdenas near Calle Galeana.

HOURS OF OPERATION

Most stores are open daily 10–8 or even later in high season. A few close for siesta at 1 PM or 2 PM, then reopen at 4 PM. Fewer than half of PV's shops close on Sunday; those that do usually close up by 2 or 3 on Saturday afternoon as well. Many shops close altogether during the low season (August or September through mid-October). We've noted this whenever possible; however, some shops simply close up for several weeks if things get excruciatingly slow. In any case, low-season hours are usually reduced, so call ahead during that time of year.

WATCH OUT Watch that your credit card goes through the machine only once, so that no duplicates of your slip are made. If there's an error and a new slip needs to be drawn up, make sure the original is destroyed. Another scam is to ask you to wait while the clerk runs next door ostensibly to use another business's phone or to verify your number—but really to make extra copies. Don't let your card leave a store without you. While these scams aren't common in Puerto Vallarta and we don't advocate excessive mistrust, taking certain precautions doesn't hurt.

Don't buy items made from tortoiseshell or any sea turtle products—it's illegal (Mexico's turtle species are endangered or threatened, and these items aren't allowed into the United States, Canada, or the United Kingdom anyway). Cowboy boots, hats, and sandals made from the leather of endangered species such as crocodiles may also be taken from you at customs, as will birds (such as squawking parrots) or stuffed iguanas. Both the U.S. and Mexican governments also have strict laws and guidelines about the import-export of antiquities. Check with customs beforehand if you plan to buy anything unusual or particularly valuable.

Galeria Dante is one of the largest fine art galleries in Puerto Vallarta and shows mainly paintings and sculptures.

Although Cuban cigars are readily available, American visitors aren't allowed to bring them into the United States and will have to enjoy them while in Mexico. However, Mexico produces some fine cigars from tobacco grown in Veracruz. Mexican cigars without the correct Mexican seals on the individual cigars and on the box may be confiscated.

PUERTO VALLARTA

ZONA ROMÁNTICA

ART

Fodor's Choice
★

Galleria Dante. Classical, contemporary, and abstract works are displayed and sold in this 6,000-square-foot gallery—PV's largest—and sculpture garden. Check out the marvelous large-format paintings of indigenous people in regional costumes by Juana Cortez Salazar, whimsical statues by Guillermo Gómez, and the startlingly realistic paintings of nature by James Knowles along with the work of nearly 50 other talented artists. ⊠ *Calle Basilio Badillo 269, Col. E. Zapata* ☎ *322/222–2477.*

BOOKS AND PERIODICALS

A Page in the Sun. Folks read books they've bought or traded at this outdoor café, and there are almost always people playing chess. The large selection of tomes is organized according to genre and then alphabetized by author. ⊠ *Calle Olas Altas 399, Col. E. Zapata* ☎ *322/222–3608.*

Chocoholics beware: it's hard to resist chocolates by Xocodiva.

CANDY

Fodor'sChoice ★ **Xocodiva.** Exquisite truffles and molded chocolates are all stylishly arranged on immaculate glass shelves at this classic Canadian chocolatier. The chocolate itself is European; among the different mousse fillings are some New World ingredients, including lime, coconut, cinnamon, Kahlúa, espresso, and a few dozen more. Stop by after dinner for a fab dessert; it's open until 10 PM. During holidays, out come the molded Santas or Day of the Dead skulls, some packaged as pretty gifts. ⊠ *Calle Rodolfo Gómez 118, Col. E. Zapata* ✛ *Between Calle Amapas and Calle Olas Altas* ☎ *322/113–0352* ⊕ *www.xocodiva.com* ☾ *Closed Sun. and some evenings July–early Oct.*

CERAMICS, POTTERY, AND TILE

★ **Mundo de Azulejos.** Buy machine- or handmade tiles starting at about $1 each at this large shop. You can get mosaic tile scenes (or order your own design), a place setting for eight, hand-painted sinks, or any number of soap dishes, cups, saucers, plates, or doodads. Around the corner and run by family members, Mundo de Cristal (⇨ *below*) has more plates and tableware in the same style. ⊠ *Av. Venustiano Carranza 374, Col. E. Zapata* ☎ *322/222–2675* ⊕ *www.talavera-tile.com.*

Talavera Etc. Buy reproductions of tiles from Puebla churches and small gift items or choose made-to-order pieces from the catalog. Note that hours are 10 to 3 only, and it's closed during lunch. ⊠ *Av. Ignacio L. Vallarta 266, Col. E. Zapata* ☎ *322/222–4100* ☾ *Open 10–3; closed lunch, Sun., two weeks in Sept.*

SHOPPING IN SPANISH

bakery: *panadería*

bookseller: *librería*

butcher shop: *carnicería*

candy store: *dulcería* (often sells piñatas)

florist: *florería*

furniture store: *mueblería*

grocery store: *abarrotes*

hardware store: *ferretería*

health-food store: *tienda naturista*

ice cream parlor: *heladería*

jewelry store: *joyería*

market: *mercado*

notions store: *mercería*

shoe store: *zapatería*

stationery store: *papelería*

tobacconist: *tabaquería*

toy store: *juguetería*

undergarment store: *bonetería*

CLOTHING

Etnica Boutique. This shop has a well-edited collection of cotton and linen dresses, shawls, purses, hats, sandals, and jewelry. A few items from Indonesia are mixed in with things from different regions of Mexico and Central America. ⊠ *Av. Olas Altas 388, Col. E. Zapata* ☎ *322/222–6763.*

★ **La Bohemia.** Some of the elegant clothing sold here was designed by the equally elegant owner, Toody. You'll find unique jewelry, accessories, and the San Miguel shoe—the elegant yet comfortable footwear designed for walking on cobblestone streets like those of San Miguel and Puerto Vallarta. ⊠ *Calle Constitución, at Calle Basilio Badillo, Col. E. Zapata* ☎ *322/222–3164* ⊠ *Plaza Neptuno, Av. Francisco M. Ascencio, Km 7.5, Marina Vallarta* ☎ *322/221–2160* ⊗ *Closed Sun. (both branches).*

Myskova Beachwear Boutique. Myskova has its own extensive line of sexy bikinis, plus cover-ups, nylon slacks, and some items for children (sunglasses, bathing suits, flip-flops). There's a small line of jewelry, and Brazilian flip-flops for adults in a rainbow of colors. The shop is open daily until 10 PM. ⊠ *Calle Basilio Badillo 278, Col. E. Zapata* ☎ *322/222–6091.*

Rebeca's. You can browse through its large selection of beachwear daily until late. Look for shorts, pseudo-Speedos, and bathing trunks for men, and sandals, fashionable flip-flops, attractive tankinis, lots of bikinis, and a few one-piece suits

TRUE MEXICAN TALAVERA

Talavera ceramics are named for the Spanish town where the style originated; indigenous artisans in the New World added rust, green, black, and ochre to the original blue-and-white palate. Authentic Mexican Talavera is produced in Puebla and parts of Tlaxcala and Guanajuato. The glazing process follows centuries-old "recipes." Look on the back or bottom of the piece for the factory name and state of origin. Manufacturers throughout Mexico produce Talavera-style pieces, which should sell for much less.

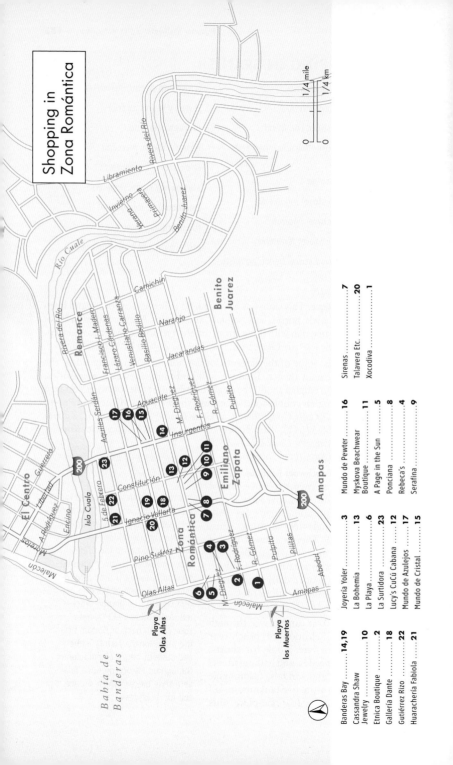

Shopping in Zona Romántica

Bahía de
Banderas

1/4 mile
1/4 km

Beaded figurines decorated with colorful Huichol symbols are practically de rigeur on any first timer's shopping list.

for women. Most of the goods are manufactured in Mexico. ⊠ *Olas Altas 403, Col. E. Zapata* ☎ *322/222–2320.*

Serafina. This is the place to go for over-the-top ethnic clothing; stamped leather purses from Guadalajara; belt buckles from San Miguel; and clunky necklaces and bracelets of quartz, amber, and turquoise. It also sells wonderful tchotchkes. The shop doubled in size in 2008, taking over the adjacent store. ⊠ *Calle Basilio Badillo 260, Col. E. Zapata* ☎ *322/223–4594* ⊘ *Closed Sun.*

★ **Sirenas.** It's affiliated with Serafina and geared to women with eclectic tastes. Creative sisters from Tamaulipas State create chic and unusual, exuberant fantasy jewelry. Colorful clutches and makeup bags made from recycled packaging are an innovation from Mexico City. At this writing, the shop was filled with tight-fitting, ribbed T-shirts edged in sequins and an assortment of ethnically inspired yet edgy and contemporary blouses and skirts from Indonesia and elsewhere. ⊠ *Calle Basilio Badillo 252B, Col. E. Zapata* ☎ *322/223–1925* ⊘ *Closed Sun.*

FOLK ART AND CRAFTS

★ **Lucy's CuCú Cabana.** Here you can shop for inexpensive, one-of-a-kind folk art from Guerrero, Michoacán, Oaxaca, and elsewhere at this very small shop. Note that Lucy closes during lunch. ✉ *Calle Basilio Badillo 295, Col. E. Zapata* ☎ *322/222–1220* ⊘ *Closed Sun. and Sept.–mid-Oct.*

Mundo de Cristal. Come for the glassware from Jalisco and Guanajuato states in sets or individually. Also available are Talavera place settings and individual platters, pitchers, and decorative pieces. Look in the back of the store for high-quality ceramics with realistic portrayals of fruits and flowers. You can have your purchase packed and shipped through the store. ✉ *Av. Insurgentes 333, at Calle Basilio Badillo, Col. E. Zapata* ☎ *322/222–1426* ⊘ *Closed Sat. afternoon and Sun.*

Mundo de Pewter. Relatives of the owners of Mundo de Cristal and Mundo de Azulejos *(⇨ above)* own this shop, which is wedged in between the other two stores. Attractive, lead-free items in modern and traditional designs are sold here at reasonable prices. The practical, tarnish-free pieces can go from stovetop or oven to the dining table and be no worse for wear. ✉ *Av. Venustiano Carranza 358, Col. E. Zapata* ☎ *322/222–0503.*

GROCERY STORE

Gutiérrez Rizo. The most convenient market to the Romantic Zone has an ample liquor section, American-brand cereals, canned food, condiments, and ground-to-order coffee. Naturally it's a bit more expensive than its megasize chain competitors. ✉ *Av. Constitución 136, between Av. 5 de Febrero and Aquiles Serdan, Col. E. Zapata* ☎ *322/222–1367.*

HOME FURNISHINGS

★ **Banderas Bay.** The American owners, who also own Daiquiri Dick's restaurant *(⇨ Chapter 5)*, travel around the country for months in search of antiques, collectibles, handicrafts, and other unique household items. About two-thirds of the merchandise is new. The shop will pack and ship your purchases. ✉ *Av. Lázaro Cárdenas 263, Col. E. Zapata* ☎ *322/223–4352* ✉ *Constitución 319–A, Col. E. Zapata* ☎ *322/223–9871* ⊘ *Closed Sun (both branches).*

Ponciana. You can find things here that you won't find at other stores, like porcelain replicas of antique dolls or an old reliquary transformed into wall art. Leaving room for creative license means that some "antiques" here may only have a few original parts (say, a cupboard that only has original doors). Also look for tablecloths and place mats from Michoacán, place settings, arty statuettes, matchboxes decorated with Frida Kahlo and Mexican movie themes, and other decorative items. ✉ *Calle Basilio Badillo 252–A, Col. E. Zapata* ☎ *322/222–2988.*

JEWELRY

Fodor's Choice ★ **Cassandra Shaw Jewelry.** It's hard to ignore the huge, chunky rings, bracelets, and necklaces here. In the back of the shop are more delicate items of pure silver set with various stones in artful ways. All are unusual. There's a small selection of hats, handbags, tunics, and other items, and, up the spiral staircase, the owner's oil paintings, mainly non-representational portraits. ✉ *Calle Basilio Badillo 276, Col. E. Zapata* ☎ *322/223–9734.*

Joyería Yoler. Manager Ramon Cruz proudly shows off the store's collection of the Los Castillo family's silver jewelry made with lost-wax casting as well as hammering and burnishing techniques, small silver pitchers with lapis lazuli dragonfly handles, napkin rings, abalone pillboxes, and other lovely utilitarian pieces. The merchandise—which includes an extensive yet not overwhelming array of silver and semi-precious-stone jewelry—is nicely arranged in the ample shop. It's open daily from 9 AM to 10 PM (even on Sunday). ⊠ *Calle Olas Altas 391, Col. E. Zapata* ☎ *322/222–8713 or 322/222–9051.*

ALL THAT GLITTERS ISN'T SILVER

There's a great selection of Mexican silver in PV, but watch out for "German silver" (aka *alpaca* or *chapa*), an alloy of iron, zinc, and nickel. Real silver is weightier and is marked "925" (indicating a silver content of at least 92.5%) for sterling and "950" (at least 95% silver content) for finer pieces. When size permits, the manufacturer's name and the word "Mexico" should also appear.

LEATHER, SHOES, AND HANDBAGS

★ **Huarachería Fabiola.** Longtime visitors to Puerto Vallarta will remember this shop. Buy huaraches off the rack or order custom sandals for men or women. Most styles can be made in one to three days. There are limited hours (roughly 10–3) on Sunday, and credit cards aren't accepted. ⊠ *Av. Ignacio L. Vallarta 145, at Calle A. Serdán, Col. E. Zapata* ☎ *322/222–9154.*

CENTRO AND ENVIRONS

ART

★ **ARTE 550.** Wonderful ceramic pieces and sculptures are found at this shop a few blocks in from the malecón. Co-owner/artist Patricia Gawle digs her own clay outside El Tuito. Her monotypes are colorful, cheerful, and tropical-themed. You can browse through the catalogue of hand-painted tile work to order pieces for a kitchen or bathroom mural. Business partner Kathleen Carrillo paints equally cheerful acrylics, and the two lead tours combining whale-watching, snorkeling, or other activities with journaling and other types of artistic expression. ⊠ *Calle Hidalgo at Corona, Centro* ☎ *322/222–7365* ⊕ *www.yourcreativeawakening.com* ⊗ *Closed Sun.–Mon.*

Art Gallery Millan. It's a breath of fresh air in the gallery scene, with cheeky oils by Eduardo Eguía, sculpture by Benito Arciniegas, and affordable, fun ceramic cyclist statuettes created by Rodo Padilla. ⊠ *Calle Aldama 209, Centro* ☎ *322/137–3519* ⊕ *www.artgallerymillan.com.*

Galería Arte Latinoamericana. This gallery sells contemporary art, primarily paintings. There are representative Indian portraits by Marta Gilbert and chunky village scenes—a cross between the Flintstones and Chagall—by Celeste Acevedo. ⊠ *Calle Josefa O. de Domínguez 15, between Av. Juárez and Calle Morelos, Centro* ☎ *322/222–4406* ⊕ *www.galeriaal.com* ⊗ *Closed Sun.*

T. Fuller Fine Art. With shows changing monthly, this downtown focuses on contemporary fine art. The current show features the wonderful gilded, textured oils and silverpoints (the latter a technique employed by DaVinci and other masters) of constructivist painter Chad Buck and the delightful high-fire glazeware of Michoacán ceramist Manuel Morales. There's usually a photography exhibition in May highlighting the work of different international artists. In an effort to help maintain classic Mexican folk art, the gallery is currently inviting Mexican legends to the gallery to

display their wares and demonstrate their techniques. At the back of the gallery, the store-within-a-store Caballito de Mar sells wonderful antique and vintage Mexican silver jewelry. ⊠ *Calle Corona 169, Centro* ☎ *322/222–8196* ⊕ *www.tfullerfineart.com* ⊗ *Closed Sun.–Mon. and* Aug.–Sept.

Galería 8 y Más. It started with eight Guadalajara artists and has expanded under new ownership to 45 artists from or residing in Jalisco. The large old building has glass, bronze, chalk, and oil paintings. The Miramar Street gallery is open 10–5 and the Calle Corona gallery 10–2 and 5–8. Both close after 2 on Saturday and all day Sunday. ⊠ *Calle Miramar 237, Centro* ☎ *No phone* ⊠ *Calle Corona 186, Centro* ☎ *322/223–9700* ⊕ *www.artismexico.com* ⊗ *Closed Sun.*

Galería Pacífico. Open since 1987, Pacífico features the sculpture of Ramiz Barquet, who created the bronze *Nostalgia* piece on the malecón. Brewster Brockmann paints contemporary abstracts; Marco Alvarez, Alejandro Mondria, and Alfredo Langarica are other featured artists. ⊠ *Calle Aldama 174, Centro* ☎ *322/222–1982* ⊕ *www.galeriapacifico.com.*

Sergio Bustamante. Internationally known Sergio Bustamante—the creator of life-size brass, copper, and ceramic animals, mermaids, suns, and moons—has a team of artisans to execute his never-ending pantheon of creative and quirky objets d'art, such as pots shaped like human torsos that sell for more than $1,000. Paintings, purses, shoes, and jewelry are sold here as well. It's across the street from the statue by the same artist, on the malecón. ⊠ *Av. Juárez 275, at Calle Corona, Centro* ☎ *322/223–1405* ⊠ *Paseo Diaz Ordaz 542, at Calle Corona, Centro* ☎ *322/222–5480* ⊕ *www.sergiobustamante.com.mx.*

CANDY

★ **Dulces Típicos Mexicanos.** Passersby are yanked almost involuntarily into the shop by the eye-popping displays, and the stock of candies and cookies from around the republic creates a strong sense of nostalgia in Mexicans. Shop for coconut cookies by the bag, sugar-encrusted nuts and seeds by weight, or bars of sweet *ate* or *membrillo* (fruit pastes) in a variety of tropical flavors. ⊠ *Av. Juárez 1449, at Calle Mina, Centro* ☎ *322/223–0707* ⊗ *Closed Sun.*

CERAMICS, POTTERY, AND TILE

Alfarería Tlaquepaque. This is a large store with a ton of red-clay items traditional to the area—in fact, their predecessors were crafted before the 1st century AD. After a recent dip in quality, there's been a return to

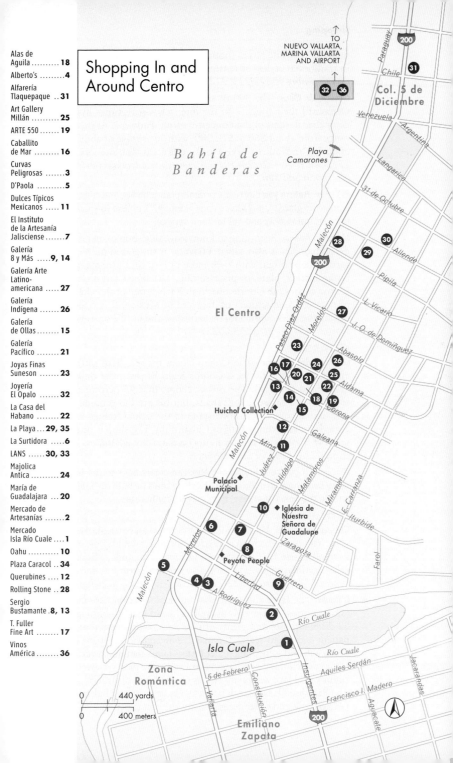

Shopping In and Around Centro

more worthwhile pieces (both rustic pottery and glazed ceramic pieces in traditional styles) at reasonable prices. ⊠ *Av. México 1100, Col. 5 de Diciembre* ☎ *322/223–2121.*

Galería de Ollas. The 300 or so potters from the village of Juan Mata Ortiz add their touches to the intensely—sometimes hypnotically—geometric designs of their ancestors from Paquimé. At this shop pieces range from about $60 to $10,000, with an average of about $400. Stop in during artWalk, or have a look at its great Web site. ⊠ *Calle Corona 176, Centro* ☎ *322/223–1045* ⊕ *www.galeriadeollas.com* ☉ *Closed Sat. afternoon and Sun.*

■**TIP**➡ Before you buy rustic ceramic plates, bowls, and cups, ask if there's lead in the glaze ("*¿hay plomo en el vidriado?*"), unless you plan to use them for decoration only and not for food service.

★ **Majolica Antica.** According to knowledgeable shop owner Antonio Cordero, majolica is also called Talavera or tin-glazed pottery. You get a certificate of origin with each piece of beautiful ornamental tile, utilitarian pitcher, plate, or place setting. The shop's latest claim to fame: It now carries the Uriarte line from Puebla, one of the oldest and most respected manufacturers of Talavera in Mexico. It is open until 8 PM during the week, until 5 PM on Saturday, and until 2 on Sunday. ⊠ *Calle Corona 191, Centro* ☎ *322/222–5118*

CIGARS

La Casa del Habano. The Cuban cigars for sale here start at $4 each and top out at $200 for a Cohiba Siglo VI (by order only; they don't keep these in stock). The owner claims that 95 percent of the cigars sold in Vallarta are fake Cubans, but his are the genuine article. You can smoke your stogie downstairs in the casual lounge while sipping coffee or a enjoying a shot of Cuban rum. The shop is open weekdays noon to 9 PM, with shorter hours on Saturday. ⊠ *Aldama 170, Centro* ☎ *322/223–2758* ☉ *Closed Sun.*

■**TIP**➡ If you're bringing any Mexican cigars back to the United States, make sure they have the correct Mexican seals on both the individual cigars and on the box. Otherwise, they may be confiscated.

CLOTHING

Curvas Peligrosas. Here it's all about beachwear, particularly nice bathing suits. The emphasis is on plus sizes, but you can find some items that are as small as size 12. Choose from Jantzen, Longitude, Miracle Suits, and other quality brands. The shop also has cute cover-ups and skirts. ⊠ *Av. Juárez 178, Centro* ☎ *322/223–5978* ⊕ *www.curvaspeligrosaspv.com*

★ **D'Paola.** The large and somewhat unusual selection here includes pashminas, purses, and shawls as well as lots of muslin clothing. You'll find 32 different lines and plenty of plus sizes. We'd guess that any woman patient enough to search the massive inventory (the main shop has the most) will find something to her taste—here's that much variety. Complement your clothing purchases with a signature piece of jewelry, perhaps a chunky necklace with giant stones or one made of strands of tiny beads. The Paradise Plaza branch has sexy resort wear and halter dresses from Gecko Batik and other designers, but the best experience on the whole is at the main branch, where the owners' warm friendliness is contagious. ⊠ *Calle Agustín Rodriguez 289, Centro* ☎ *322/222–1120* ⊙ *Closed Sun.* ⊠ *Paradise Plaza, Local 11–A, Nuevo Vallarta* ☎ *322/297–1030.*

☼ **La Surtidora.** At first glance the items in this long-established shop seem mainly matronly, but plowing through the racks will unearth fashionable cocktail dresses, trendy tops, and T-shirts, plus men's guayaberas and slacks. The location near the bridge in Colonia E. Zapata has the larger selection; it also has shoes (high heels to flip-flops) and children's clothing. ⊠ *Calle Morelos 256, at Guerrero, Centro* ☎ *322/222–1439* ⊠ *Av. 5 de Febrero at Av. Insurgentes, Col. E. Zapata* ☎ *322/222–0355.*

☼ **Oahu.** One of the best places in Puerto Vallarta to shop for children's casual wear not only has things like pint-size Hawaiian shirts but also water gear like board shorts and rash guards. It's also a good place for men's surf and casual wear, including well-made flip-flops and high-quality T-shirts. It's open daily from 10 AM to 9 PM. ⊠ *Calle Juárez 314, Centro* ☎ *322/223–1058.*

DEPARTMENT STORE

☼ **LANS.** At this multilevel department store for men, women, and children, look for Perry Ellis khakis and Levi's, Lee, and Dockers shirts and trousers, and jeans. The store also sells housewares; purses and Swatch watches; Samsonite luggage; ladies' perfume and makeup (Chanel, Gucci, Estée Lauder); and men's undies. Both locations offer parking, which is especially nice in crowded downtown Vallarta. ⊠ *Calle Juárez 867, at Pípila, Centro* ☎ *322/226–9100* ⊠ *Plaza Caracol, near Soriana supermarket, Blvd. Francisco M. Ascencio 2216, Zona Hotelera* ☎ *322/226–0204* ⊕ *www.lans.com.mx.*

FOLK ART AND CRAFTS

Alas de Aguila. In addition to pewter there's a wide selection of Talavera-style objects—from soap holders and liquid-soap dispensers to pitchers, platters, and picture frames—in a variety of patterns. Quality is middle-of-the-road; prices are excellent. ⊠ *Av. Juárez 547, at Calle Corona, Centro* ☎ *322/222–4039* ⊙ *Closed Sun.*

El Instituto de la Artesanía Jalisciense. This shop promotes Jalisco State's handicrafts, selling burnished clay bowls signed by the artist, blown glass, plates and bowls from Tonalá, and other items at fair prices. That said, Bustamante knockoffs and Huichol pieces in less-than-traditional themes (smiley faces not being one of the Huichol's typical motifs) are indications that quality is slipping. Still, there's a representative sampling of the state's ceramics, blue and red glassware, and *barro bruñido*: clay pieces finished by burnishing only. It's catercorner from La Plaza de Armas and is open 9 to 9 daily. ⊠ *Calle Juárez 284, Centro* ☎ *322/222–1301.*

Galería Indígena. The assortment of handicrafts here is huge: Huichol yarn paintings and beaded bowls and statuettes, real Talavera ceramics from Puebla, decorative pieces in painted wood, and many other items. The owner likes offering customers a drink of water or other refreshment, no strings attached. ⊠ *Av. Juárez 628, Centro* ☎ *322/223–0800.*

Continued on page 198

THE ART OF THE HUICHOL

Updated by
Georgia de Katona

The intricately woven and beaded designs of the Huichols' art are as vibrant and fascinating as the traditions of its people, best known as the "Peyote People" for their traditional and ceremonial use of the hallucinogenic drug. Peyote-inspired visions are thought to be messages from God and are reflected in the art.

Like the Lacandon Maya, the Huichol resisted assimilation by Spanish invaders, fleeing to inhospitable mountains and remote valleys. There they retained their pantheistic religion in which shamans lead the community in spiritual matters and the use of peyote facilitates communication directly with God.

Roads didn't reach larger Huichol communities until the mid-20th century, bringing electricity and other modern distractions. The collision with the outside world has had pros and cons, but art lovers have only benefited from their increased access to intricately patterned woven and beaded goods. Today the traditional souls that remain on the land—a significant population of perhaps 6,000 to 8,000—still create votive bowls, prayer arrows, jewelry, and bags, and sell them to finance elaborate religious ceremonies. The pieces go for as little as $5 or as much as $5,000, depending on the skill and fame of the artist and quality of materials.

(left) Huichol yarn painting, National Museum of Anthropology, (top) Huichol art, Puerto Vallarta

UNDERSTANDING THE HUICHOL

When Spanish conquistadors arrived in the early 16th century, the Huichol, unwilling to work as slaves on the haciendas of the Spanish or to adopt their religion, fled to the Sierra Madre. They lived there, disconnected from society, for nearly 500 years. Beginning in the 1970s, roads and electricity made their way to tiny Huichol towns. Today, about half of the population of perhaps 12,000 continues to live in ancestral villages and *rancheritas* (tiny individual farms).

THE POWER OF PRAYER

They believe that without their prayers and offerings the sun wouldn't rise, the earth would cease spinning. It is hard, then, for them to reconcile their poverty with the relative easy living of "free-riders" (Huichol term for non-spiritual freeloaders) who enjoy fine cars and expensive houses thanks to the Huichols efforts to sustain the planet. But rather than hold our reckless materialism against us, the Huichol add us to their prayers.

THE PEYOTE PEOPLE

Visions inspired by the hallucinogenic peyote plant are considered by the Huichol to be messages from God and to help in solving personal and communal problems. Indirectly, they provide

Huichol artisans and beadwork

inspiration for their almost psychedelic art. Just a generation or two ago, annual peyote-gathering pilgrimages were done on foot. Today the journey is still a man's chief obligation, but they now drive to the holy site at Wiricuta, in San Luis Potosi State. Peyote collected is used by the entire community—men, women, and children—throughout the year.

SHAMANISM

A Huichol man has a lifelong calling as a shaman. There are two shamanic paths: the path of the wolf, which is more aggressive, demanding, and powerful (wolf shamans profess the ability to morph into wolves); and the path of the deer, which is playful—even clownish—and less inclined to prove his power. A shaman chooses his own path.

Huichol bird, Jalisco

HOW TO READ THE SYMBOLS

Spiders that come out at dawn are thought to welcome the rising sun.

The deer is the animal manifestation of the god Kahumari, who intercedes in heaven on earthlings' behalf.

Anything with horns or antlers symbolizes communion and oneness with God.

Yarn painting

6

■ The trilogy of corn, peyote, and deer represents three aspects of God. According to Huichol mythology, peyote sprang up in the footprints of the deer. Depicted like stylized flowers, peyote represents communication with God. Corn, the Huichol's staple

Corn symbol

food, symbolizes health and prosperity. An image drawn inside the root ball depicts the essence of God within it.

■ The double-headed eagle is the emblem of the omnipresent sky god.

Peyote

■ A nierika is a portal between the spirit world and our own. Often in the form of a yarn painting, a nierika can be round or square.

■ Salamanders and turtles are associated with rain; the former provoke the clouds. Turtles maintain underground springs and purify water.

■ A scorpion is the soldier of the sun.

Scorpion

■ The Huichol depict raindrops as tiny snakes; in yarn paintings they descend to enrich the fields.

Snakes

Jose Beníctez Sánchez, (1938—) may be the elder statesman of yarn painters and has shown in Japan, Spain, the U.S., and at the Museum of Modern Art in Mexico City. His paintings sell for upward of $3,000 a piece.

TRADITION TRANSFORMED

The art of the Huichol was, for centuries, made from undyed wool, shells, stones, and other natural materials. It was not until the 1970s that the Huichol began incorporating bright, zingy colors, without sacrificing the intricate patterns and symbols used for centuries. The result is strenuously colorful, yet dignified.

YARN PAINTINGS
Dramatic and vivid yarn paintings are highly symbolic, stylized visions of life.

MASKS AND ANIMAL STATUETTES
Bead-covered wooden or ceramic masks and animal statuettes are other adaptations made for outsiders.

PRAYER ARROWS
Made for every ceremony, prayer arrows send petitions winging to God.

VOTIVE BOWLS
Ceremonial votive bowls, made from gourds, are decorated with bright, stylized beadwork.

WOVEN SHOULDER BAGS
Carried by men, the bags are decorated with traditional Huichol icons.

For years, Huichol men as well as women wore BEADED BRACELETS; today earrings and necklaces are also made.

Diamond-shape GOD'S EYES of sticks and yarn protect children from harm.

SMART SHOPPING TIPS

BEADED ITEMS: The smaller the beads, the more delicate and expensive the piece. Beads with larger holes are fine for stringed work, but if used in bowls and statuettes cheapen the piece.

Items made with iridescent beads from Japan are the priciest. Look for good-quality glass beads, definition, symmetry, and artful use of color.

Beads should fit together tightly in straight lines, with no gaps.

Bead-covered ram figurine

YARN PAINTINGS: Symmetry is not necessary, although there should be an overall sense of unity. Thinner thread results in finer, more costly work. Look for tightness, with no visible gaps or broken threads. Paintings should have a stamp of authenticity on the back, including artist's name and tribal affiliation.

PRAYER ARROWS: Collectors and purists should look for the traditionally made arrows of brazilwood inserted into a bamboo shaft. The most interesting ones contain embroidery work, or tiny carved icons, or are painted with copal symbols indicative of their original, intended purpose, for example protecting a child or ensuring a successful corn crop.

6

IN FOCUS THE ART OF THE HUICHOL

WHERE TO SHOP

Huichol who make art to supplement farming tend to work more slowly and with a higher degree of artistry than their city-dwelling brethren. Shopping at stores like the ones listed here supports artisans who live in their ancestral villages and practice the ancient traditions.

Peyote People. Here the Huichol are treated as a people, not a product. At their downtown Vallarta shop, the owners—a Mexican-Canadian couple—are happy to share with customers their wealth of info about Huichol art and culture. They work with just a few farming families, providing all the materials and then paying for the

finished product. ⊠ *Calle Juárez 222, Centro, Puerto Vallarta* ☎ *322/222–2303.*

Hikuri. Near the north end of Banderas Bay, Hikuri is run by a British couple that pays asking prices to their Huichol suppliers and employs indigenous men in the adjoining carpentry and screen-printing shops. The men initially have little or no experience, and the jobs give them a leg up to move on to more profitable work. The excellent inventory includes fine yarn paintings large and small, beaded bowls and jewelry, and feathered prayer wands. An onsite patio restaurant called Abalón

(closed Wed. and 2–6 PM) offers international dishes and sometimes live music. ⊠ *Calle Coral 66A, Puerto Vallarta* ☎ *329/295–5071* ⊕ *www.hikuri.com.*

Huichol Collection. Native artisans working on crafts and wearing their stunning and colorful clothing draw customers in. The shop has an excellent inventory, with some museum-quality pieces. Though the merchandise is genuine, the shop is also a venue for timeshare sales—albeit with a soft sales pitch. ⊠ *Paseo Diaz Ordaz 732, Centro, Puerto Vallarta* ☎ *322/223–0661* ⊠ *Morelos 490, Centro, Puerto Vallarta* ☎ *322/223–2141.*

Querubines. An old house that once belonged to Jesús Langarica, PV's first mayor, is the setting for this shop selling woven goods from Guatemala and southern Mexico. Items include tablecloths, napkins, place mats, and *rebozos* (stoles) made of rayon, cotton, and sometimes silk. The structure's stone, cement, and brick floors make interesting backdrops for painted gourds from Michoacán, carved gourds from the Costa Chica (northern Oaxaca coast), and Talavera pottery. ⊠ *Av. Juárez 501–A, at Calle Galeana, Centro* ☎ *322/223–1727.*

JEWELRY

Caballito de Mar. Lynn Auch and Carol Simonton own and operate this small store at the back of T. Fuller Fine Arts. At the heart of the collection of vintage and antique silver jewelry are pieces acquired by their mother over 40 years of collecting beginning in the 1940s. The sisters continue to add select, handmade jewelry to their small but stellar collection, and they offer a small selection of folk art as well. ⊠ *Calle Corona 169, Centro* ☎ *322/129–5209 (cell)* ⊙ *Closed Sun.– Mon. and Aug.–Sept.*

Alberto's. This family-run shop has been in business for three generations. The inventory has been revived with the introduction of lovely one-of-a-kind pieces designed by young designer Emerson. Each of his baroque pieces—most with opals, pearls, amethysts, topaz, and other semi-precious stones—is stamped with Emerson's copyrighted logo and guaranteed to be one-of-a-kind. ⊠ *Av. Juárez 185, Centro* ☎ *322/222– 8317* ⊙ *Closed Sun.*

★ **Joyería El Opalo.** It's a bright spot in a nearly abandoned mall that has stayed afloat through its cruise-ship contacts. Look for it near the northern entrance to the open-air mall, across the street from Gold's Gym. Silver jewelry ranges in price from $3 per gram for simpler pieces to $30 a gram for the lighter, finer-quality, more complex pieces. There's high-grade "950" silver jewelry in addition to the usual "925" sterling silver. Look for gold settings as well. Most of the semiprecious stones— amethyst, topaz, malachite, black onyx, and opal in 28 colors—are of Mexican origin. They sell blue diamond jewelry and increasingly rare tanzanite. The diamond-cut necklaces are magnificent. If you want to comparison-shop, there are three or four other jewelry stores in the immediate vicinity. ⊠ *Local 13–A, Plaza Genovesa, Col. Las Glorias* ☎ *322/224–6584* ⊙ *Closed Sun.*

★ **Joyas Finas Suneson.** Some of Mexico's finest designers create the unusual silver jewelry and objets d'art that are sold here. Most items have modern rather than traditional motifs. ⊠ *Calle Morelos 593, Centro* ☎ *322/222–5715* ⊙ *Closed Sun.*

LEATHER, SHOES, AND HANDBAGS

Rolling Stone. It's good for custom-made boots, sandals, and shoes in a wide variety of leathers. But the help is often unhelpful, letting customers wait while they attend to other duties—real or imagined. ⊠ *Paseo Diaz Ordaz 802, Centro* ☎ *322/223–1769.*

MALL

Plaza Caracol. Caracol is lively and full on weekends and evenings, even when others are dead. Its anchors are the Soriana (formerly Gigante) supermarket and the adjacent LANS department store. Surrounding these are tiny stores dispensing electronics, ice cream, and fresh flowers. This is also a good place for manicures and haircuts. Adding to the commercial center's appeal is the six-theater CineMark cinema. ⊠ *Blvd. Francisco M. Ascencio, Km 2.5, across from Fiesta Americana hotel, Zona Hotelera* ☎ *322/224–3239.*

> ### DO WEAR THEM OUT
>
> *Huaraches* are woven leather sandals that seem to last several lifetimes. Traditionally worn by peasants, they're now sold by fewer shops, but in a slightly larger assortment of styles. Once broken in—and that takes a while—this classic, sturdy footwear will be a worthwhile addition to your closet.

MARKETS

Mercado de Artesanías. Flowers, piñatas, produce, and plastics share space in indoor and outdoor stands with souvenirs and lesser-quality crafts. Upstairs, locals eat at long-established, family-run restaurants. ⊠ *Calle Agustín Rodríguez, between Calles Matamoros and Miramar, at base of bridge* ☎ *No phone.*

Mercado Isla Río Cuale. Small shops and outdoor stalls sell an interesting mix of wares at this informal and fun market. Harley-Davidson kerchiefs, Che paintings on velvet, and Madonna icons compete with the usual synthetic lace tablecloths, shell and quartz necklaces, and silver jewelry amid postcards and key chains. The market is partially shaded by enormous fig and rubber trees and serenaded by the rushing river; a half-dozen cafés and restaurants provide sustenance. ⊠ *Dividing El Centro from Colonia E. Zapata, access at Calle Morelos, Calle I. Vallarta, Calle Matamoros, Calle Constitución, Calle Libertad, Av. Insurgentes, and the malecón* ☎ *No phone.*

WINE, BEER, AND SPIRITS

La Playa. Yes, it has tequila. But it also has wines from Chile, California (Gallo), and Spain; imported vodka and other spirits; and the cheapest beer around. ⊠ *Blvd. Francisco M. Ascencio, Km 1.5, across from IMSS (Mexican Social Security Agency), Zona Hotelera* ☎ *322/224–7130* ⊠ *Calle Morelos at Calle Pípila, Centro* ☎ *322/223–1818* ⊠ *Olas Altas 246 at Calle Basilio Badillo, Col. E. Zapata* ☎ *322/222–5304.*

Vinos América. A huge and excellent inventory of wine from Germany, Spain, France, Argentina, Chile, California, Australia, and elsewhere makes this a natural stop for lovers of the grape. The shop sells champagne and other sparkling vintages, sherry, port, and two Napa Valley non-alcoholic wines. There's no shortage of Mexican wines, of course, as well as tequila, *raicilla* (green agave liquor), *Agavero* (Damiana liqueur with tequila), and other hard liquor. ⊠ *Av. de las Américas 433, Col. Lázaro Cárdenas* ☎ *322/223–3334.*

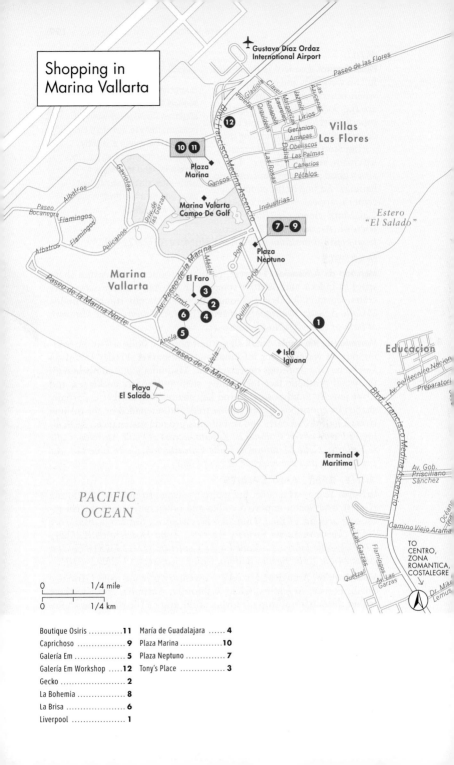

Shopping in Marina Vallarta

MARINA VALLARTA

ART

Galería Em. This shop sells art glass, stained glass, and glass sculpture and also has a small selection of eccentric jewelry made by local artists. The shop offers fully insured international shipping, too. **By appointment only, you can commission a piece at the Galería Em workshop** (✉ *ArtBlvd. Francisco M. Ascencio 2758, Marina Vallarta* ☎ *322/332–1728*). ✉ *Marina Las Palmas II, Local 17, Marina Vallarta* ☎ *322/221–2228* ☉ *Closed Sun. and Sept.–Oct. 2–5* PM.

CLOTHING

Boutique Osiris. The inventory may wax and wane a bit, but at its best this shop has a nice selection of simple gauze, cotton, and linen clothing for day or evening wear, although it's more practical than formal or fancy. ✉ *Plaza Marina, Local F–6, Marina Vallarta* ☎ *322/221–0732*.

Caprichoso. Sizes here range from XS to 2X, and it's the only PV store to stock the Oh My Gauze line of women's resort wear. Also look for Dunes, Juanita Banana, and unusual clothing by Chalí, with cutout, painted flowers. Most of the inventory is cotton, including a smaller selection of clothing for men. ✉ *Plaza Neptuno, Av. Francisco M. Ascencio, Km 7.5, Marina Vallarta* ☎ *322/221–3067*.

Gecko. This is the place to go in Marina Vallarta for beach togs for kids and teens. The selection of any one type of item isn't large, but there are bikinis, sunglasses, flip-flops, nice ball caps, and T-shirts. Board shorts and rash guards are stocked for surfers and wannabes. ✉ *Condominios Puesto del Sol, Marina Vallarta* ☎ *322/221–2165*.

★ **María de Guadalajara**. It's DIY chic here. You choose the colorful, cotton, triangular sash of your liking, miraculously transforming pretty but baggy dresses into flattering and stylish frocks. The color palette is truly inspired, although the selection for men is limited. ✉ *Puesta del Sol condominiums, Local 15–A, Marina, Marina Vallarta* ☎ *322/221–2566* ✉ *Calle Morelos 550, Centro* ☎ *322/222–2387* ⊕ *www.mariadeguadalajara.com*.

DEPARTMENT STORE

Liverpool. Locals were giddy about this department store anchoring 73,000 square feet of shopping on two floors at Plaza Galerías—until they caught a look at the price tags. This and the surrounding shops are mainly visited by cruise-ship passengers and Mexican out-of-towners looking for everything from sporting goods to clothing to housewares. Plaza Galerías has two escalators; restaurants; parking; a 12-theater cinema; and a fast-food court with the ubiquitous McDonald's, Dominos Pizza, Chili's, and Starbucks (it also has the most slippery polished-stone flooring known to man). ✉ *Av. Francisco M. Ascencio 2920, Plaza Galerías, Marina Vallarta* ☎ *322/226–2400*.

JEWELRY

La Brisa. La Brisa's friendly staff, fair prices, and no-pressure sales approach make shopping here a pleasure. They have everything from $5 bracelets to items costing several hundred dollars, including some unique designs. They have a small selection of Talavera pottery and

other gifts as well. ⊠ *Condominios Puesta del Sol, Local 11–B, Marina Vallarta* ☎ *322/221–2516.*

LEATHER

Tony's Place. This shop facing the private marina offers a nice selection of boots, shoes, purses, belts, and wallets in different types of leather, including pigskin, cow, shark, alligator, and ostrich. ⊠ *Royal Pacific, Loc. 117 at Marina Vallarta, Marina Vallarta* ☎ *322/221–0156* ⊘ *Closed Sun.*

MALLS

Plaza Marina. One long block north of Plaza Neptuno, this mall has several banks with ATMs, a dry cleaner, a photo-developing shop, a pharmacy, a café, an Internet café, and several bars and shops. The whole place is anchored by the Comercial Mexicana supermarket. ⊠ *Carretera al Aeropuerto, Km 8, Marina Vallarta* ☎ *322/221–0490.*

Plaza Neptuno. This small mall in the heart of the marina district is home to a number of fine-home-furnishing shops, several classy clothing boutiques, and, just behind it, a few good, casual restaurants. ⊠ *Carretera al Aeropuerto, Km 7.5, Marina Vallarta* ☎ *No phone.*

RIVIERA NAYARIT

NUEVO VALLARTA

BOOKS

★ **NV Bookstore.** It may be small, but it has the area's best-distilled selection of English-language books. There are guidebooks; books about Mexican culture, history, and arts; and best-selling titles to read around the pool. ⊠ *Paradise Plaza, 2nd floor, Nuevo Vallarta* ☎ *322/297–2274.*

CLOTHING

★ **Guayaberass.** This shop has wonderful men's shirts that are great for the tropical heat. You'll find *guayaberas* (pleated men's shirts with collars made to be worn without a tie) in sizes 0 to 54 and a hundred different colors. The shop specializes in linen, cotton, and cotton-poly blends. Custom orders can be produced within 10 to 14 days. ⊠ *Paradise Plaza, Nuevo Vallarta* ☎ *322/297–5668.*

GROCERIES

Mega Comercial Nuevo Vallarta. The area's first large supermarket is almost as convenient for people in Bucerías as for those in Nuevo Vallarta. It has the full range of grocery, liquor, and deli items, and more. ⊠ *Hwy. 200, Fracc. Flamingos, just south of Flamingos Country Club, Nuevo Vallarta.*

One Man's Metal

In less than a decade after William Spratling arrived in the mining town of Taxco—275 km (170 mi) north of Acapulco—he had transformed it into a flourishing silver center, the likes of which had not been seen since colonial times. In 1929 the writer-architect from New Orleans settled in the then-sleepy, dusty village because it was inexpensive and close to the pre-Hispanic Mexcala culture that he was studying in Guerrero Valley.

In Taxco—Mexico's premier "Silver City"—marvelously preserved white-stucco, red-tile-roof colonial buildings hug cobblestone streets wind up and down the foothills of the Sierra Madre. Taxco (pronounced "TAHS-ko") is a living work of art. For centuries its silver mines drew foreign mining companies. In 1928 the government made it a national monument.

For hundreds of years Taxco's silver was made into bars and exported overseas. No one even considered developing a local jewelry industry. Journeying to a nearby town, Spratling hired a couple of goldsmiths and commissioned them to create jewelry, flatware, trays, and goblets from his own designs.

Ever the artist, with a keen mind for drawing, design, and aesthetics, Spratling decided to experiment with silver using his designs. Shortly afterward, he set up his own workshop and began producing highly innovative pieces. By the 1940s Spratling's designs were gracing the necks of celebrities and being sold in high-end stores abroad.

Spratling also started a program to train local silversmiths; they were soon joined by foreigners interested in learning the craft. It wasn't long before there were thousands of silversmiths in the town, and Spratling was its wealthiest resident. He moved freely in Mexico's lively art scene, befriending muralists Diego Rivera (Rivera's wife, Frida Kahlo, wore Spratling necklaces) and David Alfaro Siqueiros as well as architect Miguel Covarrubios.

The U.S. ambassador to Mexico at the time, Dwight Morrow, father of Anne Morrow, who married Charles Lindbergh, hired Spratling to help with the architectural details of his house in Cuernavaca. American movie stars were frequent guests at Spratling's home; once, he even designed furniture for Marilyn Monroe. Indeed, when his business failed in 1946, relief came in the form of an offer from the U.S. Department of the Interior: Spratling was asked to create a program of native crafts for Alaska. This work influenced his later designs.

Although he never regained the wealth he once had, he operated the workshop at his ranch and trained apprentices until he died in a car accident in 1969. A friend, Italian engineer Alberto Ulrich, took over the business and replicated Spratling's designs using his original molds. Ulrich died in 2002, and his children now operate the business.

Each summer PV shop owners travel to Taxco to procure silver jewelry.

6

BUCERÍAS

FOLK ART

Jan Marie's Boutique. The gift items here include small housewares and tin frames sporting Botero-style fat ladies. The classy selection of Talavera pottery is both decorative and utilitarian. An extension half a block down the street has an even larger inventory, and the merchandise is larger, too, including classy leather settees, lamps, desks, and other furnishings as well as decorative and utilitarian pieces from various parts of Mexico. Neither shop is for bargain hunters, but prices are reasonable given the high quality of the merchandise. ⊠ *Av. Lázaro Cárdenas 56 and 58, Bucerías* ☎ *329/298–0303.*

Arte Oaxaca. Brothers from the weaving town of Teotitlán del Valle, in Oaxaca, work on the loom while they wait for customers and produce custom rugs, bedspreads, and tablecloths to order. (Allow about 4 weeks for a 3' x 5' rug or large tablecloth to make it to your address back home.) All dyes are derived from minerals, plants, or animal parts, as they were by the weavers' ancestors. Wool handbags with wooden handles bring the shop's inventory up to date. ⊠ *Av. México 17–A, Bucerías Centro* ☎ *951/120–9528 (cell)* ۞ *Closed Sun. and June–mid-Sept.*

Casa del Artesano. Bucerías's best folk art shop, on the south side of town near the gallery and restaurant district, sells modern and traditional ceramicware from Tonalá, lovely burnished pottery from Michoacán, wooden frames and boxes of fine wood from the owner's native state of San Luis Potosí, and many other fine crafts. Find handmade, artsy, inexpensive items for gifts alongside paintings of indigenous people in native dress by Carlos Zavala. It's often closed by 2 PM, so plan to visit in the morning. ⊠ *Av. Lázaro Cárdenas 29, Bucerías* ☎ *329/298–0232* ۞ *Closed June–mid-Sept.*

GROCERY STORES

Frutería Chabacano. Chabacano has the reputation of selling the freshest fruits and vegetables in town to both casual street traffic and longstanding restaurant buyers alike. ⊠ *Calle Hidalgo 15, Bucerías* ☎ *329/298– 0692* ۞ *Open until 3 PM Mon.–Sat., until 1 PM Sun.*

SAYULITA

FOLK ART

Fodor'sChoice ★ **Galería Tanana.** The beauty of its glistening glass-bead (Czech) jewelry in iridescent and earth colors may leave you weak in the knees. Sometimes a Huichol artisan at the front of the store works on traditional yarn paintings, pressing the fine filaments into a base of beeswax and pine resin to create colorful and symbolic pictures. Money from sales supports the owner's nonprofit organization to promote cultural sustainability for the Huichol people. ⊠ *Av. del Palmar 8, Sayulita* ☎ *329/291–3889* ⊕ *www.thehuicholcenter.org.*

★ **La Hamaca.** The inventory of folk art and utilitarian handicrafts is large, and each piece is unique. Scoop up masks and pottery from Michoacán, textiles and shawls from Guatemala, hammocks from the Yucatán, and

lacquered boxes from Olinalá. The store is open daily 9 to 9. ⊠ *Calle Revolución 110, Sayulita* ☎ *329/291–3039.*

Mexica Teahui. It smells of incense and seems to have the usual shell-and-bead bric-a-brac. Closer investigation reveals inventive jewelry in 0.950 silver, obsidian statuettes of modern design, and freshwater pearl necklaces, among other treasures. The surfer-girl cotton Ts and gauzy blouses, shorts, and skirts are cute, but consider some of the more glamorous dresses for that big party or special date. ⊠ *Av. Revolución 53, Centro* ☎ *329/291–3764* ⊙ *Closed Aug.–Sept.*

SAN FRANCISCO

FOLK ART

Galería Corazón. The emphasis at this small shop is on high-end Mexican arts and crafts, the likes of which have found their way to the Smithsonian and other well-regarded museums. One section holds unique designs of Huichol beaded sculptures; the owners supply artisans with Bali-carved mini masks and the highest-quality beeswax and tinier-than-standard beads in order to ensure both innovation and a superior product. The results are excellent and reasonably priced. During the summer months store owners travel to folk-art-rich states to purchase directly from artisans—such as Manuel Morales, a well-known Michoacán ceramist. Shop hours are 11–6. ⊠ *Calle Cuba at Av. Tercer Mundo, San Pancho* ☎ *322/779–3710 (cell)* ⊙ *Closed Mon. and May–Oct.*

HOME FURNISHINGS

Anthony Chetwynd Collection. The British owner of the same name travels to Mexican villages and estates to stock his interesting shop. Some of the pieces are antiques or collectibles, but more than half the inventory is new and used Mexican housewares and furnishings. Look for distressed kitchen tables, sideboards, cupboards, free-standing closets, antique masks, chandeliers, reliquaries, and sometimes copies of well-known paintings. ⊠ *Calle Las Palmas 130, Col. Costa Azul, San Francisco* ☎ *311/258–4407.*

After Dark

WORD OF MOUTH

"Muertos is PV's most popular beach and very swimable most days. You will be in the heart of shops, cafés, bars and much nightlife. About a half mile from the main Malecon where the more 'infamous' drinking spots are."

—stewbear

Outdoorsy Vallarta switches gears after dark and rocks into the wee hours. When the beachgoers and sightseers have been showered and fed, Vallarta kicks up its heels and puts the baby to bed. Happy hour in martini lounges sets the stage for an evening that might include a show, live music, or just hobnobbing under the stars at a rooftop bar.

Many hotels have Mexican fiesta dinner shows, which can be lavish affairs with buffet dinners, folk dances, and even fireworks. Tour groups and individuals—mainly middle-age and older Americans and Canadians—make up the audience at the Saturday-night buffet dinner show at Playa Los Arcos and other hotels. *Vaqueros* (cowboys) do rope tricks and dancers perform Mexican regional or pseudo-Aztec dances. The late-late crowd gets down after midnight at dance clubs, some of which stay open until 6 AM.

The scene mellows as you head north and south of Puerto Vallarta. In Punta Mita (aka Punta de Mita), Bucerías, Sayulita, and San Francisco (aka San Pancho), local restaurants provide live music; the owners usually scare up someone good once or twice a week in high season. Along the Costalegre, tranquility reigns. Most people head here for relaxation, and nightlife generally takes the form of stargazing, drink in hand. If you're visiting June through October (low season), attend live performances whenever offered, as they are few and far between.

Although there's definitely crossover, many Mexicans favor the upscale bars and clubs of the Hotel Zone and Marina Vallarta hotels, while foreigners tend to like the Mexican flavor of places downtown and the south side (the Zona Romántica), where dress is decidedly more casual.

NIGHTLIFE OPTIONS

BARS AND PUBS

Like any resort destination worth its salt—the salt on the rim of the margarita glass, that is—PV has an enormous variety of watering holes. Bars on or overlooking the beach sell the view along with buckets of

beer. Martini bars go to great lengths to impress with signature drinks, and sports bars serve up Canadian hockey and Monday-night football. Hotels have swim-up bars and lobby lounges, and these, as well as restaurant bars, are the main options in places like Nuevo Vallarta, Marina Vallarta, and most of the small towns to the north and south.

DANCE CLUBS

You can dance salsa with the locals, groove to rock in English or *en español*, or even tango. Things slow down in the off-season, but during school vacations and the winter, clubs stay open until 3, 5, or even 6 AM. Except those that double as restaurants, clubs don't open until 10 PM. ■TIP➔ If you care about looking hip, don't show up at a club before midnight—it will most likely be dead. Arriving around 10 PM, however, could save you a cover charge.

Have a late and leisurely dinner, take a walk on the beach and get some coffee, and then stroll into the club cool as a cucumber at 12:30 AM or so.

MUSIC CLUBS

Most of Puerto Vallarta's live music is performed in restaurants and bars, often on or overlooking the beach. ■TIP➔ Musical events happening anywhere in Vallarta are listed in *Bay Vallarta* (⊕ *www.bayvallarta.com*). This twice-monthly rag is an excellent source of detailed information for who's playing around Old Vallarta, the Zona Hotelera Norte, Marina Vallarta, and even as far north as the Riviera Nayarit. More detail-oriented than most similar publications, *Bay Vallarta* lists showtimes, venues, genres, and cover charges. Live music is much less frequent in the smaller towns to the north and south of PV; to find out what's happening there, ask in tourist-oriented bars, restaurants, or hotels.

MOVIES

Movie tickets here are less than half what they are in the United States and Canada. Many theaters have discounted prices on Wednesday. See theater Web sites or ⊕ *www.vallartaonline.com/cinema.*

SHOWS

Most hotels have lounge music, and many hotels have buffet dinners with mariachis, folkloric dancers, and *charros* (elegantly dressed horsemen, who, in this case, perform mostly roping tricks, as horses are a bit too messy for the stage and most of their feats on horseback involve running at top speed in a specially designed arena called a *lienzo charro*). All-inclusive hotels generally include nightly entertainment in the room price. Drag shows are crowd pleasers—whether the crowd is straight or gay.

PUERTO VALLARTA

ZONA ROMÁNTICA

BARS, PUBS, AND LOUNGES

Andale. Most nights, crowds spill out onto the sidewalk as party-hearty men and women shimmy out of the narrow saloon, drinks in hand, to the strains of Chubby Checker and other vintage tunes. For

a laugh, intoxicated or less inhibited patrons sometimes take a bumpy ride on the burro just outside Andale's door (a handler escorts the burro). Andale opens at 8 AM. ⊠ *Av. Olas Altas 425, Col. E. Zapata* ☎ *322/222–1054.*

★ **Apaches.** It's gay friendly, lesbian friendly, *people* friendly. Heck, super-women Mariann and her partner, Endra, would probably welcome you and your pet python with open arms and give you both a squeeze. PV's original martini bar, Apaches is the landing zone for expats reconnoitering after a long day, and a warm-up for late-night types. When the outside tables get jam-packed in high season, the overflow heads into the narrow bar and the adjacent, equally narrow bistro. It opens at 4 PM; happy hour is 5 to 7. If you're alone, this is the place to make friends of all ages. ⊠ *Av. Olas Altas 439, Col. E. Zapata* ☎ *322/222–5235.*

Burro's Bar. Right on the sand across from Parque Lázaro Cárdenas, this restaurant-bar has bargain brewskis and equally inexpensive fruity margaritas by the pitcher. The seafood is less than inspired, but nachos and other munchies are good accompaniments to the drinks. Watch the waves and listen to Bob Marley and the Gypsy Kings among lots of gringo couples and a few middle-age Mexican vacationers. It opens daily at 10 AM. ⊠ *Av. Olas Altas at Calle Lázaro Cárdenas, Col. E. Zapata* ☎ *No phone.*

★ **Encuentros.** At this darkly atmospheric gay lounge (which is open from 6 PM to 1 AM), take a seat at one of the comfortable faux-suede barstools surrounding the horseshoe-shaped bar; small tables face equally comfortable banquets. The small pizzas are a perfect snack, or try the beef and chicken satay, chicken wings, or spring rolls. ⊠ *Calle Lázaro Cárdenas 312, Col. E. Zapata* ☎ *322/222–0643* ⊕ *www.encuentrosbar.com.*

Garbo. This isn't necessarily the kind of place where you'll strike up a conversation with the guy on the next barstool; rather, it's an upscale place to go with friends for a sophisticated, air-conditioned drink or two. A musician plays piano or gentle jazz on weekend nights at 10:30 during high season, less often the rest of the year. Garbo is primarily a gay club, is straight friendly, is renowned for its martinis, and is open nightly after 6. ⊠ *Púlpito 142, at Av. Olas Altas, Col. E. Zapata* ☎ *322/223–5753* ⊕ *www.garbobar-vallarta.com.*

Steve's Bar. With NASCAR on Sunday morning, NFL on Monday night, hockey, indispensable motocross, and welterweight fights, Steve's is a sports mecca. Five feeds and nine television sets guarantee broadcasts of many sporting events from various continents, simultaneously. There are piles of board games, too, and the burgers and fries couldn't be better. ⊠ *Calle Basilio Badillo 286, Col. E. Zapata* ☎ *322/222–0256.*

GAY BARS

Blue Chairs. In addition to its famous beach scene, Blue Chairs has the popular **Blue Sunset Rooftop Bar,** which is the perfect place to watch the sunset. Nightly late-afternoon and evening entertainment ranges from "Blue Balls" Bingo to the biweekly drag show and the Saturday-night "Blue Hombre Review." It's open to the public between 3 and 11; after that, it's hotel guests only. ⊠ *Almendro 4 at the malecón, south end of Los Muertos Beach, Col. E. Zapata* ☎ *322/222–5040.*

Frida. We've heard this place described as "the gay Cheers of Mexico." It's a friendly neighborhood cantina where you'll meet middle-aged to older queens, many Mexicans, a few foreigners, and maybe even some straights. Show up a few times for $1 beers (served daily between 1 and 7 PM) and everyone is sure to know your name. It has moved around the corner from its original location and now serves daily lunch specials in the small second-story restaurant. ✉ *Av. Insurgentes 301, Col. E. Zapata* ☎ *322/222–3668* ⊕ *barfrida.com.*

> **HANGOVER CURES**
>
> For a hangover, *menudo* (tripe stew) and pozole are recommended, both with the addition of chopped fresh onions and cilantro, a generous squeeze of lime, and as much chili as one can handle. Ceviche is another popular cure, with the same key ingredients: lime and chili.

La Noche. This charming martini lounge has red walls and a huge, eye-catching chandelier. Gringo-owned, it attracts a crowd of gay 20- to 40-year-old men (a mix of foreigners and Mexicans). Electronica and house music are the favorites; speaking of which, the house makes excellent cocktails, and not too expensive, either. There's usually happy hour between 7 and 9 PM. ✉ *Calle Lázaro Cárdenas 257, Col. E. Zapata* ☎ *322/222–3364.*

COFFEEHOUSES

Café San Angel. It's moody, romantic, and a favorite with locals and the gay crowd. It has tables along the sidewalk and comfortable couches and chairs inside. The menu includes soups, sandwiches, salads, and a great frappuccino. ✉ *Av. Olas Altas 449, at Calle Francisca Rodriguez, Col. E. Zapata* ☎ *322/223–1273.*

Pie in the Sky Vallarta (✉ *Calle Lázaro Cárdenas 247, Col. E. Zapata* ☎ *322/223–8183*). Come for the excellent coffee as well as *the* most scrumptious pies, cookies, and cakes. There's free Wi-Fi for those with their trusty laptops.

SHOWS

La Iguana. Enjoy Vallarta's original dinner show Thursday nights at 7 PM. Large troupes of professional mariachis entertain, beautiful women dance in colorful costumes, couples cut a rug, kids whack piñatas, and fireworks light up the sky. The simulated cockfight is supposed to be painless for the roosters, and nearly so for alarmed foreign visitors. There's an open bar (domestic Mexican beer and well drinks only), and the buffet has 40 selections. Most folks deem this party worth the price of $57.50 per person (about half that for kids). Reservations are generally made through tour operators or streetside vendors; employees at La Iguana rarely answer their phone except around show time. ✉ *Calle Lázaro Cárdenas 311, Col. E. Zapata* ☎ *322/222–0105.*

Playa Los Arcos. This place has a theme dinner show Monday and Saturday 8–9 PM. The show, which costs 215 pesos (around US$17), includes a buffet and one cocktail. The most popular theme night is Saturday's Mexico Night, with mariachis, rope tricks, and folkloric dance. Mon-

Take in a charrería, or Mexican rodeo performance, at Mundo Cuervo in Tequila.

day is Tex-Mex food and a pre-Hispanic show. ⊠ *Av. Olas Altas 380, Col. E. Zapata* ☎ *322/226–7100.*

CENTRO AND ENVIRONS

BARS, PUBS, AND LOUNGES

Constantini Wine Bar. Bon vivants should head for the latest innovation of hotshot restaurant Café des Artistes. Order one of 50 wines by the glass (more than 300 by the bottle, from 10 countries) and snack on caviar, bruschetta, and carpaccio—or go directly to dessert. Wine tastings are scheduled from time to time. There's live music most every night of the week except Sunday. ⊠ *Café des Artistes, Av. Guadalupe Sánchez 740, Centro* ☎ *322/222–3229.*

La Cantina. Although La Cantina isn't especially hip, it has a good view of Banderas Bay and the boardwalk from its second floor. It also has canned (and sometimes live) Mexican tunes, especially *ranchera, norteño, grupera,* and *cumbia.* ⊠ *Calle Morelos 709, at J.O. de Dominguez, Centro* ☎ *322/222–1734.*

★ **Le Bistro Jazz Café.** It's a mellow, grown-up venue with a good

DRINKS ON THE BEACH

Playa Los Muertos is the destination of choice for a sunset cocktail and dinner on the beach. Strolling mariachi bands or trios playing romantic ballads serenade diners overlooking the sand. Candles and torches light the scene, along with the moon. After dinner you can take a stroll or sit on the beach, or head to another restaurant bar for a coffee or after-dinner digestif to the tunes of marimba, folk music, or jazz.

restaurant. There's usually bossa nova or jazz Wednesday or Thursday through Saturday after 8 PM in high season. ⊠ *Isla Río Cuale 16–A, Centro* ☎ *322/222–0283* ⊕ *www.lebistro.com.mx.*

Party Lounge. This place is open daily after 1 PM for stop-and-go drinks: mainly *litros,* that is, 34-ounce tequila sunrises, Long Island ice teas, piña coladas, and the like. The upstairs bar is open 8 PM to 4 AM and plays '70s, '80s, and lounge music, making it popular with an older set, foreign and domestic. ⊠ *Av. México 993, across from Parque Hidalgo, Centro* ☎ *No phone.*

La Regadera. Talent at this karaoke spot varies; it's open Monday through Saturday (except during low season, when the schedule is less consistent) after 9 PM. Come practice your standard Beatles tunes or hip-hop before your next official recording session. ⊠ *Calle Morelos 666, Centro* ☎ *322/221–3970.*

Señor Frog's. What's called simply "Frog's" by the locals is a good old-fashioned free-for-all for the young and the restless. There are black lights on the walls, bar stools shaped like thong-clad women's butts, and a giant-screen TV above the dance floor. Expect foam parties; ladies'-night Fridays; or, in the high season, beach parties with bikini contests and other shenanigans. ⊠ *Calle Morelos 518, Centro* ☎ *322/222–5171.*

The Shamrock. At this Irish-owned pub, open daily after 11 AM, the Wi-Fi flows freely throughout the chummy bar, and the chips, batter-fried cod, cottage pies, and burgers are great. When the number of customers warrants it during busy season, the more sophisticated (and peaceful) upstairs lounge is opened. ⊠ *Av. México 27, Bucerías* ☎ *329/298–3073.*

Ztai. Beyond its garden restaurant, multilevel Ztai offers curtained poster beds, supersoft bar stools, and backless sofas in addition to more standard club seating. The minimalist bar is imbued with a peachy glow and overlooks the ocean: muy cool! There's usually a small cover or none at all—except on ladies' night (at this writing, Thursday), when the gals can spend $8 and then attempt to maintain their decorum over unlimited drinks between 11 PM and 3 AM; guys pay three times that much. *Banda* music is currently in vogue with the young hip crowd, and Ztai has bands play this brand of Mexican classics several times a week beginning at 11 PM, reverting to DJ-spun tunes about an hour after midnight. ⊠ *Calle Morelos 737, Centro* ☎ *322/222–0364.*

DANCE AND MUSIC CLUBS

Fodor's Choice
★
Bebotero (⊠ *Paseo Díaz Ordaz 522, Centro* ☎ *322/113–0099*). This upscale, second-story nightclub has live rock. Although it opens nightly after 7, music doesn't start until 10 or 11; closing time is 4 AM. There's no cover charge.

Blanco y Negro (⊠ *Calle Lucerna at Calle Niza, behind Blockbuster Video store, Zona Hotelera* ☎ *322/293–2556*). Here's a wonderful place for

Mexican Rhythms and Roots

Salsa, merengue, *cumbia*—do they leave you spinning before you even hit the dance floor? This primer is designed to help you wrap your mind around Latin beats popular in Pacific Mexico. Unfortunately, it can't cure two left feet, and these flat-footed styles of dancing can be difficult for anyone not accustomed to Latin beats. In Puerto Vallarta, the dance club J.B. is great for lessons.

Latin dance rhythms were born of African drumming. Dancing was vital to West African religious ceremonies; these rhythms spread with importation of slaves to the New World. Evolving regional tastes and additional instruments have produced today's Latin music.

From Colombia, wildly popular **cumbia** combines vocals, wind, and percussion instruments. With a marked rhythm (usually 4/4 time), the sensual music is relatively easy to dance to. Hip-hop and reggae influences have produced urban cumbia, with up-tempo, accordion-driven melodies. Popular artists include Kumbia Kings, La Onda, Control, and Big Circo.

Fast-paced and with short, precise rhythms, **merengue** originated in the Dominican Republic. Although the music sounds almost frantic, the feet aren't meant to keep pace with the melody. Check out Elvis Crespo's 2004 album *Saboréalo.*

Born in Cuba of Spanish and African antecedents, **son** is played on accordion, guitar, and drums. The folkloric music was translated to various dialects in different parts of Mexico. "La Bamba" is a good example of *son jarrocho* (from Veracruz).

American Prohibition sent high rollers sailing down Cuba way, and they came back swinging to son, mambo, and rumba played by full orchestras—think Desi Arnaz and his famous song "Babalou." In New York these styles morphed into **salsa**, popularized by such luminaries as Tito Puente and Celia Cruz and carried on today by superstars like Marc Anthony.

Mexicans love these African-inspired beats but are especially proud of homegrown genres, like **música norteña**, which has its roots in rural, northern Mexico (in Texas, it's called *conjunto*). The traditional instruments are the *bajo sexto* (a 12-string guitar), bass, and accordion; modern groups add the trap drums for a distinctive rhythmic pulse. It's danced like a very lively polka, which is one of its main influences.

A subset of música norteña is the **corrido**, popularized during the Mexican Revolution. Like the ballads sung by wandering European minstrels, corridos informed isolated Mexican communities of the adventures of Emiliano Zapata, Pancho Villa, and their compatriots. Today's "narco-corridos" portray dubious characters: the drug lords who run Mexico's infamous cartels.

But the quintessential Mexican music is **mariachi**, a marriage of European instruments and native sensibilities born right here in Jalisco, Mexico. Guitars, violins, and trumpets are accompanied by the *vihuela* (a small, round-backed guitar) and the larger, deep-throated *guitarrón*. Professional mariachis perform at birthdays and funerals, engagements, anniversaries, and life's other milestones. ⇨ *For more about mariachi, see "Mariachi: Born in Jalisco" in Chapter 8.*

DID YOU KNOW?

Many types of traditional Mexican dancing can be broken down into some basic steps that you can learn yourself, but it's often more fun to sit back and watch the professionals do their thing in colorful, flowing clothing that can seem a part of the dance itself.

a quiet drink. The intimate café-
bar is comfortable yet rustic, with
equipale (leather-and-wood) love
seats and traditional round cocktail tables. At around 10:30, *trova*
(think Mexican Cat Stevens) by
Latino legends Silvio Rodríguez and
Pablo Milanés begins; songs composed and sung by the owner liven

> **ROCK ON**
>
> The sound system at de Santos is
> top-notch, not surprising since one
> of the principal partners is Alex
> González, the drummer from Mexi-
> co's venerable rock band Maná.

up the atmosphere. There's never a cover. It opens after 8 PM every night
but Sunday (Sunday and Monday in low season).

La Bodeguita del Medio (⊠ *Paseo Díaz Ordaz 858, Centro* ☎ *322/223–
1585*). It's a wonderful Cuban bar and restaurant with a friendly vibe.
People of all ages come to salsa and drink mojitos made with Cuban
rum. The small dance floor fills up as soon as the house sextet starts
playing around 9:30 PM. There's no cover.

★ **Christine.** Christine has a spectacular light shows set to bass-thumping
music that ranges from techno and house to disco, rock, and Mexican
pop. Most people (young boomers and Gen-Xers) come for the duration
(it doesn't close until 6 AM), as this is the top of the food chain for the PV
dancing experience. The dance club is open Wednesday through Sunday
after 10 PM, and the cover is typically $20. Exceptions include ladies'
nights (no set night), when women get in free. On open-bar nights, the
$36-per-person cover gets you unlimited drinks. ⊠ *Krystal Vallarta, Av.
de las Garzas s/n, Zona Hotelera* ☎ *322/224–6990.*

Fodor's Choice **de Santos.** In addition to having a pretty good Mediterranean dinner in
★ the ground-floor restaurant, you can start an evening here with chill-
out and lounge music that appeals to an upscale, slightly older crowd
of locals, gringos, local gringos, and Spanish-speaking travelers. Later,
local and guest DJs spin the more danceable, beat-driven disco and
house tunes that appeal to slightly younger folks. If the smoke and noise
get to you, head upstairs to the rooftop bar, where you and your friends
can fling yourselves on the giant futons for some stargazing. This is a
see-and-be-seen place for locals, and the kitchen is generally open until 2
AM; the whole place shuts down at 4 AM, or 6 AM in high season. ⊠ *Calle
Morelos 771, at Leona Vicario, Centro* ☎ *322/223–3052.*

Hilo. Popular with young, hip *vallartenses,* Hilo attracts a mix of locals
and visitors. It's mainly a young crowd, serving up house, techno, hip-
hop, electronic, and Top 40. The ceiling is several stories high, and enormous bronze-color statues give an epic feeling. It's open from 4 PM to 6
AM but doesn't get rolling until midnight. The cover is $7–$10, or $30
with open bar. ⊠ *Paseo Díaz Ordaz 588, Centro* ☎ *322/223–5361.*

★ **J&B Dance Club.** People call it "Hota Bay" (it's how you pronounce
the letters "j" and "b" in Spanish), and it's the best club in town for
salsa. The age of the crowd varies but tends toward thirty- and forty-
somethings. J&B is serious about dancing, so it feels young at heart.
There's usually a band Friday and Saturday nights, DJ music the rest
of the week. Those with *dos patas zurdas* (two left feet) can attend
salsa lessons Thursday and Friday 8 to 9 PM (50 pesos) or take tango

lessons for the same price on Monday at 8 PM. The dance club's cover is $8 when there's live music, otherwise about $4 and free on Monday and Tuesday. ⊠ *Blvd. Francisco M. Ascencio 2043, Zona Hotelera* ☎ *322/224–4616.*

Zoo Bar & Dance. Ready to party? Then head here for DJ-spun techno, Latin, reggae, and hip-hop. The adventurous can dance in the cage. It attracts a mixed crowd of

mainly young locals and travelers, though after midnight the median age plunges. It's open until 6 AM when things are hopping. The restaurant fills with cruise-ship passengers early in the evening. ⊠ *Paseo Díaz Ordaz 630, Centro* ☎ *322/222–4945.*

MOVIES

Cinemark. This easy-to-access cinema is in the heart of the Hotel Zone, on the second floor at the south end of the Plaza Caracol mall. The latest films are shown on its 10 screens. Tickets are less than $4, with a 25% Wednesday discount. ⊠ *Av. de los Tules 178, Plaza Caracol, Zona Hotelera* ☎ *322/224–8927* ⊕ *www.cinemark.com.mx.*

Cinépolis. Until Cinemark showed up, this was PV's newest theater. Next to Soriana department stores at the south entrance to El Pitillal, it has 15 screens and shows movies in English and Spanish. Tickets are $4, less on Wednesday. ⊠ *Plaza Soriana, Av. Francisco Villa 1642–A, Pitillal* ☎ *322/225–1251* ⊕ *www.cinepolis.com.mx.*

SHOW

El Mariachi Loco. It's the place to see mariachi musicians and dance to Latin tunes—all at a price that locals can afford (and it's geared to them, not so much to foreign tourists). The schedule changes frequently, but on a typical night you'll hear mariachis at 11 PM followed by a comedian (in Spanish, of course). A ranchera group then takes over, and couples dance until the wee hours. There is no live entertainment Sunday or Monday. The cover is under $5 most nights; sometimes there's a minimum consumption of around $7. ⊠ *Calle Lázaro Cárdenas 254, at Calle I. Vallarta, Centro* ☎ *322/223–2205.*

MARINA VALLARTA

BARS, PUBS, AND LOUNGES

El Faro. Here you can admire the bay and marina from atop a 110-foot lighthouse. It's mainly a baby-boomer crowd (think yachters) and open daily after 6 PM. During high season, especially on weekends, there's mellow music (including Mexican folk, or trova) after 10 PM. ⊠ *Royal Pacific Yacht Club, Paseo de la Marina 245, Marina Vallarta* ☎ *322/221–0541.*

Tribu Bar Lounge. Locals decided that this was a bit out-of-the-way to become a serious hot spot, but Mexicans and foreigners in the Marina

TEQUILA TOURS

Near Boca de Tomatlán, **Agave Don Crispín** (⊠ *Las Juntas y Los Veranos, 6 km (10 mi) south of PV* ☎ *322/223–6002*) is a small but proud producer of 100% agave tequila. Learn the basics of tequila production, and see the pit ovens and old-fashioned stills. Ask for the day's guide, who will give you a short tour and tasting at no charge, although they prefer to cater to groups. One of the most complete tequila country tours is with **Hacienda San José, del Refugio** (⊠ *Calle Comercio 172, Amatitán, about 400 km (250 mi) east of PV* ☎ *33/3942–3900* ⊕ *www.herradura. com*), producer of the Herradura brand. It offers 90-minute tours with tastings weekdays between 9 and 3. The 60-peso price includes a sip

of three different tequilas, all of which are—surprise!—available in the adjacent gift shop. On the nine-hour **Tequila Express** (☎ *33/3880–9090; 33/3818–3800 Ticketmaster* ⊕ *www. tequilaexpress.com.mx*) train ride, blue agave fields zip by as you sip tequila and listen to roving mariachis. After a distillery tour, there's lunch, folk dancing, and charro (cowboy) demonstrations. Make reservations up to a month ahead; from outside Mexico you'll need to use Ticketmaster, which adds an 8 percent surcharge.

Of course, you might want to just cut to the chase: **La Casa de Tequila** (⊠ *Calle Morelos 589, Centro* ☎ *322/222–2000*) is staffed with a bartender who can educate you as you taste a few of the 80 tequilas on hand.

district find it atmospheric. DJ-spun music pulses house, lounge, techno, disco, or '80s music—whatever the crowd demands, but only until 11 PM. There's also a billiards table. Wednesday is usually salsa night, though the music isn't live; head here Thursday for karaoke. In high season it's open Tuesday to Sunday from 5 PM, often earlier if there's an important ball game on. In low season (generally August through mid-November) it's open Thursday and Friday only. There's never a cover. ⊠ *Paseo de la Marina 220, Mayan Palace Marina, Marina Vallarta* ☎ *322/226–6000 Ext. 4786.*

Victor's Place (Café Tacuba). This inexpensive restaurant doubles as a bar and is as casual as could be. Beer for a buck-fifty (or less, depending on the peso's fluctuations) and cheap tequila with beer chasers are practically a house rule. You can check it out nightly until 11 PM, a bit later on weekends. The outside deck overlooks the yachts in the marina. ⊠ *Condominios Las Palmas, Local 9, Marina Vallarta* ☎ *322/221–2808.*

MOVIES

MMCinema. Across from the cruise-ship pier in the Liverpool shopping complex is the newest of Puerto Vallarta's cinemas. It has 10 screens and $4 tickets. The nearly PV-wide Wednesday discount of 25% means prohibitively large crowds at this particular theater; we suggest coming on a full-price day. ⊠ *Blvd. Francisco M. Ascencio 2920, Galerías Vallarta Local 234, Col. Educación* ☎ *322/221–0095* ⊕ *www.mmcinema.com.*

Continued on page 226

TEQUILA AND MEZCAL—¡SALUD!

If God were Mexican, tequila and mezcal would surely be our heavenly reward, flowing in lieu of milk and honey. Before throwing back your first drink, propose a toast in true Mexican style and wave your glass accordingly— *"¡Arriba, abajo, al centro, pa' dentro!"* ("Above, below, center, inside!")

Historians maintain that, following Spanish conquest and the introduction of the distillation process, tequila was adapted from the ancient Aztec drink *pulque*. Whatever the true origin, Mexico's national drink long predated the Spanish, and is considered North America's oldest spirit.

When you think about tequila, what might come to mind are spaghetti-Western-style bar brawls or late-night teary-eyed confessions. But tequila is more complex and worldly than many presume. By some accounts it's a digestive that reduces cholesterol and stress. Shots of the finest tequilas can cost upward of $100 each, and are meant to be savored as ardently as fine cognacs or single-malt scotches.

Just one of several agave-derived drinks fermented and bottled in Mexico, tequila rose to fame during the Mexican Revolution when it became synonymous with national heritage and pride. Since the 1990s tequila has enjoyed a soaring popularity around the globe, and people the world over are starting to realize that tequila is more than a one-way ticket to (and doesn't necessitate) a hangover.

Harvesting agave in Jalisco.

TEQUILA AND MEZCAL 101

Harvesting blue agave to make tequila.

WHICH CAME FIRST, TEQUILA OR MEZCAL?

Mezcal is tequila's older cousin. Essentially, all tequila is mezcal but only some mezcal is tequila. The only difference between tequila and mezcal is that the tequila meets two requirements: 1) it's made only from blue agave (but some non-agave sugar can be added) and 2) it must be distilled in a specific region in Jalisco or certain parts of neighboring Guanajuato, Michoacán, Nayarit, and Tamaulipas. Unlike tequila, all mezcal must be made from 100 percent agave and must be bottled in Mexico.

CHOOSE YOUR LIQUOR WISELY

Your first decision with tequila is whether to have a *puro* or a *mixto*. You'll know if a bottle is *puro* because it will say so prominently on the label; if the words "100% de agave" don't appear, you can be sure you're getting mixto. Don't be fooled by bottles that say, "Made from agave azul," because all tequila is made from agave azul; that doesn't mean that cane sugar hasn't been added. Popular wisdom holds that puro causes less of a hangover than mixto, but we'll leave that to your own experimentation.

Even among *puros*, there's a wide range of quality and taste, and every fan has his or her favorite. For sipping straight (*derecho*), most people prefer *reposado*, *añejo*, or extra *añejo*. For mixed drinks you'll probably want either a *blanco* or a *reposado*.

Herradura

TEQUILA TIMELINE

Aztec ritual human sacrifice as portrayed on the Codex Magliabechiano.

Pre-Columbian	Aztecs brew pulque for thousands of years; both priests and the sacrificial victims consume it during religious rituals.
1600	The first commercial distillery in New Spain is founded by Pedro Sanches de Tagle, the father of tequila, on his hacienda near the village of Tequila.
1740	*Mezcal de Tequila* earns an enthusiastic following and King Philip V of Spain grants José Antonio Cuervo the first royal license for a mezcal distillery.

THE MAKING OF MEZCAL

1 To make both mezcal and tequila, the agave may be cultivated for as long as ten years, depending on growing conditions and the variety of plant.

2 When the agave is ripe, the leaves, or *pencas*, are removed and the heavy core (called a *piña*, Spanish for "pineapple," because of its resemblance to that fruit) is dug up, **3** cut into large chunks, and cooked to convert its starches into sugars.

4 The *piñas* are then crushed and their juice collected in tanks; yeast is added and the liquid ferments for several days.

After the fermentation, the resulting *mosto* generally measures between 4 and 7 percent alcohol. **5** Finally it's distilled (usually twice for tequila, once for mezcal). This process of heating and condensing serves to boost the alcohol content.
6 And finally, the alcohol is aged in barrels.

While the process is the same, there are a few critical differences between tequila and mezcal: mezcal is made in smaller distilleries and still retains more of an artisanal quality; mezcal magueys are grown over a wider area with more diverse soil composition and microclimate, giving mezcals more individuality than tequila; and lastly, the *piñas* for mezcal are more likely to be baked in stone pits, which imparts a distinctive smoky flavor.

The World's Columbian Fair in Chicago, 1893.

1800s	As the thirst for mezcal grows, wood (used to fire the stills) becomes scarce and distilleries shift to more efficient steam ovens.
1873	Cenobio Sauza exports mezcal to the United States via a new railroad to El Paso, Texas.
1893	*Mezcal de Tequila* (now simply called tequila) receives an award at Chicago's Columbian Exposition.

TEQUILA COCKTAILS

Margarita: The original proportions at Rancho La Gloria were reportedly 3 parts tequila, 2 parts Triple Sec, and 1 part lime juice, though today recipes vary widely. In Mexico an orange liqueur called Controy is often substituted for the Triple Sec. The best margaritas are a little tart and are made from fresh ingredients, not a mix. Besides deciding whether you want yours strained, on the rocks, or frozen, you have dozens of variations to choose from, many incorporating fruits such as strawberry, raspberry, mango, passion fruit, and peach. To salt the rim or not to salt is yet another question.

Sangrita: The name meaning "little blood," this is a very Mexican accompaniment, a spicy mixture of tomato and orange juice that's sipped between swallows of straight tequila (or mezcal).

Tequila refresca: Also very popular in Mexico, this is tequila mixed with citrus soft drinks like Fresca, or Squirt. Generally served in a tall glass over ice.

Tequila Sunrise: Invented in the 1950s, this is a distant runner-up to the margarita, concocted from tequila, orange juice, and grenadine syrup. The grenadine sinks to the bottom, and after a few refills you might agree that the resulting layers resemble a Mexican sky at dawn.

Bloody Maria: One to try with brunch, this is a bloody Mary with you-know-what instead of vodka.

DID YOU KNOW?

Aging mezcal and Tequila imparts a smoothness and an oaky flavor, but over-aging can strip the drink of its characteristic agave taste.

TEQUILA TIMELINE

Mexican revolutionaries

1910–1920	During the Mexican Revolution, homegrown tequila becomes a source of national pride, associated with the hard-riding, hard-drinking rebels.
1930s	Federal land reforms break up the great haciendas and Mexico's agave production slumps by two thirds. To make up for the shortfall, the government allows distillers to begin mixing non-agave sugars into their tequila. This blander drink, called mixto, is better suited to American tastes and sales surge.

TEQUILA AND MEZCAL VOCABULARY

pulque: an alcoholic drink made by the Aztecs

mexcalmetl: Nahuatl word for agave

mixto: a type of tequila that is mixed with non-agave sugars

puro: tequila made with no non-agave sugars

reposado: aged between two months and a year

añejo: aged between one and three years

extra añejo: aged longer than three years

blanco: tequila that is aged less than two months

joven: young tequila, usually a mixto with colorings and flavors

caballito: tall shot glass

pechuga: mezcal flavored with raw chicken breast

cremas: flavored mezcal

aguamiel: agave juice

piña: the agave core

salmiana: a type of agave

pencas: agave leaves

mosto: fermented agave before it is distilled

gusano: the larva found in mescal bottles

WHAT'S WITH THE WORM?

Some mezcals (never tequila) are bottled with a worm (*gusano*), the larva of one of the moths that live on agave plants. Rumor has it that the worm was introduced to ensure a high alcohol content (because the alcohol preserves the creature), but the truth is that the practice started in the 1940s as a marketing gimmick. The worm is ugly but harmless and the best mezcals are not bottled *con gusano*.

Early 1940s	The history of mixology was forever altered when Carlos Herrera invented the margarita for American starlet Marjorie King.
2004	The agave fields around Tequila become a UNESCO World Heritage Site.

Agave fields

CHOOSING A BOTTLE

Reposado (rested)

Silver

Añejo (mature)

Corralejo

BUYING TEQUILA

There are hundreds of brands of tequila, but here are a baker's half dozen of quality *puros* to get you started; generally these distillers offer blanco, reposado, añejo, and extra añejo.

Corralejo—An award winner from the state of Guanajuato, made on the historic hacienda once owned by Pedro Sanchez de Tagle, "the father of tequila" and birthplace of Miguel Hidalgo, the father of Mexican independence.

Corzo—Triple distilled, these tequilas are notably smooth and elegant.

Don Julio—This award-winning tequila, one of the most popular in Mexico, is known for its rich, smooth flavor; the *blanco* is especially esteemed.

Espolón—A relative newcomer founded only in 1998, this distiller has already won several international awards.

Herradura—This is a venerable, popular brand known for its smoky, full body.

Patrón—Founded in 1989, this distiller produces award-winning tequilas. The *añejo* is especially noteworthy for its complex earthiness.

Siete Leguas—Taking their name ("Seven Leagues") from the horse of Pancho Villa, a general in the Mexican Revolution, these quality tequilas are known for their big, full flavor.

TYPES OF TEQUILA AND MEZCAL

Three basic types of tequila and mezcal are determined by how long they've been aged in oak barrels.

Blanco (white) is also known as **plata** or silver. It's been aged for less than two months.

Reposado ("rested") is aged between two months and a year.

añejo ("mature") is kept in barrels for at least a year and perhaps as long as three. Some producers also offer an extra *añejo* that is aged even longer.

Herradura

Don Julio

Gusano Rojo

BUYING MEZCAL

As for enjoying mezcal, it can be substituted in any recipe calling for tequila. But more often it's drunk neat, to savor its unique flavor. Like tequila, straight mezcal is generally served at room temperature in a tall shot glass called a *caballito*.

Some producers now add flavorings to their mezcals. Perhaps the most famous is *pechuga*, which has a raw chicken breast added to the still, supposedly imparting a smoothness and subtle flavor. (Don't worry, the heat and alcohol kill everything.) Citrus is also a popular add-in, and *cremas* contain flavorings such as peaches, mint, raisins, or guava, along with a sweetener such as honey or *aguamiel* (the juice of the agave).

Part of the fun of mezcal is stumbling on smaller, less commercial brands, but here are a few recognized, quality producers. Most make *blancos*, *reposados*, and *añejos*, and some offer extra *añejos*, flavored mezcals, and *cremas* as well.

El Señorio—Produced in Oaxaca the traditional way, with stone ovens and a stone wheel to crush the *piñas*.

El Zacatecano—Founded in 1910 in the northern state of Zacatecas; in a recent competitive tasting, their añejo was judged the best in its category.

Gusano Rojo—This venerable Oaxaca distillery makes the number-one-selling mezcal in Mexico. Yes, there's a worm in the bottle.

Jaral de Berrio—From Guanajuato, this distiller uses the *salmiana* agave. Their *blanco* recently garnered a silver medal.

Real de Magueyes—From the state of San Luis Potosí, these fine mezcals are also made from the local *salmiana* agave. Try the flavorful añejo.

Scorpion—More award-winning mezcals from Oaxaca. Instead of a worm, there's a scorpion in the bottle.

RIVIERA NAYARIT

BARS, PUBS, AND LOUNGES

★ **The Bar Above.** It's difficult to categorize this little place above Tapas del Mundo. It's a martini bar without a bar: the owner, Buddy, prefers that people come to converse with friends at tables rather than hang out at a bar. Desserts are a focus here; come for the signature molten chocolate soufflé, the charred-pineapple-bourbon shortcake, cardamom-laced bread pudding, or any of the other delicious innovations. Lights are dim, the music is romantic, and there's an eagle's view of the ocean from the rooftop crow's nest. It's open daily after 7 PM in high season (November through April). The rest of the year, it's open Tuesday and Thursday only, 8 PM–11 PM. ⊠ *Av. México at Av. Hidalgo, Bucerías* ☎ *329/298–1194.*

La Rosa Chueca. By day an open patio bar selling good burgers (including crocodile and ostrich) and fries, by night a live music hotspot, La Rosa Chueca is a winner. Most exciting for Latin lovers is a dance band playing son, cha-cha, meringue, and salsa; other nights see Latin jazz or other mellow tunes. There's music Tuesday through Saturday in high season, Thursday and Saturday during the sleepy summer months. Candles on the tables and dim overhead lights throw the shadows of lacy palms and looming fig trees onto deep red walls to create a Caribbean ambience that matches the tropical tunes. They have a kid's menu; during the slow rainy season they offer specials (such as Monday drink specials or "kids eat free" days) to drum up business. ⊠ *Av. Hidalgo at Av. México, Bucerías* ☎ *322/146–3023* ⊙ *www.twistedrose.com.mx* ⊙ *Closed Sun.*

MUSIC CLUBS

Philo's. It's the unofficial cultural center and meeting place of La Cruz, with music, food, a large-screen TV, and a pool table. The owner Philo, a former record producer, also has a small recording studio here. The space is plain, but there's excellent live music (a blend of Roots Rock, country, and blues) after 8:30 PM Thursday through Saturday year-round. Get down to the music or chow down on good pizza or barbecue. ⊠ *Calle Delfín 15, La Cruz de Huanacaxtle* ☎ *329/295–5068.*

Overnight Excursions

WORD OF MOUTH

"We took a bus into Guadalajara for a day and then a taxi back to Tlaquepaque. We were glad we were staying there as Guadalajara was big and busy. One day we hired a driver to take us and pick us up in Ajijic, the cute little town where a friend lives. She showed us some of her town; we had a nice lunch and walked along lake Chapala."

—judi

WELCOME TO OVERNIGHT EXCURSIONS

TOP REASONS TO GO

★ **Alchemic atmosphere:** San Blas's basic but charismatic attractions—beaches, markets, churches, and boat trips—combine like magic for a destination that's greater than the sum of its parts.

★ **Highland rambles:** Drop-dead-gorgeous hills and river valleys from Talpa de Allende to San Sebastián get you out into nature and away from coastal humidity.

★ **Amazing photography:** In the mountain towns like San Sebastián, Mascota, and Talpa, even amateurs can capture excellent small-town and nature photos.

★ **Palpable history:** Soak up Mexican history and culture in Guadalajara's churches, museums, and political murals.

★ **Getting the goods:** Guadalajara has excellent housewares and handicrafts at great prices for sale in its megamalls as well as in nearby pre-Hispanic townships.

1 San Blas. Change happens slowly in San Blas, which has yet to experience a tourism boom. Cruise wide dirt streets on one-speed bikes, read books in the shade, dig your toes in the sand, and just enjoy life— one lazy day at a time. Blue mountains and green hills provide a beautiful backdrop.

2 The Mountain Towns.
The former mining and supply towns within the Sierra Madre—Talpa de Allende, Mascota, and tiny San Sebastián—were isolated for centuries by narrow roads and dangerous drop-offs and remain postcards of the past. Soak up the small-town atmosphere and alpine air.

3 Greater Guadalajara.
Home to cherished archetypes like mariachi, charrería (elegant "rodeos"), and tequila, Guadalajara is often called "the Mexican's Mexico." The metropolitan area includes former farming community Zapopan and two districts known for crafts: Tlaquepaque and neighboring Tonalá. Outside the city are unique archaeological digs at Teuchitlán, lakeside retreat Chapala, artists' and expats' enclave Ajijic, and Tequila, famous for…do we even need to say it?

GETTING ORIENTED

About 156 km (95 mi) north of PV, mountain-backed San Blas has beaches and birding. Inland 340 km (211 mi) or so from PV, Jalisco capital Guadalajara (pop. 4 million) sits in the Atemajac Valley, circled by Sierra Madre peaks. Sleepy mountain towns Talpa de Allende, Mascota, and San Sebastián lie about halfway between PV and Guadalajara; each offers a glimpse of rural life from centuries long gone.

8

OVERNIGHT EXCURSIONS PLANNER

Coming and Going

If you plan to visit both Puerto Vallarta and Guadalajara, consider flying into one and out of the other. Some open-jaw trips cost even less than a round-trip flight to/from PV. If you plan your trip right, travel between PV and Guadalajara by bus is $32–$37. One-way drop-off charges for rental cars are steep. Access to Mascota and Talpa from Guadalajara is more direct than from PV, although the latter road is now paved, with new bridges in place. Nonetheless, this windy mountain route is occasionally impassable in rainy season. Buses take you directly from PV to San Blas, or you can get off at nearby beaches. That said, a car is handier for exploring the coast. The mostly two-lane PV–San Blas road is curvy but otherwise fine.

■TIP→ Most small towns that don't have official stations sell gas from a home or store. Ask around before heading out on the highway if you're low on gas.

Day Trips Versus Extended Stays

The San Blas area is best as an overnight unless you go with an organized tour, though you could easily drive to Platanitos, south of San Blas, for a day at the beach.

If busing or driving to the mountain towns, plan to overnight unless you take the day tour with Vallarta Adventures or another PV tour company. Alternatively, you can fly on your own with **Aerotaxis de la Bahía** (☎ 322/221–1990) for a day trip or an overnight stay.

Guadalajara is too far to go for the day from Vallarta or San Blas; we recommend at least three nights if you're doing a round trip.

How Much Can You Do?

What you can (physically) do and what you should do are very different things. To get the most out of your excursion from Puerto Vallarta, don't overdo it. It's a vacation—it's supposed to be relaxing! If you'll be in the Sayulita, San Francisco, and Chacala areas in Nayarit, it's easy to do an overnight jaunt up to San Blas, enjoying the myriad beaches and small towns as you travel up and back. Or make San Blas your base and explore from there.

You could also feasibly spend one night in San Blas and two in Guadalajara, about 4½ hours by rental car and 6 hours by bus. For lovers of the road less traveled, two to three nights gives you ample time to explore the mountain towns of San Sebastián, Mascota, and Talpa as well as the surrounding countryside. Or you could spend one night in the mountains and continue to Guadalajara the next day. To fully appreciate Guadalajara, plan to spend at least three nights as traveling there takes half a day.

DRIVING TIMES FROM PUERTO VALLARTA	
San Blas	3–3½ hours
San Sebastián	1½–2 hours
Mascota	2½–3 hours
Talpa de Allende	3–3½ hours
Guadalajara	4½–6 hours

Tour Companies

Contact the **Cámera de Comercio** (Chamber of Commerce ✉ *Av. Vallarta 4095, Zona Minerva, Guadalajara* ☎ *33/3880–9090 or 01800/503–9720 toll-free in Mexico* ⊕ *www.tequilaexpress.com.mx*) for information about the all-day tour aboard the ***Tequila Express Train.*** The cost is about $80, including lunch, factory tour, mariachi serenades, and tequila.

The bilingual guides of Ajijic's **Charter Club Tours** (✉ *Carretera Chapala–Jocotepec at Calle Colón, Plaza Montana mall, Ajijic* ☎ *376/766–1777, 408/626–7479 in U.S.* ⊕ *www.charterclubtours.com.mx*) lead tours of Guadalajara, shopping and factory trips in Tlaquepaque and Tonalá, Tequila, the Teuchitlán archaeological site, and treks to Jalisco's lesser-known towns.

TB Tours (✉ *Calle Cisne 129, Fracc. Los Sauces* ☎ *322/209–1655*) leads tours to San Blas, with a visit to the old fort and the town, and to La Tovara mangroves and the crocodile farm. It's a full-day tour, including breakfast en route, the boat tour, guide, lunch, and hotel pick-up and return. The cost is about $100 per person. There are tours year-round, but only on Thursday. TB also has a San Sebastián tour, at about $75, Tuesday through Thursday.

Highly recommended **Vallarta Adventures** (✉ *Edificio Marina Golf, Local 13–C, Calle Mástil, Marina Vallarta, Puerto Vallarta* ☎ *322/297–1212, 888/526–2283 in U.S. and Canada* ⊕ *www.vallarta-adventures.com*) has daily, seven-hour jeep tours to San Sebastián ($80).

WHAT IT COSTS IN U.S. DOLLARS

	¢	$	$$	$$$	$$$$
Restaurants	under $5	$5–$10	$11–$15	$16–$25	over $25
Hotels	under $50	$50–$75	$76–$150	$151–$250	over $250

Restaurant prices are for a median main course at dinner, excluding tax, drinks, and service. Hotel prices are for a standard room, generally excluding taxes and service charges.

When to Go

Thanks to a springlike climate, Guadalajara is pleasant at most times of year, though May and June can be uncomfortably hot for some. Book well in advance to visit during the October Festival or other holidays. Roads can be dangerous during summer rains; June through October isn't the best time to visit the mountain towns by land.

San Blas and the coast begin to heat up in May; during the late June through October rainy season both the ambient and ocean temps are highest. In Guadalajara, rain tends to be limited to the late afternoon and evening.

Festivals and Special Events

8

Guadalajara's major events include the International Mariachi Festival in September, the Tequila Festival in March, and a cultural festival in May. Also in Guadalajara, the entire month of October is given up to mariachis, *charreadas* (rodeos), soccer matches, and theater.

At the San Blas Festival (February 3), a statue of the town's patron saint gets a boat ride around the bay and the town invests in a major fireworks show. In the Sierra Madre, Talpa's equally admired icon brings the faithful en masse four times a year for street dances and mariachi serenades.

Puerto Vallarta's location means lots of variety. You can explore little-visited beaches and miles of mangrove canals in San Blas. You can shop and "get culture" in historic Guadalajara. Or you can head to the mountains for a look at mining towns and long walks down country lanes.

Although San Blas is now the northern terminus of the so-called Riviera Nayarit (the new term for the stretch of coast from San Blas to the southern Nayarit State border at Nuevo Vallarta), thus far it's changed little. Things here are low-key and friendly—a nice change from bustling Vallarta and environs, where traffic sometimes snarls. There are no supermarkets; everyone shops at mom-and-pop groceries or the daily market for tropical fruits and vegetables, tortillas, and hot or cold snacks. Many of the restaurants around the plaza are relatively simple and inexpensive.

Founded by the Spanish but soon all but abandoned for busier ports, San Blas has several historic structures to visit, including the old customs and counting houses, and original churches. But more of a draw are its miles of sandy beaches and La Tobara, a serpentine series of mangrove-lined channels leading to a freshwater spring.

Even less sophisticated than San Blas are a handful of former silver-mining towns and supply centers in the hills behind Puerto Vallarta. Until a 21st-century road improvement, Mascota, Talpa de Allende, San Sebastián, and other villages en route to Guadalajara were accessible only by narrow, treacherous, snaky mountain road or small plane. Today sunny, unpolluted days and crisp nights lure people out of the fray and into a more relaxed milieu, where lingering over coffee or watching kids play in the town plaza are the activities of choice. If this sounds too tame, there's horseback riding, hiking, and fishing at Presa Coriches, among other activities.

Guadalajara—Mexico's second-largest city—makes an excellent add-on to a Vallarta beach vacation. You can shop in megamalls or in surrounding towns, where artisans were producing pottery centuries before the Spanish invasion. You can take in modern Russian ballet or Mexican folkloric dances; see a fast-paced *charrería,* with men and women on

well-groomed Arabian horses; listen to a 12-piece mariachi band; or visit one of a dozen museums. Although at times overwhelming, this modern city provides an excellent overview of all Mexico has to offer. For a foray outside the metropolis, head for Lago de Chapala, Mexico's largest natural lake, or to Tequila, land of the blue agave, where the country's national drink is produced and bottled.

SAN BLAS AND ENVIRONS

The cool thing about San Blas and the surrounding beaches is that they're untouristy and authentic. Sure, there's an expat community, but it's minuscule compared to that of Puerto Vallarta. Parts of San Blas itself are deliciously disheveled or, should we say, ungentrified. The lively square is a nice place to polish off an ice-cream cone and watch the world. If you're looking for posh restaurants and perfect English speakers, this isn't the place for you.

Most people come to the San Blas area for basic R&R, to enjoy the long beaches and seafood shanties. The town's sights can be seen in a day, but stay for a few days at least to catch up on your reading, visit the beaches, and savor the town as it deserves. La Tovara jungle cruise through the mangroves should not be missed.

SAN BLAS

Many travelers come here looking for Old Mexico, or the "real Mexico," or the Mexico they remember from the 1960s. New Spain's first official Pacific port has experienced a long, slow slide into obscurity since losing out to better-equipped ports in the late 19th century. But there's something to be said for being a bit player rather than a superstar. Industrious but not overworked, residents of this drowsy seaside city hit the beaches on weekends and celebrate their good fortune during numerous saints' days and civic festivals. You can, too.

8

GETTING HERE AND AROUND

If you want to head directly to San Blas from outside Mexico, fly to Mexico City and on to Tepic (69 km [43 mi] from San Blas), capital of the state of Nayarit, on Aeromar (affiliated with Mexicana de Aviación). To get to San Blas by road from Tepic, head north on Highway 15D, then west on Highway 11. Most visitors, however, make San Blas a road trip from PV.

The Puerto Vallarta bus station is less than 5 km (3 mi) north of the PV airport; there are usually four daily departures for San Blas ($10; three hours). These buses generally don't stop, and most don't have bathrooms. Departure times vary throughout the year, but at this writing, there were no departures after 4:30 PM. To get to Platanitos Beach, about an hour south of San Blas, take the Puerto Vallarta bus. ■TIP➔ Always check the return schedule with the driver when taking an out-of-town bus. A taxi from Puerto Vallarta or from the airport costs about $100.

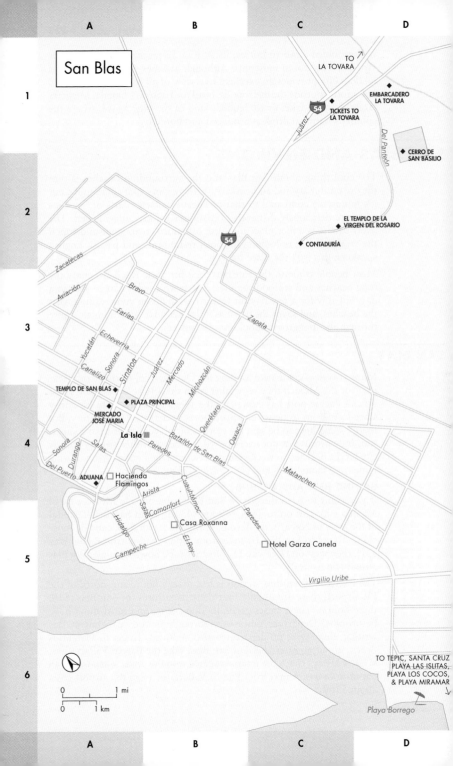

San Blas

A **B** **C** **D**

1

TO
LA TOVARA

54
Juárez

TICKETS TO
LA TOVARA

EMBARCADERO
LA TOVARA

Del Panteón

CERRO DE
SAN BÁSILIO

2

54

EL TEMPLO DE LA
VIRGEN DEL ROSARIO

CONTADURÍA

Zacatecas

Aviación

Bravo

3

Farías

Zapata

Echeverría

Yucatán

Canalizo

Sonora

Sinaloa

Juárez

Mercado

Michoacán

TEMPLO DE SAN BLAS

PLAZA PRINCIPAL

MERCADO
JOSÉ MARÍA

Querétaro

Oaxaca

4

La Isla

Sonora

Durango

Salas

Batallón de San Blas

Del Puerto

ADUANA

Hacienda
Flamingos

Matanchén

Arista

Salas
Comonfort

Cuauhtémoc

Paredes

Hidalgo

El Rey

Casa Roxanna

5

Campeche

Hotel Garza Canela

Virgilio Uribe

6

0   1 mi

0   1 km

TO TEPIC, SANTA CRUZ
PLAYA LAS ISLITAS,
PLAYA LOS COCOS,
& PLAYA MIRAMAR

Playa Borrego

A **B** **C** **D**

A car is handy for more extensive explorations of the coast between PV and around San Blas. Within San Blas, the streets are wide, traffic is almost nonexistent, and, with the exception of the streets immediately surrounding the main plaza, parking is easy. From Puerto Vallarta, abandon Highway 200 just past Las Varas in favor of the coast road. (Follow the sign toward Zacualpan, where you must go around the main plaza to continue on the unsigned

> ### BIRDER'S PARADISE
>
> More than 500 species of birds settle in the San Blas area; 23 are endemic. Organize a birding tour through Hotel Garza Canela (⇨ *below*). In late January, you can attend the International Festival of Migratory Birds for bird-watching tours and conferences with experts and fellow enthusiasts.

road. Ask locals "San Blas?" and they'll point you in the right direction). The distance of about 160 km (100 mi) takes 3 to 3½ hours.

From Guadalajara, you can take 15D (the toll road, about $40) to the Miramar turnoff to San Blas. It's actually much faster and less congested, however, to take Highway 15 at Tequepexpan and head west through Compostela on Highway 68 (toll about $5); merge with Highway 200 until Las Varas, and then head north on the coastal route (Highway 66) to San Blas.

To really go native, rent a bike from Wala Restaurant, a half block up from the plaza on Calle Juárez, and cruise to your heart's content. To get to the beaches south of town, to Matanchén Bay, and to the village of Santa Cruz, take a bus (they usually leave on the hour) from the bus station across the street from the church on the main plaza. To come back, just stand by the side of the road and flag down a passing bus.

ESSENTIALS

Air Contacts Aeromar (☏ *55/5133–1111 in Mexico* ⊕ *www.aeromar.com.mx*). **Mexicana** (☏ *800/531–7921 in U.S., 866/281–3049 in Canada, 01800/502–2000 in Mexico* ⊕ *www.mexicana.com*).

Bank Banamex (✉ *Calle Juárez 26, 1 block east of plaza, San Blas* ☏ *323/285–0031*).

Bus Contact Transportes Norte de Sonora (☏ *55/5729–0807*) .

Medical Assistance Centro de Salud San Blas (✉ *Calle H. Batallón at Calle Yucatán, San Blas* ☏ *323/285–0232*). **Emergency Hotline** (☏ *066*). **Farmacia Económica** (✉ *Calle H. Batallón at Calle Mercado, San Blas* ☏ *323/285–0111*) closes between 2 and 4:30 PM and for the night at 9 PM.

Tourist Board Oficina de Turismo de San Blas (✉ *Calle Canalizo at Calle Sinaloa in Municipal Palace, 2nd fl., on main plaza, San Blas*).

EXPLORING

If you need a break from all-out relaxation, visit some of these locations. However, keep in mind that, like the town itself, the sites of San Blas are very low key.

Templo de San Blas, called *La Iglesia Vieja* ("the old church") by residents, is on the town's busy plaza. It's rarely open these days, but you can admire its diminutive beauty and look for the words to Henry

Take in the expansive landscape from San Blas Fort at Cerro de San Basilio.

Wadsworth Longfellow's poem "The Bells of San Blas," inscribed on a brass plaque. (The long-gone bells were actually at the church dedicated to the Virgin of the Rosary, on Cerro de San Basilio.)

Browse for fruits or good photo-ops at the market, **Mercado José María** (⊠ *Calle H. Battalón de San Blas, between Calles Sonora and Sinaloa*), where you can take a load off at Chito's for a milk shake or fresh fruit juice.

The old **Aduana** (*Customs House* ⊠ *Calle Juárez, near Calle del Puerto*) has been partially restored and is now a cultural center with sporadic art or photography shows and theatrical productions.

For a bird's-eye view of town and the coast, hike or drive up Calle Juárez, the main drag, to **Cerro de San Basilio**. Cannons protect the ruined **Contaduría** (*Counting House* ⊠ *Cerro de San Basilio*), built during colonial times when San Blas was New Spain's first official port.

Continuing down the road from the Contaduría brings you to **El Templo de la Virgen del Rosario**. Note the new floor in the otherwise ruined structure; the governor's daughter didn't want to soil the hem of her gown when she married here in 2005. A bit farther on, San Blas's little cemetery is backed by the sea and the mountains.

WHERE TO EAT AND STAY

$ ✗ **La Isla.** Shell lamps; pictures made entirely of scallops, bivalves, and star-
SEAFOOD fish; shell-drenched chandeliers—every inch of wall space is decorated in different denizens of the sea. Service isn't particularly brisk (pretty much par for the course in laid-back San Blas), but the seafood, filet mignon, and fajitas are all quite good. Afterward stroll over to the main plaza a

few blocks away. ⊠ *Calle Mercado at Calle Paredes* ☎ *323/285–0407* ▭ *No credit cards* ⊘ *2–9* PM; *closed Mon. except holidays* ⊹ *B4.*

$ ⊡ **Casa Roxanna.** This is an attractive little enclave of cozy and clean (albeit basic) cottages with screened windows. Full kitchens with lots of pots and pans invite cooking, but the real draws are the lovingly tended gardens surrounding the

lodgings, the covered patio, and the sparkling, three-lane lap pool. If you love it, settle in awhile; monthly rates are usually available. **Pros:** personable staff; great lap pool. **Cons:** so-so a/c units; lackluster interior decor. ⊠ *Callejón El Rey 1, San Blas* ☎ *323/285–0573* ⊕ *www.casaroxanna. com* ⇆ *6 cottages* ⚹ *In-room: no phone, kitchen (some), refrigerator (some). In-hotel: pool, laundry facilities, Wi-Fi hotspot, parking (free)* ▭ *No credit cards* |○| *EP* ⊹ *B5.*

$$ ⊡ **Hacienda Flamingos.** Built in 1882, this restored mansion-turned-hotel was once part of a large hacienda. The restoration is stunning: surrounding a pretty, plant-filled courtyard is a covered veranda of lovely floor tiles, with lazily rotating ceiling fans, antique furniture, and groupings of chairs for a casual conversation. Opening off the veranda, elegant suites have also been restored to their original glory. It's right across from the cultural center and near the market and town plaza. **Pros:** lovely decor; close to town center. **Cons:** sometimes eerily devoid of other guests; staff can be chilly. ⊠ *Calle Juárez 105, San Blas* ☎ *323/285–0930; 669/985– 1818 for information in English* ⊕ *www.sanblas.com.mx* ⇆ *20 rooms* ⚹ *In-room: no phone, DVD (some). In-hotel: pool, gym, laundry facilities, Wi-Fi hotspot, parking (free)* ▭ *MC, V* |○| *EP* ⊹ *A4.*

$$ ⊡ **Hotel Garza Canela.** Opened decades ago by a family of dedicated bird-
★ watchers, this meandering, three-story hotel with expansive grounds is the home base of choice for birding groups. Rooms have small balconies and polished limestone floors; junior suites have large whirlpool tubs. Betty Vasquez, who runs El Delfín French restaurant here, studied at Le Cordon Bleu in France; she prepares elegant and very tasty meals. **Pros:** very good French restaurant; suites have hot tub; babysitters. **Cons:** estuary location means there are some biting bugs; one shared computer for checking Internet in lobby; no Internet access, including Wi-Fi, after 8 PM. ⊠ *Calle Paredes 106 Sur, San Blas* ☎ *323/285–0112, 01800/713–2313 toll-free in Mexico* ⊕ *www.garzacanela.com* ⇆ *44 rooms, 6 suites* ⚹ *In-room: no phone. In-hotel: restaurant, pool, Wi-Fi hotspot, parking (free)* ▭ *AE, MC, V* |○| *EP* ⊹ *C5.*

SPORTS AND THE OUTDOORS

BOAT TOUR A series of narrow waterways wends through the mangroves to **La**
☾ **Tovara,** San Blas's most famous attraction. Turtles on logs, crocs that
★ *look* like logs, birds, iguanas, and exotic orchids make this maze of mud-brown canals a magical place. Begin the tranquil ride ($8 per person; four-person minimum or $27 [360 pesos] total for fewer than four) at the El Conchal Bridge, at the entrance-exit to San Blas, or the village

DID YOU KNOW?

When you travel down the Río Tovara on your way to Tovara Springs, you can ask the guide to help you spot wildlife—he or she will likely slow down for easier photographing. What might be harder to get help with is child-size life vests; know that the one supplied might not be helpful in the event it's needed.

of Matanchén. Boats depart when there are enough customers, which isn't usually a problem. Either way you'll end up, after a 45-minute boat ride, at the freshwater pool fed by a natural spring. Rest at the snack shop overlooking the water or jump in using the rope swing, keeping an eye out for the allegedly benign resident croc. There's

> **CAUTION**
>
> The fierce biting *jejenes* (no-see-ums) of San Blas are legendary; luckily, early afternoon breezes keep them (relatively) at bay. They're worst during full and new moons, when the tide is highest.

an optional trip to a crocodile farm for a few dollars more, making it a three-hour instead of a two-hour tour.

ECOTOUR   **Singayta** (⊠ *8 km [5 mi] from San Blas on road to Tepic* ⊕ *www. singayta.com*) is a typical Nayarit village that is attempting to support itself through simple and ungimmicky ecotours. The basic tour includes a look around the town, where original adobe structures compete with more practical but less picturesque structures with corrugated tin roofs. Take a short guided hike through the surrounding jungle, and a boat ride around the estuary ($6 per person). This is primo birding territory. The townspeople are most geared up for tours on weekends and during school holidays and vacations: Christmas, Easter, and July, and August. The easiest way to book a tour is to look for English-speaking Juan Bananas, who sells banana bread from a shop called Tumba de Yako (look for the sign on the unmarked road Avenida H. Batallón between calles Comonfort and Canalizo, en route to Playa Borrego). He can set up a visit and/or guide you there. Groups of five or more can call ahead to make a reservation with Juan (☎ *323/285–0462* ✎ *ecomanglar@ yahoo.com*) or with Santos (☎ *323/100–4191*); call at least a day ahead if you want to have a meal.

8

THE BEACHES NEAR SAN BLAS

Like San Blas itself, the surrounding beaches attract mostly local people and travelers fleeing glitzier resort scenes. Beaches here are almost uniformly long, flat, and walkable, with light brown sand, moderate waves, and seriously bothersome no-see-ums, especially around sunrise and sunset (and during the waxing and waning moons). Almost as ubiquitous as these biting bugs are simple *ramadas* (open-sided, palm-thatch-roof eateries) on the beach whose owners don't mind if you hang out all day, jumping in the ocean and then back in your shaded hammock to continue devouring John Grisham or leafing through magazines. Order a cold lemonade or a beer, or have a meal of fillet of fish, ceviche, or chips and guacamole. Don't expect a full menu, rather what's fresh and available. All these beaches are accessible by bus from San Blas's centrally located bus station.

☾   You can walk or ride a bike to long, lovely **Playa Borrego**, 1 km (½ mi)
Fodor's Choice   south of town. Rent a surfboard at Stoners' or Mar y Sol restaurant to
★   attack the year-round (but sporadic) shore or jetty breaks here, or stroll down to the southern end to admire the lovely, palm-fringed estuary.

About 6 km (4 mi) south of Playa Borrego, at the northern edge of Bahía de Matanchén, **Playa Las Islitas** used to be legendary among surfers for its long wave, but this has diminished in recent years; the beach is now suitable for swimming, body-surfing, and boogie boarding.

★ At the south end of the Matanchén Bay, **Playa Los Cocos and Playa Miramar** are both great for taking long walks and for hanging out at ramadas.

Adjacent to Miramar Beach is the well-kept fishing village of **Santa Cruz**. Take a walk on the beach or around the town; buy a soft drink, find the bakery, and pick up some banana bread. Outdoor dances are occasionally held on the diminutive central plaza.

★ Beyond Matanchén Bay the road heads inland and reemerges about 8 km (5 mi) later at **Playa Platanitos**, a lovely little beach in a sheltered cove. Fishermen park their skiffs here and simple shacks cook up the catch of the day.

WHERE TO STAY

¢ ⊞ **Casa Mañana**. Some of the pleasant rooms overlook the beach from a
☺ balcony or terrace, but most people stay here for easy access to the good burgers, guacamole, and seafood platter for two ($13) at the adjoining El Alebrije restaurant. The bar, with its cool, brick-floor interior open to the beach, is also popular. Other perks: the long beach, large pool, and hiking and other outdoor activities. **Pros:** good burgers; nice beachfront location. **Cons:** must take a bus or taxi to and from San Blas. ⊠ *South end of Playa Los Cocos, 13 km (8 mi) south of San Blas* ☎ *323/254–9070; also 800/202–2079 in Mexico only* ⊕ *www.casa-manana.com* ⇗ *26 rooms* ⅛ *In-hotel: restaurant, bar, pool, beachfront, parking (free)* ⊟ *MC, V* ⅋⊙⅋ *EP.*

THE MOUNTAIN TOWNS

A trip into the Sierra Madre is an excellent way to escape the coastal heat and the hordes of vacationers. The Spanish arrived to extract ore from these mountains at the end of the 16th century; after the Mexican Revolution the mines were largely abandoned in favor of richer veins. The isolation of these tiny towns has kept them old-fashioned.

The air is crisp and clean and scented of pine, the valley and mountain views are spectacular, and the highland towns are earthy, unassuming, and charming. Whitewashed adobe homes radiate from plazas where old gents remember youthful exploits. Saturday night boys and girls court each other alfresco while oompah bands entertain their parents from the bandstand. Although most of the hotels in the region have only basic amenities (construction on a massively improved road from PV is encouraging entrepreneurs, however), the chill mountain air and pounds of blankets can produce a delicious night's sleep.

GREAT ITINERARIES

If you're not joining an organized day tour, there are many possible itineraries, depending on whether you leave from PV or from Guadalajara, your tolerance for driving mountain roads, and your desire to explore (i.e., either to see lots or just relax and enjoy the tranquility, mountain-and-valley views, and quaint lifestyle).

From Puerto Vallarta, consider a two-day trip to the area beginning in San Sebastián and returning to PV (or Guadalajara) from Talpa de Allende. There are many ways to go; keys are not driving at night and enjoying the slow pace. Drive to San Sebastián, enjoying the mountain scenery en route. After a look around the quaint old mining village and an early lunch, continue to Mascota,

the area's largest town and a good base. Spend the night in Mascota. The Sierra Lodge on Lake Juanacatlán, which serves excellent food, can be added as an overnight trip, but it doesn't take day-trippers. If you prefer, take a day trip from Mascota to Talpa de Allende, whose raison d'être is the tiny, beloved Virgin statue in the town's ornate basilica.

Each of the three towns has hills to climb for excellent vistas and photos. Otherwise, activities include wandering the streets, visiting small museums and Catholic churches, tasting regional food, and drinking in the mountain air and old-fashioned ambience. Make sure you get where you're going before dark, as mountain roads are unlighted and narrow and in many cases have sheer drop-offs.

GETTING HERE AND AROUND

For an effortless excursion, go on a tour through Vallarta Adventures. It has excellent day trips ($80) to San Sebastián by bus or jeep, depending on the number of passengers.

To have more flexibility or to spend the night in a cozy, no-frills hotel or a refurbished hacienda, charter a twin-engine Cessna through Aerotaxis de la Bahía in PV. For one to seven passengers the rate is about $700 split among them to San Sebastián, $750 to Mascota or Talpa de Allende. Add to these fares 15% sales tax and $20 per person air travelers' tax. ■TIP➜ The return flight is usually free if you fly back with the pilot within three hours of arrival.

ATM (Autotransportes Talpa–Mascota) buses depart from their bus station in PV three times a day around 9 AM, 2:30, and 6:30 PM, stopping at La Estancia (11 km [7 mi] from San Sebastián; 1½ hours), then Mascota (2 to 2½ hours) and Talpa (3 to 3½ hours). Cost is about $5 one way to San Sebastián (La Estancia); $9 to Mascota; and $10 to Talpa.

Buses also depart several times a day from Guadalajara's new bus station (Entronque Carretera Libre a Zapotlanejo, modules 3 and 4). Note that the bus doesn't enter San Sebastián; you'll be dropped at a small rest area, where taxis usually are available to transport you to town. The cost for the short drive is a bit steep at about $12. Share the cab with others on the bus to split the cost; or get a lift with a local and offer to pay (note that many will decline or ask just a small amount to help out with gas).

8

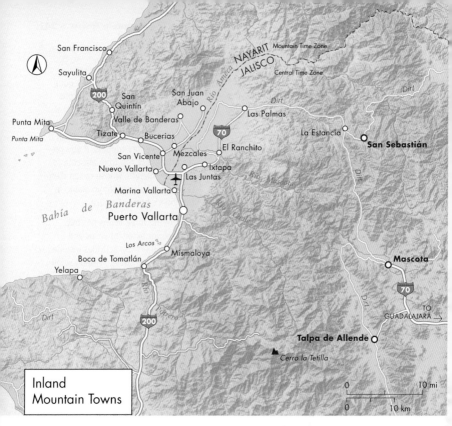

From Puerto Vallarta the road to San Sebastián is paved now, but those going to San Sebastián still have to get off the bus at La Estancia and take a taxi those last few miles. A suspension bridge was inaugurated in early 2007 to cover the last 8 km (5 mi) of the road to Mascota, which used to get washed out regularly in the rainy season. (Note that this road still may become dangerous or at least frightening during the rainy season, when landslides can occur.) Lago Juanacatlán is an hour from Mascota on a rough one-lane road of dirt and rock.

Taxis hang out near the main square in Talpa, Mascota, and San Sebastián.

ESSENTIALS

Air Contact Aerotaxis de la Bahía (☎ 322/221–1990).

Banks Bancomer (✉ Calle Constitución at Av. Hidalgo, Mascota ☎ 388/386–0387). **Banco HSBC** (✉ Calle Independencia, across from la presidencia [town hall], Talpa ☎ 388/385–0197).

Bus Contact Autotransportes Talpa–Mascota (ATM ☎ 388/386–0093 in Mascota, 388/385–0015 in Talpa, 33/3619–7549 in Guadalajara).

Medical Assistance Centro de Salud de Mascota (✉ Francisco J Madero 299, Mascota ☎ 388/386–0174). **Farmacia del Oeste** (✉ Calle Hidalgo 20, across from plaza, San Sebastián ☎ 322/297–2833). **Farmacia San Miguel**

(✉ *Calle Independencia 16, at Calle Anahuac, across from square, Talpa* ☎ *388/385–0085*).

Tour and Visitor Information Oficina de Turismo de Mascota (✉ *La Presidencia [Town Hall], Calle Ayuntamiento, at Calle Constitución, facing plaza, Mascota* ☎ *388/386–1179*). **Oficina de Turismo de San Sebastián** (✉ *Calle López Mateos, around corner from la presidencia [town hall], San Sebastián* ☎ *322/297–2938*). **Oficina de Turismo de Talpa** (✉ *La Presidencia [Town Hall], Calle Independencia s/n, 2 blocks north of plaza, Talpa de Allende* ☎ *388/385–0009 or 388/385–0287*). **Vallarta Adventures** (☎ *322/297–1212; 888/526–2238* ⊕ *www.vallarta-adventures.com*).

SAN SEBASTIÁN

If, physically, there are only about 80 km (50 mi) between Puerto Vallarta and San Sebastián, metaphorically they're as far apart as the Earth and the moon. Sleepy San Sebastián is the Mayberry of Mexico, but a little less lively. It's the kind of place where you feel weird walking past people without saying hello, even though you don't know them from Adam. The miners who built the town have long gone, and more recently, younger folks are drifting away in search of opportunity. Most of the 800 or so people who have stayed seem perfectly content with life as it is, although rat-race dropouts and entrepreneurs are making their way here along improved roads.

EXPLORING

The most interesting thing to see in San Sebastián is the town itself. Walk the cobblestone streets and handsome brick sidewalks, admiring the white-faced adobe structures surrounding the plaza. Take any side street and wander at will. Enjoy the enormous walnut trees lining the road into town, and diminutive peach trees peaking over garden walls. The reason to go to this cozy, lazy, beautiful town at 5,250 feet above sea level is to look inward, reflecting on life, or outward, greeting or chatting as best you can with those you meet. Look anywhere, in fact, except at a laptop or, if possible, a television screen. That's just missing the point.

San Sebastián has a few things to do, although none of them are the reason to visit.

Stop in the *abarrotes* (general store) on the north side of the square for a beverage or a spool of thread; then head directly behind it to **Iglesia de San Sebastián**, a typically restored 1800s-era church that comes to life in the days preceding its saint's day, January 20.

You're welcome any time at the **Casa Museo de Doña Conchita** (✉ *Calle Juárez 2* ☎ *322/297–2860* ✍ *$1*). The aged but affable lady loves to show visitors photos of her venerable family—which she traces back six generations. See bank notes from the mining days, bloomers, shirts made by hand by the lady for her many children, and other old memorabilia. If you speak Spanish, ask Doña Conchita to tell you about the ghosts that haunt her house, which is right on the square between the basketball court and *la presidencia*, or town hall. Hours are somewhat flexible, but stated hours are Monday through Saturday 10:30–3 and 5–7, Sunday noon–3.

8

San Sebastian is beautiful at dusk; get to higher ground for the full effect.

WHERE TO EAT AND STAY

$
MEXICAN
✗ **Fonda de Doña Lupita.** Typical food of the countryside—enchiladas, tamales, pozole, beefsteak with beans and tortillas, and so on—is served in an equally typical family home. The house has been enlarged to welcome guests, and the friendly owner does her part. Straw-bottom chairs are comfortable enough, and the oilcloths shiny and new. The small bar is at the back behind the large, open kitchen. It's open for breakfast, too. ⊠ *Calle Cuauhtemoc 89* ☎ *322/297–2803* ⊘ *9:30 AM–8:30 PM* ▭ *No credit cards.*

$$
▦ **La Galerita de San Sebastián.** A pair of displaced *tapatíos* (Guadala-jarans) have created a cluster of pretty cabins on their property about four blocks from the plaza. Comfortable futons in each room provide a place to sleep, nap, or watch TV. The double-sided fireplace heats the bedroom and adjoining sitting room. Bed coverings and matching drapes of earthy, muted colors are all good quality. This is the most modern place to stay in San Sebastián and is geared to adults but accepts children, too, for an additional charge of about $20 per child. **Pros:** stylish; has in-room fireplaces. **Cons:** pricey compared to other area digs; extra charge for each child. ⊠ *Camino a Las Galeritas 62, Bar-rio La Otra Banda* ☎ *322/297–3040* ⊕ *www.lagalerita.com.mx* ⟳ *3 bungalows* ♿ *In-room: no a/c, no phone, refrigerator, Wi-Fi. In-hotel: restaurant, parking (free), Wi-Fi hotspot* ▭ *MC, V* ❍❙ *BP.*

$
▦ **Real de San Sebastián.** Small rooms are dominated by snug king beds in curtained alcoves in this interesting B&B. It has a (somewhat cramped) shared main living space with a cushy, plush couch facing a large-screen sat-ellite TV, and more formal round tables where hot drinks like tea or cocoa may be served in the afternoon. In the morning, you get complimentary

coffee or hot chocolate and rolls in bed, served through a small service window. The manager, Margarito Salcedo, is friendly and solicitous. At this writing, the Web site was still under construction. **Pros:** friendly, helpful hosts; good value. **Cons:** living room is dated; guest rooms are dominated by the bed and don't have phones; credit cards aren't accepted. ⊠ *Calle Zaragoza 41* ☎ *322/297–3224* ⊕ *www.sansebastiandeloeste. com* ⇌ *6 rooms* ⚐ *In-room: no a/c, no phone, no TV. In-hotel: restaurant* ⊟ *No credit cards* |◎| *CP.*

SPORTS AND THE OUTDOORS

Local men can be hired for a truck ride up to **La Bufa**, a half-dome visible from the town square. One such man is **Obed Dueña** (☎ *322/297–2864*), who charges about $46 for the trip, whether for two or eight passengers; it's about $62 for up to 15 people in a larger vehicle. It's the same price if you return with him or hike back. The truck will wait while you climb—about 15 minutes to the top—and enjoy the wonderful view of the town, surrounding valleys, and, on a clear day, Puerto Vallarta. San Sebastián was founded as a silver- and gold-mining town; ask the driver to stop for a quick visit to a mine en route. The excursion takes about three hours. Or you can hike both ways; it takes most folks two to two and a half hours to reach the top, and half to two-thirds that time to return.

> **WARM CUPPA CORN?**
>
> For an authentic experience, pop into any *fonda* or *lonchería* (simple eateries, the former usually in someone's home, the latter open for lunch only) for a typical *atole con piloncillo* (hot corn drink sweetened with unrefined brown sugar) and a simple meal. Some, like the **Fonda Doña Leo** (⊠ *Calle Paso del Norte* ☎ *322/297–2909* ☙ *Breakfast only, 9 AM–11 AM*), down the street from the basketball court, don't even have signs out front.

MASCOTA

Mascota's cool but sunny climate is perfect for growing citrus, avocados, nuts, wheat, corn, and other crops. Fed by the Mascota and Ameca rivers and many springs and year-round streams, the blue-green hills and valleys surrounding town are lusciously forested; beyond them rise indigo mountains to form a painterly tableau. This former mining town and municipal seat is home to some 13,000 people. Its banks, shops, and hospital serve surrounding villages. On its coat of arms are a pine tree, deer, and rattlesnake. The town's name derives from the Nahuatl words for "deer" and "snake."

EXPLORING

★ Mascota's pride is **La Iglesia de la Preciosa Sangre** (Church of the Precious Blood), started in 1909 but unfinished due to the revolution and the ensuing Cristero Revolt. Weddings, concerts, and plays are sometimes held here under the ruins of Gothic arches. Note the 3-D blood squirting from Jesus's wound in the chapel—you could hardly miss it.

Walk around the **plaza**, where old gents share stories and kids chase balloons. Couples dance the stately *danzón* on Thursday and Saturday evenings as the band plays in the wrought-iron bandstand. The town

produces ceramics, saddles, and *raicilla*, a relative of tequila made from the green agave plant (tequila comes from the blue one).

On one corner of the plaza is the town's white-spire **Iglesia de la Virgen de los Dolores**. The Virgin of Sorrow is feted on September 15, which segues into Mexican Independence Day on the 16th.

A block beyond the other end of the plaza, the **Museo de Mascota** (⊠ *Calle Morelos, near Calle Allende*) is worth a look. It's open Monday through Saturday 10–3 and 5–8.

> **MASCOTA'S MARTYR**
>
> In 1927, during the anticlerical Cristero movement, Mascota's young priest refused to abandon his post. Soldiers peeled the skin from his hands and feet before forcing him to walk to a large oak tree, where he was hanged. Mascota's hero, José María Robles, was canonized in 2000 by Pope John Paul II.

Around the corner from the Mascota Museum, the **Casa de la Cultura** (⊠ *Calle Allende 115*) has rotating exhibits of photography and art. It's open 10–2 and 4–7 Monday through Saturday.

WHERE TO EAT

$ ✕ **Café Napolés**. Originally a coffee-and-dessert stop and fashionable
CAFÉ hangout for Mascotans, this snug little eatery serves big breakfasts and now main dishes at lunch and dinner, too. Sit on the small street-facing patio, in the diminutive dining room, or facing the glass case featuring fantastic-looking cakes, pies, and tarts. You can get wine and beer as well as pizza, barbecue, spaghetti, and other Italian food. ⊠ *Calle Hidalgo 105, Centro* ☎ *388/386–0051* ⊙ *9 AM– 9 PM Wed.–Sun.; closed Mon. and Tues.* ⊟ *No credit cards.*

$ ✕ **La Casa de Mi Abuela**. Everyone and his mother likes "Grandma's
MEXICAN House," which is conveniently open all day (and evening), every day, starting at around 8 AM with breakfast. In addition to beans, rice, carne asada, and other recognizable Mexican food, there are backcountry recipes that are much less familiar to the average traveler. ⊠ *Calle Corona, at Calle Zaragoza* ☎ *No phone.*

WHERE TO STAY

$ ⌨ **Mesón de Santa Elena**. Beautiful rooms in this converted 19th-century
★ house have lovely old tile floors, beige cotton drapes covering huge windows, rag-rolled walls, and wonderful tile floors and sinks. The dining room has old-fashioned cupboards, and there are dining tables inside and out on two patios festooned with flowers and large potted plants. Second-floor rooms have views of fields and mountains to the west. **Pros:** two blocks from the town square; feels like you're a guest in someone's home; Internet café about a block away. **Cons:** Internet intermittent in some rooms; feels like you're a guest in someone's home. ⊠ *Hidalgo 155* ☎ *388/386–0313* ⊕ *www.mesondesantaelena.com* ⤴ *10 rooms, 2 suites* ♿ *In-room: no a/c, no phone, no TV. In-hotel: restaurant (breakfast only), Wi-Fi hotspot* ⊟ *MC, V* ⌸ *BP, EP.*

$ ⌂ **Rancho La Esmeralda.** Catering to small groups and father-and-son outings, this ranch-style lodging near the entrance to town also accepts individual travelers. All interiors are pine-wood simple, with ceiling beams and tile roofs, and plain furnishings. The villas have kitchens, and most have a porch and fireplace; many sport a king-size bed. This working ranch offers horseback riding and also rents bicycles and ATVs. Because most guests are Guadalajarans on weekends, prices are discounted 20% Sunday through Thursday. **Pros:** newer construction; fireplaces and king-size beds; midweek discount. **Cons:** 10-minute drive from town center; bumpy cobblestone entry road. ⊠ *Calle Salvador Chavez 47* ☎ *388/386–0953* ⊕ *www.rancholaesmeralda.com.mx* ⇆ *10 rooms, 7 cabins* ☖ *In-room: kitchen (some), refrigerator (some), Wi-Fi (some). In-hotel: Wi-Fi hotspot, parking (free)* ▭ *MC, V.*

$$$ ⌂ **Sierra Lago Resort & Spa.** An hour north of Mascota, this lodge of knotty pine is a tranquil lakeside retreat. Sail or kayak or just read a book in the steamy hot tub. The spa isn't as expansive as those in some of Sierra Lago's Villa Group sister properties, but it does have massage, a steam room, and an outdoor hot tub. If you choose the all-inclusive plan, drinks are included, as are activities like horseback riding, kayaking, and mountain biking. There's also fishing, and, if he has time, the chef will cook up your freshly caught fish. **Pros:** beautiful scenery and mountain air; activities included in all-inclusive room rate. **Cons:** no phone in room; no Internet access. ⊠ *Domicilio Conocido, Lago Juanacatlán* ☎ *866/622–3418 in U.S. and Canada, 01800/823–4488 toll-free in Mexico* ⊕ *www.sierralago.com* ⇆ *24 suites* ☖ *In-room: no phone. In-hotel: restaurant, bar, tennis court, pool, spa, bicycles, parking (free)* ▭ *MC, V* ❙◎❙ *AI, EP.*

SPORTS AND THE OUTDOORS

★   The countryside just outside town is ideal for hikes and drives. From Mascota's plaza you can walk up Calle Morelos out of town to **Cerro de la Cruz**. The hike to the summit takes about a half hour and rewards with great valley views. **Presa Corinches**, a dam about 5 km (3 mi) south of town, has bass fishing, picnic spots (for cars and RVs), and a restaurant where locals go for fish feasts on holidays and weekend afternoons. To get to the dam, head east on Calle Juárez (a block south of the plaza) and follow the signs to the reservoir. Take a walk along the shore or set up a tent near the fringe of pine-oak forest coming down to meet the cool blue water, which is fine for swimming when the weather is warm. **Lago Juanacatlán** is a lovely lake in a volcanic crater at 7,000 feet above sea level. Nestled in the Galope River valley, the pristine lake is surrounded by alpine woods, and the trip from Mascota past fields of flowers and self-sufficient *ranchos* is bucolic.

SHOPPING

Stores in town sell homemade preserves, locally grown coffee, raicilla (an alcoholic drink made of green agave), and sweets. A good place to shop for local products and produce is the **Mercado Municipal** (⊠ *Calle P. Sánchez, at Hidalgo, 1 block west of plaza*).

8

TALPA DE ALLENDE

Another tranquil town surrounded by pine-oak forests, Talpa, as it's called, has just over 7,000 inhabitants but welcomes 4 million visitors a year. They come to pay homage or ask favors of the diminutive Virgen del Rosario de Talpa, one of Jalisco's most revered Virgins. Some people walk three days from Puerto Vallarta as penance or a sign of devotion; others come by car, horse, bicycle, or truck but return annually to show their faith.

HOLY CITY

During several major annual fiestas, the town swells with visitors. The Fiesta de la Candelaria culminates in Candlemass, February 2. The town's patron saint, St. Joseph, is honored March 19. May 12, September 10, September 19, and October 7 mark rituals devoted to the Virgen del Rosario de Talpa.

EXPLORING

★ On the large plaza, the **Basílica de Talpa** is the main show in town. The twin-spire limestone temple is Gothic with neoclassic elements. After visiting the diminutive, royally clad Virgin in her side chapel, stroll around the surrounding square. Shops and stalls sell sweets, miniature icons of the Virgin in every possible presentation, T-shirts, and other souvenirs. *Chicle* (gum) is harvested in the area, and you'll find small keepsakes in the shapes of shoes, flowers, and animals made of the (nonsticky) raw material.

WHERE TO EAT

$$ ╳ **Casa Grande**. This steak house also serves grilled chicken and seafood.
STEAKHOUSE Under a roof but open on all sides and with an incredible view, it's highly recommended by visitors and locals. In fact, it's a popular place for locals' reunions and family parties. ⊠ *Calle Juárez 53* ☎ *388/385–0709* ▭ *MC, V* ☺ *1–10; Closed Tues.*

$ ╳ **El Herradero**. "The Blacksmith" will win no awards for cuisine or, for
MEXICAN that matter, decoration. But it's often filled with families of pilgrims, and the locals recommend it, too. The menu offers mainly meat dishes, including burgers with fries, plus *antojitos, gorditas,* and *sopes* (all cornmeal based, fried concoctions stuffed with meat or beans and, in the case of the latter, topped with beans and salsa), pozole, and quesadillas. The tortillas are made fresh at the back of the restaurant. Half orders are available, and there's a bar serving national booze and beer. ⊠ *Calle 23 de Junio 8* ☎ *388/385–0376* ▭ *No credit cards.*

WHERE TO STAY

$ 🏨 **Hacienda Jacarandas**. The charming, two-story building has high ceilings, wide corridors, and comfortable guest rooms with fine and folk art. Bougainvillea in shades of purple and pink climb up the cream-color exterior walls, and the rooftop terrace—with a terrific view—is a nice place to laze away a morning or afternoon, in the sun or under the covered portion. The 62-acre property has a small lake. **Pros:** you get to stay in a restored hacienda; savvy hoteliers who know how to treat foreign guests. **Cons:** has been for sale for some years; no elevator; credit cards not accepted. ⊠ *Rancho Portrellos, just over bridge at southeast end of town* ☎ *388/102–7078* ⊕ *hacienda-jacarandas.com*

🛏 *5 rooms, 1 casita* ☖ *In-hotel: restaurant, bar, pool, Wi-Fi hotspot* 🖃 *No credit cards* ☾ *Closed Easter–June* ⦿ *BP.*

¢ ▦ **Renovación.** Basic yet comfortable rooms in this three-story hotel (opened in 2007) have king-size beds with dark blue, hunting-theme spreads and desks of shiny lacquered wood. The property is on the main road into town, just a few short blocks from the plaza and town hall. The price goes up slightly on weekends, although only January through May. **Pros:** newer property; a couple of blocks from the main plaza. **Cons:** no elevator; no credit cards accepted. ✉ *Calle Independencia 45, Centro* ☎ *388/385–1412* 🛏 *18 rooms* 🖃 *No credit cards.*

THE GUADALAJARA REGION

Guadalajara rests on a mile-high plain of the Sierra Madre Occidental, surrounded on three sides by rugged hills and on the fourth by the spectacular Oblatos Canyon. Mexico's second-largest city has a population of 4 million and is the capital of Jalisco State. This cosmopolitan if traditional and quintessentially Mexican city offers a range of activities. Shop for handicrafts, housewares, and especially fine ceramics in smart shops or family-owned factories. Dress up for drinks, dinner, and dancing in smart Zona Minerva, in downtown Guadalajara, or put on your comfy walking shoes to visit satellite neighborhoods of indigenous origin. For shoppers and metropolis lovers, this is a great complement to a Puerto Vallarta vacation.

An hour's drive in just about any direction from Guadalajara will bring you out of the fray and into the countryside. Due south is Lake Chapala, Mexico's largest natural lake. Bordering it are several villages with large expat communities, including Chapala and Ajijic, a village of bougainvillea and cobblestone roads. Tequila, where the famous firewater is brewed, is northwest of Guadalajara. Teuchitlán, south of Tequila, has the Guachimontones ruins. The placid lakeside area around Chapala makes for a weeklong (expats would say lifelong) getaway, while Tequila and Teuchitlán are great for day-trippers.

8

GUADALAJARA

The Guadalajara region's must-see sights can be found in four major areas: Guadalajara city itself, Zapopan, Tlaquepaque, and Tonalá. Each can be navigated on foot in a few hours, hitting the major sites, though to get a good feel for these places one must devote at least a day to each, and more to Guadalajara city.

In Guadalajara city, the historic Guadalajara Centro houses many of the city's key tourist attractions, but several of the surrounding neighborhoods are also worth a visit. In Zona Minerva, due west of the Centro; Plaza del Sol, southwest; and Providencia, northwest, you'll find modern hotels, boutique shops, and some of the city's best cafés, bars, and restaurants. Sample the Zona Minerva district by strolling down the Avenida Juárez–Avenida Vallarta corridor; Avenida Vallarta is shut to vehicular traffic from 8 AM to 2 PM every Sunday for Via Recreativa, where locals and tourists gather to walk or bike.

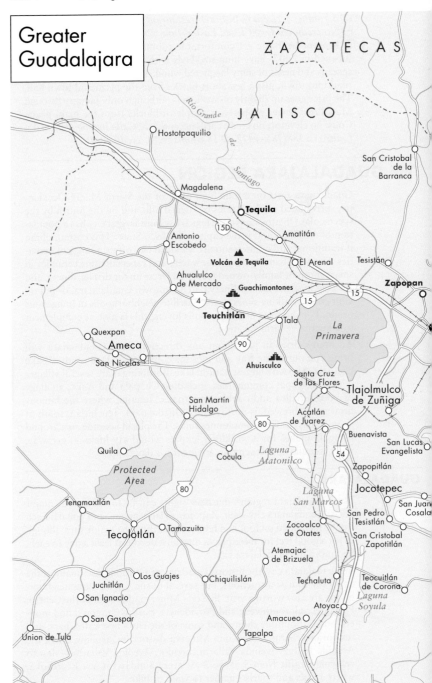

Greater
Guadalajara

ZACATECAS

JALISCO

Río Grande

Hostotpaquilio

de

San Cristobal
de la
Barranca

Santiago

Magdalena

Tequila

15D

Amatitán

Antonio
Escobedo

Volcán de Tequila

El Arenal

Tesistán

Ahualulco
de Mercado

Guachimontones

Zapopan

4

15

15

Teuchitlán

Tala

La
Primavera

Quexpan

Ameca

90

San Nicolas

Ahuisculco

Santa Cruz
de las Flores

Tlajolmulco
de Zuñiga

San Martín
Hidalgo

80

Acatlán
de Juarez

Buenavista

San Lucas
Evangelista

Quila

Cocula

Laguna
Atatonilco

54

Zapopitlán

Protected
Area

80

Laguna
San Marcos

Jocotepec

San Juan
Cosala

Tenamaxtlán

Zocoalco
de Otates

San Pedro
Tesistlán

San Cristobal
Zapotitlán

Tecolotlán

Tamazuita

Atemajac
de Brizuela

Juchitlán

Los Guajes

Chiquilislán

Techaluta

Teocuitlán
de Corona

San Ignacio

Laguna
Soyula

San Gaspar

Atoyac

Amacueo

Union de Tula

Tapalpa

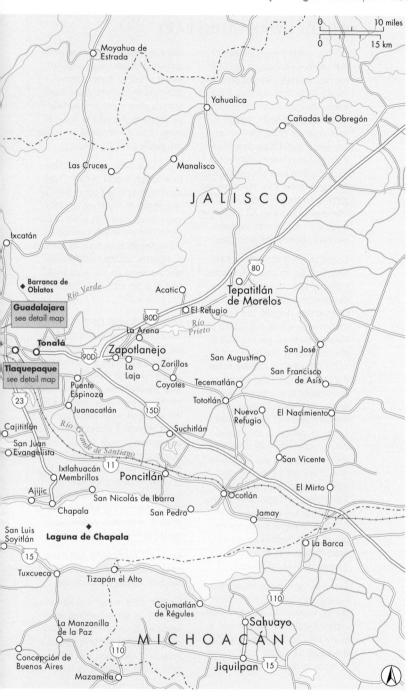

0   10 miles
0   15 km

Moyahua de Estrada

Yahualica

Cañadas de Obregón

Las Cruces

Manalisco

J A L I S C O

Ixcatán

80

Barranca de Oblatos

Río Verde

Acatic

Tepatitlán de Morelos

Guadalajara
see detail map

80D
El Refugio

Río Prieto

La Arena

Tonalá

Zapotlanejo

San José

Tlaquepaque
see detail map

90D

La Laja

Zorillos

San Augustín

San Francisco de Asís

8

23

Puente Espinoza

Coyotes

Tecematlán

Juanacatlán

15D

Tototlán

Nuevo Refugio

El Nacimiento

Río Grande de Santiago

Suchitlán

Cajititlán

San Juan Evangelista

Ixtlahuacán Membrillos

San Vicente

11

Poncitlán

El Mirto

Ajijic

San Nicolás de Ibarra

Ocotlán

Chapala

San Pedro

Jamay

San Luis Soyitlán

Laguna de Chapala

La Barca

15

Tuxcueca

Tizapán el Alto

Cojumatlán de Régules

110

La Manzanilla de la Paz

Sahuayo

M I C H O A C Á N

110

Concepción de Buenos Aires

Jiquilpan

15

Mazamitla

GUADALAJARA ITINERARY

The four primary municipalities of metropolitan Guadalajara are Guadalajara, Zapopan, Tlaquepaque, and Tonalá. Aside from Zapopan, areas of interest to visitors can be navigated on foot in a few hours, though each deserves at least half a day. Zapopan requires more time since it's a sprawling suburb with lots of shopping. Due west of Guadalajara's Centro Histórico, Zona Minerva is the place to go for great restaurants and after-dark action. Plan on a third day if you want to visit outlying areas like Lake Chapala and Teuchitlán.

On the morning of Day 1, visit historic Guadalajara, checking out the cathedral and other landmarks on the interconnecting plazas. Mercado Libertad (aka Mercado San Juan de Dios) is several long blocks east of Plaza Fundadores; you can walk or take the subway two blocks south of the cathedral on Avenida Juárez. If it's Sunday, see a charreada; otherwise head to Zapopan to see the basilica, the Huichol Museum, and the Art Museum of Zapopan, and spend 15 minutes at *la presidencia municipal* (city hall) to admire the mural inside. If you have more time, check out the market, two blocks west at Calles Eva Briseño and Hidalgo, and some surrounding churches before grabbing a drink or a bite on Paseo Teopinztle, two blocks south. Freshen up at your hotel, then dine in downtown Guadalajara or the Zona Minerva.

Spend the second day shopping and visiting churches and museums in the old towns of Tonalá and in more compact, walkable Tlaquepaque. If you're here on Thursday or Sunday, don't miss the Tonalá crafts market. El Parián in Tlaquepaque is a great place to enjoy a mariachi serenade and refreshments. Have lunch or dinner in one of Tlaquepaque's charming restaurants. If you don't want to shop, consider spending an afternoon listening to mariachi music, seeing a charrería, or visiting the gardens at Parque Azul.

If you have three days, you'll have time to visit Tequila or Lake Chapala. It's refreshing to get out of the city and admire the relatively dry hills and valleys, noting the fields of blue agave that are Tequila's reason for being. Tequila is en route to San Blas and Puerto Vallarta. Lake Chapala and the towns on the shore work well as a day excursion, especially if you have a car.

LOGISTICS AND TIPS

You need at least three hours for the Centro Histórico, longer if you really want to enjoy the sculptures and street scene. Mornings are the least crowded time of day, although the light is particularly beautiful in the afternoon, when the jugglers, street musicians, and other informal entertainers emerge. Take advantage of free walking tours in the historical district. Accompanied by mariachis or other musicians, the two-hour tours meet most evenings around dusk in front of city hall. Show up at about 7 PM (an hour earlier during winter) to register.

Beware of heavy traffic and *topes* (speed bumps). Traffic circles are common at busy intersections.

Tonalá's crafts market and Mercado Libertad are the region's top marketplaces. El Trocadero is a weekly antiques market at the north end of Avenida Chapultepec. Feel free to drive a hard bargain at all three.

As with nearly all of Mexico, Guadalajara has no shortage of religious iconography in public spaces.

GETTING HERE AND AROUND

BY AIR   Many major airlines fly nonstop from the United States to Guadalajara. Aeropuerto Internacional Libertador Miguel Hidalgo is 16½ km (10 mi) south of the city, en route to Chapala. Autotransportaciones Aeropuerto operates a 24-hour taxi stand with service to any place in the Guadalajara area; buy tickets at the counters at the national and international exits. Some hotels also offer airport pickup shuttles; these need to be arranged in advance.

BY BUS AND SUBWAY   Although flying from your hometown to Guadalajara, then back home from PV can be a good deal, flying round-trip to Guadalajara from Puerto Vallarta is not. The bus is much cheaper, scenic, and efficient. Luxury buses between PV and Guadalajara take 4½ hours and cost $30–$35. With one wide seat on one side of the aisle and only two on the other, ETN is the most upscale line and has about nine trips a day to and from PV, except Sunday, which has only one. Within Mexico, it accepts advance reservations with a credit card. Estrella Blanca is an umbrella of different bus lines, many of which head straight for Guadalajara. TAP (Transportes al Pacifico) is a first-class line that serves major Pacific Coast destinations between Ixtapa/Zihuatanejo and the U.S. border, including service to Guadalajara, Puerto Vallarta, and Tepic. ■TIP➔ Many bus lines do not accept credit cards. Guadalajara's Nueva Central Camionera (New Central Bus Station) is 10 km (6 mi) southeast of downtown.

Most city buses (45¢) run from every few minutes to every half hour between 6 AM and 9 PM; some run until 11 PM. ⚠ The city's public transit buses are infamously fatal; drivers killed more than 100 pedestrians

8

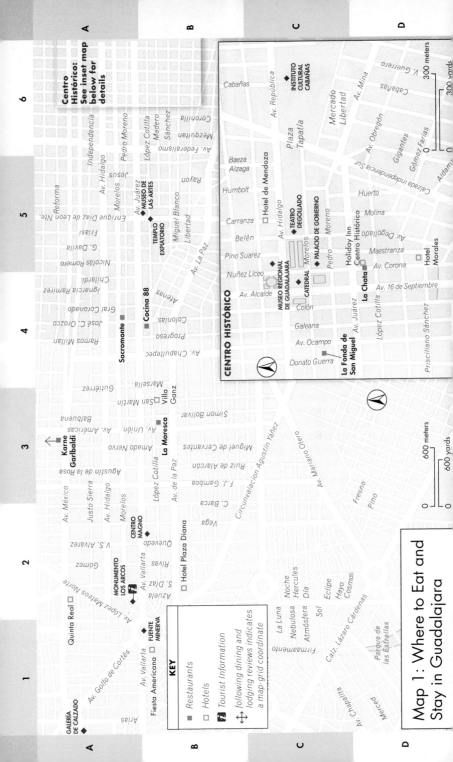

Map 1: Where to Eat and Stay in Guadalajara

KEY

■ Restaurants
□ Hotels
🛈 Tourist Information
↔ following dining and lodging reviews indicates a map-grid coordinate

CENTRO HISTÓRICO

- Cabañas
- INSTITUTO CULTURAL CABAÑAS
- Av. República
- Plaza Tapatía
- Av. Mina
- V. Guerrero
- Cabañas
- Mercado Libertad
- Av. Obregón
- Gigantes
- Gómez Farías
- Baeza Alzaga
- Humbolt
- Hotel de Mendoza
- TEATRO DEGOLLADO
- Av. Hidalgo
- PALACIO DE GOBIERNO
- Huerto
- Molina
- Calzada Independencia Sur
- Aldama
- Carranza
- Belén
- Pino Suarez
- Nuñez
- MUSEO REGIONAL DE GUADALAJARA
- Liceo
- Morelos
- Pedro Moreno
- CATEDRAL
- Holiday Inn Centro Histórico
- Av. Degollado
- Maestranza
- Av. Corona
- Hotel Morales
- La Chata
- Av. Alcalde
- Colón
- Galeana
- Av. 16 de Septiembre
- Av. Ocampo
- La Fonda de San Miguel
- Av. Juárez
- López Cotilla
- Prisciliano Sánchez
- Donato Guerra

300 meters / 300 yards

Main map

- Galería de Calzado
- Arias
- Av. Gollo de Cortés
- Quinta Real
- Av. Vallarta
- Fiesta Americana
- Av. López Mateos Norte
- Gómez
- V.S. Alvarez
- Av. México
- Justo Sierra
- Av. Hidalgo
- Morelos
- Reforma
- Enrique Díaz de León Nte.
- Frías
- G. Dávila
- Nicolás Romero
- Chilardi
- Ignacia Ramírez
- Gral Coronado
- José C. Orozco
- Ramos Millán
- Independencia
- Jesús
- Morelos
- Miguel Blanco
- Libertad
- Av. La Paz
- Museo de las Artes
- Av. Juárez
- Templo Expiatorio
- Pedro Moreno
- López Cotilla
- Madero
- Mezquitan
- Sánchez
- Coronilla
- Av. Federalismo
- Rayon
- Atenas
- Colonias
- Progreso
- Av. Chapultepec
- Marsella
- Cocina 88
- Sacromonte
- Monumento Los Arcos
- Centro Magno
- Quevedo
- Rivas
- S. Díaz
- Azuela
- Hotel Plaza Diana
- Av. Vallarta
- Fuente Minerva
- Karne Garibaldi
- Amado Nervo
- Av. Américas
- Av. Unión
- La Moresca
- Balbuena
- Gutiérrez
- San Martín
- Villa
- Ganz
- Simon Bolivar
- Agustín de la Rosa
- López Cotilla
- Av. de la Paz
- Miguel de Cervantes
- Ruiz de Alarcón
- F.J. Gamboa
- C. Barca
- Vega
- Circunvalación Agustín Yañez
- Av. Mariano Otero
- Fresno
- Pino
- Noche
- Hercules
- Día
- Eclipse
- Hayo
- Cosmos
- La Luna
- Nebulosa
- Atmósfera
- Sol
- Firmamento
- Calz. Lázaro Cárdenas
- Av. Chapalita
- Merced
- Parque de las Estrellas

**Centro Histórico:
See inset map below for details**

600 meters / 600 yards

annually in the late 1990s before the government intervened. These poorly designed, noisy, noxious buses are still driven ruthlessly and cause at least a dozen deaths per year.

Large mint-green Tur and red Cardinal buses are the safest, quickest, and least crowded and go to Zapopan, Tlaquepaque, and Tonalá for around 10 pesos. Wait for these along Avenida 16 de Septiembre.

Autotransportes Guadalajara–Chapala serves the lakeside towns from Guadalajara's new bus station (Central Camionera Nueva) and from the old bus station (Antigua Central Camionera); cost is around $4. It's 45 minutes to Chapala and another 15 minutes to Ajijic; there are departures every half hour from 6 AM to 9:30 PM. Make sure you ask for the *directo* (direct) as opposed to the *clase segunda* (second-class) bus, which stops at every little pueblo en route.

Guadalajara's underground *tren ligero* (light train) system is clean and efficient. Trains run every 10 minutes from 5 AM to midnight; a token for one trip costs about 40¢.

BY CAR Metropolitan Guadalajara's traffic gets intense, especially at rush hour, and parking can be scarce. Streets shoot off at diagonals from round-abouts (called *glorietas*), and on main arteries, turns (including U-turns and left turns) are usually made from right-side lateral roads (called *laterales*)—which can be confusing for drivers unfamiliar with big city traffic. ■TIP→ Ubiquitous and inexpensive, taxis are the best way to go in Guadalajara.

BY TAXI Taxis are easily hailed on the street in the Centro Histórico, Zapopan, Tlaquepaque, and most other areas of Guadalajara. All cabs are sup-posed to use meters (in Spanish, *taxímetro*)—you can insist the driver use it or else agree on a fixed price at the outset. Many hotels have rate sheets showing the fare to major destinations and parts of town.

Taxi is the best way to get to Tonalá or Tlaquepaque (about $7). To continue from Tlaquepaque to Tonalá, take a taxi from Avenida Río Nilo southeast directly into town and the intersection of Avenida de los Tonaltecas ($4–$6; 5–10 minutes depending on traffic).

ESSENTIALS

Air Contacts Aeroméxico (☎ 01800/021–4000, 01800/021–4010 toll-free in Mexico, 800/237–6639 toll-free in U.S. or Canada ⊕ www.aeromexico.com). **American Airlines** (☎ 33/3616–4090, 33/3688–5518 at airport, 01800/904–6000, 800/443–7300 in U.S. and Canada ⊕ www.aa.com). **Continental** (☎ 33/3647–4251, 33/3688–5141 at airport, 01800/900–5000, 800/523–3273 in U.S. and Canada ⊕ www.continental.com). **Mexicana** (☎ 55/2881–0000 in Mexico City, 01800/801–2030 toll-free in Mexico, 800/531–7921 in U.S. and Canada ⊕ www.mexicana.com).

Airport Transfers Autotransportaciones Aeropuerto (☎ 33/3688–5293).

Bus Contacts Autotransportes Guadalajara Chapala (☎ 33/3619–5675). **Estrella Blanca** (☎ 55/5729–0807 in Mexico City, 33/3619–2309 ⊕ www. estrellablanca.com.mx). **ETN** (☎ 33/3600–0477; 33/3770–3777; 01800/360–4200 toll-free in Mexico ⊕ www.etn.com.mx). **Primera Plus** (☎ 33/3600–0014; 01800/375–7587 toll-free in Mexico ⊕ www.primeraplus.com.mx). **Transportes al Pacifico** (☎ 33/3668–5920 ⊕ www.tap.com.mx).

Internet Compu-Flash (✉ *Calle Priciliano Sánchez 402, Centro Histórico* ☎ *33/3614–7165*). **La Vaca Loca** (✉ *Juárez 145, Tlaquepaque* ☎ *33/3838–6860*).

Medical Assistance Hospital Puerta De Hierro (✉ *Av. Empresarios #150, Col. Puerta de Hierro, Zapopan* ☎ *33/3669–0222; 01800/263–CMPDH toll free in Mexico*). **Hospital San Javier** (✉ *Av. Pablo Casals 640, Col. Providencia, Zona Minerva* ☎ *33/3669–0222*).

Rental Cars Alamo (✉ *Av. Niños Héroes 982, south of Centro Histórico* ☎ *01800/849–8001 toll-free in Mexico; 33/3688–8078 at airport* ⊕ *www.alamo-mexico.com.mx*). **Avis** (✉ *Hilton, Av. de las Rosas 2933, Rinconda del Bosque* ☎ *33/3671–3422; 33/3688–5784 at airport* ⊕ *www.avis.com.mx*). **Budget** (✉ *Hotel Misión Carlton, Av. Niños Héroes 125, at Av. 16 de Septiembre, Centro Histórico* ☎ *01800/700–1700 toll-free in Mexico; 33/3688–5216 at airport* ⊕ *www.budget.com.mx*).

Taxis Taxi Plaza del Sol (☎ *33/3631–5262*). **Taxi Sitio Minerva no. 22** (☎ *33/3630–0050*).

Visitor and Tour Info Guadalajara Municipal Tourist Office (✉ *Calle Morelos 1596, Centro Histórico* ☎ *33/3668–1600*). **Jalisco State Tourist Office** (✉ *Calle Morelos 102, Centro Histórico* ☎ *33/3668–1600; 01800/363–2200 toll-free in Mexico* ⊕ *visita.jalisco.gob.mx* ✉ *Palacio de Gobierno, Av. Corona 31, Centro Histórico* ☎ *33/3668–1601 Ext. 34730* ✉ *Calle Madero 407–A, 2nd fl., Chapala* ☎ *376/765–3141*). **Tlaquepaque Municipal Tourist Office** (✉ *Calle Morelos 288, top fl., Tlaquepaque* ☎ *33/3662–7050 Ext. 2319*). **Tonalá Municipal Tourist Office** (✉ *Av. de los Tonaltecas Sur 140, Tonalá* ☎ *33/3284–3092 or 33/3284–3093*). **Tourist Board of Zapopan** (✉ *Calle Eva Brisena s/n, next to Basilica, Zapopan* ☎ *33/3818–2200 Ext. 1102 or 1103* ⊕ *www.zapopan.gob.mx*).

EXPLORING
CENTRO HISTÓRICO

The downtown core is a mishmash of modern and old buildings connected by a series of large plazas, four of which were designed to form a cross when viewed from the sky, with the cathedral in the middle. Though some remain, many colonial-era structures were razed before authorities got serious about preserving them. Conservation laws, however, merely prohibit such buildings from being altered or destroyed; there are no provisions on upkeep, as plenty of abandoned, crumbling buildings indicate.

Must-visit sights include the Palacio del Gobierno and the Instituto Cultural Cabañas; both have phenomenal murals by José Clemente Orozco. Even if you're not in the mood to shop, you should experience the bustling Mercado Libertad. Explore the district in the morning if you dislike crowds; otherwise, you'll get a more immediate sense of Mexico's vibrant culture if you wait for street performers and vendors to emerge around the huge Plaza Tapatía in the afternoon.

Allot at least three hours for the Centro, longer if you really want to absorb the main sights and stroll along the pedestrian streets.

★ **Catedral.** Begun in 1561 and consecrated in 1618, this downtown focal point is an intriguing mélange of baroque, Gothic, and other styles. Its emblematic twin towers replaced the originals, felled by the earthquake

of 1818. Ten of the silver-and-gold altars were gifts from King Fernando VII for Guadalajara's financial support of Spain during the Napoleonic Wars. Some of the world's most magnificent *retablos* (altarpieces) adorn the walls; above the sacristy (often closed to the public) is Bartolomé Esteban Murillo's priceless 17th-century painting *The Assumption of the Virgin*. In a loft above the main entrance is a magnificent 19th-century French organ. ⊠ *Av. 16 de Septiembre, between Av. Hidalgo and Calle Morelos, Centro Histórico* ☎ *33/3614–5504; 33/3614–3058* 🖃 *Free* 🕙 *Daily 8–8.*

🕓 **Instituto Cultural Cabañas.** Financed
Fodor'sChoice by Bishop Juan Ruiz de Cabañas
★ and constructed by Spanish architect-sculptor Manuel Tolsá, this neoclassical-style cultural center, also known as Hospicio Cabañas,
was originally opened in 1810 as a shelter for widows, orphans, and the elderly. The Instituto's 106 rooms and 23 flower-filled patios now house art exhibitions (ask for an English-speaking guide). The main chapel displays murals by José Clemente Orozco, including *The Man of Fire*, his masterpiece. In all, there are 57 murals by Orozco, plus many of his smaller paintings, cartoons, and drawings. Kids can wonder at the murals, some which appear as optical illusions, and investigate the labyrinthine compound. The center, named a UNESCO World Heritage site in 1997, is closed Monday. ⊠ *Calle Cabañas 8, Centro Histórico* ☎ *33/3818–2800* 🖃 *$7; free Tues.* 🕙 *Tues.–Sun. 10–6.*

Museo Regional de Guadalajara. Constructed as a seminary and public library in 1701, this has been the Guadalajara Regional Museum's home since 1918. First-floor galleries contain artifacts tracing western Mexico's history from prehistoric times through the Spanish conquest. Five 19th-century carriages, including one used by General Porfirio Díaz, are on the second-floor balcony. There's an impressive collection of European and Mexican paintings. ⊠ *Calle Liceo 60, Centro Histórico* ☎ *33/3614–9957* 🖃 *$3.50* 🕙 *Tues.–Sat. 9–5:30, Sun. 9–4:30.*

★ **Palacio de Gobierno.** The adobe structure of 1643 was replaced with this churrigueresque and neoclassical stone structure in the 18th century. Within are Jalisco's state offices and two of José Clemente Orozco's most passionate murals, both worth the visit alone. One just past the entrance depicts a gigantic Father Miguel Hidalgo looming amid figures representing oppression and slavery. Upstairs, the other mural (look for a door marked CONGRESO) portrays Hidalgo, Juárez, and other Reform-era figures. ⊠ *Av. Corona 31, between Calle Morelos and Pedro Moreno, Centro Histórico* ☎ *33/3668–1800* 🖃 *Free* 🕙 *Daily 9–8.*

OPEN-AIR BUSES

The **Tapatío Tour** (⊠ *Calle Morelos 231, Centro Histórico* ☎ *33/3613–0887; 33/3614–7430; 01800/001–1827 toll-free in Mexico* ⊕ *www.tapatiotour.com/*) is an easy way to get an overview of the city and its history. The open-air, double-decker buses leave every 30 minutes from Rotunda de los Jaliscienses Ilustres (to the left of the cathedral) and cost 90 pesos (less than $9) per person. The one-hour tour is narrated in six different languages via headphones; the Texas accent and unintended slip-ups of the English version are very entertaining. There's also a trip to Tlaquepaque; buses back leave every 30 min.

LIVE PERFORMANCE

The State Band of Jalisco and the municipal band usually play at the bandstand Tuesday through Friday at around 6:30 PM. Small, triangular Plaza de los Mariachis, south of the Mercado Libertad, was once the ideal place to tip up a beer and experience mariachi, the most Mexican of music, at about $15 a pop. Now boxed in by a busy street, a market, and a run-down neighborhood, it's safest to visit in the day or late afternoon.

For about the same amount of money but a more tourist-friendly atmosphere, mariachis at El Parián, in Tlaquepaque, will treat you to a song or two as you sip margaritas at this enormous, partly covered conglomeration of 17 cantinas diagonal from the town's main plaza. Once a marketplace dating from 1883, it has traditional *cazuela* drinks, which are made of fruit and tequila and served in ceramic pots.

After a brief transfer of affection to the newer Teatro Diana, the internationally acclaimed **Ballet Folclórico of the University of Guadalajara** (⊕ *www.ballet.udg.mx*) has returned to perform its traditional Mexican folkloric dances and music in the **Teatro Degollado** (✉ *Calle Belén s/n* ☎ *33/3614–4773*) most Sundays at 12:30 PM; tickets are $5–$25. The state-funded **Orquesta Filarmónica de Jalisco** (*Philharmonic Orchestra of Jalisco* ⊕ *www.ofj.com.mx*) performs pieces by Mexican composers mixed with standard orchestral fare. When in season (it varies), the OFJ usually performs Sunday afternoons or weeknights (usually Wednesday and Friday at 8:30 PM) at Teatro Degollado; tickets are $8–$35.

★ **Teatro Degollado.** Inaugurated in 1866, this magnificent theater was modeled after Milan's La Scala. The refurbished theater preserves its traditional red-and-gold color scheme, and its balconies ascend to a multitier dome adorned with Gerardo Suárez's depiction of Dante's *Divine Comedy*. The theater is home to the Jalisco Philharmonic. ✉ *Av. Degollado between Av. Hidalgo and Calle Morelos, Centro Histórico* ☎ *33/3614–4773* 🎫 *$8–$35* ⊙ *Hours vary.*

ZONA MINERVA

Also known as Zona Rosa (Pink Zone), this district west of the Centro Histórico is arguably the pulse of the city. At night a seemingly endless strip of the region's trendiest restaurants and watering holes lights up Avenida Vallarta east of Avenida Enrique Díaz de León. Victorian mansions, art galleries, a striking church, and two emblematic monuments—the Fuente Minerva (Minerva Fountain) and the Monumento Los Arcos—are scattered throughout the tree-lined boulevards.

The best way to get here from the Centro is by cab. Museo de las Artes requires two hours when all its exhibits are open. Budget an hour for the Templo Expiatorio across the street.

Museo de las Artes. The University of Guadalajara's contemporary-art museum is in this exquisite early-20th-century building. The permanent collection includes several murals by Orozco. Revolving exhibitions have contemporary works from Latin America, Europe, and the United

States. ✉ *Av. Juárez 975, Centro Histórico* ☎ *33/3134–1664* ⊕ *www. museodelasartes.udg.mx* ✆ *Free* ⊙ *Tues.–Fri. 10–6, weekends 10–4.*

Templo Expiatorio. The striking neo-Gothic Church of Atonement is Guadalajara's most breathtaking church. Modeled after Italy's Orvieto Cathedral, it has phenomenal stained-glass windows—observe the rose window above the choir and pipe organ. ✉ *Calle Díaz de León 930, at Av. López Cotilla, Centro Histórico* ☎ *33/3825–3410* ✆ *Free* ⊙ *Daily 6:30 AM–10:30 PM.*

TLAQUEPAQUE

Local arts and handicrafts fill the showrooms and stores in this touristy town, where you'll find carved wood furniture, colorful ceramics, and hand-stitched clothing among other goods. Pedestrian malls and plazas are lined with more than 300 shops, many run by families with generations of experience. One of Guadalajara's most exceptional museums, which draws gifted artists for its annual ceramics competition in June, is also here.

But there's more to Tlaquepaque than shopping. The downtown area has a pleasant square and many pedestrian-only streets, making this a good place to take a stroll, even if you're not interested in all the crafts for sale. There are several good restaurants, some with outdoor seating perfect for people-watching.

■ TIP→ Many tourists come to Tlaquepaque via the **Tapatío Tour,** an open-air bus that leaves from Guadalajara's historic center.

Fodor's Choice ★ **Museo del Premio Nacional de la Cerámica Pantaleon Panduro.** The museum is named after Pantaleon Panduro, who's considered the father of modern ceramics in Jalisco. On display are prizewinning pieces from the museum's annual ceramics competition, held every June. It's possibly the best representation of modern Mexican pottery under a single roof. You can request an English-speaking guide. ✉ *Calle Priciliano Sánchez 191, at Calle Flórida* ☎ *33/3562–7036* ✆ *Free* ⊙ *Tues.–Sat. 10–6, Sun. 10–3.*

Museo Regional de la Cerámica. The frequently changing exhibits at the Regional Museum of Ceramics are in the many rooms surrounding a central courtyard. Track the evolution of ceramic wares in the Atemajac Valley during the 20th century. The presentation isn't always strong, but the Spanish-language displays discuss six common processes used by local ceramics artisans, including *barro bruñido,* which involves polishing large urns with smoothed chunks of the mineral pyrite. Items in the gift shop are surprisingly uninteresting. ✉ *Calle Independencia 237, at Calle Alfareros* ☎ *33/3635–5404* ⊕ *www.artesanias.jalisco.gob. mx/ubicacion.html* ✆ *Free* ⊙ *Tues.–Sun. 10–6.*

ZAPOPAN

Mexico's former corn-producing capital is now a municipality of wealthy enclaves, modern hotels, and malls surrounded by hills of poor communities (as is much of metropolitan Guadalajara). Farther out, some farming communities remain. The central district, a good 25-minute cab ride from downtown Guadalajara, has two worthwhile museums, an aged church that's home to the city's most revered religious icon, and a pedestrian corridor punctuated by restaurants and watering holes popular with young Tapatíos.

Continued on page 268

MARIACHI: BORN IN JALISCO

By Sean Mattson

It's 4 AM and you're sound asleep somewhere in Mexico. Suddenly you're jolted awake by trumpets blasting in rapid succession. Before you can mutter a groggy protest, ten men with booming voices break into song. Nearby, a woman stirs from her slumber. The man who brought her the serenade peeks at her window from behind the lead singer's sombrero, hoping his sign of devotion is appreciated— and doesn't launch his girlfriend's father into a shoe-throwing fury.

Left and top right: Mariachis in traditional attire. Above: Mariachi strumming the guitarrón.

At the heart of Mexican popular culture, mariachi is the music of love and heartache, of the daily travails of life, and nationalistic pride. This soundtrack of Mexican tradition was born in the same region as tequila, the Mexican hat dance, and *charrería* (Mexican rodeo), whose culture largely defines Mexican chivalry and machismo.

Today, mariachi bands are the life of the party. They perform at weddings, birthdays, public festivals, restaurants, and city plazas. The most famous bands perform across the globe. Guadalajara's annual mariachi festival draws mariachis from around the world.

WHY IS IT CALLED "MARIACHI"?

The origin of the word mariachi is a source of some controversy. The legend is that it evolved from the French word *mariage* (marriage), stemming from the French occupation in the mid-1800s. But leading mariachi historians now debunk that myth, citing evidence that the word has its origins in the Nahuatl language of the Coca Indians.

Flying mariachi skeleton formed out of paper, used to celebrate Day of the Dead.

8

THE RISE OF MARIACHI

Historians trace the roots of mariachi to Cocula, a small agricultural town south of Guadalajara. There, in the 17th century, Franciscan monks trained the local indigenous populations in the use of stringed instruments, teaching them the religious songs to help win their conversion.

The aristocracy, who preferred the more refined contemporary European music, held early mariachi groups in disdain. But by the late 19th century, mariachi had become enormously popular among peasants and indigenous people in Cocula, eventually spreading throughout southern Jalisco and into neighboring states.

MODERN MARIACHI INSTRUMENTS

Traditional mariachi groups consisted of two violins (the melody), and a vihuela and guitarrón (the harmony). Some long-gone groups used a *tambor* or drum, not used in modern mariachi. All members of the group shared singing responsibilities.

THE FOLK HARP
Longstanding mariachi instrument, used today by large ensembles and by some traditional troupes

VIOLINS
Essential to any mariachi group

GUITARS
The round-backed vihuela is smaller and higher-pitched than the standard guitar

5-string Vihuela   6-string guitar

TRUMPETS
Added to the traditional mariachi lineup in the 1930s when mariachis hit the big screen, at the insistence of a pioneer in Mexican radio and television

THE GUITARRÓN
A large-bellied bass guitar

In 1905, Mexican dictator Porfirio Díaz visited Cocula and was received with a performance of a mariachi group. Impressed with the performance, Diaz invited the group to Mexico City where, after a few years and a revolution, mariachi flourished. Over the next two decades, more groups followed to Mexico City. Mariachi groups gained wide popularity by the 1930s, when movie stars as Jorge Negrete and Pedro Infante began portraying mariachi musicians in their films.

MARIACHI STYLE

The mariachi *traje* (suit) consists of matching vest, *chaleco* (short jacket), and form-fitting pants, and *moño* (large bow tie). Simple *trajes* have soutache trim or embroidery; finer versions have suede patterns on the jacket with metal buttons down the pants legs. Trajes come in all colors, but formal costumes are black.

Sombreros made from pressed rabbit fur are the highest quality.

The modern mariachi's dress is an adaptation of *charro*, or Mexican cowboy attire, first worn by the members of an early mariachi group led by Cirilo Marmolejo and adopted for Mexican movies of the 1930s–50s. A complete formal outfit can cost as much as US$3,000.

Botonaduras (decorative buttons on the pants legs) can be simple, or ornate, made of silver or gold. A brooch on the front of the jacket often matches the botonadura.

Black leather *botines* (half-boots) are standard mariachi footwear.

WHERE AND HOW TO HEAR MARIACHI

HIRE A MARIACHI GROUP

There may be no better way to thoroughly surprise (or embarrass) your significant other than with a mariachi serenade. Hiring a band is easy. Just go to Plaza de los Mariachis, beside Mercado Libertad in downtown Guadalajara. Pablo Garcia, whose Mariachi Atotonilco has been working the plaza for almost 40 years, says a serenade runs about 2,000 pesos, or just under US$155. Alternatively, you can ask for a recommendation at Casa Bariachi (⊠ *Av. Vallarta 2221 at Calderon de la Barca*, ☎ *33/3616–9900*). Negotiate price and either leave a deposit (ask for a business card and a receipt) and have the band meet you at a determined location, or, as Mexicans usually do, accompany the band to the unexpecting lady.

HIT THE INTERNATIONAL MARIACHI FESTIVAL

The last weekend of every August, some 700 mariachi groups from around the world descend upon Guadalajara for this event. Mexico's most famous mariachi groups—Mariachi Vargas de Tecalitlán, Mariachi los Camperos, and Mariachi de América—play huge concerts in the Degollado Theater, accompanied by the Jalisco Philharmonic Orchestra. The weeklong annual charro championship is held simultaneously, bringing together the nation's top cowboys and mariachis.

THE WORLD'S BEST MARIACHI BAND

At least, the world's most *famous* mariachi band, Mariachi Vargas de Tecalitlán was founded in 1897, when the norm was four-man groups with simple stringed instruments. Started by Gaspar Vargas in Tecalitlán, Jalisco, the mariachi troupe shot to fame in the 1930s after winning a regional mariachi contest, which earned them the favor of Mexican president Lázaro Cárdenas. The group quickly became an icon of Mexican cinema, performing in and recording music for films. Now in its fifth generation, Mariachi Vargas performs the world over and has recorded more than 50 albums, and music for more than 200 films.

The *gabán* (poncho) was worn traditionally for warmth.

CATCH YEAR-ROUND PERFORMANCES

If you miss Guadalajara's mariachi festival you can still get your fill of high-quality mariachi performances on street corners, in city plazas, and at many restaurants. An estimated 150 mariachi groups are currently active in the City of Roses.

Restaurants, most notably Guadalajara's Casa Bariachi chain, hire mariachi groups, whose performance is generally included with your table (though tips won't be refused). On occasion, mariachis perform free nighttime concerts in Guadalajara's Plaza de Armas. Another venue, the Plaza de Mariachi, beside Guadalajara's landmark Mercado Libertad, is a longstanding attraction, albeit during the day—at night it's better known for crime than mariachi.

Tlaquepaque's El Parían, a former market turned series of bars around a tree-filled central patio, is a fantastic intimate setting for mariachi music. Between free performances in the central kiosk, you can request serenades at about $15–18 per song or negotiate deals for longer performances for your table.

ALL ABOARD THE TEQUILA TRAIN!

To experience the Jalisco quartet of traditions—mariachi, charreria, folkloric dance, and tequila—in one adventure, take the Tequila Express. It includes a train ride from Guadalajara through fields of blue agave to a tequila-making hacienda, live mariachi music, all the food and drink you can handle, and a charro and folkloric dance performance.

WORKING HARD FOR THE MONEY

It is becoming harder for mariachi groups to make a living at the trade. The increasing cost of living has made nighttime serenades, once a staple of a mariachi's diet of work, expensive ($200 and up) and out of the reach of many locals. Performers generally work day jobs to make ends meet.

THE COWBOY CONNECTION

Mariachi and Mexican rodeo, or *charreada* (Mexico's official sport), go together like hot dogs and baseball. Both charreada and mariachi music evolved in the western Mexican countryside, where daily ranching chores like branding bulls eventually took on a competitive edge. The first of Mexico's 800 charro associations was founded in Guadalajara in 1920, and to this day holds a two-hour rodeo every Sunday. Throughout the competition, mariachi music is heard from the stands, but the key mariachi performance is at the end of a competition when female riders called *escaramuzas* perform synchronized moves, riding side-saddle in traditional ribboned and brightly colored western Mexican dresses.

8

IN FOCUS MARIACHI: BORN IN JALISCO

TONALA

Among the region's oldest pueblos is bustling Tonalá, a unique place filled with artisan workshops small and large. Although it's been swallowed by ever-expanding Guadalajara, Tonalá remains independent and industrious. More geared to business than pleasure, it doesn't have the folksy character of nearby Tlaquepaque. There's a concentration of stores on Avenida Tonalá and Avenida de los Tonaltecas, the main drag into town, and many more shops and factories can be found spread throughout Tonalá's narrow streets. ■TIP➔ The town has unusually long blocks, so wear your most comfortable shoes.

While Tonalá and its shops may not be as quaint or as touristy as Tlaquepaque, this is where you'll find the best bargains since most local goods—from furniture to glassware and ceramics—are made here. Most stores are open daily 10–5. On Thursday and Sunday, bargain-price merchandise is sold at a street market (⊠ *Av. Tonaltecas at Calle Benito Juárez* ☎ *No phone*) packed with vendors from 9 AM to 5 PM. Vendors set up ceramics, carved wood, candles, glassware, furniture, metal crafts, and more. Look for *vajilla* (ceramic place settings), but note that the more high-end ceramic offerings are at more formal stores.

★ **Basílica de Zapopan.** This vast church with an ornate plateresque facade and *mudéjar* (Moorish) tile dome was consecrated in 1730. It's home to the Virgin (or Our Lady) of Zapopan: a 10-inch-high, corn-paste statue venerated as a source of many miracles. Every October 12 more than a million people crowd the streets around the basilica, where the Virgin is returned after a five-month tour of Jalisco's parish churches. It's an all-night fiesta capped by an early-morning procession. ⊠ *Av. Hidalgo at Calle Morelos, Zona Zapopan Norte* ☎ *33/3633–6614* ⊡ *Free* ☉ *Daily 7 AM–9 PM.*

Museo de Arte de Zapopan. Better known by its initials, MAZ, the large and modern Art Museum of Zapopan is Guadalajara's top contemporary-art gallery. The museum regularly holds expositions of distinguished Latin American painters, photographers, and sculptors, as well as occasional international shows. ⊠ *Andador 20 de Noviembre 166, at Calle 28 de Enero* ☎ *33/3818–2575* ⊕ *www.mazmuseo.com* ⊡ *$1, free Tues.* ☉ *Tues.–Sun. 10–6.*

★ **Museo Huichol Wixarica de Zapopan.** The Huichol Indians of northern Jalisco and neighboring states of Zacatecas and Nayarit are famed for their fierce independence and exquisite beadwork and yarn "paintings." This small museum has rather hokey mannequins wearing the intricately embroidered clothing of both men and women. Bilingual placards explain the Huichol religion and worldview. The gift shop sells a small inventory of beaded items, prayer arrows, and god's eyes. ⊠ *Av. Hidalgo 152, Centro Histórico Zapopan* ☎ *33/3636–4430* ⊡ *2 pesos* ☉ *Mon.–Sat. 9:30–1 and 3–6, Sun. 10–2.*

WHERE TO EAT

The most popular international restaurants are scattered about west Guadalajara, but some of the best Mexican food is near the main attractions in downtown Guadalajara, Tlaquepaque, and Tonalá.

If sitting down to a meal before 8 PM, you may find you don't need reservations—and you might even have the restaurant to yourself. By around 10 PM, the locals will start filling up the place, and reservations become a must. Good food tends to be very low-priced compared to comparable food in the States, even at the best restaurants in town. A main course is $6 to $15, and alcoholic beverages start at $2. Some of the best food in the city can be found at smaller taco shops and stands, where you can come away full having spent under $5 for four tacos and a soda. It's important to be careful when eating food from street vendors, however; the best sign of a stand worth trying is a long line of locals waiting to order.

CENTRO HISTÓRICO

$ ✕ **La Chata**. At high meal times, travelers will find lines of locals and

MEXICAN

Fodor's Choice

★

tourists alike extending out the door of this traditional Mexican restaurant in El Centro. While the decor is plain, the food is the best in the city. Items worth testing include the *queso fundido* (cheese fondue) and the enchiladas. If you're staying in West Guadalajara, there's a second restaurant at 405 Terranova in Providencia. ✉ *Corona 126, between Av. López Cotilla and Juárez, Centro Histórico* ☎ *33/3613–1315* ⊕ *www. lachata.com.mx* ▭ *No credit cards* ✚ *1:D5.*

$$ ✕ **La Fonda de San Miguel**. La Fonda, in a former convent, is perhaps the

MEXICAN

★

Centro's most exceptional eatery. Innovative, high-end Mexican dishes are presented in a soaring courtyard, the middle of which is dominated by a stone fountain and hung with a spectacular array of shining tin stars and folk art from Tlaquepaque and Tonalá. Relish the freshly made tortillas with the *molcajete,* a steaming stew of chicken, seafood, or beef that comes in a three-legged volcanic stone bowl. *Camarones en mole* (shrimp in mole) is another good dish. There's piano or saxophone music every evening except Monday. Piano music accompanies a breakfast buffet 8:30–noon on Saturday and Sunday. ✉ *Donato Guerra 25, Centro Histórico* ☎ *33/3613–0809* ⊕ *www.lafondadesanmiguel.com* ▭ *AE, MC, V* ✪ *Closes at 6 PM Mon. and 9 PM Sun.* ✚ *1:C4.*

ZONA MINERVA

$$$ ✕ **Cocina 88**. Teeming with a crowd of well-dressed local yuppies and

ECLECTIC

Fodor's Choice

★

business travelers every night of the week, this hip restaurant housed in a converted 90-year-old mansion not only serves fresh, wonderfully prepared steaks and seafood, it also provides a unique experience. If you arrive at gringo time, before 9 PM, you'll likely encounter the owner, Enrique, a character who likes to show off the wine store and food selections, which you can choose yourself in the front kitchen area. Ask him if he can make a sampler plate. Margaritas come complete with their own miniature bottles of Don Julio. And if you plan to return during your trip, you can buy a bottle of tequila or other liquor and store the leftovers in the wine cellar to await your next visit. ✉ *Av. Vallarta 1342, Zona Minerva* ☎ *33/3827–5996 or 33/3827–5998* ⊕ *www.cocina88. com* ▭ *AE, MC, V* ✚ *1:B4.*

8

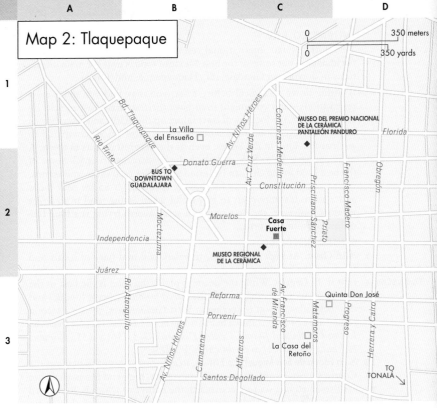

Map 2: Tlaquepaque

A   B   C   D

0 ___ 350 meters
0 ___ 350 yards

1

La Villa
del Ensueño □

MUSEO DEL PREMIO NACIONAL
DE LA CERÁMICA
PANTALEÓN PANDURO ◆   Florida

Bd. Tlaquepaque
Río Tinto

Av. Niños Héroes
Av. Cruz Verde
Contreras Medellín
Priscilliano Sánchez
Prieto
Francisco Madero
Obregón

Donato Guerra

BUS TO
DOWNTOWN
GUADALAJARA ◼

Constitución

2

Morelos

Casa
Fuerte ▣

Moctezuma

Independencia

MUSEO REGIONAL
DE LA CERÁMICA ◆

Juárez

Río Atenguillo

Reforma

Porvenir

Av. Francisco
de Miranda

Matamoros

Quinta Don José □

Progreso

Herrera y Cairo

3

Av. Niños Héroes

Camarena

Alfareros

La Casa del
Retoño □

Santos Degollado

TO
TONALÁ ↘

$

MEXICAN

✕ **Karne Garibaldi.** In the *1996 Guinness Book of World Records,* this Tapatío institution held the record for world's fastest service: 13.5 seconds for a table of six. Lightning service is made possible by the menu's single item: *carne en su jugo,* a combination of finely diced beef and bacon simmered in rich beef broth and served with grilled onions, tortillas, and refried beans mixed with corn. Don't be put off by the somewhat gritty area surrounding the restaurant at the original location on Calle Garibaldi. There also are three other locations in Zapopan. ⊠ *Calle Garibaldi 1306, Zona Minerva* ☎ *33/3826–1286* ⊕ *www. karnegaribaldi.com.mx* ⊟ *AE, MC, V* ⊠ *Mariano Otero 3019, Zona Plaza del Sol, Zapopan* ☎ *33/3123–2607* ⊠ *Av. Vallarta 3959, Jardines del los Arcos, Zapopan* ☎ *33/3621–1600* ⊠ *Plaza Galerias, Vallarta Norte, Zapopan* ☎ *33/3165–2042* ✛ *1:A3.*

$$

ITALIAN

★

✕ **La Moresca.** While this modern Italian restaurant comes alive at night when it turns into a hip martini bar, don't pass up a meal before partaking in the revelry. It has the best Italian food in town. The twentysomething Tapatíos like to take their dates here for delicious pasta and pizza dinners and stick around for the scene that follows. Birthday gatherings are common, too, as are simple be-seen excursions. However you do it, this place is Guadalajara at its trendiest, including music played at decibel levels that can sometimes make conversation difficult. Luckily, the Italian kitchen is up to the task. ⊠ *Av. López Cotilla 1835, Zona*

Mariachis stroll along Tlaquepaque's Calle Independencia playing requests for restaurant patrons.

Minerva ☎ 33/3616–8277 ▭ AE, MC, V ⊙ Closed Sun. ⊠ Blvd. Puerto de Hierro 4965, Plaza Andares, Zapopan ✛ 1:B3.

$$$ ✕ **Sacromonte.** An elegant atmosphere, decor, and dishes make for a
MEXICAN wonderful dining experience. This isn't the choice if you're looking for
★ an atmosphere that feels Mexican—a significant portion of the other diners will likely be other English-speaking visitors—but the food's delicious anyway. The waiters offer menus in Spanish and in English. If you're into trying local favorites, this is the place to order *la lengua*—the beef tongue—or the chicken mole, which has a sweet twist. The pork loin and barbecue ribs are also worth a taste. For dessert order the flan with *cajeta* (a local soft caramel sauce); it's homemade—literally made in someone's house and delivered nightly to the restaurant. One waiter's wife claims it's the best she's had. ⊠ *Pedro Moreno 1398, Col. Americana* ☎ 33/3825–5447 ▭ MC, V ⊙ No dinner Sun. ✛ 1:A4.

TLAQUEPAQUE

$$ ✕ **Casa Fuerte.** Relax with tasty Mexican dishes at the tables along the
MEXICAN sidewalk or under the palms and by the fountain on the patio. You'll
★ be tempted by the tables scattered around the sidewalk, but before you decide take a peek at those on the oversize garden patio surrounding a magnificent old tree. Try the house specialty: chicken stuffed with *huitlacoche* (a corn fungus that's Mexico's answer to the truffle) and shrimp in tamarind sauce. Live musicians accompany *comida* (2:30 to 6 PM, approximately) every day except Monday. ⊠ *Calle Independencia 224, Tlaquepaque* ☎ 33/3639–6481 or 33/3639–6474 ▭ AE, MC, V ⊙ Daily noon–8 ✛ 2:C2.

TONALÁ

$　　✕ **El Rincón del Sol**. A covered patio invites you to sip margaritas while
MEXICAN　listening to live trova (romantic ballads). Musicians play Tuesday to
Friday evenings between 7 and 9 and on weekends during the leisurely
lunch hour (roughly 3 to 5). Try one of the steak or chicken dishes, the
burrito, or the classic *chilies en nogada* in the colors of the Mexican
flag. The staff is friendly and helpful. ✉ *Av. 16 de Septiembre 61, Tonalá*
☎ *33/3683–1989 or 33/3683–1940* ▭ *MC, V.*

WHERE TO STAY

Choosing a place to stay is a matter of location, price, and comfort.
Tourists are often drawn to the Centro, where colonial-style hotels are
convenient to the historical center and other sights. But hotels in the
center tend to be a bit run down and don't offer the amenities available
at those farther west. Businesspeople and those looking for more modern digs head for the area around Avenida López Mateos Sur, a 16-km
(10-mi) strip extending from the Minerva Fountain to the Plaza del Sol
shopping center, or Avenida Americas in Providencia where they can take
advantage of newer facilities and four-star comforts. Several hotels, like
the polished Hilton, are near the Expo Guadalajara convention center.

CENTRO HISTÓRICO

$$　🏨 **Holiday Inn Centro Histórico**. This branch of the reliable international
chain sits in the heart of historic Guadalajara. Though the hotel's pub-
lic areas could use some updating, it has a grand entrance—with a
restaurant and a men's shop—leading guests up to the check-in area.
Rooms have nice touches like plasma TVs; the bathrooms have glassed-
in showers, but no tubs. The breakfast buffet is a good deal, and the
restaurant serves national and international dishes. **Pros:** helpful busi-
ness center; free Wi-Fi in rooms and public spaces; some free items in
the minibar. **Cons:** no heat; small, old gym; no pool. ✉ *Av. Juárez 211,
Centro Histórico* ☎ *33/3560–1200* ⊕ *www.holidaycentrogdl.com* 🛏 *45
rooms, 45 suites* ♿ *In-room: safe, Wi-Fi. In-hotel: restaurant, room
service, bar, laundry facilities, laundry service, Internet terminal, Wi-Fi
hotspot, parking (free), no-smoking rooms* ▭ *AE, MC, V* ✛ *1:D5.*

$$　🏨 **Hotel de Mendoza**. Elegant with its postcolonial architecture, this hotel
is on a calm side street a block from Teatro Degollado. Hand-carved
furniture and doors and wrought-iron railings adorn the public areas
and the rooms. Standard rooms are small, making suites worth the
extra cost. Balconies overlook the courtyard pool from some rooms.
Pros: great location; comfortable rooms. **Cons:** standard rooms lack
tubs; most rooms don't have balconies. ✉ *Calle Venustiano Carranza
16, Centro Histórico* ☎ *01800/361–2600 toll-free in Mexico; 33/3942–
5151* ⊕ *www.demendoza.com.mx* 🛏 *86 rooms, 18 suites* ♿ *In-room:
safe, Wi-Fi. In-hotel: restaurant, pool, gym, Internet terminal, Wi-Fi
hotspot, parking (paid)* ▭ *AE, MC, V* ✛ *1:C5.*

$　🏨 **Hotel Morales**. After being abandoned for 30 years, this downtown
Fodor'sChoice　hotel—originally a 19th-century rooming house—has been transformed
★　into one of the city's most luxurious lodgings. No wonder it's the choice
of celebrities ranging from movie stars to soccer heroes. Demure guest
rooms have crown molding, blond-wood floors, and gold-and-beige
furnishings with an old-world style. Café tables on the rooftop terrace

make for a casual retreat. The lobby and restaurant are much more formal. **Pros:** relaxed elegance; double-paned windows keep out the noise. **Cons:** lobby restaurant isn't cozy; no Wi-Fi in rooms. ☒ *Ave. Ramón Corona 243, Centro Histórico* ☏ *33/3658–5232* ⊕ *www.hotelmorales. com.mx* ☛ *59 rooms, 7 suites* ♿ *In-room: safe, Wi-Fi (some; first floor only). In-hotel: restaurant, parking (free)* ▭ *AE, MC, V* ✛ *1:D5.*

ZONA MINERVA

$$ ★ 🛏 **Fiesta Americana.** The dramatic glass facade of this high-rise faces the Minerva Fountain and Los Arcos monument. Four glass-enclosed elevators ascend dizzyingly above a 14-story atrium lobby to the guest rooms, which have dignified modern furnishings, small marble bathrooms with bathtub, and, for the most part, arresting views (rooms 1211 through 1217 have the absolute best). The lobby bar has live music every night. Executive-floor rooms come with Continental breakfast and canapes, and there's a fully equipped business center. **Pros:** airport shuttle (fee); 24-hour room service; ample parking; nice bathroom amenities; AAA discount. **Cons:** some rooms have unpleasant views of roof and generators; no swimming pool. ☒ *Av. Aurelio Aceves 225, Col. Vallarta Poniente, Zona Minerva* ☏ *33/3818–1400* ⊕ *www.fiestamericana.com. mx* ☛ *309 rooms* ♿ *In-room: Wi-Fi. In-hotel: restaurant, bar, gym, laundry service, Internet terminal, Wi-Fi hotspot, parking (paid), no-smoking rooms* ▭ *AE, DC, MC, V* ✛ *1:B1.*

$$ ★ 🛏 **Hotel Plaza Diana.** At this modest hotel two blocks from the Minerva Fountain, the rooms are on the small side. One suite has a sauna. Stay on the upper floors in the rear for the quietest rooms. The expansive, café-style restaurant specializes in Argentine-style cuts of beef. The huge indoor pool is good for swimming laps. **Pros:** free Internet; heated indoor pool; free airport shuttle. **Cons:** gym is on the small side. ☒ *Av. Agustín Yáñez 2760, Zona Minerva* ☏ *33/3540–9700; 01800/248–1001 toll-free in Mexico* ⊕ *www.hoteldiana.com.mx* ☛ *127 rooms, 24 suites* ♿ *In-room: safe, Wi-Fi. In-hotel: restaurant, room service, bar, pool, gym, Internet terminal, Wi-Fi hotspot* ▭ *AE, DC, MC, V* ✛ *1:B2.*

$$$ ★ 🛏 **Quinta Real.** Stone-and-brick walls, colonial arches, and objets d'art fill this luxury hotel's public areas. Suites are plush, though on the small side, with neocolonial-style furnishings, original art, and faux fireplaces. Master suites have separate seating areas with love seats and marble-top desk. For a bit more the Grand Class suites have luxurious touches like round whirlpool tubs. You can arrange in-room massages from one of two nearby spas. The wood-floor gym is outfitted with the latest equipment and plasma-screen TVs. **Pros:** elegant rooms; stately grounds; in-room spa services. **Cons:** pricey rates; no on-site spa. ☒ *Av. México 2727, at Av. López Mateos Norte, Zona Minerva* ☏ *33/3669–0600; 866/621–9288 toll-free from U.S.; 01800/500–4000 in Mexico* ⊕ *www. quintareal.com* ☛ *76 suites* ♿ *In-room: safe, Internet. In-hotel: restaurant, bar, pool, gym, laundry service, Internet terminal, Wi-Fi hotspot, parking (free), no-smoking rooms* ▭ *AE, MC, V* ✛ *1:A2.*

$$$$ Fodor'sChoice ★ 🛏 **Villa Ganz.** Staying in this neighborhood full of restaurants and nightlife yet away from the gritty historic center might be just the ticket. But location is just one of the many virtues of this gracious mansion. We loved the spacious rooms, the hunting-lodge-like sitting area with

8

fireplace, and a candlelit, tree-shaded garden that will make you want to book an extended stay. Private dinners in the garden can be arranged in advance and make for Guadalajara's most romantic dining. **Pros:** great location; inviting patios; free early-evening wine and canapes. **Cons:** suites must be paid in full when booked; high-season cancellations charged tax as well as 100% of room fee. ⊠ *Av. López Cotilla 1739, Zona Minerva* ☎ *33/3120–1416* ⊕ *www.villaganz.com* ⋧ *9 suites* ⟁ *In-room: safe, Wi-Fi (some). In-hotel: bar, Wi-Fi hotspot, no kids under 12* ⊟ *AE, MC, V* ⵏ⃝ *CP* ✛ *1:B3.*

TLAQUEPAQUE

$$ ⛶ **La Casa del Retoño.** On a quiet street several blocks from the shopping district is this B&B. Rooms are made of painted cinder block but are clean and cheerful. Rooms in the back overlook a large but uninspired garden, while the ones upstairs have small private terraces. There's an open-air reading area, and complimentary Continental breakfast is served in the courtyard. **Pros:** quiet neighborhood; private terraces in some rooms. **Cons:** smallish rooms; lackluster garden. ⊠ *Matamoros 182, Tlaquepaque* ☎ *33/3639–6510 or 33/3635–7636* ⊕ *www. lacasadelretono.com.mx* ⋧ *8 rooms, 1 suite* ⟁ *In-room: Wi-Fi. In-hotel: Internet terminal, Wi-Fi hotspot* ⊟ *AE, MC, V* ⵏ⃝ *CP* ✛ *2:C3.*

$$ ⛶ **La Villa del Ensueño.** A 10-minute walk from Tlaquepaque's center, this intimate B&B is near lots of shopping. The restored 19th-century hacienda has thick, white adobe walls; exposed-beam ceilings; and plants in huge unglazed pots. Smokers should request a room with private balcony; smoking isn't allowed anywhere inside the hotel. Room rates include a full, hot breakfast. **Pros:** hot tub; take-out food available from adjacent Mexican restaurant; friendly staff. **Cons:** only junior suites have bathtubs. ⊠ *Florida 305, Tlaquepaque* ☎ *33/3635–8792* ⊕ *www.villadelensueno.com* ⋧ *16 rooms, 4 suites* ⟁ *In-room: refrigerator (some), Wi-Fi. In-hotel: restaurant, bar, pools, parking (free), no-smoking rooms* ⊟ *AE, MC, V* ⵏ⃝ *BP* ✛ *2:B1.*

$$ ⛶ **Quinta Don José.** One block from Tlaquepaque's main plaza and shopping area, this B&B has a great location. Natural lighting and room size vary; suites face the pool and are spacious but a bit dark. There's remarkable tile work in the master suite. Hearty Continental breakfasts—with fruit, cereal, toast, and sweet breads plus juice and coffee—are served in an inner courtyard and are included in the room rate. Tasty pizzas are baked in the brick oven at the hotel's Mexican-Italian restaurant (closed Monday). If you stay three nights or more, they'll shuttle you to and from the airport or bus station. **Pros:** central location; friendly staff who speak excellent English; free calls worldwide; free Wi-Fi; free parking. **Cons:** pool is chilly; some rooms are small. ⊠ *Calle Reforma 139, Tlaquepaque* ☎ *33/3635–7522; 01800/700–2223 toll-free in Mexico; 866/629–3753 in U.S. and Canada* ⊕ *www. quintadonjose.com* ⋧ *18 rooms* ⟁ *In-room: Wi-Fi (some). In-hotel: restaurant, bar, pool, laundry service, Internet terminal, Wi-Fi hotspot* ⊟ *AE, MC, V* ⵏ⃝ *BP* ✛ *2:C3.*

NIGHTLIFE

With the exception of a few well-established nightspots like La Maestranza, downtown Guadalajara quiets down relatively early. The existing nightlife centers on Avenida Vallarta, favored by the well-to-do under-30 set; Avenida Patria, full of bars for young people who party until early in the morning; or the somewhat seedy Plaza del Sol. Bars in these spots open into the wee hours, usually closing by 3 AM. Dance clubs may charge a $15–$20 cover, which includes an open bar, on Wednesday and Saturday nights. Dress up for nightclubs; highly subjective admission policies hinge on who you know or how you look. The local music scene is less formal and centers on more intimate digs.

■ TIP→ For the latest listings, grab a Público newspaper on Friday and pull out the weekly Ocio cultural guide.

BARS

One of Guadalajara's hot spots, **I Latina** (⊠ *Av. Inglaterra 3128, at López Mateos, Col. Vallarta Poniente, Centro* ☎ *33/3647–7774*) is where you will spot a cool, upscale local and international crowd having cocktails.

★ Appealing and unpretentious, **La Fuente** (⊠ *Calle Pino Suarez s/n at Hidalgo, Centro Histórico* ☎ *No phone* ☉ *Closed Mon.*) opened in this location in 1950. The cantina draws business types, intellectuals, and blue-collar workers, all seeking cheap drinks, animated conversation, and live music. Above the bar, look for an old bicycle. It's been around since 1957, when, legend has it, one of a long list of famous people (most say it was the father of local newspaper baron Jesús Álvarez del Castillo) left the bike to pay for his drinks. The bar opens at 8—arrive soon after to avoid crowds.

For some local color, stop at **La Maestranza** (⊠ *Calle Maestranza 179, between López Cotillo and Madero, Centro Histórico* ☎ *33/3613–5878*), a renovated 1940s cantina full of bullfighting memorabilia.

LIVE MUSIC

★ **Rusty Trombone** (⊠ *Lerdo de Tejada 2166, Col. Americana* ☎ *33/3630–2294*) is a great place to relax and enjoy a variety of hip bands.

Sun, surf, and sand rule **Wall Street** (⊠ *Av. Américas 1419, Col. Providencia* ☎ *33/3817–1743*), a spring-break-themed bar and dance club drawing crowds of twentysomethings and featuring live music, including pop, ska, and rock.

SPORTS AND THE OUTDOORS

GOLF Clubs are less crowded on Wednesday and Thursday; all rent equipment for around $20 to $30. Golf carts typically cost around $40. Guadalajara's top golf clubs—El Cielo and Santa Anita—are technically for members only, but hotels can get you in.

Atlas Country Club (⊠ *Carretera Guadalajara–Chapala, Km 6.5, El Salto* ☎ *33/3689–2620*) is an 18-hole, par-72 course designed by Joe Finger and is on the way to the airport. Greens fees are about $92 on weekdays, $104 on weekends and holidays.

The private **El Cielo Country Club** (⊠ *Paseo del Cello 1, Zapopan* ☎ *33/3684–4436*), on a hill outside town, is an 18-hole, 6,765-yard, par-72 course blissfully removed from the city's din and with challenging holes and

water features. For non-members it's $115 for 18 holes, including cart.

HEALTH CLUBS **Gold's Gym** (✉ *Av. Xóchitl 4203, Zona Plaza del Sol* ☎ *33/3122–6541* ✉ *Av. México 3370, Local Ancla 1–A PB, Col. Monraz* ☎ *33/1201–1485 or 33/1201–1486* ⊕ *www. goldsgymmexico.com*) has two locations. Day passes are $8 at both. Weekday hours are 6 AM–11 PM at both; the Plaza del Sol location (which has a pool) is open 9–5 on weekends, while the Colonia Monraz location, near Plaza México, is open 7–3 on Saturday and is closed on Sunday.

SHOPPING

The Centro Histórico is packed with shops as well as ambulatory vendors, who compete with pedestrians for sidewalk space. You'll find the most products under one roof at labyrinthine Mercado Libertad, one of Latin America's largest markets. Tlaquepaque and Tonalá are arts-and-crafts meccas. Shoe stores and silver shops are ubiquitous in Guadalajara.

Stores tend to open Monday–Saturday from 10 or 11 until 8, and Sunday 10–2; some close during lunch, usually 2–4 or 2–5, and others close on Sunday. Bargaining is customary in Mercado Libertad, and you can talk deals with some crafts vendors in Tlaquepaque and Tonalá. The ticketed price sticks just about everywhere else, with the exception of antiques shops.

Neighborhood street markets, called *tianguis*, also abound in Guadalajara. They take place at various times throughout the week, with a larger share on Sunday morning. Some focus on specific items like antiques or art, but many have a variety of vendors selling everything from chicken, homemade mole sauce, and fruits and vegetables to flowers, clothing, and housewares.

MARKETS

Tonalá's crafts market, Tlaquepaque's crafts and housewares shops, and Mercado Libertad are the region's top marketplaces. Allot yourself plenty of time and energy to explore both. El Trocadero is a weekly antiques market at the north end of Avenida Chapultepec. Feel free to drive a hard bargain.

Mercado Libertad. Better known as San Juan de Dios, this is one of Latin America's largest covered markets. Its three expansive floors, with shops organized thematically, tower over downtown's east side. Fluctuating degrees of government intervention dictate the quantity of contraband electronics available. Avoid the food on the second floor unless you have a stomach of iron. Be wary of fakes in the jewelry stores. The

market opens Monday–Saturday 10–8, but some stores close at 6; the few shops open on Sunday close by 3. ⊠ *Calz. Independencia Sur; use pedestrian bridge from Plaza Tapatía's south side, Centro Histórico* ☏ *No phone.*

SPECIALTY SHOPS

ART AND HANDICRAFTS

Ana Lucia Pewter (⊠ *Av. Tonalá 230, Tonalá* ☏ *33/3683–2794* ⊕ *www.analuciapewter.com*) sells beautiful locally made pewter items—from decorative tableware to picture frames—at ridiculously low prices.

Arte Jimenez (⊠ *Cruz Blanca 264-F, Tonalá* ☏ *33/3690–8509* ⊕ *www.artejimenez.com*) is a unique shop specializing in decorative art made from fired copper and other metals.

Cadi (⊠ *Juárez 174, Tlaquepaque* ☏ *33/3343–3682*) sells awesome stained-glass lamps and other decorative items for the home.

Fodor'sChoice
★

Sergio Bustamante's work is in galleries around the world, but you can purchase his sculptures of human, animal, and fairy-tale creatures in bronze, ceramic, or resin for less at **Galería Sergio Bustamante** (⊠ *Calle Independencia 238, Tlaquepaque* ☏ *33/3639–5519, 33/3657–8354, or 33/3659–7110*). You'll also find his designs in silver- and gold-plated jewelry. Don't expect a bargain, however; most pieces range from hundreds to thousands of dollars.

The government-run **Instituto de la Artesanía Jalisciense** (⊠ *Calz. González Gallo 20, at Calz. Independencia Sur, Centro Histórico* ☏ *33/3030–9090*), on the northeast side of Parque Agua Azul, has exquisite blown glass and hand-glazed pottery typical of Jalisco artisans. Prices are fixed here.

TEQUILA

56 km (35 mi) northwest of Guadalajara.

The drive to tequila country is a straightforward and easy trip. Head west from Guadalajara along Avenida Vallarta for about 25 minutes until you hit the toll road junction (it will say Puerto Vallarta Cuota). The whole trip takes about an hour by car. Take either the toll road (*cuota*) or the free road (*libre*) toward Puerto Vallarta. The toll road is faster, safer, and costs about $10. You can also catch a bus to Tequila from the Antigua Central Camionera (Old Central Bus Station), northeast of the Parque Agua Azul on Avenida Dr. R. Michel, between Calle Los Angeles and Calle 5 de Febrero. Buses marked AMATITÁN–TEQUILA are easy to spot from the entrance on Calle Los Angeles.

TRAIN

Another option is to take the Tequila Express train from Guadalajara to Tequila and back for about $80. One of the few passenger trains left in Mexico takes guests on an all-day tour starting and ending with free

Tequila isn't just about the local drink; you can easily spend an afternoon taking in the town's colonial architecture.

canned-tequila mixed drinks (like *palomas* and *sangrita*), accompanied by mariachi music. Upon arrival in Tequila, the tour takes visitors to a distillery to learn about the process of making the liquor; the day includes tastings at the distillery, a show of traditional Jalisco dancing and music, and a delicious all-you-can-eat-and-drink Mexican buffet.

TOURS Tours of the city that include stops at distilleries and agave fields are available from two providers found under the porticos to the left of the cathedral. Tranvias Turisticos De Tequila leaves every 30 minutes daily, 10–4:30, except for Tuesday; the $8 tour lasts 2 hours. Servi-Tours Agave Azul offers three different tours every 30 minutes that range from $7 to $11, adding additional stops and time—from one and a half to two hours—depending on what level you choose.

ESSENTIALS

Train **Tequila Express** (☎ 33/3880–9090 Ext. 2099 ⊕ www.tequilaexpress.com.mx).

Tours **Servi-Tours Agave Azul** (☎ 37/4742–0851). **Tranvias Turisticos De Tequila** (☎ 33/1299–7536).

Tequila Express Contacts **Guadalajara Chamber of Commerce** (⊠ *Av. Vallarta 4095, at Niño Obrero, Guadalajara* ☎ 33/3880–9099 or 33/3122–7920). **Guadalajara Train Station** (⊠ *Av. Washington at Calzada Independencia, Guadalajara* ☎ 33/3641–3141). **TicketMaster** (⊕ www.ticketmaster.com.mx).

EXPLORING

The **Sauza Museum** (⊠ *Calle Albino Rojas 22* ☎ 37/4742–0247) has memorabilia from the Sauza family, a tequila-making dynasty second only to the Cuervos. The museum opens daily 10–3. Admission costs

about 6 pesos; for this low price, they offer tours in English as well as Spanish, depending on the needs of the crowd.

Opened in 1795, the **José Cuervo Distillery** (⊠ *Calle José Cuervo 73* ☎ *37/4742–2442*) is the world's oldest tequila distillery. Every day, 150 tons of agave hearts are processed into 80,000 liters of tequila here. Tours are given daily every hour from 10 to 4. The tours at noon and 3 PM are in English, but English-speakers can often be accommodated at other times. The basic tour, which includes one margarita cocktail, costs $8. It's $12 for tours with a few additional tastings as well as an educational catalog, or $20 if you want to add special reserve tequilas to your tasting. Tours including round-trip transportation can be arranged through the major hotels and travel agencies in Guadalajara. This is a good deal, including several tequila tastings, a complimentary margarita, and time for lunch for about $22. Call 33/3343–4481 at least a day in advance to make arrangements. ■ TIP➔ Make sure to ask the guide for coupons for an additional margarita as well as discounts at an area restaurant and in the gift shop.

WHERE TO EAT

$ ✕ **Fonda Cholula.** This typical Mexican restaurant owned by Jose Cuervo
MEXICAN serves up decent quesadillas and other local favorites without leaving your wallet empty. The margaritas are not bad, either. ⊠ *Ramón Corona 55* ☎ *37/4742–1079* ⊙ *Daily noon–6.*

TEUCHITLÁN

🔺 *50 km (28 mi) west of Guadalajara.*

Teuchitlán itself isn't much to see: a small Mexican town like many others, with a few small eateries surrounding a central plaza. But its main draw, the mysterious Guachimontones Ruins, is growing in popularity, and preservation efforts are moving apace. Near the ruins, there are nice lakeside restaurants with decent food and better atmosphere than in town; spending some time here after seeing the ruins makes for a lovely afternoon.

GETTING HERE AND AROUND

To get to Teuchitlán from Guadalajara, drive west out along Avenida Vallarta for 25 minutes to the toll-road junction to Puerto Vallarta, then take the free (*libre*) Route 70 toward Vallarta. Head west along Route 15 for a couple of miles; then turn left onto Route 70 and continue until you reach the town of Tala. Two kilometers (1 mi) past the sugar mill, turn right onto Route 27. Teuchitlán is 15 minutes from the last junction. If you prefer not to drive yourself, it's also possible to hire a car from Guadalajara.

EXPLORING

Guachimontones Ruins. For decades, residents in this sleepy village of sugarcane farmers had a name for the funny-looking mounds in the hills above town, but they never considered the Guachimontones to be more than a convenient source of rocks for local construction projects. Then in the early 1970s an American archaeologist asserted that the mounds were the remnants of a long-vanished, 2,000-year-old community. It

took Phil Weigand nearly three decades to convince authorities in far-off Mexico City that he wasn't crazy. Before he was allowed to start excavating and restoring this monumental site in the late 1990s, plenty more houses and roads were produced with Guachimonton rock—and countless tombs were looted of priceless art.

This UNESCO World Heritage Site is most distinctive for its sophisticated concentric architecture—a circular pyramid surrounded by a ring of flat ground, surrounded by a series of smaller platforms arranged in a circle. The "Teuchitlán Tradition," as the concentric circle structures are called, is unique in world architecture. While little is known about the ancient settlement, Weigand believes the formations suggest the existence of a pre-Hispanic state in the region, whereas it was previously held that only socially disorganized nomads inhabited the area at the time. Similar ruins are spread throughout the foothills of the extinct Tequila Volcano, but this is the biggest site yet detected.

Until late 2009, visitors had to find their way to the ruins by asking locals and driving up a hill on an unmarked dirt road. But construction of a large visitor center and museum was nearing completion at this writing, and there are now signs along the highway and through the town of Teuchitlán directing visitors to the site.

WHERE TO EAT

$$
MEXICAN
✕ **Restaurant Montecarlo.** This outdoor restaurant is one of a handful of eateries along the lakeside in Teuchitlán. While not fancy, it offers a variety of Mexican dishes, including fish, molcajetes, and fajitas, and provides a grand view of the lake teeming with fish and birds—including herons and pelicans. There's also a fish pond where kids can borrow a homemade rod for some catch and release. As you turn into the street, don't feel pressured by the parking attendants at the other restaurants who will make attempts to get you into their locales. ⊠ *Carretera Guadalajara–Tala–San Marcos, Km 49* ☎ *38/4733–0257.*

AROUND LAGO DE CHAPALA

48 km (30 mi) southeast of Guadalajara.

Mexico's largest natural lake is a one-hour drive southeast of Guadalajara. Surrounded by jagged hills and serene towns, Lake Chapala is a favorite Tapatío getaway and a haven for thousands of North American retirees. The name probably derives from Chapalac, who was chief of the region's Taltica Indians when the Spaniards arrived in 1538.

The area's main town, Chapala, is flooded with weekend visitors and the pier is packed shoulder-to-shoulder most Sundays. Its *malecón* is often packed with local families and couples on the weekends. Eight kilometers (5 mi) west is Ajijic, a picturesque village that's home to the bulk of the area's expatriates. Farther west, San Juan Cosalá is popular for its thermal-water pools.

GETTING HERE AND AROUND

Driving from Guadalajara, take Avenida Lázaro Cárdenas or Dr. R. Michel to Carretera a Chapala. The trip takes about an hour. The Carretera a Chapala is the quickest route to Chapala and Ajijic.

Autotransportes Guadalajara Chapala (☎33/3619–5675) serves the lakeside towns for about $4. It's 30 minutes to Chapala and another 15 minutes to Ajijic; there are departures every half hour from 6 AM to 9:30 PM. Make sure you ask for the *directo* (direct) as opposed to *clase segunda* (second-class) bus, which makes frequent stops along the highway en route.

CHAPALA
45 km (28 mi) south of Guadalajara.

Chapala was a placid weekend getaway for aristocrats in the late 19th century, but when then-president Porfirio Díaz got in on the action in 1904, other wealthy Mexicans followed suit. More and more summer homes were built, and in 1910 the Chapala Yacht Club opened. Avenida Madero, Chapala's main street, is lined with restaurants, shops, and cafés. Three blocks north of the promenade, the plaza at the corner of López Cotilla is a relaxing spot to read a paper or succumb to sweets from surrounding shops. The Iglesia de San Francisco (built in 1528), easily recognized by its blue neon crosses on twin steeples, is two blocks south of the plaza.

On weekends Mexican families flock to the shores of the (for now, at least) rejuvenated lake. Vendors sell refreshments and souvenirs, while lakeside watering holes fill to capacity.

> ### WATER LEVELS
>
> Fifty miles wide but less than 30 feet deep when full, Lake Chapala is the vestige of an ancient inland sea. It's at the tail end (in geological terms) of a natural death from millennia of silt accumulation. This drying process has been accelerated in recent decades by overexploitation of the Lerma River feeding the lake. In 2002, Lake Chapala plummeted to an average depth of 4 feet, exposing a mile of lake bed stretching from the Chapala pier. Several years of heavy summer rain brought the lake back to near pre-2002 water levels, but what once was a clean place to enjoy lake activities is now much less pristine.

WHERE TO EAT AND STAY

$$ ✕ **Restaurant Cazadores.** This grandly turreted brick building was once
MEXICAN the summer home of the Braniff family, former owners of the defunct airline. The menu includes slightly overpriced seafood and beef dishes. The house specialty is *chamorro*, pork shank wrapped in banana leaves. A patio overlooks the boardwalk and is inviting in the evening. ⊠ *Paseo Ramón Corona 18* ☎ *376/765–2162* ═ *AE, MC, V* ☉ *Closed Mon.*

$$ 🏨 **Hotel Villa Montecarlo.** Built on a Mediterranean-style villa nearly a century old, this hotel has well-maintained grounds with plenty of places for picnics or for the kids to play. One of the two swimming pools (the biggest in the area) is filled water from the nearby hot springs; it's usually open only on weekends and holidays. The simple, clean rooms all have patios or terraces. Popular with Mexican families, the hotel has packages that are often good deals. For about $20 more than a standard room you can get a suite with larger terrace or balcony, a kitchenette, and king-size bed. **Pros:** huge pools; extensive grounds; outdoor dining under a flowering tree. **Cons:** can be noisy. ⊠ *Av. Hidalgo 296, about 1 km (½ mi) west of Av. Madero* ☎ *37/6765–2024* ⊕ *www.hoteles.udg.mx/montecarlo*

🛏45 rooms, 2 suites & In-room: no a/c. In-hotel: restaurant, bar, tennis courts, pools, laundry service, parking (free) ☰ AE, MC, V.

$$ 🛏 **Lake Chapala Inn.** Three of the four
★ rooms in this restored mansion face the shore; all have high ceilings and whitewashed oak furniture. Rates include an English-style breakfast (with a Continental breakfast on Sunday). **Pros:** solar-heated lap

> **CAUTION**
>
> On both ends of the highway are precarious hilly stretches. Care should be taken while returning to Guadalajara from Chapala on Sunday night, when the largely unlighted highway fills with tipsy drivers.

pool; English-speaking host; sunny reading room. **Cons:** dated furnishings; square tubs not conducive to long soaks. ⊠ *Paseo Ramón Corona 23* ☎ *37/6765–4786 or 37/6765–4809* ⊕ *www.chapalainn.com* 🛏 *4 rooms* & *In-room: no a/c, Wi-Fi. In-hotel: restaurant, pool, laundry service, Wi-Fi hotspot, parking (free)* ☰ *No credit cards* ⦿⊨ *BP.*

AJIJIC

8 km (5 mi) west of Chapala; 47 km (30 mi) southwest of Guadalajara.

Ajijic has narrow cobblestone streets, vibrantly colored buildings, and a gentle pace—with the exception of the considerably trafficky main highway through the town's southern end. The foreign influence is unmistakable: English is widely (though not exclusively) spoken, and license plates come from far-flung places like British Columbia and Texas.

The Plaza Principal (also known as Plaza de Armas) is a tree- and flower-filled central square at the corner of Avenidas Colón and Hidalgo. The Iglesia de San Andrés (Church of St. Andrew) is on the plaza's north side. In late November the plaza and its surrounding streets fill for the saint's nine-day fiesta. From the plaza, walk down Calle Morelos (the continuation of Avenida Colón) toward the lake and peruse the boutiques. Turn left onto Avenida 16 de Septiembre or Avenida Constitución for art galleries and studios. Northeast of the plaza, along the highway, the hub of local activity is the soccer field, which doubles as a venue for concerts.

WHERE TO EAT

$$ ✕ **Ajijic Tango.** Considered one of the top, if not the top, restaurants in
ARGENTINE   Ajijic, this Argentine favorite sees locals and tourists waiting in a line down the block to get inside. Many go for the *arrachera* (flank steak), lamb, or carpaccio. Reservations are a must on weekdays—but the eatery doesn't take them on weekends, so get there early. ⊠ *Calle Morelos 5* ☎ *37/6766–2458* ⊕ *www.ajijictango.com* ☰ *MC, V* ⊗ *Wed.–Sat. and Mon. 12:30–10, Sun. 12:30–6.*

$–$$ ✕ **Johanna's.** Come to this intimate bit of Bavaria on the lake for German
GERMAN   cuisine like sausages and goose or duck pâté. Main dishes come with soup or salad, applesauce, and cooked red cabbage. For dessert indulge in plum strudel or blackberry-topped torte. Come on the early side, though; this restaurant closes at 8 PM. ⊠ *Carretera Chapala–Jocotepec, Km 6.5* ☎ *37/6766–0437* ☰ *No credit cards* ⊗ *Closed Mon.*

$$ ✕ **La Bodega de Ajijic.** Eat on a covered patio overlooking a grassy lawn
ECLECTIC   and a small pool at this low-key restaurant. In addition to Mexican standards, the menu has Italian dishes such as pastas; the food here

is a bit meager and overpriced. Still, service is friendly, and there's live music—ranging from Mexican pop and rock to blues, jazz, guitar, and harp—most nights. It opens at 8 AM, in time for breakfast, every day but Thursday, when it opens later. ⊠ *Av. 16 de Septiembre 124* ☎ *376/766–1002* ☐ *AE, MC, V.*

$$ ✕ **Number 4.** This trendy two-level outdoor restaurant on one of Ajijic's
ECLECTIC   charming side streets offers beautifully presented dishes, many with an Asian twist. Diners can sit in the modern interior or chose to enjoy the upstairs patio, surrounded by trees and the night sky. Fabulous live piano music accompanies lunch Saturday and Sunday, and there's live music nightly. The bar offers special concoctions, such as a cranberry mandarin martini. ⊠ *Donato Guerra 4* ☎ *37/6766–1360; 416/907–0609 in U.S. and Canada* ⊕ *www.number4.com.mx* ☐ *MC, V* ☉ *Hours fluctuate seasonally.*

WHERE TO STAY

$–$$ ▦ **Casa Blanca.** Gracious gardens, tinkling fountains, bright colors, and arched windows give the traveler a sense of sleeping in a Mexican hacienda while also enjoying the comforts of home. The hotel's basic rooms are cheerful and tastefully decorated with blond-wood furnishings, and the grounds include two patios for guest use. A small, upscale bar provides drinks of your choice, a few quick food options, and flat-screen TVs for watching sports games. Continental breakfast is included, and four of the eight rooms have a kitchenette. **Pros:** full of character; manicurist and massage therapist by reservation; complementary shoe shine; on-site Internet service. **Cons:** small rooms. ⊠ *Calle 16 de Septiembre 29, Centro* ☎ *376/766–4440 or 800/436–0759* ⊕ *www.casablancaajijic. com* ⇆ *8 rooms* ⌂ *In-room: kitchen (some). In-hotel: Internet terminal, Wi-Fi hotspot, bar* ☐ *AE, MC, V* ⏹ *CP.*

$$ ▦ **La Nueva Posada.** The well-kept gardens framed in bougainvil-
★   lea define this inviting inn. Rooms are large, with high ceilings and local crafts. Villas share a courtyard and have tile kitchenettes. The bar has jazz or Caribbean music some weekend evenings. Out in the garden restaurant, strands of tiny white lights set the mood for an evening meal. **Pros:** uniquely decorated, airy rooms; great restaurant; discounts given for paying with cash. **Cons:** TVs in rooms are small. ⊠ *Calle Donato Guerra 9* ⌂ *A.P. 30, 45920* ☎ *37/6766–1344* ⊕ *www. hotelnuevaposada-ajijic.com* ⇆ *19 rooms, 4 villas* ⌂ *In-room: TV. In-hotel: restaurant, bar, pool, laundry service* ☐ *MC, V* ⏹ *BP.*

NIGHTLIFE

La Bodega de Ajijic (⊠ *Calle 16 de Septiembre 124* ☎ *376/766–1002* ⛁ *$3 cover Fri. and Sun.*) has dancing on the weekends and live guitar the rest of the week. It's closed Thursday.

SPORTS AND THE OUTDOORS

The **Rojas family** (⊠ *Paseo de los Caballos and Calle Los Carriles* ☎ *376/766–4261*) has been leading horseback trips for more than 30 years. A ride along the lakeshore or in the surrounding hills costs around $8 an hour.

UNDERSTANDING PUERTO VALLARTA

HISTORY

PRE-COLUMBIAN MEXICO

The first nomadic hunters crossed the Bering Straight during the Late Pleistocene Era, some 30,000 or 40,000 years ago, fanning out and finding niches in the varied landscape of North America. In the hot and arid "Great Chichimeca," as the vast area that included the Sonora and Chihuahua deserts and the Great Plains of the United States was known, lived far-flung tribes whose circumstances favored a nomadic lifestyle. Even the unassailable Aztecs were unable to dominate this harsh wilderness and its resilient people.

Mesoamerica, the name given posthumously to the great civilizations of mainland Mexico, spanned as far south of the Great Chichimeca as Honduras and El Salvador. Here, trade routes were established, strategic alliances were formed through warfare or marriage, and enormous temples and palaces were erected on the backs of men, without the aid of beasts of burden or the wheel. Some cultures mysteriously disappeared, others were conquered but not absorbed.

It was in northern Mesoamerica that the continent's first major metropolis, Teotihuacán—which predated the Aztec capital of Tenochtitlán by more than half a century—was built. The gleaming city with beautifully decorated pyramids, palaces, homes, and administrative buildings covered miles and administered to some 175,000 souls; it was abandoned for unknown reasons around AD 700. On the Yucatán Peninsula, great and powerful Maya cities rose up, but like Teotihuacán were abandoned one by one, seemingly at the height of civilization.

During the rise and fall of these great cities, small, loosely organized bands of individuals occupied Mesoamerica's western Pacific coast. By 1200 BC, the culture that archaeologists call Capacha occupied river valleys north and south of what would later be named Bahía de Banderas. From well-positioned settlements, they planted gardens and took advantage of animal and mineral resources from the sea and the surrounding foothills.

These cultures—centered primarily in the present-day states of Nayarit, Jalisco, and Colima—built no large, permanent structures and left few clues about their society. Some of the most compelling evidence comes from artifacts found in tombs. Unlike their more advanced neighbors, the Pacific coast people housed these burial chambers not in magnificent pyramids but in the bottom of vertical shafts deep within the earth. Lifelike dog sculptures were sometimes left to help their deceased owners cross to the other side; servants, too, were buried with their masters for the same purpose. Realistically depicted figures involved in myriad rituals of daily and ceremonial life, most of them excavated only since the 1970s, have given more clues about pre-Hispanic civilizations of western Mexico.

Only so much information can be gleaned, however, especially since the majority of tombs were looted before archaeological research began. North and south of Banderas Bay, the Aztatlán people seem to have established themselves primarily in river valleys between Tomatlán, in southern Jalisco, and northern Nayarit. In addition to creating utilitarian and ceremonial pottery, they appear to have been skilled in at least rudimentary metallurgy. Aside from the Purépecha of Michoacán, to whom the Aztatlán (or Aztlán) are related, no other Mesoamerican societies were skilled in making or using metal of any kind.

The Colonial Period

History favors those who write it, and the soldier-priest-scribe who documented the discovery of Banderas Bay in 1525 gave it a decidedly European spin. According to Padre Tello, four years after the Spanish demolished the Aztec capital at Tenochtitlán, about 100 Spanish troops met 10,000 to 20,000 Aztatlán at Punta Mita (aka Punta de Mita), the bay's northernmost

point. Then, by Tello's fantastic account, the sun's sudden illumination of a Spanish battle standard (a large pennant) bearing the image of the Virgin of the Immaculate Conception caused the armed indigenous peoples to give up without a fight. When they lay their colorful battle flags at the feet of Francisco Cortés de Buenaventura, the Spanish commander named the site Bahía de Banderas, or Bay of Flags.

Subsequent adventurers and explorers rediscovered and used the region around the bay, but it wasn't colonized until three centuries later. The name Bahía de Banderas is seen on maps from the 1600s, although whalers in the 1800s called it Humpback Bay, after their principal prey. Boats were built on the beach in today's Mismaloya for a missionary expedition to Baja California, and the long, deep bay was used as a pit stop on other long sailing voyages.

To a lesser extent, Banderas Bay was a place of refuge and refueling for pirates. Around the end of the 16th century, Sir Francis Drake lay in wait here for the Manila galleon—sailing south along the coast laden with wares from the Orient. He sent the booty to his patron, Queen Elizabeth of England.

The Formative Years

Although adventurers made use of the area's magnificent bay, Puerto Vallarta's story started inland and made its way to the coast. Mining in this part of the Sierra Madre wasn't as profitable as in Zacatecas and Guanajuato, but there was plenty of gold and silver to draw the Spaniards' attention. At the vanguard of Spanish exploration in 1530, the infamous conquistador Nuño Beltrán de Guzmán arrived in the region with a contingent of Spanish soldiers and indigenous allies.

During his tenure in Nueva Galicia (which included today's Jalisco, Zacatecas, and Durango states), de Guzmán seized land that was settled by native peoples and parceled out *encomiendas* (huge grants of land) to lucky *encomendados* (landholders) in return for loyalty and favors to the Crown. The landholders were entitled to the land and everything on it: the birds of the trees; beasts of the forest; and the unlucky indigenous people who lived there, who were consequently enslaved. De Guzmán's behavior was so outrageous that by 1536 he had been stripped of authority and sent to prison.

In exchange for their forced labor, the native population received the "protection" of the encomendado, meaning food and shelter, that they had enjoyed previously without any help from the Spanish. Abuse was inevitable, and many overworked natives died of famine. Epidemics of smallpox, diphtheria, scarlet fever, influenza, measles, and other imported diseases had a disastrous effect. The region's native population was reduced by about 90% within the first 100 years of Spanish occupation.

By the early 17th century, gold and silver were being mined throughout the region; there were bases of operation at San Sebastián del Oeste, Cuale, and Talpa. After the War for Independence (1810–21), Mexican entrepreneurs began to extract gold, silver, and zinc previously claimed by the Spanish. In the mid-1800s, the coast around today's Vallarta was under the jurisdiction of the mountain municipalities.

Independence from Spain brought little contentment to average people, who were as disenfranchised and poor as ever. A prime topic of the day among the moneyed elite was the growing conflict between Liberals and Conservatives. Liberals, like the lawyer Benito Juárez, favored curtailing the Church's vast power. When the Liberals prevailed and Juárez became Mexico's first indigenous president (he was a Zapotec from Oaxaca), a host of controversial reforms were enacted. Those regarding separation of church and state had immediate and lasting effects.

Settlers on the Bay

The power struggles of the first half of the 19th century had little real impact on relatively unpopulated coastal areas like Banderas Bay. In 1849, a few men from the fishing hamlet of Yelapa camped out at the mouth of the Cuale River, in present-day Puerto Vallarta. A few years later, young Guadalupe Sánchez, his wife, and a few friends were the first official settlers. This entrepreneur made his money by importing salt, vital for extracting mineral from rock. From this business grew the tiny town Las Peñas de Santa María de Guadalupe.

When silver prices dipped between the two World Wars, some of the mountain-based miners returned to their farming roots, relocating to the productive lands of the Ameca River basin (today, Nuevo Vallarta) at the southern border of Nayarit. The fecund land between the mountains and the bay produced ample corn crops, and the growing town of Las Peñas—renamed Puerto Vallarta in honor of a former Jalisco governor—became the seat of its own municipality in 1918.

Development came slowly. By the 1930s there was limited electricity; a small airstrip was built in the 1950s, when Mexicana Airlines initiated the first flights and electricity was finally available around the clock. Retaining the close-knit society and values brought down from the mining towns, each family seemed to know the others' joys and failures. They sat outside their adobe homes to discuss the latest gossip and the international news of the day.

THE MODERN ERA

Honoring a promise made to the Mexican government by John F. Kennedy, President Richard Nixon flew into an improved PV airport in 1970 to sign a treaty settling boundary disputes surrounding the Rio Grande, meeting with his Mexican counterpart, Gustavo Díaz Ordaz. Upon asking for an armored car,

he was cheerfully told that the convertible that had been arranged would do just fine. After riding parade-style along the roadway lined with cheering citizens and burros garlanded in flowers, the American leader is said to have asked why, if he was a Republican, the road was lined with donkeys. To which his host sensibly responded, "Well, where in the world would we get all those elephants?"

It took about 500 years for Puerto Vallarta to transition from discovery to major destination, but the city is making up for lost time. "When I was a child here, in the 1950s, Puerto Vallarta was like a big family," the town's official chronicler, the late don Carlos Munguía, said. "When I married, in 1964, there were about 12,000 people." By the early '70s the population had jumped to 35,000 and continued to grow steadily.

Today the greater Puerto Vallarta area has some 220,368, a significant number of them expat Americans and Canadians who vacationed here and never left. The metropolitan area has three universities and a vast marina harboring yachts, tour boats, and the Mexican navy. In 2005 the harbor was expanded to accommodate three cruise ships; the overflow has to anchor offshore. While many folks lament the loss of the good old days before tourism took off, some things haven't changed: Most *vallartenses* (Puerto Vallarta natives) are still intimately acquainted with their neighbors and the man or woman who owns the corner taco stand, which is likely to have been there for years, maybe even generations.

CHRONOLOGY

ca. 350 BC Oldest evidence of civilization—a ceramic piece from Ixtapa (northwest of Puerto Vallarta)—dates to this time

ca. 1100 Indigenous Aztatlán people dominate region from present-day Sinaloa to Colima states; create first-known settlement in area

1525 First Spanish–Indian confrontation in the region, at Punta Mita. By Spanish accounts, 100 Spanish soldiers prevailed over tens of thousands armed native peoples. Bahía de Banderas (Bay of Flags) was named for the battle flags of the indigenous army that were (or so claimed the Spanish) thrown down in defeat

1587 Pirate Thomas Cavendish attacks Punta Mita, looting pearls gathered from Mismaloya and the Marietas Islands

1664 Mismaloya serves as a shipyard for vessels bound for exploration and conquest of Baja California

1849 Yelapa fishermen are said to have found excellent fishing at the mouth of the Cuale River, making them the first unofficial settlers

1851 Puerto Vallarta founded, under the name Las Peñas de Santa María de Guadalupe, by the salt merchant Guadalupe Sánchez

1918 The small but growing seaside town becomes county seat and is renamed Puerto Vallarta in honor of former Jalisco State governor Ignacio Luis Vallarta (1871–75)

1922 Yellow fever kills some 150 people

1925 Flood and landslides during a great storm form narrow Cuale Island in the middle of the Cuale River in downtown PV

1931 Puerto Vallarta gets electricity (7–10 PM only)

1951 Reporters covering centennial celebrations—marked with a 21-gun naval salute and a wealthy wedding—capture the small-town charm, exposing this isolated coastal gem to their countrymen

1963 Hollywood film *The Night of the Iguana*, directed by John Huston and starring Richard Burton and Ava Gardner, puts PV on the world map, due to the much-publicized affair between Burton and Elizabeth Taylor (who was not in the movie) during the filming here

1970 Vallarta builds a new airport, and improves the electrical and highway systems for Richard Nixon's official visit with President Díaz Ordaz

2000 Census reports the city's population as 159,080

2005 Population rapidly increases to 220,368 in greater metropolitan area

2006 Ground is broken for the 385-slip luxury-yacht marina at La Cruz de Huanacaxtle, north of Bucerías, continuing the trend of converting quiet fishing villages into big-bucks vacation destinations

2007 The "Riviera Nayarit," referring to the real estate between San Blas and Nuevo Vallarta, is officially launched as a newly branded destination

2008   On May 31, Puerto Vallarta celebrates its 40th anniversary as a full-fledged city. Although Puerto Vallarta is largely unaffected, in 2008 gang-related violence escalates on both sides of the U.S.–Mexican border, with the fatality count reaching into the thousands by year's end

2009   In April, U.S. President Barack Obama and Mexican President Felipe Calderon meet to discuss ways to curb gang violence on both sides of the border. Late April also sees outbreaks of H1N1 influenza (swine flu), with Mexico City as the epicenter. Health clubs, nightclubs, stadiums, and many businesses in the Distrito Federal and elsewhere go dark for days, and several international air carriers temporarily suspend service in an effort to prevent the spread of the virus

2010   Anticipated at this writing, in December Mexico plays a role in finalizing a successor for the Kyoto Protocol by hosting the UN Framework Convention on Climate Change (UNFCCC) to create the next global agreement on climate change

BOOKS AND MOVIES

Books

Those interested in Mexican culture and society have a wealth of books from which to choose. *The Mexicans: A Personal Portrait of a People,* by Patrick Oster, is a brilliant nonfiction study of Mexican persona and personality. Like Patrick Oster, Alan Riding, author of *Distant Neighbors: A Portrait of the Mexicans,* was a journalist for many years in Mexico City whose insight, investigative journalism skills, and cogent writing skills produced an insightful look into the Mexican mind and culture.

Written by poet, essayist, and statesman Octavio Paz, *The Labyrinth of Solitude,* is classic, required reading for those who love Mexico or want to know it better. *The True Story of the Conquest of Mexico,* by Bernal Diaz de Castillo, is a fascinating account of the conquest by one of Cortés's own soldiers.

A collection of essays, *First Stop in the New World,* by David Lida, has contemporary Mexico City as its muse. *The Last Prince of the Mexican Empire,* by C.M. Mayo, explores the motivations and repercussions of Maximilian von Habsburg's disastrous reign as Emperor of Mexico in the mid-19th century. Barbara Kingsolver's *The Lacuna* is an epic set in the Yucatan Peninsula and Mexico City.

There are a few recommended books specifically about Puerto Vallarta. *La Magia de Puerto Vallarta,* by Marilú Suárez-Murias, is a bilingual (English and Spanish) coffee-table book discussing beaches, history, people, and places of Puerto Vallarta. The information is interesting, but the photographs are terribly grainy. For a lighthearted look at life in PV through the eyes of an expat, read *Puerto Vallarta on 49 Brain Cells a Day* and *Refried Brains,* both by Gil Gevins. Along these same lines is *Gringos in Paradise,* by Barry Golson, which evolved out of an assignment for *AARP* magazine and provides a lighthearted look at building the author's dream house in Sayulita, Nayarit. Those interested in Huichol art and culture might read *People of the Peyote: Huichol Indian History, Religion and Survival,* by Stacy Shaefer and Peter Furst. Also by Stacy Shaefer is *To Think With a Good Heart: Wixarica Women, Weavers and Shamans.*

Movies

The Night of the Iguana (1964), directed by John Huston, is the movie that alerted the world to Puerto Vallarta's existence. Set on the beach and bluffs of Mismaloya, the haunting movie features Richard Burton as a cast-out preacher-turned-tour-guide, Sue Lyons and Deborah Kerr as his clients, and Ava Gardner as the sexy but lonely proprietress of the group's idyllic Mexican getaway. There's no better mood-setter for a trip to Vallarta.

Like Water for Chocolate (Como Agua Para Chocolate) (1992) is a magic-realism glance into rural Mexico during the Mexican Revolution. This visual banquet will make your mouth water for the rose-petal quail and other recipes that the female lead, Tita, prepares. It's based on the novel of the same name by Laura Esquivel, which is equally wonderful. Academy Award winner *The Treasure of the Sierra Madre* (1948), with Humphrey Bogart, is a classic with great mountain scenery. For more fantastic scenery and a great town fiesta, see *The Magnificent Seven* (1960), starring Yul Brynner and Eli Wallach. Nominated for best foreign-language film in 2000, the dark *Amores Perros (Love's a Bitch)* is three intertwined stories portraying corruption and class distinction in urban Mexico. Set in Mexico City with Pierce Brosnan as a failing hit man, *The Matador* (2005) has some good scenes of the Camino Real in Mexico City, a great bullfighting sequence, and is a good drama. More recently, *Rudo y Cursi (Rude and Tacky)* (2008) is a melancholy comedy that follows small-town brothers who become national soccer heroes.

SPANISH VOCABULARY

	ENGLISH	SPANISH	PRONUNCIATION
BASICS			
	Yes/no	Sí/no	see/no
	Please	Por favor	pore fah-**vore**
	May I?	¿Me permite?	may pair-**mee**-tay
	Thank you (very much)	(Muchas) gracias	(**moo**-chas) **grah**-see-as
	You're welcome	De nada	day **nah**-dah
	Excuse me	Con permiso	con pair-**mee**-so
	Pardon me	¿Perdón?	pair-**dohn**
	Could you tell me?	¿Podría decirme?	po-dree-ah deh-**seer**-meh
	I'm sorry	Lo siento	lo see-**en**-toh
	Good morning!	¡Buenos días!	**bway**-nohs **dee**-ahs
	Good afternoon!	¡Buenas tardes!	**bway**-nahs **tar**-dess
	Good evening!	¡Buenas noches!	**bway**-nahs **no**-chess
	Good-bye!	¡Adiós!/¡Hasta luego!	ah-dee-**ohss/ah** -stah **lwe**-go
	Mr./Mrs.	Señor/Señora	sen-**yor**/sen-**yohr**-ah
	Miss	Señorita	sen-yo-**ree**-tah
	Pleased to meet you	Mucho gusto	**moo**-cho **goose**-toh
	How are you?	¿Cómo está usted?	**ko**-mo es-**tah** oo-**sted**
	Very well, thank you.	Muy bien, gracias.	**moo**-ee bee-**en**, **grah**-see-as
	And you?	¿Y usted?	ee oos-**ted**
	Hello (on the telephone)	Diga	**dee**-gah
NUMBERS			
	1	un, uno	oon, **oo**-no
	2	dos	dos
	3	tres	tress
	4	cuatro	**kwah**-tro
	5	cinco	**sink**-oh

ENGLISH	SPANISH	PRONUNCIATION
6	seis	saice
7	siete	see-**et**-eh
8	ocho	**o**-cho
9	nueve	new-**eh**-vey
10	diez	dee-**es**
11	once	**ohn**-seh
12	doce	**doh**-seh
13	trece	**treh**-seh
14	catorce	ka-**tohr**-seh
15	quince	**keen**-seh
16	dieciséis	dee-**es**-ee-**saice**
17	diecisiete	dee-**es**-ee-see-**et**-eh
18	dieciocho	dee-**es**-ee-**o**-cho
19	diecinueve	**dee-es**-ee-new-**ev**-eh
20	veinte	**vain**-teh
21	veinte y uno/ veintiuno	**vain**-te-**oo**-noh
30	treinta	**train**-tah
32	treinta y dos	train-tay-**dohs**
40	cuarenta	kwah-**ren**-tah
43	cuarenta y tres	kwah-**ren**-tay-**tress**
50	cincuenta	seen-**kwen**-tah
54	cincuenta y cuatro	seen-**kwen**-tay **kwah**-tro
60	sesenta	sess-**en**-tah
65	sesenta y cinco	sess-**en**-tay **seen**-ko
70	setenta	set-**en**-tah
76	setenta y seis	set-**en**-tay **saice**
80	ochenta	oh-**chen**-tah
87	ochenta y siete	oh-**chen**-tay see-**yet**-eh
90	noventa	no-**ven**-tah
98	noventa y ocho	no-**ven**-tah-**o**-choh

ENGLISH	SPANISH	PRONUNCIATION
100	cien	see-**en**
101	ciento uno	see-**en**-toh **oo**-noh
200	doscientos	doh-see-**en**-tohss
500	quinientos	keen-**yen**-tohss
700	setecientos	set-eh-see-**en**-tohss
900	novecientos	no-veh-see-**en**-tohss
1,000	mil	meel
2,000	dos mil	dohs meel
1,000,000	un millón	oon meel-**yohn**

COLORS

black	negro	**neh**-groh
blue	azul	ah-**sool**
brown	café	kah-**feh**
green	verde	**ver**-deh
pink	rosa	**ro**-sah
purple	morado	mo-**rah**-doh
orange	naranja	na-**rahn**-hah
red	rojo	**roh**-hoh
white	blanco	**blahn**-koh
yellow	amarillo	ah-mah-**ree**-yoh

DAYS OF THE WEEK

Sunday	domingo	doe-**meen**-goh
Monday	lunes	**loo**-ness
Tuesday	martes	**mahr**-tess
Wednesday	miércoles	me-**air**-koh-less
Thursday	jueves	hoo-**ev**-ess
Friday	viernes	vee-**air**-ness
Saturday	sábado	**sah**-bah-doh

	ENGLISH	SPANISH	PRONUNCIATION
MONTHS			
	January	enero	eh-**neh**-roh
	February	febrero	feh-**breh**-roh
	March	marzo	**mahr**-soh
	April	abril	ah-**breel**
	May	mayo	**my**-oh
	June	junio	**hoo**-nee-oh
	July	julio	**hoo**-lee-yoh
	August	agosto	ah-**ghost**-toh
	September	septiembre	sep-tee-**em**-breh
	October	octubre	oak-**too**-breh
	November	noviembre	no-vee-**em**-breh
	December	diciembre	dee-see-**em**-breh
USEFUL PHRASES			
	Do you speak English?	¿Habla usted inglés?	**ah**-blah oos-**ted** in-**glehs**
	I don't speak Spanish	No hablo español	no **ah**-bloh es-pahn-**yol**
	I don't understand (you)	No entiendo	no en-tee-**en**-doh
	I understand (you)	Entiendo	en-tee-**en**-doh
	I don't know	No sé	no seh
	I am American/ British	Soy americano (americana)/inglés(a)	soy ah-meh-ree-**kah**-no (ah-meh-ree-**kah**-nah)/in-**glehs(ah)**
	What's your name?	¿Cómo se llama usted?	koh-mo seh **yah**-mah oos-**ted**
	My name is . . .	Me llamo . . .	may **yah**-moh
	What time is it?	¿Qué hora es?	keh **o**-rah es
	It is one, two, three . . . o'clock.	Es la una/Son las dos, tres . . .	es la **oo**-nah/sohnahs dohs, tress
	Yes, please/No, thank you	Sí, por favor/No, gracias	**see** pohr fah-**vor**/no **grah**-see-us
	How?	¿Cómo?	**koh**-mo

ENGLISH	SPANISH	PRONUNCIATION
When?	¿Cuándo?	**kwahn**-doh
This/Next week	Esta semana/ la semana que entra	**es**-teh seh-**mah**-nah/ lah seh-**mah**-nah keh **en**-trah
This/Next month	Este mes/el próximo mes	**es**-teh mehs/el **proke**-see-mo mehs
This/Next year	Este año/el año que viene	**es**-teh **ahn**-yo/el **ahn**-yo keh vee-**yen**-ay
Yesterday/today/ tomorrow	Ayer/hoy/mañana	ah-**yehr**/oy/mahn-**yah**-nah
This morning/ afternoon	Esta mañana/ tarde	**es**-tah mahn-**yah**-nah/ **tar**-deh
Tonight	Esta noche	**es**-tah **no**-cheh
What?	¿Qué?	keh
What is it?	¿Qué es esto?	keh es **es**-toh
Why?	¿Por qué?	pore **keh**
Who?	¿Quién?	kee-**yen**
Where is . . . ?	¿Dónde está . . . ?	**dohn**-deh es-**tah**
the train station?	la estación del tren?	la es-tah-see-on del trehn
the subway station?	la estación del tren subterráneo?	la es-ta-see-**on** del trehn la es-ta-see-**on** soob-teh-**rrahn**-eh-oh
the bus stop?	la parada del autobus?	la pah-**rah**-dah del ow-toh-**boos**
the post office?	la oficina de correos?	la oh-fee-**see**-nah deh koh-**rreh**-os
the bank?	el banco?	el **bahn**-koh
the hotel?	el hotel?	el oh-**tel**
the store?	la tienda?	la tee-**en**-dah
the cashier?	la caja?	la **kah**-hah
the museum?	el museo?	el moo-**seh**-oh
the hospital?	el hospital?	el ohss-pee-**tal**
the elevator?	el ascensor?	el ah-**sen**-sohr
the bathroom?	el baño?	el **bahn**-yoh

ENGLISH	SPANISH	PRONUNCIATION
Here/there	Aquí/allá	ah-**key**/ah-**yah**
Open/closed	Abierto/cerrado	ah-bee-**er**-toh/ ser-**ah**-doh
Left/right	Izquierda/derecha	iss-key-**er**-dah/ dare-**eh**-chah
Straight ahead	Derecho	dare-**eh**-choh
Is it near/far?	¿Está cerca/lejos?	es-**tah** sehr-kah/ **leh**-hoss
I'd like . . .	Quisiera . . .	kee-see-ehr-ah
a room	un cuarto/una habitación	oon **kwahr**-toh/ **oo**-nah ah-bee- tah-see-**on**
the key	la llave	lah **yah**-veh
a newspaper	un periódico	oon pehr-ee-**oh**-dee-koh
a stamp	un sello de correo	oon **seh**-yo deh korr-ee-oh
I'd like to buy . . .	Quisiera comprar . . .	kee-see-**ehr**-ah kohm-**prahr**
cigarettes	cigarrillos	ce-ga-**ree**-yohs
matches	cerillos	ser-**ee**-ohs
a dictionary	un diccionario	oon deek-see-oh-**nah**-ree-oh
soap	jabón	hah-**bohn**
sunglasses	gafas de sol	**ga**-fahs deh sohl
suntan lotion	Loción bronceadora	loh-see-**ohn** brohn-seh-ah-**do**-rah
a map	un mapa	oon **mah**-pah
a magazine	una revista	**oon**-ah reh-**veess**-tah
paper	papel	pah-**pel**
envelopes	sobres	**so**-brehs
a postcard	una tarjeta postal	**oon**-ah tar-**het**-ah post-**ahl**
How much is it?	¿Cuánto cuesta?	**kwahn**-toh **kwes**-tah
It's expensive/ cheap	Está caro/barato	es-**tah kah**-roh/ bah-**rah**-toh

ENGLISH	SPANISH	PRONUNCIATION
A little/a lot	Un poquito/ mucho	oon poh-**kee**-toh/ **moo**-choh
More/less	Más/menos	mahss/**men**-ohss
Enough/too	Suficiente/	soo-fee-see-**en**-teh/
much/too little	demasiado/ muy poco	deh-mah-see-**ah**-doh/ **moo**-ee poh-koh
Telephone	Teléfono	tel-**ef**-oh-no
Telegram	Telegrama	teh-leh-**grah**-mah
I am ill	Estoy enfermo(a)	es-**toy** en-**fehr**-moh(mah)
Please call a doctor	Por favor llame a un medico	pohr fah-**vor ya**-meh ah oon **med**-ee-koh

ON THE ROAD

Avenue	Avenida	ah-ven-**ee**-dah
Broad, tree-lined boulevard	Bulevar	boo-leh-**var**
Fertile plain	Vega	**veh**-gah
Highway	Carretera	car-reh-**ter**-ah
Mountain pass	Puerto	poo-**ehr**-toh
Street	Calle	**cah**-yeh
Waterfront promenade	Rambla	**rahm**-blah
Wharf	Embarcadero	em-bar-cah-**deh**-ro

IN TOWN

Cathedral	Catedral	cah-teh-**dral**
Church	Templo/Iglesia	**tem**-plo/ee-**glehs**-see-ah
City hall	Casa de gobierno	kah-sah deh go-bee-**ehr**-no
Door, gate	Puerta portón	poo-**ehr**-tah por-**ton**
Entrance/exit	Entrada/salida	en-**trah**-dah/sah-**lee**-dah
Inn, rustic bar, or restaurant	Taverna	tah-**vehr**-nah
Main square	Plaza principal	plah-thah prin-see-**pahl**

ENGLISH	SPANISH	PRONUNCIATION

DINING OUT

Can you recommend a good restaurant?	¿Puede recomendarme un buen restaurante?	**pweh**-deh rreh-koh-mehn-**dahr**-me oon bwehn rrehs-tow-**rahn**-teh?
Where is it located?	¿Dónde está situado?	**dohn**-deh ehs-**tah** see-**twah**-doh?
Do I need reservations?	¿Se necesita una reservación?	seh neh-seh-**see**-tah oo-nah rreh-sehr- bah-**syohn**?
I'd like to reserve a table . . .	Quisiera reservar una mesa . . .	kee-**syeh**-rah rreh-sehr-**bahr** oo-nah **meh**-sah . . .
for two people.	para dos personas.	**pah**-rah dohs pehr-**soh**-nahs
for this evening.	para esta noche.	**pah**-rah **ehs**-tah **noh**-cheh
for 8 PM	para las ocho de la noche.	**pah**-rah lahs **oh**-choh deh lah **noh**-cheh
A bottle of . . .	Una botella de . . .	**oo**-nah bo-**teh**-yah deh
A cup of . . .	Una taza de . . .	**oo**-nah **tah**-thah deh
A glass of . . .	Un vaso de . . .	oon **vah**-so deh
Ashtray	Un cenicero	oon sen-ee-**seh**-roh
Bill/check	La cuenta	lah **kwen**-tah
Bread	El pan	el pahn
Breakfast	El desayuno	el deh-sah-**yoon**-oh
Butter	La mantequilla	lah man-teh-**key**-yah
Cheers!	¡Salud!	sah-**lood**
Cocktail	Un aperitivo	oon ah-pehr-ee-**tee**-voh
Dinner	La cena	lah **seh**-nah
Dish	Un plato	oon **plah**-toh
Menu of the day	Menú del día	meh-**noo** del **dee**-ah
Enjoy!	¡Buen provecho!	bwehn pro-**veh**-cho
Fixed-price menu	Menú fijo o turistico	meh-**noo fee**-hoh oh too-**ree**-stee-coh

ENGLISH	SPANISH	PRONUNCIATION
Fork	El tenedor	el ten-eh-**dor**
Is the tip included?	¿Está incluida la propina?	es-**tah** in-cloo-**ee**-dah lah pro-**pee**-nah
Knife	El cuchillo	el koo-**chee**-yo
Large portion of savory snacks	Raciónes	rah-see-**oh**-nehs
Lunch	La comida	lah koh-**mee**-dah
Menu	La carta, el menú	lah **cart**-ah, el meh-**noo**
Napkin	La servilleta	lah sehr-vee-**yet**-ah
Pepper	La pimienta	lah pee-me-**en**-tah
Please give me	Por favor déme	pore fah-**vor deh**-meh
Salt	La sal	lah sahl
Savory snacks	Tapas	**tah**-pahs
Spoon	Una cuchara	**oo**-nah koo-**chah**-rah
Sugar	El azúcar	el ah-**thu**-kar
Waiter!/Waitress!	¡Por favor Señor/ Señorita!	pohr fah-**vor** sen-**yor**/ sen-yor-**ee**-tah

Travel Smart
Puerto Vallarta

WORD OF MOUTH

"We were in many taxis and talked to many drivers. They complimented me on my willingness to try out my infant Spanish."

—jetsetj

GETTING HERE AND AROUND

■ BY AIR

Flights with stopovers in Mexico City tend to take the entire day. There are nonstop flights from a few U.S. cities, including Atlanta (Delta), Los Angeles (Alaska Air, American Airlines via Mexicana de Aviación), San Francisco (Alaska Air, United, Mexicana), Seattle (Alaska Air), Phoenix (US Airways), Houston (Continental), Dallas (American), Denver (Frontier Air, United), Chicago ORD (American Airlines), and Kansas City, Missouri (Frontier Air).

Air Canada has nonstop flights from Toronto and connecting flights (via Toronto) from all major cities. Web-based Volaris is a Tijuana-based airline with reasonable fares. It flies direct to Puerto Vallarta from Tijuana and between Guadalajara and San Francisco, Los Angeles, and Cancun. You can fly to Manzanillo, just south of the Costalegre, via many airlines with a stop in Mexico City.

If you plan to include Guadalajara in your itinerary, consider an open-jaw flight to Puerto Vallarta with a return from Guadalajara (or vice versa). There's almost no difference in price when you fly a Mexican airline like Aeroméxico, even when factoring in bus fare; sometimes the open jaw is even cheaper.

Flying times are about 2¾ hours from Houston, 3 hours from Los Angeles, 3½ hours from Denver, 4 hours from Chicago, and 8 hours from New York.

Airline and Airport Links Airline and Airport Links.com (⊕ *www.airlineandairportlinks.com*).

Airlines Aeroméxico (☎ *800/237–6639 in U.S. and Canada, 01800/021–4000 or 01800/021–4010 in Mexico, 322/221–1204 in PV* ⊕ *www.aeromexico.com*). **Air Canada** (☎ *888/247–2262 in U.S. and Canada, 322/221–1823 in PV* ⊕ *www.aircanada. com*). **Alaska Airlines** (☎ *800/252–7522 in Mexico, 322/221–2610 in PV* ⊕ *www.alaskaair.*

com). **American Airlines** (☎ *800/433–7300, 800/904–6000 in Mexico, 322/221–1799 in PV* ⊕ *www.aa.com*). **Continental Airlines** (☎ *800/523–3273 for U.S. and Mexico reservations, 01800/900–5000 in Mexico, 322/221–1025 in PV* ⊕ *www.continental.com*). **Delta Airlines** (☎ *800/221–1212* ⊕ *www.delta.com*). **Frontier** (☎ *800/432–1359 in U.S.* ⊕ *www.frontierairlines.com*). **Mexicana** (☎ *800/531–7921 in U.S., 866/281–3049 in Canada, 01800/801–2010 in Mexico, 322/224–6252 in PV* ⊕ *www.mexicana.com*). **US Airways** (☎ *800/428–4322 in U.S., 322/221–1333 in PV* ⊕ *www.usairways.com*). **Volaris** (☎ *55/1102–8000 in Mexico City, 01800/122–8000 in Mexico* ⊕ *www.volaris.com.mx*).

Airline Security Issues Transportation Security Administration (⊕ *www.tsa.gov*).

AIRPORTS

The main gateway, and where many PV-bound travelers change planes, is Mexico City's large, modern Aeropuerto Internacional Benito Juárez (airport code: MEX), infamous for pickpocketing and taxi scams; watch your stuff.

Puerto Vallarta's small international Aeropuerto Internacional Gustavo Díaz Ordáz (PVR) is 7½ km (4½ mi) north of downtown.

Airport Information Aeropuerto Internacional Benito Juárez (*MEX* ☎ *55/2482–2424 or 55/2482–2400* ⊕ *www.aicm.com.mx*). **Aeropuerto Internacional Gustavo Díaz Ordáz** (*PVR* ☎ *322/221–1298* ⊕ *vallarta. aeropuertosgap.com.mx*).

GROUND TRANSPORTATION

Vans provide transportation from the airport to PV hotels; there's a zone system with different prices for the Zona Hotelera (Hotel Zone), downtown PV, and so on. Outside the luggage collection area, vendors shout for your attention. It's a confusing scene. Purchase the taxi vouchers sold at the stands inside the terminal, and be sure to avoid the time-share

vendors who trap you in their vans for a high-pressure sales pitch en route to your hotel. Avoid drivers who approach you, and head for an official taxi kiosk, which will have zone information clearly posted. As in any busy airport, don't leave your luggage unattended for any reason.

Before you purchase your ticket, look for a taxi-zone map (it should be posted on or by the ticket stand), and make sure your taxi ticket is properly zoned; if you need a ticket only to Zone 3, don't pay for a ticket to Zone 4 or 5. Taxis or vans to the Costalegre resorts between PV and Manzanillo are generally arranged through the resort. If not, taxis charge about 200 to 250 pesos an hour—more if you're traveling beyond Jalisco State lines.

▌ BY BUS

LONG-DISTANCE SERVICE

PV's Central Camionero, or Central Bus Station, is 1 km (½ mi) north of the airport, halfway between Nuevo Vallarta and downtown.

First-class Mexican buses (known as *primera clase*) are generally timely and comfortable, air-conditioned coaches with bathrooms, movies, and reclining seats—sometimes with seat belts. Deluxe (*de lujo* or *ejecutivo*) buses offer the same—sometimes with fewer, roomier seats—and usually have refreshments. Second-class (*segunda clase*) buses are used mainly for travel to smaller, secondary destinations.

A lower-class bus ride can be interesting if you're not in a hurry and want to experience local culture; these buses make frequent stops and keep less strictly to their timetables. Often they will wait until they fill up to leave, regardless of the scheduled time of departure. Fares are up to 15%–30% cheaper than those for first-class buses. The days of pigs and chickens among your bus mates are largely in the past. ▌TIP➔ Unless you're writing a novel or your memoir, there's no reason to ride a second-class bus if a first-class or better is available. Daytime trips are safer.

Bring snacks, socks, and a sweater—the air-conditioning on first-class buses is often set on high—and toilet paper, as restrooms might not have any. Smoking is prohibited on all buses.

Estrella Blanca goes from Mexico City to Manzanillo, Mazatlán, Monterrey, Nuevo Laredo, and other central, Pacific coast, and northern-border points. ETN has the most luxurious service—with exclusively first-class buses that have roomy, totally reclining seats—to Guadalajara, Mexico City, Barra de Navidad, Chamela, and Manzanillo. Primera Plus connects Mexico City with Manzanillo and Puerto Vallarta along with other central and western cities.

TAP serves Mexico City, Guadalajara, Puerto Vallarta, Tepic, and Mazatlán. Basic service, including some buses with marginal or no air-conditioning, is the norm on Transportes Cihuatlán, which connects the Bahía de Banderas and PV with southern Jalisco towns such as Barra de Navidad.

You can buy tickets for first-class or better in advance; this is advisable during peak periods, although the most popular routes have buses on the hour. You can make reservations for many, though not all, of the first-class bus lines, through the Ticketbus central reservations agency. Rates average 35–76 pesos per hour of travel, depending on the level of luxury. Plan to pay in pesos, although most of the deluxe bus services accept Visa and MasterCard.

Bus Contacts Central Camionero (✉ *Puerto Vallarta–Tepic Hwy., Km 9, Las Mojoneras* ☎ *322/290–1009).* **Estrella Blanca** (☎ *01800/507–5500 toll-free in Mexico, 322/290–1001 in Puerto Vallarta* ⊕ *www. estrellablanca.com.mx).* **ETN** (☎ *01800/800–0386 toll-free in Mexico, 322/290–0997 in PV* ⊕ *www.etn.com.mx).* **Primera Plus** (☎ *322/290–0715 in PV).* **Transportes Cihuatlán** (☎ *322/290–0994 in PV).* **Transporte del Pacifico (TAP)** (☎ *322/290–0119 in PV).*

CITY BUSES

City buses (5.5 pesos) serve downtown, the Zona Hotelera Norte, and Marina Vallarta. Bus stops—marked by blue-and-white signs—are every two or three long blocks along the highway (Carretera al Aeropuerto) and in downtown Puerto Vallarta. Green buses to Playa Mismaloya and Boca de Tomatlán (6 pesos) run about every 15 minutes from the corner of Avenida Insurgentes and Basilio Badillo downtown.

Gray ATM buses serving Nuevo Vallarta and Bucerías (20 pesos), Punta Mita (30 pesos), and Sayulita (50 pesos) depart from Plaza las Glorias, in front of the HSBC bank, and Wal-Mart, both of which are along Carretera Aeropuerto between downtown and the Zona Hotelera.

■TIP➜ It's rare for inspectors to check tickets, but just when you've let yours flutter to the floor, a figure of authority is bound to appear. So hang on to your ticket and hat: PV bus drivers race from one stoplight to the next in jerky bursts of speed.

There's no problem with theft on city buses aside from perhaps an occasional pickpocket that might be at work anywhere in the world.

▌BY CAR

From December through April—peak season—traffic clogs the narrow downtown streets, and negotiating the steep hills in Old Vallarta (sometimes you have to drive in reverse to let another car pass) can be unnerving. Avoid rush hour (7–9 AM and 6–8 PM) and when schools let out (2–3 PM). Travel with a companion and a good road map or atlas. Always lock your car, and never leave valuable items visible in the body of the car. The trunk is generally safe, although any thief can crack one open if he chooses.

■TIP➜ It's absolutely essential that you carry Mexican auto insurance for liability, even if you have full coverage for collision, damages, and theft. If you injure anyone in an accident, you could well be jailed until culpability is established—whether it was your fault or not—unless you have insurance.

GASOLINE

Pemex (the government petroleum monopoly) franchises all of Mexico's gas stations, which you can find at most junctions and in cities and towns. Gas is measured in liters. Stations in and around the larger towns may accept U.S. or Canadian credit cards (or dollars).

Premium unleaded gas (called *premium,* the red pump) and regular unleaded gas (*magna,* the green pump) are available nationwide, but it's still best to fill up whenever you can and not let your tank get below half full. Fuel quality is generally lower than that in the United States, but it has improved enough so that your car will run acceptably. At this writing gas was about 7.8 pesos per liter (about $2.26 per gallon) for the cheap stuff and 10 pesos per liter ($2.91 per gallon) for super. Some people bring fuel additive and add every third tank or so.

Attendants pump the gas for you and may also wash your windshield and check your oil and tire air pressure. A small tip is customary (from just a few pesos for pumping the gas only to 5 or 10 for the whole enchilada of services). Keep an eye on the gas meter to make sure the attendant is starting it at "0" and that you're charged the correct price.

PARKING

A circle with a diagonal line superimposed on the letter *E* (for *estacionamiento*) means "no parking." Illegally parked cars may have the license plate removed, requiring a trip to the traffic-police headquarters for payment of a fine. When in doubt, park in a lot rather than on the street; your car will probably be safer there anyway. There are parking lots in PV at Parque Hidalgo (✉ *Av. México at Venezuela, Col. 5 de Diciembre*), just north of the Cuale River at the malecón between Calle A. Rodríguez and Calle Encino, and in the Zona Romántica at Parque Lázaro Cárdenas. Fees vary depending on time of day, ranging from

12 pesos (just under US$1) per hour to 20 pesos (about US$1.50) per hour.

ROAD CONDITIONS

Several well-kept toll roads head into and out of major cities like Guadalajara—most of them four lanes wide. However, these *carreteras* (major highways) don't go too far into the countryside, and even the toll-roads have *topes* (speed bumps) and toll booths to slow you down. *Cuota* means toll road; *libre* means no toll, and such roads are often two lanes and not as well-maintained. A new 33½-km (21-mi) highway between Tepic and San Blas will shorten driving time to about 20 minutes.

Roads leading to, or in, Nayarit and Jalisco include highways connecting Nogales and Mazatlán; Guadalajara and Tepic; and Mexico City, Morelia, and Guadalajara. Tolls between Guadalajara to Puerto Vallarta (207 mi [334 km]) total about $25.

In rural areas roads are sometimes poor; other times the two-lane, blacktop roads are perfectly fine. Be extra cautious during the rainy season, when rock slides and potholes are a problem.

Watch out for animals, especially untethered horses, cattle, and dogs, and for dangerous, unrailed curves. *Topes* (speed bumps) are ubiquitous; slow down when approaching any town or village and look for signs saying TOPES or VIBRADORES. Police officers often issue tickets to those speeding through populated areas.

Generally, driving times are longer than for comparable distances in the United States and Canada. Allow extra time for unforeseen occurrences as well as for traffic, particularly truck traffic.

ROADSIDE EMERGENCIES

To help motorists on major highways, the Mexican Tourism Ministry operates a fleet of more than 250 pickup trucks, known as the Angeles Verdes, or Green Angels, reachable by phone throughout Mexico by dialing 078 or, in some areas near Puerto Vallarta, 066. In either case, ask the person who answers to transfer the call to the Green Angels hotline. The bilingual drivers provide mechanical help, first aid, radio-telephone communication, basic supplies and small parts, towing, tourist information, and protection.

Services are free, and spare parts, fuel, and lubricants are provided at cost. Tips are always appreciated (around $5–$10 for big jobs and $3–$5 for minor stuff; a souvenir from your country can sometimes be a well-received alternative). The Green Angels patrol the major highways twice daily 8–8 (usually later on holiday weekends). If you break down, pull off the road as far as possible, and lift the hood of your car. If you don't have a cell phone, hail a passing vehicle and ask the driver to notify the patrol. Most drivers will be quite helpful.

Emergency Services Angeles Verdes (☎ *078*).

RULES OF THE ROAD

When you sign up for Mexican car insurance, you may receive a booklet on Mexican rules of the road. It really is a good idea to read it to familiarize yourself with not only laws but also customs that differ from those of your home country. For instance: if an oncoming vehicle flicks its lights at you in daytime, slow down: it could mean trouble ahead; when approaching a narrow bridge, the first vehicle to flash its lights has right of way; right on red is not allowed; one-way traffic is indicated by an arrow; two-way, by a double-pointed arrow. (Other road signs follow the widespread system of international symbols.)

⚠ On the highway, using your left turn signal to turn left is dangerous. Mexican drivers—especially truck drivers—use their left turn signal on the highway to signal the vehicle behind that it's safe to pass. Conversely they rarely use their signal to actually make a turn. Foreigners signaling a left turn off the highway into a driveway or onto a side road have been killed by cars or trucks behind that mistook their turn signal for a signal to pass. To turn left

from a highway when cars are behind you, it's best to pull over to the right and make the left turn when no cars are approaching, to avoid disaster.

Mileage and speed limits are given in kilometers: 110 KPH and 80 KPH (66 MPH and 50 MPH, respectively) are the most common maximums on the highway. However, speed limits can change from curve to curve, so watch the signs carefully. In cities and small towns, observe the posted speed limits, which can be as low as 20 KPH (12 MPH).

Seat belts are required by law throughout Mexico. Drunk driving laws are fairly harsh in Mexico, and if you're caught you may go to jail immediately. It's difficult to say what the blood-alcohol limit is since everyone we asked gave a different answer, which means each case is probably handled in a discretionary manner. The best way to avoid any problems is simply to not drink and drive.

If you're stopped for speeding, the officer is supposed to take your license and hold it until you pay the fine at the local police station. But the officer will usually prefer a *mordida* (small bribe). Just take out a couple hundred pesos, hold it out discreetly while asking politely if the officer can "pay the fine for you." Conversely, a few cops might resent the offer of a bribe, but it's still common practice.

If you decide to dispute a charge that seems preposterous, do so courteously and with a smile, and tell the officer that you would like to talk to the police captain when you get to the station. The officer usually will let you go rather than go to the station.

SAFETY ON THE ROAD
Never drive at night in remote and rural areas. *Bandidos* are one concern, but so are potholes, free-roaming animals, cars with no working lights, road-hogging trucks, drunk drivers, and difficulty in getting assistance. It's best to use toll roads whenever possible; although costly, they're safer, too.

Off the highway, driving in Mexico can be nerve-wracking for novices, with people sometimes paying little attention to marked lanes. Most drivers pay attention to safety rules, but be vigilant. Drunk driving skyrockets on holiday weekends.

A police officer may pull you over for something you didn't do; unfortunately a common scam. If you're pulled over for any reason, be polite—displays of anger will only make matters worse. Although efforts are being made to fight corruption, it's still a fact of life in Mexico, and for many people, it's worth the $10 to $100 it costs to get their license back to be on their way quickly. (The amount requested varies depending on what the officer assumes you can pay—the year, make, and model of the car you drive being one determining factor.) Others persevere long enough to be let off with a warning only. The key to success, in this case, is a combination of calm and patience.

RENTAL CARS
Mexico manufactures Chrysler, Ford, General Motors, Honda, Nissan, and Volkswagen vehicles. With the exception of Volkswagen, you can get the same kind of midsize and luxury cars in Mexico that you can rent in the United States and Canada. Economy usually refers to a Volkswagen Beetle or a Chevy Aveo or Joy, which may or may not come with air-conditioning or automatic transmission.

It can really pay to shop around: in Puerto Vallarta, rates for a compact car with air-conditioning, manual transmission, and unlimited mileage range from $18 a day and $120 a week to $50 a day and $300–$400 a week, excluding insurance. Full-coverage insurance varies greatly depending on the deductible, but averages $25–$40 a day. As a rule, stick with the major companies because they tend to be more reliable.

You can also hire a taxi with a driver (who generally doubles as a tour guide) through your hotel. The going rate is about $22 an hour without crossing state

lines. Limousine service runs about $65 an hour and up, with a three- to five-hour minimum.

In Mexico the minimum driving age is 18, but most rental-car agencies have a surcharge for drivers under 25. Your own country's driver's license is perfectly acceptable.

Surcharges for additional drivers are around $5 per day plus tax. Children's car seats run about the same, but not all companies have them.

CAR-RENTAL INSURANCE

You must carry Mexican auto insurance, at the very least liability as well coverage against physical damage to the vehicle and theft at your discretion, depending on what, if anything, your own auto insurance (or credit card, if you use it to rent a car) includes. For rental cars, all insurance will all be dealt with through the rental company.

Major Rental Agencies Alamo (☎ 800/522–9696 ⊕ www.alamo.com). **Avis** (☎ 800/331–1084 ⊕ www.avis.com). **Budget** (☎ 800/472–3325 ⊕ www.budget. com). **Hertz** (☎ 800/654–3001 ⊕ www.hertz. com). **National Car Rental** (☎ 800/227–7368 ⊕ www.nationalcar.com).

▮ BY TAXI

PV taxis aren't metered and instead charge by zones. Most of the larger hotels have rate sheets, and taxi drivers should produce them upon request. Tipping isn't necessary unless the driver helps you with your bags, in which case a few pesos are appropriate.

The minimum fare is 40 pesos (about $3), but if you don't ask, you'll probably be overcharged. Negotiate a price in advance for out-of-town and hourly services as well; many drivers will start by asking how much you want to pay or how much others have charged you to get a sense of your street-smarts. The usual hourly rate at this writing was 250 pesos per hour. In all cases, if you are unsure of what a fare should be, ask your hotel's front-desk personnel.

The ride from downtown to the airport or to Marina Vallarta costs about $8, $17 to Nuevo Vallarta, and $22 to Bucerías. From downtown south to Mismaloya it's about $4 to Conchas Chinas, $8 to $10 to the hotels of the Zona Hotelera, $10 to Mismaloya, and $14 to Boca de Tomatlán. You can easily hail a cab on the street. Radio Taxi PV and others provide 24-hour service.

Taxi Company Radio Taxi PV (⊠ Vallarta ☎ 322/225–0716). **Taxi Jet** (⊠ Vallarta ☎ 322/299–2608) **Sitio Valle Dorado** (⊠ Nuevo Vallarta ☎ 322/297–5407). **Sitio Bucerías** (⊠ Bucerías ☎ 329/298–0714).

ESSENTIALS

■ COMMUNICATIONS

INTERNET

Internet cafés have sprung up all over Puerto Vallarta and even small surrounding towns and villages, making e-mail by far the easiest way to get in touch with people back home. At PV Café you can enjoy a sandwich or a salad and coffee while downloading digital photos, scanning documents, or surfing the Web (30 pesos per hour). It's open daily from 8 AM to 11 PM. Get a discount when you purchase blocks of Internet time.

If you're bringing a laptop with you, check with the manufacturer's technical support line to see what service and/or repair affiliates it has in the areas you plan to visit. Carry a spare battery to save yourself the expense and headache of having to hunt down a replacement on the spot. Memory sticks and other accessories are usually more expensive in Mexico than in the United States or Europe, but are available in megastores such as Sam's Club and Office Depot as well as mom-and-pop computer shops.

The younger generation of Mexicans is computer savvy and there are some excellent repair wizards and technicians to help you with problems; many are bilingual.

Contacts Cybercafes (⊕ *www.cybercafes. com*) lists more than 4,000 Internet cafés worldwide. **PV Café** (✉ *Calle Olas Altas 246, Olas Altas* ☎ *322/222–0092*).

PHONES

The area code for PV (and the northern Costalegre) and Nuevo Vallarta is 322; San Francisco's is 311; between Bucerías and Sayulita, 329; Lo De Marcos and Rincón de Guayabitos, 327; San Blas, 323. The Costalegre from around Rancho Cuixmala to San Patricio–Melaque and Barra de Navidad has a 315 area code.

The country code for Mexico is 52. When calling a Mexico number from abroad, dial any necessary international access code, then the country code, and then all of the numbers listed for the entry. When calling a cell phone in Mexico from outside the country, dial 01152 (access and country codes) and then 1 and then the number.

Toll-free numbers in Mexico start with an 800 prefix. These numbers, however, are billed as local calls if you call one from a private phone. To reach them, you need to dial 01 before the number. In this guide, Mexico-only toll-free numbers appear as follows: 01800/123–4567. The toll-free numbers listed simply 800/123–4567 are U.S. or Canadian numbers and generally work north of the border only (though some calling cards will allow you to dial them from Mexico, charging you minutes as for a toll call). Numbers listed as 001800/123–4567 are toll-free U.S. numbers; if you're calling from Mexico, you'll be charged for an international call.

INTERNATIONAL CALLS

To make an international call, dial 00 before the country code, area code, and number. The country code for the United States and Canada is 1. Avoid phones near tourist areas that advertise in English (e.g., "Call the U.S. or Canada here!"). They charge an outrageous fee per minute. If in doubt, dial the operator and ask for rates.

CALLS WITHIN MEXICO

Directory assistance is 040 nationwide. For assistance in English, dial 090 for an international operator; tell the operator in what city, state, and country you require directory assistance, and he or she will connect you. There's no charge for the former; the latter can be dialed only from a home phone, as the charge appears on the monthly phone bill.

Much less often seen today, a *caseta de larga distancia* is a long-distance/overseas telephone service usually operated out of a store such as a *papelería* (stationery

store), pharmacy, restaurant, or other small business; look for the phone symbol on the door. Casetas may cost slightly more to use than pay phones, but you tend to be shielded from street noise, as you get your own little booth. They also have the benefit of not forcing you to buy a prepaid phone card with a specific denomination—you pay in cash according to the calls you make. Tell the person on duty the number you'd like to call, and she or he will give you a rate and dial for you. Rates seem to vary widely, so shop around. Overall, they're higher than those of pay phones and, with the extensive cell phone and Internet services now available, fewer and farther between.

PHONE CARDS

Using a prepaid phone card is a relatively inexpensive and convenient way to call long distance within Mexico or abroad. Look for a phone *booth* away from traffic noise; these phones are tucked behind three sides of Plexiglas, but street noise can make hearing difficult. If you're calling long distance within Mexico, dial 01 before the area code and number. For local calls, just dial the seven-digit number; no other prefix is necessary. If calling abroad, buy the 100-peso card, the largest denomination available.

PAY PHONES

Most pay phones only accept prepaid cards, called Ladatel or TELMEX cards, sold in 30-, 50-, and 100-peso denominations at newsstands, pharmacies, and grocery stores. These Ladatel phones are all over the place—on street corners, in bus stations, and so on.

Older, coin-only pay phones are rarely encountered; those you do find are often broken or have poor connections. Still other phones have two unmarked slots, one for a Ladatel (a Spanish acronym for "long-distance direct dialing") card and the other for a credit card. These are primarily for Mexican bank cards, but some accept Visa or MasterCard, though *not* U.S. phone credit cards.

To use a Ladatel card, simply insert it in the appropriate slot with the computer chip insignia forward and right-side up, and dial. Credit is deleted from the card as you use it, and your balance is displayed on a small screen on the phone. You'll be charged about 3 pesos per minute for local calls, 4 pesos per minute for national long-distance, and 5 pesos for calls to the United States or Canada. Most pay phones display a price list and dialing instructions.

MOBILE PHONES

If you have a multiband phone (some countries use different frequencies from those used in the United States) and your service provider uses the world-standard GSM network (as do T-Mobile, Cingular, and Verizon), you can probably use your phone abroad. Roaming fees can be steep, however: 99¢ a minute is standard. And you normally pay the toll charges for incoming and outgoing calls. It's almost always cheaper to send a text message (or at least to receive one, which is sometimes substantially cheaper than to send).

If you just want to make local calls, consider buying a new SIM card (note that your provider may have to unlock your phone for you to use a different SIM card) and a prepaid service plan in the destination. You'll then have a local number and can make local calls at local rates. If your trip is extensive, you could also simply buy a new cell phone in your destination, as they go for around $30 and sometimes come with a couple hundred prepaid minutes to start you off. The two cell phone carriers in Mexico are MovieStar and TELMEX; minutes can be purchased at their offices or more conveniently at OXXO convenience stores, Guadalajara pharmacies, or other locations.

■ **TIP→** If you travel internationally frequently, save one of your old mobile phones or buy a cheap one on the Internet; ask your cell phone company to unlock it for you, and take it with you as a travel phone, buying a new SIM card with pay-as-you-go service in each destination.

There are now companies that rent cell phones (with or without SIM cards) for the duration of your trip. You get the phone, charger, and carrying case in the mail and return them in the mailer. Daystar rents cell phones at $6 per day, with incoming calls from the United States at 22¢ a minute; it costs 30¢ a minute for domestic calls or $1.19 per minute to call the United States.

Contacts **Daystar** (☎ 888/908–4100 ⊕ www.daystarwireless.com).

■ CUSTOMS AND DUTIES

Upon entering Mexico, you'll be given a baggage declaration form and asked to itemize what you're bringing into the country. You are allowed to bring in 3 liters of spirits or wine for personal use; 400 cigarettes, 25 cigars, or 200 grams of tobacco; a reasonable amount of perfume for personal use; one video camera and one regular camera and 12 rolls of film for each; and gift items not to exceed a total of $300. If driving across the U.S. border, gift items shouldn't exceed $75, although foreigners aren't usually hassled about this. ⚠ **Although the much-publicized border violence doesn't affect travelers, it is real. To be safe don't linger long at the border.**

You aren't allowed to bring firearms, ammunition, meat, vegetables, plants, fruit, or flowers into the country. You can bring in one of each of the following items without paying taxes: a cell phone, a camera, a video cassette player, a CD player, a musical instrument, a laptop computer, and a portable copier or printer. Compact discs and/or audio cassettes are limited to 20 total and DVDs to 5.

Mexico also allows you to bring a cat or dog, if you have two things: (1) a pet health certificate signed by a registered veterinarian in the United States and issued not more than 72 hours before the animal enters Mexico; and (2) a pet vaccination certificate showing that the animal has been treated (as applicable)

for rabies, hepatitis, distemper, and leptospirosis.

For more information or information on bringing other animals, contact the Mexican consulate, which has branches in many major American cities as well as border towns. To find the consulate nearest you, check the Ministry of Foreign Affairs Web site (go to the "Servicios Consulares" option).

Information in Mexico **Mexican Embassy** (☎ 202/728–1600 ⊕ www.embassyofmexico. org). **Ministry of Foreign Affairs** (⊕ portal.sre. gob.mx/eua).

U.S. Information **U.S. Customs and Border Protection** (⊕ www.cbp.gov).

■ ELECTRICITY

For U.S. and Canadian travelers, electrical converters aren't necessary because Mexico operates on the 60-cycle, 120-volt system; however, many Mexican outlets have not been updated to accommodate three-prong and polarized plugs (those with one larger prong), so to be safe bring an adapter.

Blackouts and brownouts—often lasting an hour or so—are not unheard of, particularly during the rainy season, so bring a surge protector.

Consider making a small investment in a universal adapter, which has several types of plugs in one lightweight, compact unit.

■ EMERGENCIES

If you get into a scrape with the law, you can call your nearest consulate; U.S. citizens can also call the Overseas Citizens Services Center in the United States.

Consulate and Embassy **United States Consul** (✉ *Paseo de Cocoteros 85 Sur, 2nd fl., Centro Comercial Paradise Plaza, Nuevo Vallarta, Puerto Vallarta* ☎ 322/222–0069). **U.S. Embassy** (✉ *Paseo de la Reforma 305, Col. Cuauhtémoc, Mexico City* ☎ 55/5080–2000 ⊕ *mexico.usembassy.gov*).

LOCAL DO'S AND TABOOS

CUSTOMS OF THE COUNTRY

In the United States and elsewhere in the world, being direct, efficient, and succinct is highly valued. But Mexican communication tends to be more subtle, and the direct style of Americans, Canadians, and Europeans is often perceived as curt and aggressive. Mexicans are extremely polite, so losing your temper over delays or complaining loudly will get you branded as rude and make people less inclined to help you. Remember that things move slowly here and that there's little stigma attached to being late. You'll probably notice that local friends, relatives, and significant others show a fair amount of physical affection with each other, but you should be more retiring with people you don't know well.

GREETINGS

Learning basic phrases in Spanish such as *"por favor"* (please) and *"gracias"* (thank you) will make a big difference in how people respond to you. Also, being deferential to those who are older than you will earn you lots of points, as does addressing people as señor, señora, or señorita.

Also, saying *"Desculpe"* before asking a question of someone is a polite way of saying "Excuse me" before launching into a request for information or directions. Similarly, asking *"¿Habla inglés?"* is more polite than assuming every Mexican you meet speaks English.

SIGHTSEEING

In Puerto Vallarta, it is acceptable to wear shorts in houses of worship, but do avoid being blatantly immodest. Bathing suits and immodest clothing are also inappropriate for shopping and sightseeing in general. Mexican men don't generally wear shorts, even in extremely hot weather, although this rule is generally ignored by both Mexican and foreign men on vacation here and at other beach resorts.

OUT ON THE TOWN

Mexicans call waiters *"joven"* (literally, "young man") no matter how old they are (it's the equivalent of the word "maid" being used for the old woman who cleans rooms). Call a female waitress *señorita* ("miss") or *señora* ("ma'am"). Ask for *"la cuenta, por favor"* ("the check, please") when you want the bill; it's considered rude to bring it before the customer asks for it. Mexicans tend to dress nicely for a night out, but in tourist areas, dress codes are mainly upheld only at the more sophisticated discotheques. Smoking in bars and restaurants is now theoretically illegal, but in some smaller establishments and those with outdoor patios, people still smoke with abandon.

DOING BUSINESS

Personal relationships always come first here, so developing rapport and trust is essential. A handshake and personal greeting are appropriate along with a friendly inquiry about family, especially if you have met the family. In established business relationships, don't be surprised if you're greeted with a kiss on the cheek or a hug. Always be respectful toward colleagues in public and keep confrontations private.

Meetings may or may not start on time, but you should be patient. When you are invited to dinner at the home of a client or associate, it's not necessary to bring a gift; however, sending a thank-you note afterward scores points.

Your offers to pick up the tab at business lunches or dinners will be greatly appreciated but will probably be declined; because you are a guest in their country, most Mexicans will want to treat you to the meal. Be prepared to exchange business cards, and feel free to offer yours first. Professional attire tends to be on the conservative side. Mexicans are extremely well groomed, so you'll do well if you follow suit.

▌HEALTH

FOOD AND DRINK

Despite concerns raised by the H1N1
influenza outbreak of 2009, in Mexico
the biggest health risk is *turista* (traveler's
diarrhea), caused by consuming contami-
nated fruit, vegetables, or water. To minimize risks, avoid questionable-looking
street stands and bad-smelling food even
in the toniest establishments; and if you're
not sure of a restaurant's standards, pass
up ceviche (raw fish cured in lemon juice)
and raw vegetables that haven't been
peeled (or that *can't* be peeled, like lettuce and tomatoes).

Drink only bottled water or water that has
been boiled for at least 20 minutes, even
when you're brushing your teeth. *Agua
mineral* or *agua con gas* means mineral
or carbonated water, and *agua purificada*
means purified water. Hotels with water-
purification systems will post signs to that
effect in the rooms; even then, it's best not
to drink the stuff.

Despite these warnings, keep in mind
that Puerto Vallarta, Nuevo Vallarta, and
the Costalegre have virtually no industry beyond tourism and are unlikely to
kill (or seriously distress) the geese that
lay their golden egg. Some people choose
to bend the rules about eating at street
stands and fresh fruits and chopped lettuce or cabbage, as there's no guarantee
that you won't get sick at a five-star resort
and have a delicious, healthful meal at a
shack by the sea. If fish or seafood smells
or tastes bad, send it back and ask for
something different.

Don't fret about ice: Tourist-oriented
hotels and restaurants, and even most of
those geared toward the locals, use purified water for ice, drinks, and washing
vegetables. Many alleged cases of food

poisoning are due instead to hangovers
or excessive drinking in the strong sun.
But whenever you're in doubt, ask questions about the origins of food and water
and, if you feel unsure, err on the side
of safety.

Mild cases of turista may respond to Imo-
dium (known generically as loperamide),
Lomotil, or Pepto-Bismol (not as strong),
all of which you can buy over the counter;
keep in mind, though, that these drugs can
complicate more serious illnesses. You'll
need to replace fluids, so drink plenty of
purified water or tea; chamomile tea (*te de
manzanilla*) is a good folk remedy, and it's
readily available in restaurants throughout Mexico.

In severe cases, rehydrate yourself with
Gatorade or a salt-sugar solution (½ tea-
spoon salt and 4 tablespoons sugar per
quart of water). If your fever and diarrhea last longer than a day or two, see a
doctor—you may have picked up a para-
site or disease that requires prescription
medication.

PESTS

Mosquitoes are most prevalent during the
rainy season, when it's best to use mosquito repellent daily, even in the city; if
you're in jungly or wet places and lack
strong repellent, consider covering up well
or going indoors at dusk (called the "mosquito hour" by locals).

An excellent brand of *repelente de insec-
tos* (insect repellent) called Autan is readily available; do not use it on children
under age 2. Repellents that are not at
least 10% DEET or picaridin are not
effective here. If you're hiking in the jungle or boggy areas, wear repellent and
long pants and sleeves; if you're camping in the jungle, use a mosquito net and
invest in a package of *espirales contra
mosquitos,* mosquito coils, which are
sold in *farmacias,* or *tlalpalerías* (hardware stores).

OTHER ISSUES

According to the CDC, there's a limited risk of malaria and other insect-carried or parasite-caused illnesses in certain areas of Mexico (largely but not exclusively rural and tropical coastal areas). In most urban or easily accessible areas you need not worry about malaria, but dengue fever is found with increasing frequency. If you're traveling to remote areas or simply prefer to err on the side of caution, check with the CDC's International Travelers' Hotline. Malaria and dengue are both carried by mosquitoes; in areas where these illnesses are prevalent, use insect-repellant coiling, clothing, and sprays/lotion. Also consider taking antimalarial pills if you're doing serious adventure activities in tropical and subtropical areas.

Make sure polio and diphtheria–tetanus shots are up-to-date well before your trip. Hepatitis A and typhoid are transmitted through unclean food or water. Gamma-globulin shots prevent hepatitis; an inoculation is available for typhoid, although it's not 100% effective.

Caution is advised when venturing out in the Mexican sun. Sunbathers lulled by a slightly overcast sky or the sea breezes can be burned badly in just 20 minutes. To avoid overexposure, use strong sunscreens, sit under a shade umbrella, and avoid the peak sun hours of noon to 3 PM. Sunscreen, including many American brands, can be found in pharmacies, supermarkets, and resort gift shops.

Health Information National Centers for Disease Control & Prevention (*CDC* ☎ *800/CDC-INFO or 877/394-8747 [international travelers' health line]* ⊕ *www.cdc.gov/travel*). **World Health Organization** (*WHO* ⊕ *www.who.int*).

MEDICAL CARE

Cornerstone Hospital accepts various types of foreign health insurance and traveler's insurance and is American owned. The other recommended, privately owned hospital is Hospital San Javier Marina.

Although most small towns have at least a clinic, travelers are usually more comfortable traveling to the major hospitals than using these clinics.

Farmacias (pharmacies) are the most convenient place for such common medicines as *aspirina* (aspirin) or *jarabe para la tos* (cough syrup). You'll be able to find many U.S. brands (e.g., Tylenol, Pepto-Bismol), but don't plan on buying your favorite prescription or nonprescription sleep aid, for example. The same brands and even drugs aren't always available. Prescriptions must be issued by a Mexican doctor to be legal; you can often get prescriptions inexpensively from local doctors located near the pharmacy. The Sanborns chain stores also have pharmacies, as do the Cornerstone and San Javier Marina hospitals.

Pharmacies are usually open daily 9 AM to 10 PM; on Sunday and in some small towns they may close several hours earlier. In neighborhoods or smaller towns where there are no 24-hour drug stores, local pharmacies take turns staying open 24 hours so that there's usually at least one open on any given night—it's called the *farmacia de turno*. The CMQ chain is found throughout the Riviera Nayarit and Puerto Vallarta, and most are open 24 hours; the Web site provides a full list of all branches.

Hospitals and Clinics Cornerstone Hospital (✉ *Av. Los Tules 136, next to Plaza Caracol, Zona Hotelera Norte* ☎ *322/226-3700*). **Hospital San Javier Marina** (✉ *Blvd. Francisco M. Ascencio 2760, at María Montessori, Zona Hotelera Norte* ☎ *322/226-1010*).

Pharmacy Farmacia CMQ (✉ *Calle Basilio Badillo 365, Col. E. Zapata* ☎ *322/222-2941* ⊕ *www.cmq.com.mx*).

MEDICAL INSURANCE AND ASSISTANCE

Consider buying trip insurance with medical-only coverage. Neither Medicare nor some private insurers cover medical expenses anywhere outside of the United States. Medical-only policies typically

reimburse you for medical care (excluding that related to pre-existing conditions) and hospitalization abroad, and provide for evacuation. You still have to pay the bills and await reimbursement from the insurer, though.

Another option is to sign up with a medical-evacuation assistance company. Membership gets you doctor referrals, emergency evacuation or repatriation, 24-hour hotlines for medical consultation, and other assistance. International SOS Assistance Emergency and AirMed International provide evacuation services and medical referrals. MedjetAssist offers medical evacuation.

Medical Assistance Companies AirMed International (⊕ www.airmed.com). **International SOS Assistance Emergency** (⊕ www.intsos.com). **MedjetAssist** (☎ 800/527-7478 or 205/595-6626 ⊕ www.medjetassist.com).

Medical-Only Insurers International Medical Group (☎ 800/628-4664 ⊕ www.imglobal.com). **International SOS** (⊕ www.internationalsos.com). **Wallach & Company** (☎ 800/237-6615 or 540/687-3166 ⊕ www.wallach.com).

∎ HOURS OF OPERATION

Banks are generally open weekdays 9 to 3. In Puerto Vallarta most are open until 4, and some of the larger banks keep a few branches open Saturday from 9 or 10 to 1 or 2:30; however, the extended hours are often for deposits or check cashing only. HSBC is the one chain that stays open for longer hours; on weekdays it is open 8 to 7 and on Saturday from 8 to 3. Government offices are usually open to the public weekdays 9 to 3; along with banks and most private offices, they're closed on national holidays.

Some gas stations are open 24 hours a day. Those that are not are normally open 6 AM–10 PM daily. Those near major thoroughfares stay open 24 hours, including most holidays.

Stores are generally open weekdays and Saturday from 9 or 10 AM to 5 or 7 PM; in resort areas, those stores geared to tourists may stay open until 9 or 10 at night, all day on Saturday; some are open on Sunday as well, but it's good to call ahead before making a special trip. Some more traditional shops close for a two-hour lunch break, roughly 2–4. Airport shops are open seven days a week.

HOLIDAYS

Banks and government offices close on January 1, February 5 (Constitution Day), March 21 (Benito Juárez's birthday), May 1 (Labor Day), September 16 (Independence Day), November 20 (Revolution Day), and December 25. They may also close on unofficial holidays, such as Day of the Dead (November 1–2), Virgin of Guadalupe Day (December 12), and during Holy Week (the days leading to Easter Sunday). Government offices usually have reduced hours and staff from Christmas through New Year's Day.

∎ MAIL

The Mexican postal system is notoriously slow and unreliable; letters usually arrive in one piece (albeit late), but never send packages through the postal service or expect to receive them, as they may be stolen. Instead, use a courier service or MexPost, the more reliable branch of the Mexican Postal Service.

Post offices (oficinas de correos) are found in even the smallest villages. International postal service is all airmail, but even, so your letter will take anywhere from 10 days to six weeks to arrive. Service within Mexico can be equally slow. It costs 10.5 pesos (about 70¢) to send a postcard or letter weighing under 20 grams to the United States or Canada; it's 13 pesos ($1.17) to Europe and 14.5 pesos ($1.30) to Australia and New Zealand.

Contacts Correos (✉ Calle Mina 188, El Centro ☎ 322/222-1888).

SHIPPING PACKAGES

FedEx, DHL, Estafeta, and United Parcel Service are available in major cities and many resort areas (though PV doesn't have a FedEx office). It's best to send all packages using one of these services. These companies offer office or hotel pickup with 24-hour advance notice (sometimes less, depending on when you call) and are very reliable. From Puerto Vallarta to large U.S. cities, for example, the minimum charge is around $30 for an envelope weighing ½ pound or less.

Express Services DHL (✉ *Blvd. Francisco M. Ascencio 1046, across from Sheraton, Col. Olímpica* ☎ *322/222–4720 or 01800/765–6345* ⊕ *www.dhl.com*). **Estafeta** (✉ *Blvd. Francisco M. Ascencio 1834, across from Mega grocery store, Col. Olímpica* ☎ *322/223–2700 or 322/223–2898* ⊕ *www.estafeta.com*). **Mail Boxes Etc.** (✉ *Edifício Andrea Mar, Blvd. Francisco M. Ascencio 2180, Local 7, Zona Hotelera Norte [Col. Versalles]* ⚓ *Across from Hotel Los Tules* ☎ *322/224–9434*).

❚ MONEY

Prices in this book are quoted most often in U.S. dollars. Some services in Mexico quote prices in dollars, others in pesos. Because of the current fluctuation in the dollar/peso market, prices may be different from those listed here, but we've done our best at this writing to give accurate rates.

A stay in one of Puerto Vallarta's top hotels can cost more than $350, but if you aren't wedded to standard creature comforts, you can spend as little as $40 a day on room, board, and local transportation. Lodgings are less expensive in the charming but unsophisticated mountain towns like San Sebastián del Oeste.

You can get away with a tab of $50 for two at a wonderful restaurant (although it's also easy to pay more). The good news is that there are hotels and eateries for every budget, and inexpensive doesn't necessarily mean bargain basement. This guide will clue you in to some excellent places to stay, eat, and play for extremely reasonable prices.

Prices throughout this guide are given for adults. Substantially reduced fees are almost always available for children, students, and senior citizens.

ITEM	AVERAGE COST
Cup of Coffee	80¢–$2.50
Glass of Wine	$3.50–$8
Bottle of Beer	$1–$3
Sandwich	$2.50–$5
One-Mile Taxi Ride	$3
Museum Admission	$1

ATMS AND BANKS

ATMs (*cajeros automáticos*) are widely available, with Star, Cirrus, and Plus the most frequently found networks. Your own bank will probably charge a fee for using ATMs abroad; the foreign bank you use may also charge a fee. You'll usually get a better rate of exchange at an ATM, however, than you will at a currency-exchange office or at a teller window. And extracting funds as you need them is a safer option than carrying around a large amount of cash.

Many Mexican ATMs cannot accept PINs with more than four digits. If yours is longer, change your PIN to four digits before you leave home. If your PIN is fine yet your transaction still can't be completed, chances are that the computer lines are busy or that the machine has run out of money or is being serviced. Don't give up.

For cash advances, plan to use Visa or MasterCard, as many Mexican ATMs don't accept American Express. Large banks with reliable ATMs include Banamex, HSBC, BBVA Bancomer, Santander, Serfín, and Scotiabank Inverlat. Some banks no longer exchange traveler's checks; if you carry these, make sure they are in smaller denominations ($20s or $50s) to make it more likely that hotels or shops will accept them if need be.

Travelers must have their passport or other official identification in order to change traveler's checks.

Banks Banamex (⊠ *Calle Juárez, at Calle Zaragoza, Centro* ☎ *322/226–6110* ⊠ *Calle Emiliano Zapata 195, Pitillal* ☎ *322/224–8115* ⊠ *Paseo de los Cocoteros s/n, Paradise Plaza, Nuevo Vallarta* ☎ *322/297–1476*). **Banorte** (⊠ *Paseo Díaz Ordáz 690 at Calle L. Vicario, Centro* ☎ *322/222–4040* ⊠ *Calle Olas Altas 246, at Calle Basilio Badillo, E. Zapata* ☎ *322/223–0481* ⊠ *Blvd. Francisco M. Ascencio 500, Zona Hotelera Norte* ☎ *322/224–9744*).

CREDIT CARDS

Throughout this guide, the following abbreviations are used: **AE**, American Express; **D**, Discover; **DC**, Diners Club; **MC**, MasterCard; and **V**, Visa.

Credit cards are accepted in Puerto Vallarta and at major hotels and restaurants in outlying areas. Smaller, less expensive restaurants and shops tend to take only cash. In general, credit cards aren't accepted in small towns and villages, except in some hotels. The most widely accepted cards are MasterCard and Visa.

When shopping, you can often get better prices if you pay with cash, particularly in small shops. But you'll receive wholesale exchange rates when you make purchases with credit cards. These exchange rates are usually better than those that banks give you for changing money. U.S. banks charge their customers a foreign transaction fee for using their credit card abroad. The decision to pay cash or to use a credit card might depend on whether the establishment in which you are making a purchase finds bargaining for prices acceptable, and whether you want the safety net of your card's purchase protection. To avoid fraud or errors, it's wise to make sure that "pesos" is clearly marked on all credit-card receipts.

Before you leave for Mexico, contact your credit-card company to alert them to your travel plans and to get lost-card phone numbers that work in Mexico; the standard toll-free numbers often don't work abroad. Carry these numbers separately from your wallet so you'll have them if you need to call to report lost or stolen cards. American Express, MasterCard, and Visa note the international number for card-replacement calls on the back of their cards.

CURRENCY AND EXCHANGE

Mexican currency comes in denominations of 20-, 50-, 100-, 200-, and 500-peso bills. Coins come in denominations of 1, 2, 5, 10, and 20 pesos and 20 and 50 centavos. (Twenty-centavo coins are only rarely seen.) Many of the coins are very similar, so check carefully; bills, however, are different colors and easily distinguished.

U.S. dollar bills (but not coins) are widely accepted in tourist-oriented shops and restaurants in Puerto Vallarta. Pay in pesos where possible, however, for better prices. Although in larger hotels U.S. dollars are welcome as tips, it's generally better to tip in pesos so that service personnel aren't stuck going to the bank to exchange currency.

At this writing, the exchange rate was 12.8 pesos to the U.S. dollar. ATM transaction fees may be higher abroad than at home, but ATM exchange rates are the best because they're based on wholesale rates offered only by major banks. Most ATMs allow a maximum withdrawal of $300 to $400 per transaction. Banks and *casas de cambio* (money-exchange bureaus) have the second-best exchange rates. The difference from one place to another is usually only a few pesos.

Some banks change money on weekdays only until 1 or 3 PM (though they stay open until 4 or 5 or later). Casas de cambio generally stay open until 6 or later and often operate on weekends; they usually have competitive rates and much shorter lines. Some hotels exchange money, but they give a poor exchange rate.

You can do well at most airport exchange booths, though not as well as at the ATMs.

You'll do even worse at bus stations, in hotels, in restaurants, or in stores.

When changing money, count your bills before leaving the window of the bank or casa de cambio, and don't accept any partially torn or taped-together notes: You won't be able to use them anywhere. Also, many shop and restaurant owners are unable to make change for large bills. Enough of these encounters may compel you to request *billetes chicos* (small bills) when you exchange money. It's wise to have a cache of smaller bills and coins to use at these more humble establishments to avoid having to wait around while the merchant runs off to seek change.

PACKING

High-style sportswear, cotton slacks and walking shorts, and plenty of colorful sundresses are the palette of clothing you'll see in PV. Bring lightweight sportswear, bathing suits, and cover-ups for the beach. In addition to shorts, pack at least a pair or two of lightweight long pants.

Men may want to bring a lightweight suit or slacks and blazers for fancier restaurants (although very few have dress codes). For women, dresses of cotton, linen, or other lightweight, breathable fabrics are recommended. Puerto Vallarta restaurants are extremely tolerant of casual dress, but it never hurts to exceed expectations.

The sun can be fierce; bring a sun hat and sunscreen for the beach and for sightseeing. You'll need a sweater or jacket to cope with hotel and restaurant air-conditioning, which can be glacial, and for occasional cool spells. A lightweight jacket is a necessity in winter, and pack an umbrella for summer or unexpected rainstorms.

Bring along tissue packs in case you hit a place where the toilet paper has run out. You'll find familiar toiletries and hygiene products, as well as condoms, in shops in PV and in most rural areas.

PASSPORTS AND VISAS

Up until June 2009, you could re-enter the United States via land or sea simply by presenting a government-issued photo ID and another form of proof of citizenship, such as a birth certificate. *Nowadays it's all about the passport.* U.S. citizens reentering the United States by land or sea are required to have documents that comply with WHTI (Western Hemisphere Travel Initiative), most commonly a U.S. passport, a passport card, a trusted traveler card (such as NEXUS, SENTRI, or FAST), or an enhanced driver's license. The U.S. passport card is smaller than a traditional passport (think wallet size), cheaper, and valid for just as long, but you can't use it for travel by air.

Upon entering Mexico, all visitors must get a tourist card. If you're arriving by plane from the United States or Canada, the standard tourist card will be given to you on the plane. They're also available through travel agents and Mexican consulates and at the border if you're entering by land.

■ TIP→ You're given a portion of the tourist card form upon entering Mexico. Keep track of this documentation throughout your trip; you will need it when you depart. You'll be asked to hand it, your ticket, and your passport to airline representatives at the gate when boarding for departure.

If you lose your tourist card, plan to spend some time (and about $30) sorting it out with Mexican officials at the airport on departure.

A tourist card costs about $20. The fee is generally tacked on to the price of your airline ticket; if you enter by land or boat you'll have to pay the fee separately. You're exempt from the fee if you enter by sea and stay less than 72 hours, or by land and do not stray past the 26- to 30-km (16- to 18-mi) checkpoint into the country's interior.

Tourist cards and visas are valid from 15 to 180 days, at the discretion of the immigration officer at your point of

entry (90 days for Australians). Americans, Canadians, New Zealanders, and the British may request up to 180 days for a tourist card or visa extension. The extension fee is about $20, and the process can be time-consuming. There's no guarantee that you'll get the extension you're requesting. If you're planning an extended stay, plead with the immigration official for the maximum allowed days at the time of entry. It will save you time and money later.

■TIP➜ Mexico has some of the strictest policies about children entering the country. Minors traveling with one parent need notarized permission from the absent parent. And all children, including infants, must have proof of citizenship (the same as adults; ⇨ *above*) for travel to Mexico.

If you're a single parent traveling with children up to age 18, you must have a notarized letter from the other parent stating that the child has his or her permission to leave the country. The child must be carrying the original letter—not a facsimile or scanned copy—as well as proof of the parent/child relationship (usually a birth certificate or court document), and an original custody decree, if applicable. If the other parent is deceased or the child has only one legal parent, a notarized statement saying so must be obtained as proof. In addition, you must fill out a tourist card for each child over the age of 10 traveling with you.

Info Mexican Embassy (☏ *202/728–1600* ⊕ *portal.sre.gob.mx/usa/*).

U.S. Passport Information U.S. Department of State (☏ *877/487–2778* ⊕ *travel.state.gov/ passport*).

▌ RESTROOMS

Expect to find reasonably clean flushing toilets and cold running water at public restrooms in the major tourist destinations and attractions; toilet paper, soap, hot water, and paper towels aren't always available, though. Keep a packet of tissues with you at all times. At some tourist attractions, markets, bus stations, and the like, you usually have to pay 5 pesos to use the facilities. Since the H1N1 flu scare, many restaurants, shops, and government offices have had hand sanitizer available for customers to use.

■TIP➜ Remember that unless otherwise indicated you should put your used toilet paper in the wastebasket next to the toilet; many plumbing systems in Mexico still can't handle toilet paper.

Gas stations have public bathrooms—some tidy and others not so tidy. Alternatively, try popping into a restaurant, buying a little something (or not), and using its restroom, which will probably be simple but clean and adequately equipped.

Find a Loo The Bathroom Diaries (⊕ *www. thebathroomdiaries.com*) is flush with unsanitized info on restrooms the world over—each one located, reviewed, and rated.

▌ SAFETY

Horror stories about drug-cartel killings and border violence are making big news these days, but Puerto Vallarta is many hundreds of miles away. Imagine not going to visit the Florida Keys because of reports of violence in a bad section of New York City. Still, Puerto Vallarta is no longer the innocent of years gone by; pickpocketing and the occasional mugging can be a concern, and precaution is in order here as elsewhere. Store only enough money in your wallet or bag to cover the day's spending. And don't flash big wads of money or leave valuables like cameras unattended. Leave your passport and other valuables you don't need in your hotel's safe.

Bear in mind that reporting a crime to the police is often a frustrating experience unless you speak good Spanish and have a great deal of patience. If you're victimized, contact your local consulate or your embassy in Mexico City.

One of the most serious threats to your safety is local drivers. Although pedestrians have the right-of-way, drivers disregard this law. And more often than not, drivers who hit pedestrians drive away as fast as they can without stopping, to avoid jail. Many Mexican drivers don't carry auto insurance, so you'll have to shoulder your own medical expenses. Pedestrians should be extremely cautious of all traffic, especially city bus drivers, who often drive with truly reckless abandon.

If you're on your own, consider using only your first initial and last name when registering at your hotel. Solo travelers, or women traveling with other women rather than men, may be subjected to *piropos* (flirtatious compliments). Piropos are one thing, but more aggressive harassment is another. In the rare event that the situation seems to be getting out of hand, don't hesitate to ask someone for help. If you express outrage, you should find no shortage of willing defenders.

General Information and Warnings Transportation Security Administration (*TSA* ⊕ *www.tsa.gov*). **U.S. Department of State** (⊕ *www.travel.state.gov*).

▌TAXES

Mexico charges an airport departure tax of $18 or the peso equivalent for international and domestic flights. This tax is usually included in the price of your ticket, but check to be certain. Traveler's checks and credit cards aren't accepted at the airport as payment for this, but U.S. dollars are.

Puerto Vallarta and environs have a value-added tax of 15%, called IVA (*impuesto al valor agregado*). It's often waived for cash purchases, or it's incorporated into the price. When comparing hotel prices, be sure to find out whether yours includes or excludes IVA and any service charge. Additionally, Jalisco and Nayarit charge a 2% tax on accommodations, the funds from which are used for tourism promotion. Other taxes and

charges apply for phone calls made from your hotel room.

▌TIME

Puerto Vallarta, Guadalajara, and the rest of Jalisco State fall into Central Standard Time (the same as Mexico City). Nayarit and other parts of the northwest coast are on Mountain Standard Time.

The fact that the state of Nayarit (including Nuevo Vallarta and the rest of the Riviera Nayarit) are in a different time zone from Puerto Vallarta and points east and south leads to confusion. And to add to this confusion, Mexico does observe daylight saving time, but not on the same schedule as the United States.

▌**TIP→** Businesses in Nuevo Vallarta and most tourism-related businesses in Bucerías, La Cruz de Huanacaxtle, and Punta de Mita run on Jalisco time. Since tourism in these towns has traditionally been linked to that of Puerto Vallarta, hotels in the two areas almost always run on Jalisco time to avoid having their clients miss planes when returning home. However, as Nayarit State exerts itself as a destination in its own right with development of the Riviera Nayarit, this is no longer a given. When asking the time, checking hours of operation, or making dinner reservations, double-check whether the place runs on *hora de Jalisco* (Jalisco time) or *hora de Nayarit.*

▌TIPPING

When tipping in Mexico, remember that the minimum wage is just under $5 a day. Waiters and bellmen may not be at the bottom of that heap, but they're not very far up, either. Those who work in international chain hotels think in dollars and know, for example, that in the United States porters are tipped about $2 a bag; they tend to expect the equivalent.

TIPPING GUIDELINES FOR PUERTO VALLARTA

Bartender	10% to 15% of the bill
Bellhop	10 to 30 pesos (roughly 80¢ to $2) per bag, depending on the level of the hotel
Hotel Concierge	30 pesos or more, if he or she performs a service for you
Hotel Doorman	10 to 20 pesos if he helps you get a cab
Hotel Maid	10 to 30 pesos a day (either daily or at the end of your stay); make sure the maid gets it, and not the guy who checks the minibar prior to your departure
Hotel Room-Service Waiter	10 to 20 pesos per delivery, even if a service charge has been added
Porter/Skycap at Airport	10 to 20 pesos per bag
Restroom Attendant	5 pesos
Taxi Driver	cab drivers aren't normally tipped; give them 5 to 10 pesos if they help with your bags
Tour Guide	10% of the cost of the tour
Valet Parking Attendant	10 to 20 pesos but only when you get your car
Waiter	10% to 15%; nothing additional if a service charge is added to the bill

▮ TRIP INSURANCE

Comprehensive trip insurance is valuable if you're booking a very expensive or complicated trip (particularly to an isolated region) or if you're booking far in advance. Comprehensive policies typically cover trip cancellation and interruption, letting you cancel or cut your trip short because of a personal emergency, illness, or, in some cases, acts of terrorism in your destination. Such policies also cover evacuation and medical care. (For trips abroad you should at least have medical-only coverage). Some also cover you for trip delays because of bad weather or mechanical problems as well as for lost or delayed baggage.

Another type of coverage to look for is financial default—that is, when your trip is disrupted because a tour operator, airline, or cruise line goes out of business. Generally you must buy this when you book your trip or shortly thereafter, and it's only available to you if your operator isn't on a list of excluded companies.

Always read the fine print of your policy to make sure that you are covered for the risks that are of most concern to you. Compare several policies to make sure you're getting the best price and range of coverage available.

Insurance Comparison Sites Insure My Trip. com (☎ 800/487–4722 ⊕ www.insuremytrip. com). SquareMouth.com (☎ 800/240–0369 ⊕ www.squaremouth.com).

Comprehensive Travel Insurers Access America (☎ 800/284–8300 ⊕ www. accessamerica.com). AIG Travel Guard (☎ 800/826–4919 ⊕ www.travelguard.com). CSA Travel Protection (☎ 800/711–1197 ⊕ www.csatravelprotection.com). Travelex Insurance (☎ 800/228–9792 ⊕ www.travelex-insurance.com). Travel Insured International (☎ 800/243–3174 ⊕ www.travelinsured.com).

▮ TIP→ Okay. You know you can save a bundle on trips to warm-weather destinations by traveling in rainy season. But there's also a chance that a severe storm will disrupt your plans. The solution? Look for hotels and resorts that offer storm/hurricane guarantees. Although they rarely allow refunds, most guarantees do let you rebook later if a storm strikes.

▮ VISITOR INFORMATION

Contacts Abroad Mexican Ministry of Tourism (SECTUR) (☎ 55/3002–6300, 01800/006–8839 toll-free in Mexico ⊕ www.sectur.gob.mx). Mexican Tourism Board (U.S. and Canada)

(☎ 800/446-3942 [44-MEXICO] in U.S. and Canada ⊕ www.visitmexico.com).

PV and Jalisco Contacts Jalisco State Tourism Office (✉ Plaza Marina shopping center, Local 144, Planta Alta, Marina Vallarta ☎ 322/221-2676). **Municipal Tourist Office** (✉ Av. Independencia 123, Centro ☎ 322/223-2500 Ext. 232). **Puerto Vallarta Tourism Board & Convention and Visitors Bureau** (✉ Local 18 Planta Baja, Zona Comercial Hotel Canto del Sol, Zona Hotelera, Las Glorias ☎ 322/224-1175, 888/384-6822 in U.S., 01800/719-3276 in Mexico ⊕ www. visitpuertovallarta.com).

Riviera Nayarit Contacts Bay of Banderas/ Nuevo Vallarta Tourism Office (✉ Paseo de los Cocoteros at Blvd. Nuevo Vallarta, between Gran Velas and Maribal hotels ☎ 322/297-1006 ⊕ www.visitnayarit.com). **Riviera Nayarit Convention & Visitors Bureau** (✉ Paseo de los Cocoteros 85 Sur, Local Int. 6-A, Paradise Plaza Nuevo Vallarta ☎ 322/297-2516 ⊕ www.rivieranayarit.com).

ONLINE RESOURCES

The best of the private-enterprise Web sites are PV Mirror and Virtual Vallarta, which have tons of good info and short articles about life in PV. Bucerías, Sayulita, and Punta Mita have their own Web sites, as does the Costalegre region as a whole.

Excellent English-language sites for general history, travel information, facts, and news stories about Mexico are Mexico Online and Mexico Connect. Mexico Guru has news about PV and nearby destinations, interactive maps, and a dictionary of Mexico-specific slang and vocabulary.

The nonprofit site Ancient Mexico has information about western Mexico as well as more comprehensive information about the Maya and Aztecs.

Contacts
Ancient Mexico (⊕ www.ancientmexico.com).
Bucerías (⊕ www.buceriasmexico.com).
Costalegre (⊕ www.costalegre.ca).
Mexico Connect (⊕ www.mexconnect.com).
Mexico Guru (⊕ www.mexicoguru.com).
Mexico Online (⊕ www.mexonline.com).
Punta Mita (⊕ www.puntamita.com).
PV Mirror (⊕ www.pvmirror.com).
Sayulita Life (⊕ www.sayulitalife.com).
Virtual Vallarta (⊕ www.virtualvallarta.com).

INDEX

PHOTO CREDITS

1, Mauricio Ramos / age fotostock. 2, Franz Marc Frei / age fotostock. 5, Alija/iStockphoto. Chapter 1: Experience Puerto Vallarta: 12-13, Ambient Images Inc. / Alamy. 14, YinYang/iStockphoto. 15, Bruce Herman/Mexico Tourism Board. 16, Peggy Chen/iStockphoto. 18, YinYang/iStockphoto. 19, Richard Gunion/iStockphoto. 20 (left), Garry Adams / age fotostock. 20 (right), Museo Arqueológico del Cuale. 21 (left), Puerto Vallarta Botanical Gardens. 21 (right), toxickore/Flickr. 22, Andy Newman/Carnival Cruise Line. 23, Fidetur. 25, Starwood Hotels and Resorts Worldwide. 26, Doug Berry/iStockphoto. 27 and 28, Katherine Wessel/Royal Caribbean International. 29, YangYin/iStockphoto. 30, Andy Hwang/iStockphoto. 31, wadester16/wikipedia.org. 32, Pascal Blachier/wikipedia.org. 33 (left),Alan D. Wilson, www.naturespicsonline.com/wikipedia.org. 33 (right), Puerto Vallarta Botanical Gardens. 34, Joe Biafore/iStockphoto. 35 (left), YinYang/iStockphoto. 35 (right), Fidetur. 37 (left), David Diaz. 37 (right), Kaiser Maximilian. 38, Carlos S. Pereyra / age fotostock. Chapter 2: Beaches: 39, Keith Levit / age fotostock. 40, Mike Willis/Flickr. 44, Martin Siepmann / age fotostock. 50, Walter Bibikow / age fotostock. 54, dmealiffe/Flickr. 59, Newman Mark / age fotostock. Chapter 3: Adventure: 61, steve bly / Alamy. 62, Puerto Vallarta Tours by Johann & Sandra. 65, Vasaleks/Shutterstock. 67, Daniel Mejia/Canopy El Eden. 69, Ed Lopez. 71, Rancho El Charro. 76, Heeb Christian / age fotostock. 80, Keith Levit / age fotostock. 82, Mark Doherty/Shutterstock. 84, Irene Chan / Alamy. Chapter 4: Where to Stay: 87, El Careyes. 92, Hotel des Artistes del Mar. 93, Andres Barría. 109 (all), Dreams Puerto Vallarta Resort & Spa. 114, El Careyes Beach Resort. 115, Four Seasons Resort, Punta Mita. 116 (left), Marriott International. 116 (right), Four Seasons Resort, Punta Mita. 117 (left), Terra Noble. 117 (right), mypokcik/iStockphoto. 118 (left), Grand Velas. 118 (right), Taheima Wellness Resort & Spa, Nuevo Vallarta. 119, George Doyle/iStockphoto. 122 (top), Josef Kandoll W. 122 (bottom), Hotel des Artistes del Mar. 132 (top), El Careyes. 132 (bottom), www.mexicoboutiquehotels.com. Chapter 5: Where to Eat: 139, Andrea Gomez. 144, nicobatista/Shutterstock. 145 (top), E.B.Fladung III/waywuwei/Flickr. 145 (bottom), SanFranAnnie/Flickr. 146, Le Kliff Restaurant. 147 (top), Le Kliff Restaurant. 147 (bottom), Andrea Gomez. 148, Robyn Mackenzie/Shutterstock Shutterstock. 151, Eduardo Solórzano. 155, Hotel des Artistes del Mar. 157, El Arrayan. 172, Jill Negronida Hampton. 174, Paco Ojeda. Chapter 6: Shopping: 177, Adalberto Rios Szalay / age fotostock. 178 and 181, Gena Guarniere & Monroe Davids. 182, kokobuzz.wordpress.com. 185, tiffa130/Flickr. 192, John Mitchell / Alamy. 193 and 194 (bottom), María Lourdes Alonso. 194 (top), Danita Delimont / Alamy. 195 (top), 195 (bottom left and 2 center photos), Ken Ross/viestiphoto.com. 195 (bottom right), Jane Onstott. 196 (top left), patti haskins/Flickr. 196 (bottom left), fontplaydotcom/Flickr. 196 (top right), Wonderlane/Flickr. 196 (center right), José Zelaya Gallery/ArteDelPueblo.com. 196 (bottom right), Jane Onstott. 197, GlowImages / Alamy. 205, Wonderlane/Flickr. Chapter 7: After Dark: 207, Imagestate/age fotostock. 208, Travel Bug/Shutterstock. 212, Blaine Harrington/age fotostock. 215, Wolfgang Kaehler / Alamy. 219, csp/Shutterstock. 220 (top left), Alfredo Schaufelberger/Shutterstock. 200 (bottom left), wikipedia.org. 220 (right), Casa Herradura/Brown-Forman. 221 (top left), csp/Shutterstock. 221 (center left), Alfredo Schaufelberger/Shutterstock. 221 (bottom left), Smithsonian Institution Archives/wikipedia.org. 221 (top center), Jesus Cervantes/Shutterstock. 221 (bottom center), Blaine Harrington / age fotostock. 221 (top and bottom right), Jesus Cervantes/Shutterstock. 222 (top left), Eduard Stelmakh/Shutterstock. 222 (center left), svry/Shutterstock. 222 (bottom left), National Archives and Records Administration. 222 (top right), Andrew Penner/iStockphoto. 222 (bottom right), BlueOrange Studio/Shutterstock. 223 (top left), Keith Dannemiller / Alamy. 223 (bottom left), csp/Shutterstock. 223 (right), Patricia Hofmeester/Shutterstock. 224 (left), The Patrón Spirits Company. 224 (right), rick/Flickr. 225 (top left), Casa Herradura/Brown-Forman. 225 (bottom left), shrk/Flickr. 225 (right), Neil Setchfield / Alamy. Chapter 8: Overnight Excursions: 227, Peter Horree / Alamy. 228 (top), Holger Mette/Shutterstock.

NOTES

NOTES

ABOUT OUR WRITER

Jane Onstott was primed for adventure travel in her late teens, when she wandered Central America for six months after being stood up at the Tegucigalpa airport up by an inattentive suitor. Jane's trip to rural Honduras became an unofficial total-language-immersion course, paving the way for a love of the Spanish language and of Hispanic culture. She studied for a year at la Universidad Complutense de Madrid, Spain, and graduated from San Diego State University with a B.A. in Spanish language and literature.

She has since survived a near plunge into a gorge in the highlands of Mexico, a knife-wielding robber in Madrid, and a financial shipwreck on one of the more remote Galapagos Islands. The last led to a position as director of communications and information at the Charles Darwin Research Station on the island of Santa Cruz, where she lectured on the ecology of Ecuador's unique Galapagos archipelago.

But at age 17 this adventurer's first foray outside the United States—Southern California's concrete jungle—was to a small village in the tropical forest just a few hours north of Puerto Vallarta. The stick-and-thatch house where she stayed has since been replaced by a more modern one of cement and bright stucco, but the warm hearts of its owners have changed little in the ensuing three decades. Mexico is Jane's favorite country, and the Pacific coast is one of her more frequent destinations, whether she's traveling for business or pleasure.

In the 1990s Jane spent several years studying painting, sculpting, and the fine art of loafing in Oaxaca—ancient capital of the Zapotec nation—where she was inspired by landscape, the people, and the culture. Today Jane continues to study art and to edit and write mainly about travel and mostly about Mexico. She divides her time between Mexico's Pacific coast and its colonial heartland, with brief expeditions to visit friends and family in San Diego County, thankfully just a short hop north of the Mexican border.